SOUTHPORT
The War Years
An Island Remembers

Sarah Sherman McGrail

August 1996

ISBN: 978-1533147028

To order more copies of the book please contact the author at the address or telephone number listed below. Please keep in mind that we are a commercial fishing family, and kindly call before 7 P.M. because we turn in early. Thank you!

Sarah Sherman McGrail
P.O. Box 385
W. Southport, Maine 04576
207-633-7161

COZY
HARBOR
PRESS

Printed by CreateSpace.com
Design and production by Tim Seymour Designs, LLC; Rockport, Maine

DEDICATION

To my Dad, with the utmost respect for your service during the war. You unselfishly gave of yourself to your country, and your actions enabled me, a generation later, to speak, think, and live freely. I thank you and I love you!

AUTHOR'S NOTE

....

The following stories were compiled from personal interviews, telephone interviews, and through the mail. I have tried to write them from the veterans' point of view, including as much detail as I could whenever it was possible. All stories were checked and given the seal of approval by either the veterans, their family, or their friends. I hope you enjoy reading them as much as I enjoyed writing them.

CONTENTS

Preface vi

Acknowledgments viii

Island Statistics x

Veterans' Stories 1

Back on the Homefront 229

International Stories .309

Preface

....

Well, I finally made it! This project started January 1, 1995, and it's going to the printer a year and a half later. Considering it took us roughly three years and five months to help defeat the Axis powers during the Second World War, I think I've done alright.

Many people have asked me, "Sarah, why did you do this? How did you get the idea?" The answer to that is simple: it's my Dad's fault. Sometime in the fall of 1995 I discovered, much to my dismay, that I couldn't find the world history report I had done in high school on my Dad and the other relatives in my family who had served in the military during the Second World War, so I said to him, "You really ought to let me write down your experiences for our family history." His reply was not very enthusiastic, so I kept asking him, every time I got the chance. Finally one day he gave in, I think so I would stop asking him, and said, "Okay, when do you want to do this?" I replied, "How about tomorrow?" He thought that would be fine, and we set up a time to meet.

Meanwhile, I went home and started thinking about the questions I would ask Dad the following day. Then it dawned on me. What if no one was writing this down? It would all be lost and forgotten. That is when the idea for a book about Southport's veterans materialized. The next morning I sat Mom and Dad down at the kitchen table and said, "I've got to talk to you about something, and it's really important." They both braced themselves; I think they thought I was expecting, if you know what I mean. I began to tell them about my idea, and how important I thought it would be for the town's history records. At this point they both started to smile, and my mother said, "You can't help yourself. It's in the genes." (For those of you who don't know my mother, Evelyn, she's very involved with the historical society here on the island, and has helped write several of the town's histories.) They both agreed it was a great idea and offered to help any way they could. Looking back on it now, I bet they never imagined what they were getting themselves into.

From there we needed a starting point, so I went to the library at Newagen and copied the list of names off the veterans' honor wall. Mom and Dad helped me separate the names into three lists: living, passed on, and I don't know.

A list of questions was soon formed and I started calling people, asking them if they'd like to be interviewed. Everyone was very excited about the project and my research started to roll along nicely.

I bought a used IBM computer and printer for 300 dollars that didn't come with a manual, so I taught myself how to use it. I still haven't figured out how to make it underline words, but at the time, that didn't seem very important. Pretty soon it became evident that the list I had copied wasn't exactly complete, so I started asking around and found a few more names that I didn't have. I originally started out with 75 veterans, which later grew to 110, by the time I was finished.

My original intent was to have just stories about veterans who enlisted or were drafted from Southport, but that soon changed when I made my first "author's exception."

I realized I couldn't technically have my Uncle Earl in the book, because he was drafted from Malden, Massachusetts, so I decided I would include anyone who had been a longtime summer resident of Southport, and moved here to live after the war was over. It added a few more names to my list, but I figured what the heck, I'm preserving history.

Then I realized there were many people on the island who moved here after the war because they married residents, and had lived here for the past 50 years. I decided that I couldn't leave them out, so a second exception was made, and more names were added to the list.

My project was near completion when Gerry Gamage, one of Southport's selectmen, asked me for a list of veterans that he could use in the 1995 town report. He thought it would be nice to commemorate them, because 50 years had passed since the end of the war. I put a small disclosure at the bottom of the list, and said if I had missed anyone, it was an oversight on my part and would they please contact me, so I could add their names or their relatives to it. The response at the March 4, 1996, town meeting was tremendous: 12 people came forward, which created the third and final "town meeting exception." My self-imposed deadline to complete research for the book was March 31, 1996. The veterans and I then had a little less then four weeks to complete the project. We worked overtime, and gathered all the information needed to write their stories in record time, and ended up beating the deadline by two days.

I think a project like this could easily go on for years. One thing seems to lead to another, and there is always one more person you really ought to talk to. I think the most satisfying areas of my research have been the knowledge that this little part of Southport's history has been preserved for future generations, and also the way everyone worked together to help make this book possible. If I hadn't had the enthusiastic response and encouragement I had during my research, these pages wouldn't be nearly as interesting and colorful as they are.

We pulled together as an island, and dug out old letters and photographs. Trunks were opened that hadn't been touched in 50 years. Uniforms were unpacked from mothballs and brought to life by the memories of the men and women who served in them. For the veterans who lived out of town, and even out of state, the telephone company and postal service worked overtime for us. My phone bill alone is proof of that. I guess the point I'm trying to make is that this was a team effort from day one, and I am eternally grateful for everyone's help.

ACKNOWLEDGMENTS

First and foremost, I would like to start off by thanking the veterans, their families, and the residents of the town of Southport for all the help and support they gave me. I could not have done it without you, and I am truly honored that you entrusted me with the task of immortalizing your memories and experiences.

I would like to thank my parents, Maurice and Evelyn Sherman, who instilled in me the philosopy, anything worth doing is worth doing well; my husband, Jerry and sons, Sherm and Jake; sister Susan and her family; brother Bill and his family; Cory Chase Andrews; Jean Thompson; Evelyn "Dox" Stratton; Aunt Em and Uncle Earl Pratt; Aunt Marilyn and Uncle Ralph Spinney; Aunt Connie Gray; Uncle Neil Payson; Donald and Nora Brewer; Gram and Gramp – Leslie and Dorothy Brewer; Merle Farnham; Evelyn Blake; Betty Goulette; Dick and Louise Dill; Leland and Lucy Snowman; Lew and Franny Johnson; and Marge and Don Barter for the unlimited encouragement, advice, editing, question answering, and problem solving they provided over the course of this project.

I would like to thank Robert Mitchell and Susan Endicott for their support and the use of Bob's closeup lens, which enabled me to copy all the original photos shown in the book. If Bob hadn't given me this opportunity, there probably wouldn't have been any photographs accompanying the stories, because of the expense involved and the fact that some of the photos were one of a kind, and the owners didn't want them to leave my hands.

I would like to thank Esme McTighe, for her friendship, enthusiasm, advice, and for proofreading the entire book for me. A big hug goes to Esme's family, Jay, Niall, and Petra Janney, for allowing her the time out of their busy lives to work on this project.

Thanks to my international friends, both here and abroad for sharing their stories with me: Natalia, Ludmilia, Sergej, and Vasilij Archangelsky; Basilio Cossu; Michele and Francesca Crisi; Jan and Mimi Havinga; Enid Johnson; Ragnhild Baade; Emil Landau; Annemarie Apollonio; Ole, Laurel, and Marit Pettersen; Cary Laine; Johannes Tomasson and Minna Stefansdottir; Erna Johannesdottir; and Pranas Lape.

Thanks to Austin Wilkins, for letting me use his book, *Ten Million Acres of Timber*, as a reference for the chapter about P.O.W. camps in Maine.

Thanks to Ann Ronan, for her dedicated help proofreading at the last minute.

Thanks to Mary Patrick, who was my English teacher at Boothbay Region High School, three out of four years, and taught me to enjoy writing.

Thanks to Bill Frayer, who was my Critical Thinking instructor at Central Maine Technical College, and encouraged me to pursue my education beyond graduation.

Lastly, a special thanks and a hug to Harold Webber, for all his help and a great game of cribbage at a moment's notice.

ISLAND STATISTICS

In 1940, when the government took a census of the island, the population of Southport was 405. Out of those 405, 75 town residents served their country during the Second World War. Out of 75, three were killed in action: Leslie Swett, Norman Gaudette, and Roland Gray.

There are 110 veterans represented in this book, because I decided to include people who moved on the island after the war. The following is a breakdown of the branches of the military and the theaters of war the veterans served in.

BRANCH OF SERVICE	NUMBER SERVED
Army	32
Army Air Corps	13
Coast Guard	10
Harbor Pilot	1
Marine Corps	3
Merchant Marine	6
Navy	45

Author's note: George Poor was a Harbor Pilot in Boston Harbor during the war. I have listed him, because I believe his position would have fallen under the jurisdiction of the Navy during war time.

THEATER OF WAR	NUMBER SERVED
American Theater	36
Asiatic Pacific Theater	30
Asiatic Pacific/China Burma India Theater	1
China Burma India	1
European African Middle Eastern Theater	33
European African Middle Eastern/Asiatic Pacific	8
European African Middle Eastern/China Burma India	1

Author's note: Please keep in mind that the veterans who served overseas, originally served in the United States. That fact is not reflected under the American Theater list, because I thought it would be too repetitive.

European African Middle Eastern Theater

Ira Alley – Army Air Corps
Harold Boyd – Army
Lawrence Boyd – Army
Gerald Dill – Navy
Harold Dill, Sr. – Merchant Marine
Richard Dill – Army
* Edward Donohoe – Merchant Marine/Army Mine Planter Service
 * Robert Eaton – Army
Franklin Farmer – Merchant Marine
Lyman Farmer – Merchant Marine
 * Joe Fodera – Navy
Leslie Gamage – Army
Francis Gaudette – Coast Guard
** Norman Gaudette – Army
** Roland Gray – Army
 * Donald Harriman – Army
 * Robert Irving – Army (Southport's Principal 1968 – 1980)
 * Lewis Johnson – Army Air Corps
 * Richard W. Johnson – Army Air Corps
Paul Pierce -Navy
Kenneth Piltz – Navy
Elbridge Plummer – Army
 * Gordon Pottle – Army
Maurice Sherman – Army
Sidney Sherman – Army Air Corps
 * Olive Stratton – WAAC, Army
John Swett – Army
Raymond Swett – Navy
Maurice Taylor – Navy Seabees
Ross Stuart Thompson – Coast Guard
Edward Tibbetts – Army
Walter Tibbetts, Jr. – Army
Harold Webber – Army

European African Middle Eastern/Asiatic Pacific Theater

Richard Alley – Coast Guard
Raymond Cameron – Coast Guard
 * Robert Colby – Naval Reserves
 * Charles Collins – Army
Scott Gray – Merchant Marine
 * Weldon Lakeman – Merchant Marine
Elbridge Sherman – Coast Guard
Gerald Smith – Navy

European African Middle Eastern/China Burma India Theater

Edward Gaudette – Army Medical Corps

Asiatic Pacific Theater

Amby Alley – Army
Glendon Ayer – Navy
* Donald F. Barter – Army
David Blake – Marine Corps
Lester Boyd – Army
* Cliff Brewer – Navy
* Mason Britton – Navy
* Jack Brown – Navy
Carl Cederstrom – Navy
* Robert Chilson – Navy
* Lou Climo – Navy
Leslie Copp – Army
Roland Dyer – Navy
* Samuel Emerson – Navy
Fred Farnham – Navy
Arthur Gamage – Navy
John Gray – Navy
Ellsworth Gray – Navy
Preston Hart – Navy
Walter Hart – Navy
* Buck Hasch – Navy Seabees
* Kenneth Henderson – Army Air Corps
Wolcott Marr – Navy
Edwin McKown – Army Air Corps
Clayton Orne – Army
Franklin Payson – Army Air Corps
* Harold Roberts – Navy Seabees
* Lincoln Rockwell – Navy
Allan Smith – Navy
* Norma Clifford Smith – Navy WAVES
** Leslie Swett – Army Air Corps

China Burma India Theater

George Tibbetts – Army

Asiatic Pacific/China Burma India Theater

* Fred Cook – Marine Corps

American Theater

Ellen Cameron Berry – Navy WAVES
Niles Cameron – Coast Guard
* Frank Clifford – Navy
* Richard Conant – Navy
* Lester "Budd" Connor – Army
Harold Dill, Jr. – Army Air Corps
Leon Duprey – Navy
Walter Farmer – Navy
Gerald Fuller – Navy
Myrtle Seavey Furst – Marine Corps, Women's Reserves
Edwin Gamage – Coast Guard
Weston Gamage – Coast Guard
Arthur Hamilton – Army Air Corps (It is not known if Arthur served overseas.)
* Helen Martin Henderson – Navy WAVES
* David Hilton – Army
Walter Huskins – Navy
* Roy Jones – Army
Norman Lewis – Navy
George Marr – Army
Constance Sherman Newcomb – Army Air Corps, WACS
Kenneth Orne – Army Air Corps
Arthur Packard – Army (It is not known if Arthur served overseas.)
Lewis Dana Payson -Navy
Carl Pierce – Navy
Norman Pierce – Navy
Kenneth Pinkham – Navy
* Hazel Adams Plummer – Nurses Corps, Naval Reserves
George Poor – Harbor Pilot
* Earl Pratt – Army Air Corps
* Bodo Richter – Army
Leslie Earl Snowman – Army
Eugene Stover, Jr. – Navy
Eugene Stover, Sr. – Coast Guard
John Thompson – Navy
* Eliot Winslow – Navy/Coast Guard

* = Veterans who moved on the island after the war
** = Killed in action

VETERANS' STORIES

AMBY ALLEY
Private First Class, U.S. Army

Amby was drafted on August 27, 1941. He served with the 103rd Infantry in Guadalcanal, New Guinea, and the Northern Solomons. He was bothered by jungle rot while in the Pacific, which is a skin disease that usually begins on the feet, and stems from being wet for extended periods of time.

He was discharged from the Army on March 27, 1945, after three years and seven months of service, and was awarded the Asiatic Pacific Theater Ribbon, American Defense Service Medal, Good Conduct Medal, and the World War II Victory Medal. After the war he returned to Southport where he worked for Leslie, and later Donald Brewer seining for herring. Amby passed away in 1988 at the age of 80.

IRA ALLEY
Private First Class, Army Air Corps

Ira was drafted into the Army Air Corps on August 26, 1942, at the age of 26. He received his basic training in Reno, Nevada, and was assigned to the 565th Army Air Force Base Unit, where he was trained as a toxic gas handler. He had been a fisherman on Southport prior to that time, lobstering and sardine seining for Leslie Brewer.

Amby and Ira Alley, U.S. Army and Army Air Corps

He served in Central Europe and Rhineland during the war, and was discharged on November 14, 1945, at the separation center located at Fort Devens in Massachusetts, after three years and three months of service. He was awarded the European African Middle Eastern Theater Campaign Ribbon, American Defense Service Medal, World War II Victory Medal, and the Good Conduct Award.

After the war, Ira returned to fishing and on October 18, 1948, he married Pauline Wallace from West Point, Maine. He passed away on August 26, 1977, at the age of 70.

RICHARD ALLEY
Quartermaster, U.S. Coast Guard

Richard Alley, U.S. Coast Guard

On September 23, 1939, Richard enlisted in the Coast Guard. He was 19 years old at the time and had previously been working at Sewalls Garage in Boothbay Harbor for 11 dollars a week washing and greasing cars.

His mother took him to the U.S. Public Health Hospital in Falmouth for his physical. A Swedish doctor checked him out, and when he discovered that Richard was underweight, he told him to go eat some bananas and come back to get weighed in. So off Richard and his mother went in search of bananas. Later Richard returned after eating several bananas and passed his physical with flying colors.

Richard received his training aboard a Coast Guard tug named the *Guthrie*, which was kept in Portland Harbor. He later moved onto the *Chelan* in Boston, where he received further training. While there he ran into Maurice Sherman, who had been his next-door neighbor on Southport Island. Maurice was stationed on the *Cayouga*.

Richard was then transferred back to South Portland where he served on the *Algonquin*, which was a small Coast Guard cutter. In 1940 he received orders to report to the *Hibiscus*. She was an old steam buoy tender. Richard and her crew delivered supplies to lighthouses and set buoys up and down the coast of Maine.

On June 3, 1941, Richard was transferred to the *Wakefield* where he held the rate of quartermaster, but due to a shortage of signalmen on board took over the duty of sending and receiving signals. He became proficient in flag and light flash signaling. While enroute to Rio and Cape Town Richard received a message that Pearl Harbor had been attacked. The entire crew was angry and in shock. Meanwhile back in Southport, Richard's parents had received a letter from him stating he might be going to Pearl Harbor. You can only imagine their joy when Richard came home on leave unexpectedly after the attack. He came up over the hill whistling and as his parents heard him approaching they couldn't believe their ears. Richard was alive and well.

The *Wakefield* was transporting British and Scottish troops to Alexander to help fight against General Rommel and his troops in North Africa. Enroute they received a change of orders and took the men into Bombay for acclamation, then on to Singapore. When they were docking one of the men there told Richard, "Don't worry, the Japanese don't bomb the docks." The very next morning they were attacked at daylight and five men were killed who had been in sick bay. The British had all their guns pointing out to sea at the base on Singapore and were unable to swing them around to defend themselves from behind, so the Japanese attacked them from the rear, coming through a swamp with tanks. All the soldiers the Wakefield had just delivered were captured, as well as the men already stationed there. Richard's captain had received orders to stay there, but disobeyed them, because he thought their ship would be captured and he was right. They got out of Singapore just in time.

Richard returned to the United States via Ceylon Columbo (now Sri Lanka) where he had the tattoo of a dragon applied by hand to his leg. Later that day he began to feel really sick and discovered he had an infection in his blood from the tattoo. Back in the States the *Wakefield* picked up a shipload of Marines and received orders to deliver them to Wellington, New Zealand. Traveling alone they passed through the Panama Canal and plotted a zigzag course for New Zealand. The ship would travel a certain distance for a certain length of time, then it would switch and would travel on a new heading, creating a zigzag pattern across the ocean. There was a clock positioned over the compass which dictated when the course would be changed. This was done to try to prevent encounters with enemy submarines. Richard said this trip was very nerve-racking, because they didn't have any support traveling with them in case they ran into trouble. The crew on board were allowed one night of liberty and then they steamed back to the States to pick up more troops. It was now July of 1942.

The *Wakefield* was 794 feet long and was 80 feet wide. In August she picked up 10,000 troops for transport to the British Isles. The convoy sailing from New York, via Halifax, Nova Scotia, to Greenock, Scotland, marked the largest number of troops ever to be transported across the Atlantic in a single operation up to that time.

All the brass on board the *Wakefield* was painted gray during wartime to help camouflage the ship. Also if you were out on deck and opened a watertight door to go inside the cabin, the interior lights would auto-matically turn off. This was done to help maintain blackout conditions at night.

Enroute Richard was up on the starboard wing of the bridge smoking a cigarette. The deck below him was a sea of troops, because they couldn't all fit below deck and were rotating on 12-hour shifts. All of a sudden he heard someone calling out his name. He didn't see the man at first, but when he came closer Richard realized it was Maurice Sherman, his next-door neighbor from Southport. Richard vividly remembers Maurice approaching him wearing a blue overseas artillery hat. They arranged to meet later when Richard got off duty.

A few hours later at the prearranged location the two men met and caught up on all the news from home. Richard learned that Maurice was in a unit comprised of mostly southern soldiers and he couldn't figure how he had gotten into it, being from Maine. Maurice said to Richard, "You're lucky, you get to go home and I've got to stay." Richard remem-bers wishing he could fit Maurice in his pocket so he could go home with him. The voyage lasted 15 days and Richard never saw Maurice again during that time. There were just too many men on board. The two men didn't see each other again until after the war.

The ship anchored off Grennock, Scotland, and Richard went on lib-erty in Glasgow. He said the children would come up to him in the streets and beg for oranges, because they knew sailors had access to them on board the ship. Enroute back to New York the *Wakefield* caught on fire. Late one afternoon a fire started on the C Deck and rapidly spread throughout the ship. There were 840 passengers and 750 crew on board at the time. Richard was in his living quarters when the fire alarm was sounded. He escaped with only the clothes on his back and lost all his personal belongings including his eyeglasses. The cruiser *Brooklin* came alongside the *Wakefield*, and the crew and passengers were evacuated by climbing down cargo nets onto the other ship. The charred *Wakefield* was towed to Halifax, Nova Scotia, and the crew and passengers were taken to New York where they were fed and clothed by the Salvation Army.

A skeleton crew was formed to stand watch aboard the Wakefield as she was brought down the coast to Boston to be rebuilt. Richard volunteered for this duty and upon its completion was dispatched to Sheepshead Bay, which was a war-time boot camp. He extended his enlistment there and was reassigned to the Woodbine in Buffalo, New York, on November 20, 1942. He sailed from the Chesapeake Bay area down the East Coast where his ship commenced its duties. She was ship fitted with fire monitors, which enabled the crew to help fight fires on other ships.

The Wakefield loaded with troops.

He was later dispatched to Cuba to open sugar ports and buoy them out so American cargo ships could safely enter the harbors. Richard noticed the docks were made completely out of mahogany and was quite impressed by them. The *Woodbine* then received orders to proceed to Honolulu, traveling alone through the Panama Canal.

At this point, the *Woodbine* was unexpectedly given the chance to try out her new fire monitors, while anchored in Pearl Harbor. One night saboteurs successfully planted explosive devices on several American LSTs (landing ship tanks) that were loaded and ready to go into battle in the Pacific. Richard remembers hearing and then seeing the tremendous explosions. He said there was debris flying everywhere. The crew of the *Woodbine* immediately went into action, and started fighting the fire. Tokyo Rose, a Japanese radio personality at the time, was later heard over the airways talking about the success of the sabotage, along with her usual line of propaganda.

The *Woodbine* then received new orders, and set sail for Sai Pan. They arrived just after the Allied invasion. Army engineers had laid a discharge hose with a large plug in it out into the harbor, and it was the *Woodbine*'s job to buoy it off. Then fuel tankers could come alongside of it and pump directly to the airstrip on Sai Pan, allowing the Allied planes to refuel. Later, the bombers that carried the atomic bomb would stop here to refuel on their way to Japan.

In December of 1944, Richard boarded the *Orezaba* in Honolulu, which was a troop transport. As he was coming down the dock with his sea bag he noticed "Cracker" Page from Boothbay Harbor, leaning on the rail watching him approach the ship. He was a Third Class Radar Man on board, and he and Richard were able to visit together all the way back to San Francisco, California.

From San Francisco, Richard traveled to Constitution Wharf in Boston and was reassigned to the *Laurel*, which was an ice breaker and a buoy tender, but was being used for logistics. His next destination was Greenland. He arrived there during the summer months and the temperature was up around 68 degrees. There were strawberries growing up in the hills and the icebergs and glaciers were beautiful.

While on board, one of his shipmates won the Random House Prize for a manuscript he had written called, "Red Flannels and Green Ice." It was a humorous look at life on board a Coast Guard cutter and Richard was even portrayed as one of the characters in the winning entry. One day while on board the message came through that the United States had dropped the bomb on Japan. The Captain soon sent out the order to, "splice the main brace"; to us land lovers that means liquor was allowed on board and would be distributed by the Captain.

In August of 1950 Richard was granted leave and traveled home by train to Union Station in Portland. While there he saw a beautiful young girl crossing the railroad tracks. She boarded the train and rode to Wiscasset, where a bus met them and drove them to Boothbay Harbor. After the girl got off the bus and Richard had switched to the Southport bus, he asked Eugene Stover, who was driving, "Who was that girl?" Eugene replied, "That's Marge McDougal; she's a nice girl." Richard attended a dance at the Knicherbocker Casino later that week, and when he spotted Marge there, he asked her to dance. They were married three months later.

Richard was awarded the Good Conduct Ribbon with a bronze star, the American Area Campaign Ribbon, European African Middle Eastern Campaign Ribbon, Asiatic-Pacific Campaign Ribbon with one star, and the World War II Victory Ribbon. He was discharged from the Coast Guard in 1961 after 22 years of service at the rank of Quartermaster

The Wakefield loaded with troops.

Chief, and currently lives on Southport with his wife of 46 years, Marge.

GLENDON AYER
Seaman First Class, U.S. Navy

After months of research, I was at my wit's end, trying to find information on Glendon. For a while it seemed as if all record of him had disappeared into thin air after he married Norman Gaudette's widow Grace, and moved from Southport to California when the war ended. Then in January of 1996, I learned from Mr. Arthur Pierce of Sebasco,

Glendon Ayer, U.S. Navy, and an unidentified woman.

Maine, who was Glendon's sister's brother-in-law, that both Glendon and his sister had passed away in California some time ago.

Luckily, Marge Barter came through at the last minute for me with excerpts from her mother's diary, a photograph, and letters Glendon had written back to her during the war. From the diary I learned Glendon joined the Navy on December 14, 1941, shortly after the bombing of Pearl Harbor by the Japanese, and he came home on leave in September of 1943, having just returned from Trinidad for the second time.

The photo indicates he had achieved the rank of Seaman First Class, at the time it was taken, but it is not known when it was taken or if he earned a higher rating during the remainder of his service. Everything else I know about him comes from Marge's letters, which are listed in order below.

Author's note: *I think the censor must have been sleeping on the job to let this second letter pass through without editing it.*

April 17, 1943

Dear Marg,

I received your swell letter this evening about seven o'clock.
The officers in the Navy these days are pretty young, Marg.

We've got an Ensign aboard here that is only twenty. His name is O'Shaughnessy. Of course he is Irish. We call them ninety-day wonders. You see, they only get ninety days of training and then they are sent on active duty.

All the mail goes to New York and then its sent to where ever the ship may be. Last year when we got back from South America I had mail come that was two months old. We never know how long we will stay in one place. They never tell us anything. If they did, some of these guys would go ashore and get drunk and tell all they knew. We didn't even know we were going to Boston until we went through the Canal. We sort of guessed it then. They say we are going back there again in a few weeks. That would be swell.

I'll have to sign off here kid and get my beauty sleep. Be good and a picture will arrive soon.

Much Love,
Glendon

August 4, 1943

Dear Marg,

First we went to Safi, a city in Morocco. We stayed there for one night and a day. Nothing happened. We didn't even sight an enemy plane. We shoved off and went up to Casablanca. We got there about two hours before the battle ended. We did have a little excitement there. It was pretty hot for awhile. We can't get into actual combat, but you can bet your life we wanted to. That may sound a bit strange to you, but that's the way everyone feels when they really get that close. At least, this whole crew did.

We went into the harbor after the battle was over, and what a mess! Dead bodies were floating around everywhere. A cruiser and two destroyers (Vichy-French) had been shelled and burned. They were both on the beach. Every ship in the harbor had been scuttled. Stuck right beside the piers. We wanted to go ashore, but no soap. They had martial law there. They were afraid of snipers. They lost an awful lot of men by snipers. The first night we were there a sailor was stabbed in the back while doing patrol duty on the breakwater. We only stayed there three days. I still haven't told you what kind of a ship I'm on have I? It's a mine layer. So you see why we can't get into combat unless we really have to. There's about 120 tons of T.N.T. aboard besides the ammunition. I guess that's why they call these things the "suicide ships."

I guess that's all there is Marge. Be careful who reads this, won't you? I'm not supposed to tell things like that. Write soon.

Much Love,

Glendon

U.S.S. Monadnock

                                                        August 15, 1943

Dear Marg,

We got in yesterday noon and I was awfully glad to have a letter from you waiting for me. Liberty started at one o'clock yesterday and I decided to go ashore for a change and see a kid that is stationed at Ft. Eustis. Do you remember Walter Brewer? He used to drive one of the Cushman trucks the same time I did. I think your mother knows him. He lives over near Hazel.

Marg, please don't mention lobster to me. Good Lord, what I wouldn't give for some lobsters. You can't get them down here. They don't even know what they are. I'll be some glad to get home for more than one reason. Ah me, such is the life of a sailor! I'm glad to hear that you are on the last lap again, Marg. Keep your chin up. You just have to make it this time.

We were out on maneuvers all last week and we are going out for two or three days more. All we do is drill all day. Anyone would think we were on a battleship instead of this old mud skow.

So you like to hear these rebels beat their gums, huh? In a lot of places in the South they say, "Are you going oot?" Or rather, "Are y'all going oot?" Sho' nuff! I was in a shooting gallery quite a while ago with a rebel and you should have heard what he told me. He said, "You couldn't hit a bull in the a— with a bass fiddle." That is one of their pet expressions. They have hundreds of sayings that I could never remember. Some of them are pretty good. I think I have told you about the little guy we have from Georgia, haven't I? He is a case. One afternoon he came up to me and said, "Is y'all going ashore, Glen?" Before I thought, I said, "Is I what?" The whole crew nearly died. They razed me for a month.

I guess I have run on enough for tonight. The show starts in a few minutes and you know me. I could go to a show every night. In fact, I do. I guess the Navy has changed some since the old days. Now we have movies, a canteen, a soda fountain, baseball and football teams, etc. EVEN A LAUNDRY!! I guess the Navy is getting soft. Well, so long for now and write (agin) soon.

Much love and k——whoops!

Glendon

August 24, 1943

Dear Marg,

Second time I've been to Trinidad in the British West Indies. I wouldn't live there if they paid a dollar an hour. The locals speak some kind of language all their own as near as I could find out. Part Hindu and part French with a little English thrown in for good measure. They drive on the left side of the road as they do in England. The first time I rode there I nearly thru a fit. You can imagine how funny you would feel coming around a corner on the left side of the road and seeing another car coming. I'll take the good old U.S.A. anytime. Please write again soon and keep smiling.

Much Love,

Glendon

DONALD F. BARTER
Sergeant, U.S. Army

Don enlisted in the Army on December 30, 1942, at the age of 25. He received his basic training at Fort Bliss, Texas, over a period of three months, and became part of the 362nd Anti-Aircraft Artillery, Search Light Battalion, Battery A. Prior to that time, Don had been a Sergeant in the Civilian Conservation Corps (C.C.C.) at Camp Jefferson in North

Donald Barter, U.S. Army

Whitefield, Maine. He was a part of the 1163rd Co. from 1935 to 1938, and worked at everything from timber surveying to tree surgery, under the guidance of the State Forestry Department. Pay was one dollar a day and 25 out of the 30 dollars you earned monthly went home to help your family. Between 1938 and 1942, Don was employed at Samples Shipyard in Boothbay Harbor.

After basic training, Don left for Camp Stoneman, California, which was a debarkation camp for troops that were being coordinated to be shipped overseas. He boarded a converted liberty ship, *U.S.S. Lena Wee*, and was promptly issued a carton of cigarettes for the voyage. In two weeks he found himself in New Mear, New Caledonia, which is located off the coast of Australia, and was a French possession at that time. The island was being used as a staging area, in preparation for upcoming battles.

It was a common occurrence for the men to be put to work unloading supplies off ships until their unit had set up. Don had never bothered to get a driver's license while at home, but was assigned to drive a semi-wheeled truck just the same. He reported to the Dock Captain, the truck was loaded, and he was told to drive it off the dock. Don managed to do so, but then he had to navigate on the slippery coral roads, which proved to be quite a challenge.

A later driving assignment almost got Don into hot water. He was told to drive a unit of black soldiers to another part of the island, which seemed like an easy job. On the way, Don encountered a steep grade, which required double shifting of the gears. Don had never been taught to double shift, so he stalled the truck, and a bunch of the soldiers fell out. Boy, were they mad! Don quickly explained he didn't have much experience with this sort of thing, and they all got a good laugh out of it.

Don was trained to run a mobile, carbon search light, which was hooked up to radar. As soon as an enemy aircraft was locked on, the lights automatically came on to illuminate it, as did the automatic 40 mm and 90 mm guns. Don's battalion was credited with shooting down two enemy planes while on Guadalcanal.

Next stop was the New Hebrides, then it was onto the Solomon Islands and Guadalcanal. While there he received a letter from his mother, telling him that she had talked with Ken Gosslin's parents, and he was also stationed there. Ken was from Boothbay Harbor, so Don quickly looked him up. It was good to see a familiar face, and Ken even shared his beer and cigarette/cigar ration with Don. Ken was part of a Port Battalion stationed on Guadalcanal, and they were in charge of loading and unloading ship's cargo. The two men were able to visit several times while they were stationed there.

Don's unit set up a bivouac in a coconut plantation on Guadalcanal that was owned by the Palmolive Soap Company. There was lots of fruit growing wild, including pineapples and bananas, and pretty soon some of the men had the bright idea to try making alcohol out of coconut milk. They went to the commissary and got sugar and raisins, and before long they had created a very potent drink.

At one point in the islands, Don's outfit was transported on a cattle boat. There were no bunks for the men to sleep in, so they had to sleep on deck, along with cows, ducks, pigs, and chickens. It was quite a ride!

His outfit continued on to the Northern Solomons and landed on Green Island, where they were attached to the New Zealand Army. Years

This photo was taken on Green Island in the Northern Solomons.
Don is pictured in the back row, last man on the right.
The other men shown in the photo were part of Don's outfit and
a New Zealand outfit that was also stationed on Green Island.

later, Don would read about a one time soldier named Richard Nixon, who later became the President of the United States, and was also stationed on Green Island at the very same time Don was. Don never met him though, that he can remember.

Many of the men in Don's outfit received "Dear John" letters from home. The war took its toll on relationships and marriages, and sometimes the long separations were more than some women could bear, so they ended them. It was really rough on the guys, and made Don glad that he wasn't in a relationship before he was shipped overseas.

Green Island was overrun by land crabs. They were everywhere! One night a crab climbed up the side of a guy's tent and he thought it was a Japanese soldier attacking him, so he grabbed his gun and started shooting through the tent. Finally some of the other men got to him, and once they calmed him down, showed him what he had been shooting at. Luckily no one was hurt.

This makes a funny story now, but imagine yourself being far away from home, lying there in the darkness in your tent, and hearing all kinds of jungle noises, some which very well may be the enemy. The Japanese held up in caves all over these islands in the Pacific, and survived on next to nothing. Don said he always felt very reassured when he could hear the PT boats patrolling and our planes overhead.

There were many snakes and spiders on these tropical islands. To prevent spiders from climbing onto your army cot, the men used to put a can under each post of their cot and pour a little oil in it. There were also a lot of beautiful, tropical birds in the jungle, but you had to be careful, because the Japanese soldiers could mimic them, and would use their calls as signals to each other.

Once in a while, even though it was against Army regulations, some of the men would go fishing with hand grenades, so they could eat fresh fish for supper instead of Army rations. There were even wild pigs on some of the islands, which didn't always escape the hungry grasp of the soldiers. Don collected sea shells throughout the Pacific. He would lay them on top of anthills and let the ants eat the meat out of them, so he could save them.

While in the Pacific, Don saw several U.S.O. shows. Entertainers included Bob Hope, Francis Langford, Jerry Colona, Martha Ray, Lanny Ross, and Randolph Scott. They provided a wonderful change of pace for the soldiers, and let them forget about the war, even if it was just for a little while.

His outfit reunited with the rest of the battalion back at Guadalcanal, regrouped, and was sent to Finch Haven, New Guinea, then on to Manila as part of the liberators of the Philippines. While there Don and some of his friends found tons and tons of Japanese invasion money, which of course by this time was absolutely worthless. As the war ended the entire battalion went to the island of Hon Chu, and later took over as the Army of Occupation in the cities of Yokahama and Tokyo. His battalion was then renamed the 531st Military Police Battalion, and Don served in Company A.

Don's samurai sword, Japanese Infantry rifle, and a flag he picked up while stationed as part of the Army of Occupation in Japan.

While on patrol, Don had the authority to confiscate weapons of any sort. Obviously there was quite a language barrier between the Army of Occupation and the natives, so a Japanese interpreter was assigned to him daily, which made his job considerably easier.

American soldiers were given a book on Japanese customs, to help them adjust while they were occupying the country. Don said even so, it was mentally confusing to come out of the jungle, where you had been trained to shoot the enemy on sight, and be reassigned to upholding the peace in a city, where for the most part the inhabitants were very polite and accommodating to the soldiers. One of Don's favorite sights was Mt. Fugiyama, because the surroundings reminded him of Maine.

Don returned to the states on the troop ship *Copiapo*, AP-195. Before he left Japan, one of his interpreters gave him a samurai sword as a gift, which he carefully placed under the mattress on his bunk, and slept on the whole voyage back, so it wouldn't be confiscated. He also mailed a Japanese Infantry rifle back to the States, so he wouldn't have to carry it. While on board he met Harold Coombs, from South Bristol, Maine.

Don was discharged from the Army at Fort Devens, Massachusetts, on January 18, 1946, after three years and one month of service. He was awarded the Asiatic Pacific Campaign Ribbon, Philippines Liberation Medal with one bronze battle star, Northern Solomons Ribbon with one bronze battle star, the Good Conduct Award, World War II Victory Medal, and the Occupation Medal of Japan.

He married Marjory Gray of Newagen on May 10, 1946, and went to work at Samples Shipyard in Boothbay Harbor for the next 12 years. He then became caretaker for Mr. and Mrs. A. C. Tenner's estate in Boothbay Harbor, from 1957 to 1966.

He then was a caretaker for the Russell family, also in Boothbay Harbor, until his retirement in 1980. Don currently lives in Newagen, with his wife of 50 years, Marge.

ELLEN CAMERON BERRY
Seaman First Class, Navy WAVES

Ellen enlisted in the Navy WAVES on November 15, 1944, at the age of 21. She attended basic training at Hunter College in New York and was stationed in Norfolk, Virginia, where she worked in a transportation pool as a driver for officers on the base. She had been employed by the telephone company in Portsmouth, New Hampshire, prior to that time.

Ellen Cameron Berry,
Navy WAVES

Ellen and her brother Raymond were able to get together in Charleston, South Carolina, during the war, while he was on leave. They went out to a restaurant to get a bite to eat, and right in the middle of the meal, Raymond jumped up, out of his chair, and left the restaurant. Ellen couldn't figure out what was going on, but pretty soon Raymond returned to the table with another man in tow. It was their long time family friend, Mr. Flemming from Bath, Maine, who also had served in the Coast Guard with their father Niles. Raymond had seen him walk by the window of the restaurant, and wanted to catch him before he got lost in the crowd.

Ellen was discharged from the Navy WAVES on April 17, 1946, after two years of service, and was awarded the World War II Victory Medal. She then went into the field of nursing and was later married to Charles Berry of Cumberland, Maine. After raising a family with her husband, she went to work for New England Telephone and retired from that position in the mid 1980s. Ellen currently lives in Cumberland.

DAVID BLAKE
Sergeant, U.S. Marine Corps

David enlisted in the Marine Corps on December 7, 1941, at the age of 17. He had been working for Lawrence Boyd on Southport prior to that time doing odd jobs.

David attended boot camp at Parris Island in South Carolina, and was later sent to Camp LeJeune, North Carolina. He was in the First Marine Division, which was shipped to San Francisco, California, then overseas into battle in Guadalcanal for five months. After that

David Blake,
U.S. Marine Corps

time he was sent to Australia for R & R. David was sent into battle again in New Guinea and from there went to Pelelu, where he was in charge of ten men on a 105 Howitzer recoilless rifle. He also served in New Zealand and the Russel Islands.

After these two battles he was shipped to San Diego, California, and on to Norfolk, Virginia, where he stayed until his discharge from the Marines in December of 1945 after serving for four years. He was awarded the Asiatic Pacific Theater Campaign Ribbon and the Good Conduct Medal.

After the war David went to work at the Bath Iron Works. He later worked at the Rumford Paper Mill as a runner on a coating machine and then moved to Los Angeles, California, where he worked in maintenance for the Rex Nord Corporation, Inc., assembling cement mixers. David presently lives in Mohave Valley, Arizona, with his wife of 51 years, Shirley.

HAROLD BOYD
Staff Sergeant, U.S. Army

Harold was drafted in 1941, at the age of 21. At the time he had been working as a sheet metal worker in Boston. He received his basic training at Camp Edwards in Mashpee, Massachusetts. Harold was in the 398th Anti-Aircraft Artillery, Automatic Weapons Battalion, Battery A.

His outfit boarded the *Aquitania* in Boston Harbor on June 21st, 1944, with a destination of England. She was the fifth largest ocean liner in the world and the voyage lasted for eight

Harold Boyd,
U.S. Army

days. Harold remembers England being very cold and wet and seeing a lot of destruction there. His outfit then crossed the Channel on July 27 and arrived in France on the 29th. There were dozens of barrage balloons strung up on steel cables and a lot of equipment was being unloaded, including the half-tracks that Harold was trained on. The battery landed on the Omaha beachhead on July 30th: D-Day plus 54 days, and proceeded on to St. Germaine de Varville, where they spent their first night.

Harold was a platoon sergeant and was in charge of four squads of half-tracks, which are motorized armored vehicles. There were eight half-tracks to a platoon, and two to a squad. He was responsible for making sure they were assembled and disassembled correctly at each new location. This assignment would take Harold all over France, Germany, and the Bavarian Alps.

After four years of service, Harold shipped out of Marseille, France, in 1945 and was discharged shortly thereafter. He was in Germany when VE Day was announced and was awarded the European African Middle Eastern Campaign Ribbon and the Good Conduct Medal for his service. He worked in sheet metal and as a construction foreman all over New England after the war until his retirement in 1982. He currently lives in South Easton, Massachusetts with his wife of 20 years, Nancy.

LAWRENCE BRENTON BOYD
Corporal T-5, U.S. Army

Lawrence tried to enlist in the Navy during the winter of 1942, but was turned down for poor eyesight, yet he was drafted into the Army on March 11, 1943. He had been an apprentice machinist at the Bath Iron Works prior to that time, and when it became evident that he would probably be drafted, his status was changed to machinist helper.

Lawrence Boyd,
U.S. Army

He was trained in the anti-aircraft artillery section at Camp Callan, La Jolla, California. In June of 1943 he was sent to Camp Davis, North Carolina, to attend master gunner school. Lawrence was informed, just prior to the date when he would have graduated as a warrant officer, that the school was being phased out, because the Allies now had air superiority over the Axis powers. So he attended radar school at the same camp and graduated from that, achieving the rank of Corporal T-5.

At the time there was no place to assign new graduates, so Lawrence and the other graduates were shipped to Camp Hulen, Texas, to await reassignment. Lawrence was then sent to Fort Bliss, El Paso, Texas, where he joined approximately 10,000 other anti-aircraft artillery technicians in what had been an old Japanese American internment enclosure. The Japanese Americans had previously been removed from the camp due to its substandard conditions. Lawrence said the only improvements made when he got there was that they didn't lock the gate on him. During the winter of 1943, while he was stationed there, Lawrence worked on several communication construction projects near Las Cruces, New Mexico.

Early in the spring of 1944 he was transferred to Camp Shelby, which was located near Hattisburg, Mississippi. While there Lawrence and the other men were formed into several Engineer Maintenance Companies. He was assigned to the 982nd, and despite his other training, was made a Truck Driver Training Instructor, a position he held until he left the company.

In August the companies were relocated to a port of embarkation in New York and boarded the *Queen Elizabeth*, which took them to Grenock, Scotland. While in England, Lawrence remembers seeing the sky completely full of C-45s and C-46s pulling gliders heading for a river crossing in Germany. All morning they flew east and all afternoon they returned, some still dragging parts of the gliders.

After a month in England picking up additional equipment, the 982nd went to Omaha Beach, arriving 90 days after the D-Day invasion. They spent the winter in Paris in a large bus garage that was transformed into a repair depot for construction engineering equipment. Leaving there they were attached to the British Second Army Group and repaired equipment wherever they found it in France, Holland, and Germany.

Lawrence's unit couldn't get any supplies or fuel while they were assigned to the British Second Army Group, so every day a truck loaded with empty gas cans was sent out to find another American unit from which to beg supplies. One day Lawrence and another corporal were out on the daily search when they accidentally blundered into Venlo, Holland, before the British had succeeded in taking the town. Fortunately everyone was to busy to be concerned with them and they drove through the city without incident and then south to the American 15th Army Headquarters supply depot, where they found fuel. At the depot Lawrence and his friend were advised to return north by a different route.

The 982nd's primary duty was to provide support to the British and American combat engineer battalions by repairing their bulldozers and other heavy equipment. It was nearly impossible to get parts, and the mechanics would visit all the quartermaster dumps of damaged equipment and would return with salvaged parts or even a piece of equipment the same as what they had to repair. Often times the salvaged equipment was less damaged than the original, and the mechanics would repair it instead and then reissue it to the user, painting on it the identification numbers of the original, which in turn might later be repaired and reissued to another organization.

The 982nd were non-combatants, so they were only issued 12 rounds of ammunition for their carbines. After arriving in the British Army area most of the men in the company acquired arms they could get ammunition for. Lawrence carried a German Mauser rifle and had a case of ammo under the seat of the truck he drove.

After a few months the 982nd was ordered to leave all its equipment and move down to Marseille, France. So Lawrence returned his carbine and the 12 bullets he had been issued previously. On September 10, 1944, Lawrence was on board a troop train in Troyes, France. On the way south it was reported that the war was over, so the French train crew disconnected the engine from the rest of the train and left in the engine, thus leaving the troops stranded on the main line for 24 hours before they came back and completed their trip.

Waiting for the men at the port was the troop transport *General Richardson*, which was manned by the U.S. Coast Guard. Lawrence got on board and was sitting out on deck when Stuart Thompson recognized him. Stuart was part of the crew and was a friend from Southport. Lawrence was being returned to the United States for redeployment to the Far East when he found out the war was officially over. He was discharged from Fort Devens in Massachusetts on January 9, 1945, after two years, nine months, and 29 days of service. While there he met his brother Harold and Franklin Payson, who were on their way home. Lawrence received the European African Middle Eastern Campaign Ribbon, World War II Victory Medal, and the Good Conduct Medal.

After the war, Lawrence went to the University of Maine at Orono on the G.I. Bill and studied civil engineering.

He worked for his father one summer after college was out moving the West Southport Grammar School from the hill to its present location. Robert Eaton and Robert Colby, who were both friends from college and summer residents on the island, helped them complete the task.

He joined the Maine National Guard while at Orono, as well as attending senior R.O.T.C., and was commissioned a Second Lieutenant in the army reserve upon graduation from the University of Maine. Later in 1950, while working at Grand Coulee Dam in Washington State, Lawrence received word that his National Guard Organization had been federalized for the Korean Conflict. Upon this news Lawrence notified the National Guard of his present location and he was instructed to await further notice. To this day, he is still waiting.

Lawrence returned to Maine in March of 1951 and married his girlfriend Verna Wyman of Newcastle. Following the wedding he worked at the Bath Iron Works for one year, then started working for the Boston and Maine Railroad, which later became Gilford Transportation Industries. He retired in 1984 after 32 years with the railroad. He currently lives in Melrose, Massachusetts, with his wife of 45 years, Verna.

LESTER BOYD
Technician Fifth Grade, U.S. Army

Lester was drafted into the Army on February 14, 1945, at the age of 28. He received his basic training at Camp Gordon, Augusta, Georgia, and met a man from Warren, Maine, while he was there. He had been employed at the Bath Iron Works prior to that time. Lester was married to Charlotte Smith of North New Portland, Maine, on September 19, 1939.

When he was called into the Army, Charlotte and their five-year-old daughter moved in with her parents, until he returned home from the service.

He was enroute to Eniwetok when

Lester Boyd,
U.S. Army

the Japanese surrendered, and was rerouted to Iwo Jima for construction, repairs, and cleanup work on buildings, drainage systems, and the airport located there. Lester was discharged on August 27, 1946, after one year and six months of service, and was awarded the Asiatic Pacific Campaign Medal, World War II Victory Medal, Good Conduct Medal, and the Army Occupation Medal.

After the war he returned to the Bath Iron Works, where he was employed as a welder for about five years. The family then moved back to Southport and he went stop seining with Leslie Brewer. Several years later they moved again to Strong, Maine, and he went to work for the Fosters Manufacturing Company, located in Strong, running a wood lathe. Lester passed away in February of 1983, at the age of 66.

CLIFTON BREWER
Shipfitter Second Class, U.S. Navy

Cliff was drafted into the Navy on June 1, 1944, at the age of 25 and received his basic training at Sampson Naval Training Center in New York. He later went on to Illinois and Oakland, California, where he was assigned to a Liberty ship, which he waited for while it was put into commission. He had been employed at Samples Shipyard in Boothbay Harbor and at the Bath Iron Works prior to that time, and was married to Elsie Webber of Southport on March 25, 1939.

While in the service Cliff spent time on the *U.S.S. Montrose*, which carried troops and supplies to islands all over the Pacific

Clifton Brewer, U.S. Navy

Ocean, including the Philippines, Iwo Jima, Okinawa, Guam, Laite, and post-war Japan. He was discharged in Boston on January 20, 1946, after one year, seven months, and 20 days in the Navy. Cliff was awarded the World War II Victory Medal, American Area Medal, Asiatic Pacific Ribbon with one star, and the Philippine Liberation Ribbon with one star. After the war he returned to Southport where he started his own boatyard, which he ran until his retirement. He then went lobstering for several years until he and Elsie moved to Alna. Cliff passed away on July 2, 1985, at the age of 65.

MASON BRITTON
Ensign, U.S. Navy

In August of 1942, Mason enlisted in the Navy. He was 19 years old at the time and had been studying engineering at Cornell University, in Ithaca, New York. While at Cornell he became involved in the V-12 Program,

Mason Britton, U.S. Navy

went through midshipmen school and diesel school. He then joined the amphibious service and was sent to Guam.

Mason served on LSM #475 (landing ship medium) in the Philippines, Okinawa, Sasebo, Shanghai, and China. While in China, he traveled 1,800 miles up the Yangtze River to Chungking to deliver supplies. There were missionaries on board representing the Lutheran, Catholic, and Methodist religions. They were very knowledgeable about the area and showed the crew various pagodas and historic sights. They also pointed out artifacts you could purchase at the local markets when they docked the ship.

The crew had to try to make drinking water from the river. It was terribly polluted and proved to be a challenging task. The ship didn't carry a large supply of food on board and the crew often ate local food when they went ashore, which Mason said was very good. He discovered that in the North the fish and meat were better, and in the South the rice and vegetables were better. He said the tea was excellent throughout the country.

The LSM #475 was about 260 feet in length, and was manned by a crew of 70 men. The weather was extremely hot; when they took on a cargo of 200 horses, it became all the more noticeable. The horses were delivered to the Chinese Army further up the river, to help them fight against the Chinese Communists.

In 1946 the United States government turned over much of its equipment to the Chinese, including Mason's LSM. His crew stayed aboard for awhile and trained the Chinese Naval Officers who were assigned to it. They were used to a class system in China and didn't think they should have to get their hands dirty. They soon learned that, if they wanted to run the ship, they would have to change their way of thinking.

Mason was transferred to the inactive reserve in 1946 after over three years of service and became part of the naval reserves at this time. He was awarded the World War Two Victory Medal and the Pacific Theater of War Ribbon.

In the winter of 1950, he was called back to the amphibious service during the Korean War on LST #822. His was the first amphibious group from America to arrive in Korea and the winter weather there was extremely cold. All their operations were based in Japan, and they picked up everything from tanks to military supplies there. The cargos were then delivered to Inchon and Pusan in Korea. While in Korea Mason saw Bob Hope perform with the USO.

Japan in 1950 was an interesting place to visit, although much of it was in hard shape. You could see that the Japanese people were slowly starting to rebuild their country. It was a very poor place to visit, but it was safe for Americans to walk around in the cities and towns. Mason said it was like the Japanese had started a new chapter in their lives. General MacArthur was running the country at the time and things seemed to be coming back.

After three years of service in Korea, Mason was retired for disability in 1953 at the grade of Lieutenant-JG (junior grade). It took him 31 days to return to the United States, and he was awarded one battle star. After the war he worked for Cincinnati Micacron, Inc. in Cincinnati, Ohio, which is a machine tool business. In 1959, he married Joan Barbara, from Cincinnati. Mason has since retired and moved back to Southport, where he lives with his wife of 37 years, Joan.

One of Mason's ships loaded with cargo.

JONATHAN BROWN
Seaman First Class, U.S. Navy

Jack enlisted in the Navy on July 23, 1943, at the age of 17. He attended basic training in Newport, Rhode Island, and later became an armed guard that helped to protect merchant ships. He had attended Proctor Academy in Andover, New Hampshire, prior to that time.

He served on the *S.S. Salmon P. Chase*, which was a liberty ship; the *S. S. Fort Matanzas*, a T-2 Tanker; and the M.V. Kota Gede, a Dutch freighter. Jack spent time in the South Pacific, New Guinea, and the Philippines, and while stateside, was stationed in

Jonathan Brown,
U.S. Navy

Norfolk, Virginia; Brooklyn, New York; and San Francisco, California. He was discharged from the Navy on March 14, 1946, after two years, seven months, and 21 days and was awarded the America Area Ribbon, Asiatic Pacific Ribbon, Philippines Liberation Medal, and the World War II Victory Medal for his service. After the war Jack returned to Southport and worked at the Rendezvous gas station pumping gas, which is now the white building located between Earla Kelley's home and the Lawnmeer Inn.

He was married to Dorothy Rice, from Saugus, Massachusetts and Sprucewold – Boothbay Harbor, on August 17, 1946, at the Ocean Point Chapel. He went to work at Marine Service in Boothbay Harbor, and later started Coletti and Brown with his brother-in-law, which was a carpet cleaning business. He then took over the business and operated it by himself as Brown's Carpet Cleaning. He retired from the business in 1976. Jack passed away on September 18, 1989, at the age of 64.

NILES CAMERON
Lieutenant, U.S. Coast Guard

Niles entered the lifesaving service in 1918, which later became the U.S. Coast Guard in 1925. He was stationed at Damariscove, Burnt Island, White Head, and on a cutter which hailed from Gloucester, Massachusetts.

When the Second World War broke out he was assigned to Portsmouth, New Hampshire, where he was the Captain of the Port. He also trained men for sea duty and was in charge of communications while there. Niles was awarded the American Defense Medal and World War II Victory Medal for his service.

Niles Cameron, U.S. Coast Guard

He retired in 1948 after 30 years in the Coast Guard and worked on yachts at the Freeport Boat Yard up until June of 1959, when he passed away at the age of 65.

RAYMOND CAMERON
Chief Boatswain's Mate, U.S. Coast Guard

Raymond enlisted in the Coast Guard on March 18, 1939, at the age of 18. He served as a surfman on Damariscove Island and was later stationed in Cape Elizabeth. When the Second World War broke out, he was reassigned to the destroyer escort *U.S.S. Ramsden* DE-382, which protected troop transports and high speed tankers carrying aviation fuel while they crossed the sub-infested waters of the Atlantic Ocean and Mediterranean.

Raymond Cameron,
U.S. Coast Guard

Faced with sea and air attacks from Axis bases in Italy and Southern France, the *Ramsden* never lost a single vessel it was protecting, and in 1944, while escorting a convoy to Bizerte, North Africa, she shot down one of a flight of German Dornier bombers that was attacking the convoy. The ship crossed the Atlantic 18 times, and put in to Cardiff, Londonderry, Glasgow, Plymouth, Portsmouth, Le Havre, Cherbourg, Casablanca, and Bizerte.

While on shore leave in Scotland, Raymond met some of the local townspeople, and when it was discovered that they both shared the same last name, he was soon invited to dinner at their home along with some of his shipmates. It was a real treat, especially being so far away from home. He also was able to visit his sister Ellen during the war, while in Charleston, South Carolina, awaiting orders to ship out.

The *Ramsden* was later assigned to the Pacific Fleet, where she served as both an escort and as a plane guard, assigned to Fleet Air Wing Four, assisting Army and Navy planes on bombing and reconnaissance missions over the Kurile Island Group. During the occupation of Northern Honshu, the *Ramsden* operated as an escort for Fleet Auxiliary and as a rescue vessel for carrier and land-based planes of the occupation forces. Raymond participated in the surrender of Ominato Naval Base and as part of the occupation of northern Japan. He also made several trips to China carrying supplies after the war.

Raymond was discharged on February 25, 1947, after eight years of service in the Coast Guard, and was awarded the European African Middle Eastern Campaign Ribbon with two stars, Asiatic Pacific Campaign Ribbon, World War II Victory Medal, National Defense Service Medal, American Campaign Medal, and the Coast Guard Good Conduct Medal.

He was in the inactive reserves from 1947 until May of 1954, and was called in to help train Coast Guard recruits at Cape May, New Jersey, for a period of about three months. Raymond was later discharged on October 4, 1954, and enlisted in the Air Force on October 5, 1954.

He served in New York, Alaska, Louisiana, Illinois, and California. He retired from the Air Force on July 31, 1966, with the rank of Staff Sergeant, after over 20 years of service, and was awarded the Air Force Longevity Service Award with three oak leaf clusters.

He then moved to Gig Harbor, Washington, where he was the owner/operator of a tuna boat. Raymond passed away on December 21, 1974, at the age of 54.

CARL CEDERSTROM
Ensign, U.S. Navy

Carl Cederstrom, U.S. Navy

Carl enlisted in the Navy in May of 1943, at the age of 17. He had been attending high school in Everett, Massachusetts, prior to that time, and after his enlistment his mother and siblings moved to Southport. He attended V-12 school at Tufts and Holy Cross Colleges in Massachusetts, which were two year, accelerated college programs offered to high school seniors. Four months of additional specialized naval training and gunnery school made Carl a commissioned officer, at the age of 19.

He then went to Key West, Florida, for anti-sub warfare training, and was assigned to a destroyer escort in the Philippines. His duties included helping the navigational officer, first lieutenant, and he was an assistant to the gunnery officer. While in Hawaii he looked up his cousin Franklin Payson, who was in the Army Air Corp, and over a four-week period, was able to visit with him quite often. He also visited with Norma Clifford, who was a Navy WAVE stationed at the hospital there, and who also was from Southport.

Carl served for three years and three months, and went on inactive duty in the naval reserves in August of 1946. He was awarded the U.S. Theater of War Ribbon, Pacific Theater of War Ribbon, and the World War II Victory Medal for his service.

After the war he studied history and government at the University of Maine at Orono on the GI Bill. With two years of college already behind him, Carl graduated with a degree in 1948. He started working at the First National in Boothbay Harbor, but soon volunteered for the Korean War and served on a destroyer off the coast of Japan and Korea. Carl was now a first lieutenant on board, and was in charge of the general maintenance of the ship and served as an assistant to the gunnery officer. He was transferred to Kansas City to the Naval Reserve Training Center and was promoted to the rank of full lieutenant. He was discharged in 1964 as a lieutenant commander and was awarded the Japanese Occupation Medal, U.N. Service Medal, and the U.S./Korean Theater of Operations Medal.

Carl was married in August of 1953 to Verna Bradford. After the Korean War he attended college at the University of Missouri, where he earned a master's degree in sociology. He also earned a master's degree in city planning from Cornell University in Ithaca, New York. He later went into the field of city planning in Kansas City, Missouri, and retired from that after 17 years on the job. Carl currently lives in Blue Springs, Missouri, with his wife of 43 years, Verna.

ROBERT CHILSON
Lieutenant-JG (Junior Grade), U.S. Navy

Bob enlisted in the Navy on July 1, 1943, at the age of 17. He was trained at the Naval Operating Base in Norfolk, Virginia, and also attended Destroyer School there. He later went to Aircraft Fighter Director School at Gulfport, Mississippi. He had been a freshman at Tufts majoring in biology prior to that time.

The U.S.S. Collett DO-730

While chasing his ship across the Pacific, he was assigned temporary duty on Eniwetok Atoll, and later in Hawaii at Commander Destroyer Pacific Headquarters, or "Com-Des-Pac," as it was referred to. Bob served on the *U.S.S. Collett* DO-730 in the Pacific, and his duties included C.I.C. Officer (combat information center), which meant he was in charge of the radar and sonar plotting when the men were called to general quarters (ready for combat). He later became qualified as officer of the deck on the *Collett*.

Later, Bob's ship was sent to Shanghai and Tsing Tao, China, to patrol up and down the China Coast. He really enjoyed China, and found its country and culture to be fascinating. He was discharged in Boston on July 1, 1946, after spending exactly three years in the Navy, and was awarded the Asiatic Pacific Theater Medal, American Service Medal, and the World War II Victory Medal.

Bob returned to Tufts on the GI Bill, and graduated in 1947 with a degree in English. He then went to work for a division of the Dow Chemical Company in Cincinnati, Ohio, and later in Avon, Connecticut, in sales and marketing management. He married June Costello from Manchester, New Hampshire, and they had four children: Susan, Judy, Jeff, and Joanne. In 1977, after 30 years on the job, Bob sought a change of pace, and went into the government and public affairs branch of his company, where he stayed until 1987, when he retired, and moved to Southport with his wife, June.

FRANK CLIFFORD
Seaman First Class, U.S. Navy

Frank was 17 years old and in high school when he volunteered for the Navy. It was discovered that he was colorblind and flatfooted when he took his physical, and he was not accepted at that time. He graduated in June and was in Boothbay Harbor when VJ Day was announced. Festivities broke out all over town and

Frank Clifford,
U.S. Navy

there was soon singing and dancing in the streets. The celebration was interrupted when word spread that one of the ships in Mill Cove had caught on fire. Everyone then rushed down to the shore to watch it burn.

On September 20, 1945, Frank was drafted. He was the first one through the physical, because they did it alphabetically, and he was offered service in the Army, Navy, or Marines. Frank chose the Navy hoping to see the world.

He received his training at Camp Peary in Williamsburg, Virginia, and was later stationed on the *U.S.S. Amick*, which was a destroyer escort in Jacksonville, Florida. Frank was all set to go to sea, but instead they headed 30 miles upriver to Green Cove Springs, where he spent eight hot months chipping paint as the Navy started decommissioning ships. They rafted them up in groups of eight and went to work with the preparations necessary to put them in "mothballs." Even though the men were rafted up they still received 20% sea pay.

One of Frank's jobs was to paint the peak tanks, which are located in the bow of the ship and are in very tight quarters. They supply ballast, which is supposed to help the ship go through the water smoothly. Frank said you could only work on them for 15 or 20 minutes at a time, because there was not much ventilation and the fumes from the paint would almost knock you out. He would paint a little, then go up on deck for a half hour, then go back and paint a little more. It was an unpleasant task, to say the least.

On August 11, 1946, after ten months and 21 days, Frank was discharged from the Navy. He was awarded the World War Two Victory Medal and the Good Conduct Award. He went to the University of Maine at Orono on the GI Bill and studied business administration and psychology.

In November of 1950 he was called back for service in the Korean War. Frank tried to volunteer for the Navy, but they were looking for specialists and he was a Seaman First Class, so he was drafted into the Army. He became a Corporal at Camp Edwards in Falmouth, Massachusetts. Frank was kept there with a small nucleus of men as cadre to help train the next group of soldiers coming through. He then received orders to go to the West Coast and got on a troop train that took him from Cape Cod to San Francisco, California. He was stationed in Sausalito at Fort Barrie for a while, then was sent to Travis Air Force Base in Sacremento with an Anti-Aircraft Group. Frank said they were always on alert setting up the guns in case the Koreans flew in to attack California.

While there he specialized in the motor pool as a parts manager and a dispatcher. He was able to see a lot of the United States and even drove back to Southport to get his car with a friend of his, and then drove it back to California. He was discharged in November of 1952 after two years of service. In April of 1955, Frank married his girlfriend, Barbara Clunie, who lived in Newcastle, Maine. He went to work in the banking business and spent 38 years in it between Boston, Portland, and Damariscotta. Frank currently lives in Damariscotta with his wife of 41 years, Barbara.

LOUIS G. CLIMO
Aviation Machinist Mate First Class,
U.S. Navy

Lou enlisted in the Navy on November 1, 1941, at the age of 22. He received his basic training in Newport, Rhode Island, then went on to Aviation Mechanics School in Jacksonville, Florida. He had worked in Wakefield, Massachusetts, at odd jobs and for the railroad prior to that time.

During the war, Lou served in the North Atlantic as part of a convoy escort and in the South Pacific aboard the aircraft carrier, *U.S.S. Essex.* He was involved in battles in the Leyte

Louis G. Climo,
U.S. Navy

Gulf, Mariana Islands, and Okinawa, where his ship withstood relentless attacks by Japanese kamikaze pilots. At one point, Lou never went below deck for 45 days straight, because they were working on aircraft day and night. Sleep was a hard commodity to come by, so the men had to catch a few winks when they could on deck.

While in Jacksonville, Lou was stationed with David Smith, who would later become his brother-in-law. Both received orders to ship out to the Pacific, but they were about six weeks apart. As fate would have it they ended up on the same ship in the same squadron. Also, one day Lou heard his brother's name called over the P.A. system on the *Essex*. They were able to visit briefly, because James was in transit to another ship and was only aboard for about 48 hours.

When the war ended, Lou was awarded the European Theater Medal, Asiatic Pacific Theater Medal, World War II Victory Medal, and the Good Conduct Medal (Five Awards). He married Grace Gunn-Smith on May 13, 1946, in Minneapolis, Minnesota, and they had three children: Leslie, Smith, and Reid. He stayed in the Navy until November of 1961, when he was discharged from Brunswick Naval Air Station in Maine with the rank of ADR First Class after 20 years of service.

Lou and his family moved to the Boothbay Region from Bowdoinham, and he worked at Maine Coast Boat Sales and Boatel Boothbay in Boothbay Harbor. He was also a selectman while they lived there. In May of 1972, the Climos moved to Southport after purchasing the general store. Lou passed away on January 3, 1983, at the age of 63.

ROBERT COLBY
Petty Officer SM 2/C,
U.S. Naval Reserves

Bob enlisted on May 15th, 1942, at the age of 18. He left high school his senior year and joined the Naval Reserves, which meant he would go on active duty immediately, but would be through with his commitment when the war was over. He went to boot camp for eight weeks at Newport, Rhode Island, followed by 16 weeks at signal school at Butler University in Indianapolis, Indiana, and then spent four weeks of further training in Merchant Convoy Signals (Mersigs) in Noroton Heights, Connecticut. In November

Robert Colby,
U.S. Naval Reserves

of 1942, he was transferred to the Brooklyn Armed Guard Center in Brooklyn, New York, and was assigned to the *S.S. Denny*, a small United Fruit Company freighter under the Panamanian flag.

For the next several months Bob traveled through the Caribbean delivering various cargos, including two trips from Honduras to Northern Panama with 40 head of cattle each trip as deck cargo. Imagine hearing the mooing of cattle with no land in sight. While in the Caribbean they had a brush with an enemy submarine. The men were called to battle stations and the *Denny's* 3" gun was fired. Apparently a periscope had been sighted. Radio silence was broken, because they were traveling all alone and a Navy Kingfisher patrol plane quickly appeared on the scene, which Bob conversed with via light flash signal. Luckily that was the end of the incident, but soon enough Bob would encounter battle conditions.

He was then transferred to the Tidewater tanker, the *Tide Penn*, which spent the winter of 1943-1944 plying between ports in Venezuela, Aruba, and Columbia bringing crude oil to the Montreal pipe line in Portland, Maine. He was reassigned to the Armed Guard Center in New Orleans where he was placed on a convoy Commodore's staff making voyages to the Port of Spain, Trinidad, on the bauxite ore carriers *Felix Taussig* and the *Steel Ore*.

His next ship would be the Liberty Ship, *George L. Curry*. During the winter of 1944-1945, he made six crossings across the Atlantic carrying ammunition, bombs, airplanes, and other war supplies. They were escorted by American, British, and Canadian ships, who were on the lookout for German U-Boats and who were intent on keeping any convoy stragglers in line. All communication was visual while on convoy duty and Bob was responsible for sending and receiving messages, both by flags and flashing light.

Convoys were organized in lines so that a convoy of 50 ships might have five lines across with ten ships in each line and of course each ship was assigned a specific place in line with orders to maintain a certain distance from the ship ahead and the ships located to port and starboard. This proved to be a difficult task, because the convoy was made up of ships of varying ages and speed abilities. The Convoy Commodore then had to set a speed geared to the slower ships, perhaps seven or eight knots.

Keeping station (one's place) was particularly difficult at night because all ships were blacked out and on some nights it was necessary to tow a fog buoy, which is designed to send a jet of water into the air so that the bow lookout on the ship astern can keep the bridge informed as to their position in regard to the buoy if weather conditions don't allow the vessel ahead to be seen.

During the hurricane of the fall of 1944, Bob's ship was in convoy bound for England. The seas were 80 to 100 feet high, and maintaining convoy positions was impossible as each ship's major concern was to stay afloat. By the second day of the storm there wasn't another vessel in sight and the *Curry* finished the voyage alone. Two thirty-foot lifeboats that had been chained to the davits and a deck load of P-40 fighter planes were swept off the ship during this voyage. In a later crossing of the Atlantic, during some particularly rough winter weather, the convoy was again dispersed, and the *Curry* lost another lifeboat.

The week before Christmas of 1944 the *Curry* was in Cherbourg, France, where her cargo of bombs and ammunition was to be unloaded. Prior to unloading, the *Curry* was anchored in the harbor with the other munitions ships. All of a sudden a surface mine, which had apparently drifted through the harbor's entrance, started making its way thorough the fleet. All eyes were upon it, anxiously watching its path. Everyone held their breath, envisioning what would happen if it came in contact with one of the ships loaded with high explosives. Miraculously the mine missed the entire convoy and drifted up onto the beach, where it was exploded by rifle fire.

By this time, the Battle of the Bulge was in full swing as the Germans were making their final push for a breakthrough. Saboteurs were thought to be in the area and Bob spent his 21st birthday on Shore Patrol duty with two French sailors who didn't speak English. Bob soon found his high school French was inadequate, but none-the-less their mission was to check on servicemen who might be Germans in disguise. Needless to say, none were found.

On December 24th, the ex-Belgian liner, *Leopoldville*, serving as a troop ship, was torpedoed just outside Cherbourg Harbor with a loss of lives exceeding 700. It was the second largest troop ship loss in World War II. German U-Boats demonstrated their presence again, on the last day of 1944, when a convoy of ships, including the *Curry*, was proceeding across the Channel on a sunny winter's day. The calm was suddenly broken by the explosion of a torpedo deep in the bowels of the *Black Hawk*, which was a freighter in the left outer flank of the convoy, and was just ahead of Bob's ship. Seconds later another torpedo narrowly missed the bow of the *Curry* and struck the ship on the *Curry's* right, which had forged ahead of its proper station in line, and so received the torpedo in its stern. The explosion set off the ammunition magazine, sending flames and smoke a hundred feet or more skyward, and blew the 3" gun crew into the sea. It is a sight Bob will never forget, along with the realization that the second torpedo was meant for the *Curry*, but missed her. While the escort vessels frantically sought the U-Boat the convoy continued onward, and that night lay safely at anchor in the harbor at Swansea, Wales. The year 1945 was ushered in at midnight by the earsplitting blasts of ships' whistles saluting the New Year with their hope for peace.

The *Curry* returned to the United States, and after a brief time in dry-dock for painting and other minor repairs, received new orders. While in New York, Bob was able to visit with his cousin Steven King from Farmington, Maine, before they had to ship out. The *Curry* set forth for the Mediterranean and passed through the Gates of Hercules, as ancient sea-farers called the entrance to the Med. After short layovers in Oran Harbor in North Africa and another in the Bay of Naples, the *Curry* again in con-voy sailed up the western coast of Italy, losing one ship to a mine off Piombino, and at a last arrived at the Port of Liverno on the Liguruan Sea.

The port had been bombed extensively by the Allies when it was held by the Germans, and when they retreated they left behind a harbor full of sunken vessels. One was scuttled across the harbor's narrow entrance. Divers had to cut out the midsection of the vessel to remove it, so that ships could enter the harbor noting the bow of the ship on the port side and the stern to starboard as they passed through the open middle.

The dock where the *Curry* discharged her cargo had once been a ship, as well, but had been stripped of her superstructure and large metal gangplanks laid to the shore so that trucks could readily move cargos to the land. Leghorn was bombed by the Allies and bombed by the Germans so there was evidence of great destruction everywhere one looked. The image of the three, perhaps four-year old, girl playing by herself amidst the ruins of a one-time house with a doll as her sole com-panion is a haunting image that stays with Bob to this day.

The Germans were retreating, but still in La Spezia and Genoa, a short distance to the north, air raids from those forces were still an evening

expectation, and Bob soon learned that the noise of gunfire was oblit-
erated when he was actually firing the 20mm in the wing of the bridge.
If you weren't firing a gun the noise from the other guns was unbeliev-
ably loud, almost more than your ears could stand. Luckily the bombs
did little damage to what was already devastated. A day came when Bob
and friends had some time off the ship, and the City of Pisa was only six
miles away, so off they went via Army trucks to climb the tower made
famous by Galileo centuries before.

The return voyage to the States took the *Curry* past the Napoleonic
Isles of Corsica and Elba, past the Rock of Gibraltar, and across the
Atlantic without incident. Bob was due for leave and of course headed
for David's Island in Cozy Harbor to be with Peg, his wife to be, and his
mother. (In those days they had chaperones.) That was the May several
inches of snow fell in Maine, and in Southport in particular. Despite the
weather, the good news on the radio and in the newspapers was that the
war in Europe was over and so they, like millions of others, gave thanks.

After his leave, Bob returned to New Orleans, but soon was put on a
troop train with other veterans of the Atlantic for duty in the Pacific.
They eventually arrived at Shoemaker, California, where 10,000 Naval
personnel made up what was known as Fleet City. Here he served as
Master of Arms of his barracks while awaiting, with others, further
orders. In what seemed to be a short time the orders came, and Bob and
several hundred other Navy men found themselves on an old Dutch
liner, the *Kota Inten*, which was now used as a troop transport. Although
the vessel's destination was not known to Bob and his fellow passengers, it was generally believed that in some way they would be involved
in the invasion of Japan that was sure to come about.

It was somewhere in the mid-Pacific that the electrifying news of Japan's
surrender was announced and jubilation pervaded the ship. The remainder
of the voyage, with brief stops at the atoll islands of Ulithi and Eniwetok,
took the *Kota Inten* to the Island of Samar in the Philippines, where the trip
ended and the passengers were disembarked. Here, Bob once again did
duty as a Master at Arms, this time in a Quonset Hut known to its occupants as the Half Moon Hotel, but was soon transferred to a Squadron
commander's staff on the good ship LSM 204 (landing ship medium).

The LSM was one of a number of vessels designed to land on beaches
where the bow doors would be opened and troops, tanks, trucks, and

other invasion necessities would be spewed forth. As Bob recalls, the LSM was about 200 feet long and being for the most part flat-bottomed, behaved badly in rough seas. The builders built her well however, as was proven in the typhoon that caught the squadron in the Straits north of Luzon. Bound for Japan the squadron was soon dispersed by the gigantic wind-whipped seas, and Bob remembers wondering how the 204 could possibly survive the wracking and twisting of its hull as it was lifted, dropped, and slammed by tons of water time and time again. The welds and rivets held, and the 204 later continued on its way to Wakayama, Japan, and thence back to the Philippines where she was once again loaded with men and materials for the occupation of Japan.

This time the voyage to Nagoya through the South China Sea, where Bob's Aunt Beth had been born aboard his grandfather's ship, the *Elizabeth Cushing* in the 1870s, went smoothly with the ships in the squadron primarily concerned with which vessel had a movie that they hadn't seen. After much signaling by blinker, a trade was made as the crew sat on the deck that night and watched something from home that for the moment enriched their lives whether it was Hollywood heroics, comedy, or romance.

In November of 1945, the 204 came into Naha Bay in Okinawa and there Bob left his last Naval assignment to board a Navy AKA for transport home. After landing in Portland, Oregon, some weeks later, Bob was homeward bound, and boarded a troop train that arrived in Boston, only after derailing in Three Forks, Montana. On December 18, 1945, on his 22nd birthday, Bob was discharged having served in the Navy three years, seven months, and four days. He received the European African Middle Eastern Ribbon, Asiatic-Pacific Ribbon, American Area Ribbon, and the World War Two Victory Medal.

Upon his arrival home, Bob gathered up Peg and two of their friends, and they headed to Quincy for a pizza. Bob tried to order a beer with his, and the waitress wouldn't serve him, because she didn't think he was old enough. He felt a little put out, considering he had just spent over three years in the war effort and now he couldn't even get a beer in his own country.

After the war Bob worked various odd jobs on Southport, and was married to his long-time girl friend Peg Dawson, from Jamaica Plain, Massachusetts, in June of 1946. That fall he received a letter from Wright

Britton, who was attending Mohawk College in New York State, which was an Army Hospital that had been converted into one of the Associated Colleges of Upper New York and was being staffed by professors from around the state. Colleges in the United States had been swamped with applications due to the GI Bill, as men returned from the war, and campuses like this one were popping up all over. Bob applied and was accepted. He studied there for two years, then transferred to the University of Maine at Orono.

After graduating, he taught public school for several years, both in Maine and in New Hampshire. Then he went to work at the Hinckley School where he did everything from teaching to coaching to eventually becoming the headmaster of the school. After 21 years at Hinckley, Bob and Peg decided it was time to move back to Southport for good. Upon their return Bob managed the Canal Bank in Boothbay Harbor and later worked in various boat yards in the region. He currently lives in Southport with his wife of 50 years, Peg.

CHARLES COLLINS
Technician Fifth Grade, U.S. Army

Charlie was drafted into the Army on January 27, 1944, at the age of 24. He received his basic training at Fort Belvoir, Virginia, and was later sent to Fort Lewis in Washington state for additional training. He was assigned to the 1637th Engineer Construction Battalion, Company A and worked building bridges. He had been employed as a stage builder at Bath Iron Works prior to that time and had married Marjorie Childs on July 4, 1942. Their first son was born in 1943 and their second son was born in 1945. Marjorie really had her hands full while Charlie was away.

Charles Collins, U.S. Army

While in the Army Charlie served in Germany and in the Philippines. After two years of service he was discharged from the separation center at Fort Devens in Massachusetts on January 22, 1946, and was awarded the American Theater Campaign Ribbon, European African Middle Eastern Theater Campaign Ribbon, Asiatic Pacific Theater Campaign Ribbon, and the World War II Victory Medal for his service.

After the war Charlie went to work for Manley Reed as a carpenter and caretaker of cottages and boats on Juniper Point. He later worked for Bill Luther and Frank Connor, both from Southport, as a carpenter, and eventually became the manager of Brewer's Boat Yard, which was also located on the island. Charlie passed away on September 24, 1984, at the age of 64.

RICHARD CONANT

Electronic Technician Mate
Third Class, U.S. Navy

Rick enlisted in the Navy in August of 1945, at the age of 18. He received basic training at the Great Lakes Training Station, then Electronics Technicians training in Chicago; Biloxi, Mississippi; and Treasure Island, California. He had been attending Taft High School in Water-town, Connecticut, prior to that time.

Richard Conant, U.S. Navy

He served a total of 11 months, and was discharged in California in July of 1946. Rick was awarded the American Theater Medal, and the Good Conduct Medal for his service. He then attended Yale University in New Haven, Connecticut, on the GI Bill, and graduated in 1950, with a degree in Mechanical Engineering. He went to work for the Cincinnati Milling Machine Company for six months, but in January of 1951, was called back into the Navy during the Korean War.

Rick took a 90-day wonder course in California, and boarded the *U.S.S. Elokomin* (A055), which was a fleet tanker. He earned the rank of Ensign, and served in the position of Gunnery Officer and, later Deck Officer, while on board. The ship was used to refuel aircraft carriers and destroyers, while underway. He traveled to Scotland, and spent six months in the Mediterranean, while on the *Elokomin*.

He was discharged in October of 1952 in Norfolk, Virginia, at the rank of Lieutenant–JG, and soon went back to work for the Cincinnati Milling Machine Company. Rick later sold machine tools in Connecticut for about 16 years, then decided to change professions, and went to work for Golden Era Boats, in Noank, Connecticut, building boats.

He was married in 1952, and was later remarried in 1980 to Christine Tryon, from Glastonbury, Connecticut. They moved to Southport in 1981, and Rick went to work for Twin River Engineering in Boothbay. He later worked for Sheepscot Machine Works, where he still occasionally works part time. Rick currently lives on Southport with his wife of 16 years, Christine.

LESTER CONNOR, JR.
Private, U.S. Army

In November of 1944, Budd tried to enlist in the Air Corps, at the age of 17. He had his parents' permission, but didn't pass part of an eye examination, which was required if you wanted to fly. So he joined the Army at Fort Devens, Massachusetts, and became part of the First Service Command, 26th Division. He had attended Brown and Nichols High School in Cambridge, Massachusetts, prior to that time.

While at Fort Devens, he met a man from Eastport, Maine, and they quickly became friends, as soon as he found out Budd had summered in Maine all his life. Shortly thereafter, Budd was called in for several physicals. He was told by Army doctors that they thought he was having heart problems, and should be discharged. Budd tried to tell them there was nothing wrong with him, but it was to no avail. He was medically discharged on February 28, 1945, and was awarded the American Service Medal and the World War II Victory Medal. He went to see his family physician when he returned home, and his doctor could find nothing wrong with his heart, but surmised that his pulse might have been racing, because he was nervous being away from home for the first time, and the Army doctors diagnosed it as a heart problem instead of anxiety.

Budd attended Boston University on the GI Bill, and graduated in June of 1950, with a degree in marketing and advertising. He was married to Dorothy Harold, from West Boylston, Massachusetts in 1955, and they had two daughters, Susan and Sarah. They later divorced in 1977.

He worked for the Burroughs Corporation from 1958 to 1969, and then, over the next 13 years, worked for three different Massachusetts banks, either as treasurer or vice president. In 1982, Budd moved back to Southport, and opened Video Paradise, a movie rental store, in Bath. The business was sold in 1986, and in 1987, he purchased the Treehouse Tavern in Wiscasset, which he later sold in 1994. Budd currently lives in Southport.

FRED HOLLIE COOK
Staff Sergeant, U.S. Marine Corps

Fred Cook, U. S. Marine Corps, and his wife Phyllis.

Fred enlisted in the Marines in 1938 at the age of 21. He was trained at Parris Island, South Carolina; Jacksonville, North Carolina; and received further training at Guantanamo Bay, Cuba, as part of the First Marine Division. Prior to enlisting he had worked at various jobs in his home state of West Virginia. He met Phyllis Pinkham of Southport, Maine, in 1940 while he was in Washington, D.C., and was working for the Navy Department. They married in December of 1941, and he shipped out in May of 1942 for the Pacific.

The First Marine Division landed on Guadalcanal on August 7, 1942, and Fred served in a heavy equipment unit. It was their duty to keep the airfields open, which was quite a challenge due to heavy Japanese bombing. While he was overseas he contracted malaria, which plagued him with reoccurrences even after the war. After serving several months at Guadalcanal, Fred was sent to Australia for R&R when Army replacements arrived. He sent a letter home to Phyllis, and in it asked her, "Have you seen Victoria lately?" He was trying to let her know he was in Australia, but Phyllis couldn't figure out who Victoria was, and didn't know the answer until he came back to the United States and told her in person.

Fred was later reassigned to the D'Entrecasteaux Islands, which are located off the eastern tip of New Guinea. The Japanese forces faithfully bombed the island everyday at lunch time, but one particular night they decided to bomb under the cloak of darkness. It took Fred completely by surprise, and he got all tangled up in the mosquito net he had been sleeping under, and couldn't get to the safety of a fox hole. By the time he got untangled from the net, the raid was over.

In July of 1944, Fred was shipped back to the United States after over two years of service in the Pacific. In the Fall of 1945, he received orders to go to China, and was not very happy about them, because he would have to leave his wife and six-month-old daughter, Debbie. He served in China for about a year.

Fred was discharged in 1946 after eight years of service, and was awarded the Asiatic Pacific Campaign Ribbon, China-Burma-India Theater Ribbon, World War II Victory Medal, and the Good Conduct Award. Fred moved to Southport after the war and he and Phyllis had a second child, Fredrick. Fred went to work for Leslie Brewer seining herring, and also worked at Pinkham's Store for Phyllis' parents, Charlie and Izetta. Later he ran the contract Post Office at Southport. Fred passed away on March 7, 1968, just three days short of his 51st birthday.

LESLIE COPP

Technician Fifth Grade, U.S. Army

Leslie was drafted into the Army on March 21, 1941, at the age of 22. At the time he was a permanent resident of the United States, but not a citizen, because he had been born in Riverside, New Brunswick, and moved to Southport when he was two-years-old. This meant that the government could draft him, but could not send him overseas unless he volunteered. This being the case, Leslie volunteered, along with hundreds of other men, to become citi-

Leslie Copp, U.S. Army

zens so they could fight for the United States. After his basic training he became part of the 103rd Infantry Regiment, Company C, and served as a rifleman in Luzon, New Guinea, Guadalcanal, the Northern Solomons, and New Zealand during the war.

When it was time for him to be shipped home from New Zealand, he discovered that he had blood poisoning. Realizing that only healthy men were allowed to get on the ship, he covered his arms and never let any one know he was sick, because at this point, nothing was going to stop him from getting home to his family.

He was discharged from the separation center at Fort Devens, Massachusetts, after four years, five months, and one day in the Army and was awarded the American Defense Service Medal, Asiatic Pacific Theater Campaign Ribbon, Philippine Liberation Ribbon with one bronze star, and the Good Conduct Medal.

After the war Leslie moved to Everett, Massachusetts, where he met and married Marie Glennon. He worked as a bus driver for the Massachusetts Bay Transportation Authority until he retired in 1982. Leslie passed away on July 25, 1984, at the age of 65.

GERALD DILL

Aviation Machinist Mate Second
Class, U.S. Navy

Jerry enlisted in the Navy in the fall of 1942. He was 18 years old at the time. He had been working at Bath Iron Works, and with Elmer Payne in the milk business for Oakhurst Dairy prior to this time.

He went to boot camp in Newport, Rhode Island, and went on active duty January 1, 1943. From boot camp he was sent to Millington, Tennessee, for aviation machinist mate school. Then to Jacksonville, Florida, for gunnery

Gerald Dill, U.S. Navy

school and first flight training in PBYs (twin engine sea planes). While there he was visited by his brother Dick, who was also stationed in Florida.

At Boca Chica near Key West, Florida, he had more flight training and was assigned to the tail turret of a B-24 for battle stations. Jerry's job on the flight crew was as mechanic. The crew was made up of men ranging in age from 18 to 22. His outfit trained at several stations on the East Coast, the last being Chincoteague, Virginia, where they formed a permanent flight crew.

In February of 1945, they were sent to Dunkswell, England, south of Liverpool for anti-submarine duty. The men lived in quonset huts that each held one crew of ten men. While there Jerry had the opportunity to visit with his father, Harold, who was in the Merchant Marine. His ship docked in Portsmouth, England, and they were able to spend some time together.

Jerry's crew received briefings before daybreak, and then went on 12 to 15 hour missions flying search patterns, looking for enemy submarines. They flew at an altitude of 1200 to 1500 feet and did not need to use oxygen during these flights. One day they thought they had finally spotted a submarine, but upon closer observation realized it was a school of porpoise. When the war ended in Europe, Jerry's crew was sent to the West Coast Naval Air Station in Whidby Island, Washington, before the squadron could reform, Japan surrendered.

Jerry was discharged at Bremerton, Washington, on March 15, 1946, and he married his fiance Dorothy on March 24th.

He served for three years and four months in the Navy. Jerry received the European Theatre of War Medal and the Good Conduct Medal for his service. After the war and up until his retirement, Jerry went to work for International Harvester, maintaining logging trucks and building trailers for them. His flight crew still gets together annually, and nine of the original crew members are still living. Jerry currently lives in Southeast Everett, Washington with his wife of 50 years, Dorothy.

Jerry's flight crew circa 1944-1945.
Jerry is pictured in the front row, and is the first on the left.

Jerry's flight crew, September 1992, Harrington, Tennessee.
Jerry is in the back row, and is the second from the left.

HAROLD DILL, JR.
Sergeant, Army Air Corps

Harold went to Portland on a Friday to try to enlist in the Army, but they turned him down because he had false teeth. That Sunday an announcement came over the radio that Pearl Harbor had been bombed by the Japanese, so he returned the following Monday to the enlistment office to try again, and they took him without any question. He received his basic training at Camp Lee in Virginia, and was later transferred to the Army Air Corps, where he was trained as an aerial gunner on B-17s.

Harold Dill, Jr.,
Army Air Corps

He was then assigned to train aerial gunners, even though he really wanted to go overseas. Harold was also stationed in Meridian, Mississippi; Westover Field, Massachusetts; Tacoma and Moses Lake,

The Dill family had four members serving their country during the Second World War. Pictured from left to right: Jerry, Harold, Sr., Harold, Jr., and Dick

Washington. While in Tacoma he and his brother Gerald were able to visit. Harold was discharged in 1946, after over four years of service. He was awarded the American Theater of War Medal, World War II Victory Medal, and the Good Conduct Award.

Harold married Shirley Wooler of Holyoke, Massachusetts, in 1946 and worked for the Springfield Street Railway Co. as a diesel mechanic. After his retirement from the company he drove tour buses for Longueil Transportation, Inc. Harold passed away in March of 1993 at the age of 71.

HAROLD DILL, SR.
Merchant Marine

Harold was a veteran of the First World War, so when his three sons went off to serve their country during World War II, he decided that he ought to volunteer as well. He was 49 years old at the time, and the Army turned him down due to his age. It was then, determined to do something to help the war effort, that he joined the Merchant Marine. During the war Navy and/or Coast Guard gun crews were assigned to the merchant ships, only after many were torpedoed and sunk, to help protect the crew on board and the ship's cargo.

He went to work for the Black Diamond Steamship Company, which carried war materials all over the world and later worked for the United Fruit Company out of New York City, transporting fruit from Central America. Post war he traveled to Israel, Egypt, Germany, France, and England.

Harold left the Merchant Marine around 1959, and moved to Washington State with his wife Katherine. He worked there as a carpenter, until he passed away on January 5, 1962, at the age of 66.

RICHARD DILL
Corporal, U.S. Army

Dick enlisted in 1942 at the age of 18. He received basic training at Fort

Richard Dill, U.S. Army

Standish in Boston Harbor with the Coast Artillery Corps on ten inch disappearing rifles. The guns were positioned behind a concrete parapet and when loaded would raise their muzzle up over the embankment. Then the concussion from being fired would bring them back into place behind the parapet. Dick was really amazed by these guns when he first saw them, but later realized they were really outdated in comparison to newer artillery.

He later went on to Camp Pendleton in Norfolk, Virginia, and then was stationed in Tampa, Florida, where his duties included harbor defense. Dick's brother Jerry was stationed in Jacksonville, Florida, at the Naval Air Station. Dick was able to get a weekend pass and spent a day or two with him there. Prior to enlisting Dick had worked at the Pejepscot Paper Company in Topsham, Maine.

At this time the war department was asking for infantry volunteers. Dick was really bored after two years of harbor defense, so he signed up and was sent to Camp Adabary, Indiana, where he joined the 106th Infantry. He was very excited at this point, because now he was going to see some action. His unit soon sailed for England on the British liner *Aquitania* and anchored in Grenock, Scotland. The unit stayed in England for one month of final preparation.

In November of 1944, they sailed out of Southhampton on a British transport *H.M.T. Langliddy Castle* and anchored off Le Havre, France, for several days, because it was too rough to land. The port was in poor shape and the men were brought ashore by landing craft. They then were transported in convoys by truck. It was a wet and miserable trip due to steady rain. Early in December, they relieved the Second Infantry Division, who were on the Siegfried line (the German's western defense wall, a fortified line which ran through Belgium, Luxembourg, and France). As they moved in, the GIs moving out joked, "You've got it soft now."

On December 16th, Dick and his unit were living in bunkers made out of logs. At around 5:30 A.M. his commander, who had been on watch, came into the bunker and said, "Come out here and see what is happening; all hell is breaking loose!" German rockets were coming overhead at tree top level. The exhaust brilliantly lit up the morning sky. They were later told the bombs were aimed at Belgium. This was the beginning of The Battle of the Bulge.

Later in the day Battalion Headquarters wanted volunteers to go into "no man's land." Dick and another soldier volunteered, and were told to come back and report if they spotted anything. At 2 A.M. headquarters came and got them because their unit was moving out. All was very quiet.

On December 17th another unit had abandoned equipment and volunteers were needed to go and get it back, especially an anti-tank gun. Again Dick volunteered with some other men. When they were bringing the weapons back, they could see a German machine gun position off to one side of them. Several of the men wanted to lob a grenade into it, but the ranking officer on the mission wouldn't let them do it. He didn't know how many Germans were around, and they were not prepared to fight if there were a lot. It was a very wise move, as you will later see.

The winter weather was the coldest Europe had endured for many years. Dick's unit of about 180 men were dug into a hillside over looking Shawnburg, Belgium; two-thirds of the unit had been surrounded by the Germans. An armored U.S. division was moving in from the north to offer some relief. The unit loaded up on a convoy and tried to escape, but the lead truck hit a land mine and blew up several of the vehicles. They also were attacked by Panzer tanks and 88s (German artillery, which was used in the field or as an anti-aircraft weapon). It was at this point that Regimental Command surrendered the whole outfit. It was the biggest mass surrender of the Second World War, 7001 P.O.W.s, 1000 killed in action, and many wounded.

The men were very upset and didn't understand why they were surrendering. The officers told them to destroy their weapons and then to go stand in a nearby field. When everyone had done that, it seemed like there were German soldiers everywhere. The first thing they did was single out all the truck drivers. They made them start the trucks to ensure they were not booby trapped. Then they lined up the Americans and marched them for three days without food and with little water.

The first night the men were put in a cemetery that was surrounded by a tall stone wall. There were no blankets to keep warm and the German soldiers took their overshoes. They kept hearing horses hooves clicking; finally out of curiosity, some of the men boosted each other up to look over the wall. The German Army was bringing equipment from the First World War out of retirement, and they were using horses to transport it. The next day, as they were marching through a town, Dick noticed dead German soldiers stacked up like firewood between the gas pumps at a Shell filling station.

On the third day they arrived in Garelsteir, Germany, where they boarded a train. The boxcars had previously been used to bring the horses in and had not been cleaned out. There were at least 75 men to a boxcar and they all couldn't sit down at once, so they took turns for three days. On Christmas Eve in Limburg, Germany, the train was stopped at a railyard. The weather cleared, the moon came out, and soon after the Royal Air Force appeared and bombed the hell out of it. Several prisoners were killed because the train cars were not marked to identify they were carrying P.O.W.s. The next morning, prisoners were used to repair the tracks so the train could leave the railyard.

On Christmas Day the train arrived in Bad Orb, which appeared to be a resort town. The Americans were paraded through the streets, and children in Nazi Youth uniforms kicked and yelled at them as they passed by. Once inside the prison camp, the commander said in good English, "If you cooperate, you will be fed." Dick was handed an empty gallon paint can to eat out of. For the next three months, they were fed either potato or pea soup every day.

The stalag was IX-B, and Dick was registered as Prisoner of War #24845. The commander told the men that their dogtags would be cut in half when the Germans won the war, and the Germans would keep one half for their records and the prisoners could take the other half home to their government. The barracks at the stalag consisted of three tier bunk beds that had straw tick mattresses. It was two men to a bunk and they didn't look that bad, so the men who were exhausted chose bunks and got in. They soon found the bunks were infested with lice, which they all caught, and they spent the remainder of their time there sleeping on the floor. Quarters were so tight that when one man rolled over, they all had to roll over.

The prisoners were allowed to send one postcard a week and did not receive any mail from the outside. Many of the men were worried that their parents would find out they were taken prisoner at Christmas time and it would be hard on them. As it turned out in Dick's case, his P.O.W. postcard informed his parents about his status before the military did. The P.O.W.s were issued pages out of a used German inventory journal to use as toilet paper. Dick saved some of his and kept a daily diary on it until the camp was liberated. It has been an insightful aid to the writing of this story.

The men were served imitation coffee in the morning, soup at noon, and bread at night. The bread was dark and heavy, and one loaf was split between seven men. Once in a while there were traces of meat in the daily soup. One day Dick pulled what looked like the base of a horse's ear out of his soup. It was nothing but gristle, but it gave him something to chew on for most of the day.

They did get occasional Red Cross packages, but one box had to be shared with 20 men, so they didn't amount to much. The packages usually had cigarettes, jelly, Spam, chocolate, and sometimes even socks in them. There were 12 men in the camp from Maine and occasionally Dick would get together with them to shoot the breeze about home. There were one or two escape attempts, but neither got very far away from the camp, while Dick was there.

Halfway through Dick's stay at the camp, a good friend named Al Cardini died of malnutrition and pneumonia. Al had been part of the training cadre back at Fort Standish in Boston Harbor. Someone told Dick that he was in the dispensary at the camp, so Dick got permission to go and visit him. He was just skin and bones, and was terribly

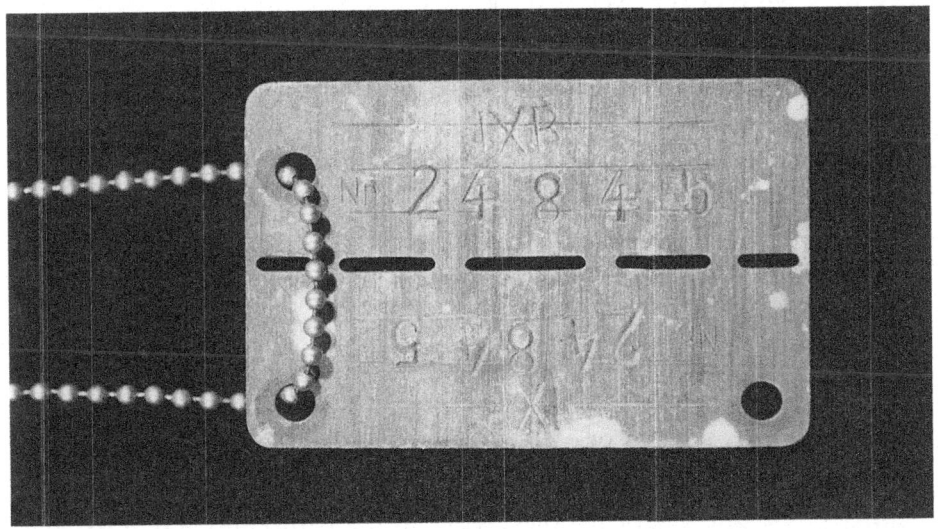

Dick's P.O.W. dogtag, number 24845. Note the perforation on it. The prisoners were told by the camp Commandant, "When we win the war, the tag will be broken in half. We will keep on half for our records, and you will give the other half to your government."

depressed. He told Dick, "We're never going to get out of here alive." Dick told him to try and eat something to keep his strength up, but within three weeks he had died. The chaplains in the camp asked for people that knew Al to help with the funeral procession. That was the only time Dick was allowed outside of the prison gate until the camp was liberated. Dick has since learned that Al is now buried in a military cemetery in St. Avold, in Belgium.

One night a guard was assaulted, when he discovered two GIs in the camp kitchen stealing food. They attacked him with a meat cleaver and nearly killed him. The next morning German SS soldiers had machine guns set up everywhere, no church was permitted, and no food would be issued until the guilty party was turned in. The men had to line up and were inspected by the German guards, who were looking for traces of blood. When none was found, the barracks were searched thoroughly and two jackets were located that were still wet from recent washing. The jackets had the serial numbers of the soldiers who owned them printed inside. Late in the day two men confessed to the assault, and the camp ate around 18:00. The two men were found guilty of assaulting the prison guard and were sentenced to death. They were allowed to appeal the case to a higher court in Berlin, which they did, and to Dick's knowledge they were never executed, because the war ended.

There was not a lot to do in the camp. The Army New Testament the men had been issued was read from cover to cover. Each barracks was allowed one armful of wood a day, so sometimes they could cut wood, but there really wasn't that much to take care of. There were a few musical instruments in the camp the prisoners were allowed to play. A man in Dick's barracks played the accordion beautifully, and when a certain guard would come into the barracks he would start playing a Strauss waltz. This seemed to sooth the savage beast, and he would leave their barracks and go into another one to start his angry tirade.

There were no medical facilities and 35 men died of malnutrition. There were men in the camp from Britain, France, Belgium, Yugoslavia, and Russia. The Russians were segregated and received the worst treatment. Thirty-eight Americans died while at the camp and 1300 Russians. The Americans who died were buried in pine boxes and received a decent burial from the Germans. The Russians were wrapped in paper and were buried.

Two American chaplains from Dick's unit were also captured. One was Protestant and the other Catholic. According to Dick they were the best morale builders in the camp. There were many Jewish Americans in the unit. They were immediately segregated and were moved out of the camp. Their fate was not known to Dick until two years ago, when he attended a P.O.W. reunion and some of them showed up. It turned out they had been sent to work in salt mines near Buchenwald and only one third of them had survived.

As the winter progressed, artillery fire and bombing could be heard. One day U.S. planes even strafed the camp a few times, because it wasn't marked as a P.O.W. camp. There were 18 casualties and several men killed that day. Speculation ran like wildfire throughout the camp as to when it would be liberated. The German soldiers, who were forbidden to give prisoners any news from the outside, even admitted the American push had begun. A few days before the liberation of Stalag IX-B, the approaching Allied forces shut off the water supply that ran to it. The Stalag had originally been a German Youth Camp and there was a pool located in it. Most of the prisoners still had Halazone tablets with them, which they used to disinfect the water so they could drink it. After Easter Sunday services, unbeknown to the men, the chaplains, "accom-

Stalag IX-B, Bad Orb, Germany

panied by German officers," went to the American lines to surrender the camp.

The next morning at daybreak the men noticed a white sheet flying from the clocktower. Soon they heard the rumble of engines and a Sherman Tank came through the front gate. They were free at last. The official time of liberation was 06:50, April 2, 1945.

The men were moved back to a small German village, where they received their first shower since January 4. They were also deloused and fed. Then they were flown to Le Havre, France, to Camp Lucky Strike where the Red Cross met them with coffee and doughnuts. In fact one man ate so many doughnuts he ate himself to death. He had been a suspected German sympathizer within the camp and was not missed.

Dick boarded an American troop ship and sailed to New York. He was home on leave on VE Day and then was sent to Lake Placid, New York, because he didn't have enough points (a system used during the war, to account for time served in the military) to be discharged. Then it was on to Fort McLellan, in Alabama, where he trained recruits. He was finally discharged in November of 1945, after serving three years, seven months, and five days.

Dick was awarded the World War II Victory Medal, Bronze Star, Good Conduct Medal, P.O.W. Medal, European African Middle Eastern Campaign Medal with three bronze stars, Presidential Unit Citation for the Battle of the Bulge, Combat Infantry Badge, and the National Defense Medal.

Dick married Louise Gaudette of Southport in 1950, and because he was in the reserves, was notified to report to Fort Williams in Portland for a physical that same year. He passed with flying colors and was informed that he was being reinstated for duty in the Korean War. Louise was due to come home from the hospital with their first child, Mary, so Dick went to talk to the officer in charge, hoping for some time to spend with his new daughter. The officer told Dick he had three weeks to get his personal affairs in order before he shipped out.

He boarded a troop train which took him to Fort Hood in Texas, where he spent three weeks. Then he went to Camp Storeman in California. On Thanksgiving he boarded a troop ship which took him to Inchon, Korea. The ship landed one night in early December and the weather was extremely cold. There had been a mix up in orders and no trucks were sent to meet the arriving troops. Dick said they waited for six hours before someone remembered to come pick them up.

Dick was reassigned to the combat engineers in Korea and he worked building pontoon bridges and airstrips while he was there. The mess sergeant in his unit was from Lewiston, Maine, and he also served with another fellow from Gray, Maine. He was sent home in August of 1951 after ten months of duty in Korea and received the Korean Service Medal with three bronze stars and the United Nations Medal.

Dick returned home and went to work for Frank Conner as a builder. He later worked for Arthur Marr building boats and at Samples Shipyard in Boothbay Harbor. While there he heard about a caretaker's job at the Newagen Inn and decided to apply for the position. In July of 1953 Dick was chosen for the job and he worked at the Inn for 35 years until his retirement in 1988. He currently is the caretaker for several cottages and lives in Southport with his wife of 46 years, Louise.

EDWARD DONOHOE
Chief Engineer, Merchant Marine,
and Warrant Officer, U.S. Army
Mine Planter Service

Ed joined the Naval Reserve in November of 1939, while a cadet at the Massachusetts Nautical School. He graduated in September of 1941, and promptly took the Third Assistant Engineer examination, and received his license from the Steamboat Inspection Service. He then served in the Merchant Marine in the Atlantic and Caribbean on the Esso Tanker *Livingston Row* and later on the *S.S. Leslie* as Third Assistant Engineer.

During the months of January and February of 1942, the Esso Company

Edward Donohoe,
U.S. Merchant Marine and
U.S. Army Mine Planter Service

began losing many tankers to submarine attack, and their crews soon began to realize just how dangerous their jobs had become. In fact, during the first six months of 1942, the United States Merchant Marine lost more tonnage and men then was lost during the Japanese attack at Pearl Harbor. The ships had no naval protection and the presence of German submarines off the East Coast of the United States was being felt.

On April 16th, the *S.S. Leslie* was making a return run from the West Indies when she was torpedoed off Cape Canaveral, Florida, by the German submarine U-123, which was commanded by Reinhard Hardegen. It was about 10 o'clock at night, and Ed was on watch in the engine room. Most of the other men on board were asleep in their bunks. He was able to get his crew of three men safely out of the engine room, up five series of ladders, but when they reached the deck, it was in a state of chaos. Ed quickly got to the starboard lifeboat, and he and the chief engineer launched it over the side. They rescued 11 men who were already overboard, treading water. There had been 27 men, serving on the *S.S. Leslie*, and five lost their lives that night.

Two hours later, after helping row the lifeboat away from the torpedoed freighter, Ed witnessed the shelling of a neutral Swedish freighter by U-123. The submarine pumped 45 shells into her hull until at last she sank. Fourteen men were believed lost during that incident. Eight hours later Ed and the rest of the crew finally reached the Florida coast, and found refuge in the home of a retired Army Captain and his wife. The other lifeboat arrived three hours later, and the men were fed by the couple. After spending two days at a naval station in Cocoa, Florida, Ed boarded the Florida Special and returned home to Lawrence by train.

It was at this point Ed decided the Merchant Marine might not be a long-time career, so he joined the U.S. Army Mine Planter Service, which was one of the more unusual organizations in the Armed Forces. While the officers and crew were all in the Army, they lived and worked on the 180 foot long Mine Planters that were steam powered and were able to go anywhere. He also married his long-time sweetheart Frances Briggs of Lawrence, Massachusetts, on November 25, 1942.

There were no commissioned officers in this branch of the service. All of the officers were warrant officers on board the ships. Their job was a tricky one, involving the servicing of anti-submarine mine fields up and down the East Coast. Keep in mind that, at this point in time, all major U.S. harbors were mined by the U.S. Army Coast Artillery, and these underwater mine fields had to be maintained by them. There were 25 mine planters and 250 men allotted to this task during the war. Ed served on the *Baird* in Boston and the *Sylvester* in the Delaware Capes.

The mines rested on the bottom of the ocean, and were electronically controlled by men in a casement on shore. This form of defense enabled the United States to set up different shipping channels everyday if they chose to do so, by simply activating one section of the mine field or another. When a mine was in need of repair, Ed's ship would radio ashore, alerting the base station to turn off the mine field. They then picked up the mine, or if they weren't able to, a diver would be sent down to assist in the process. A working mine would be laid in its place and the other would be taken back to the depot for repairs. Each mine had 5400 pounds of T.N.T. in it that had to be taken out, so the circuits could be checked, and it could be cleaned up and given a new coat of paint, before it was put back in commission.

Late in 1944, the Army decided that the threat of submarines had diminished, so orders were given to pick up all the mine fields. By March of 1945, Ed discovered that he was out of a job. He was a warrant officer, and for that reason the Army couldn't transfer him, so they put him on inactive service. He then decided to return to the only job he knew, and went back into the Merchant Marine, who by this time had gun crews on board for protection.

Ed signed on an old express freighter, the *Mexican*, with the American Hawaiian Line, and took a load of horses and cows to Marshal Josip Tito,

Pictured above, Army Mine Planter, U.S. A.M.P. Sylvester, which Ed served on from mid-1942 until early 1945.

who was the leader of the Yugoslavian forces in Europe. After the *Mexican* he signed on the *Howard Victory* as First Assistant Engineer, which was part of the J.W. Roundtree Company. The ship was transporting troops back and forth from New York, New York, to Marseilles and Le Havre, France. On a return trip they picked up 150 sailors in Naples, Italy, and returned to the Mediterranean for a load of chrome ore at Beni Saaf, Algeria. Once there, Ed heard the bomb had been dropped on Japan, and the end of the war was finally in sight.

In March of 1946, Ed was licensed as Chief Engineer (unlimited horsepower) in steam, but he left the Merchant Marine shortly thereafter to further his education. For his service he was awarded the Merchant Marine Victory Medal, Merchant Marine Combat Bar with one star (indicating a ship he served on was sunk), Merchant Marine Defense Medal, North Atlantic Theater Service Medal, and the Mediterranean Theater Service Medal. From the Army he received the American Defense Service Medal and the World War II Victory Medal.

After the war Ed attended Rensselaer Polytechnic Institute, as a student and teaching assistant, on the GI Bill. He received a degree in Mechanical Engineering in the early 1950s and continued his studies at the Massachusetts Maritime Academy, earning a B.S. in Marine and Electrical Engineering.

After his graduation in 1953, Ed joined the General Electric Company, and went to work managing the Caterpillar dealership in Venezuela, which was owned by General Electric. In 1962, he was elected Vice President of General Electric de Venezuela S.A. While in Venezuela he was one of the very few non-Venezuelans to be admitted to the Colegio De Ingenieros Venezolanos and is registered as a Professional Engineer. In 1976 after 23 years of service to Caterpillar, Ed returned to the United States and joined the faculty of General Electric's Management Development Institute at Crotonville, New York, from which he retired in 1977.

Ed currently lives in Southport with his wife of 54 years, Fran. He is very involved with the Maine Maritime Museum in Bath, and is the Bosun of the *Sherman Zwicker*, which is the last of the Grand Banks Fishing Schooners in operation today.

Author's note: *The men who served in the Merchant Marine were not officially recognized as veterans by the United States Government until January 19, 1988.*

LEON DUPREY

Aviation Machinist Mate
First Class, U.S. Navy

Leon Duprey, U.S. Navy

In September of 1942, Leon drove a truckload of lobsters from Southport to Boston for Maynard Robinson, and was all set to enlist in the Air Corps as an aerial gunner, when he ran into Commander McMillan on the street. McMillan, who was known for his expedition to the North Pole, kept his ship at Robinson's Wharf and Leon had worked on it in the spring. He pulled Leon aside and said, "I see you're not in the service yet. You've been around the water on the coast of Maine all your life. Why don't you join the Coast Guard or the Navy?" It made sense to Leon, so he and Commander McMillan walked down the street a few blocks and he enlisted in the Navy.

Before he enlisted Leon often gave servicemen from Southport rides back to Boston when he was delivering lobsters. Fred Farnham and Clayton Orne often got a lift with him when they had been home on leave.

Leon was trained at Squantum Naval Air Station in Massachusetts. There were a lot of men from Maine there, so Leon felt right at home. He was trained to work on airplane engines and, in September of 1944, was sent to Chicago to receive further training at an aircraft engine school.

Leon didn't smoke, but was rationed cigarettes anyway, so he used them when he hitchhiked from Squantum to Boston. All he had to do was hold up a pack of cigarettes and the vehicles would almost drive off the road trying to stop for him. While in Boston Leon often ran into people he knew from home at the North and South train stations. These included Arthur Barlow of Boothbay Harbor, and Evelyn Pratt, Emolyn Smith, and Jean Luther of Southport, to name a few.

While in Chicago, Leon went to see a U.S.O. show. As he was walking up a flight of stairs to get to the show, a guy came hurrying down them and almost ran him over. It turned out to be Wright Britton who summered on Southport. The two men started talking and soon went to find some coffee and a place to sit down so they could visit. Leon saw Doris Day, Vaughn Monroe, Lawrence Welk, Sammy Kaye, the Dorseys, and Guy Lombardo perform through the U.S.O. in Chicago, and he often danced with Lawrence Welk's lead singer.

Chicago held the honor, in many people's minds including Leon's, as being the best liberty town around. Often cab drivers would let servicemen ride for free or would just say, "Give me what you can afford." Restaurants and clubs were also noted for the same kind of treatment.

When he completed his training he was sent to Quonset Point, Rhode Island, and he never worked on another airplane engine again. He then went to the West Coast and was stationed at Port Hueme, which was an embarkation port for the Navy. The war ended while he was there and by this time Leon had become a section leader, which put him in charge of a large group of men.

While there he met a man who summered in Maine. He said his family had a summer cottage on Isle of Springs in Boothbay and probably Leon didn't know where that was, because it was such a small place. Leon then pulled a copy of the Boothbay Register out from under his mattress, which had been sent to him from the Knights of Pythias. The man couldn't believe it and, as it turned out, his father had bought lobsters from Leon several times during the past few summers.

Leon really enjoyed visiting the Hollywood Canteen while he was on the West Coast. He met Bette Davis there one night and there were always famous singers, actors, and actresses around volunteering their time for the war effort. There was an autograph wall, and the servicemen and women signed their names and hometowns to it. Leon found Walter Andrew's and a Paine's name from Boothbay Harbor on it. He signed his name under theirs.

One day Leon went to visit a friend who worked for Cecil B. DeMille. Mr. DeMille came out of his office and said, "You're a rugged, good looking young man; stick around and I'll give you a job after the war." Leon often wonders to this day what his life would have been like if he had.

On VJ Day Leon had been assigned to watch over a bunch of men who were deserters. During the day an announcement came over the radio saying the war had ended. Leon turned to the men he was watching and said, "Okay boys, you can go home now." Ironically, later that evening he went to a dance out in Santa Monica and happened to notice a guy from his outfit out on the dance floor that hadn't reported for muster in several days. Leon spoke to the shore patrol and the guy soon ended up in the brig.

Leon was back in Boston by September of 1945, after serving in the Navy for three years. He worked for Maynard Robinson for 15 years trucking lobsters and helping to run his lobster pound on Southport. Then he worked at Fuller's Boat Yard in East Boothbay, Oakhurst Dairy, Lincoln County Sheriff's Department, B.I.W. in security, and at the Y.M.C.A. in Boothbay Harbor, where he has been for the last 23 years and is presently employed.

ROLAND DYER
Yeoman Second Class, U.S. Navy

Roland Dyer, U.S. Navy

On February 3, 1941, Roland enlisted in the Navy. He was 18 years old at the time. He was trained in Jacksonville, Florida, and Newport, Rhode Island, and was assigned to the USN Administration School at Camp Bradford in Norfolk, Virginia, shortly thereafter.

Roland later boarded a landing craft in New Orleans which took him to the South Pacific. During his time in the service he served aboard LST 756, LST 978, and LSM 331. His job on board each ship was to maintain the records of the office and of the personnel. He also operated and maintained combat cameras, developed and processed film, and set up training syllabuses and lectures on identification of enemy ships and aircraft.

These are photographs Roland took of post-war Japan.

More photos of post-war Japan.

Roland went ashore on several islands in the South Pacific, including Saipan, Tinian, and Okinawa. He was present when the American flag was raised on Iwo Jima and, during the battle, was ashore administering first aid, giving shots of morphine to the wounded and dying. After the bomb was dropped on Japan, he was sent to Nagoya, Japan.

He was discharged on November 29, 1946, after five years, 11 months, and 19 days of service. Roland was awarded the American Theatre Ribbon, World War II Victory Medal, American Defense Ribbon with one star, Asiatic-Pacific Ribbon with one star, Philippine Liberation Ribbon with one star, the Good Conduct Award, and the Occupation Ribbon for Japan.

After the war Roland settled in California where he worked for TRW Electronics. He was married and divorced, and later remarried Paula Kint from Wichita, Kansas, in 1976, and they retired in Pahrump, Nevada. Roland passed away in April of 1993 at the age of 71.

ROBERT EATON
Second Lieutenant, U.S. Army

Robert Eaton, U.S. Army

Bob was drafted at the age of 18 on July 3, 1944. At the time, he had been a participant in an accelerated high school course and had finished his senior year in May before his class graduated. He had just started his freshman year at the University of Maine at Orono, studying engineering and forestry, when he was called into the service.

He was stamped to go into the U.S. Navy, but ended up in the U.S. Army in the field artillery operating 105mm Howitzers. Bob received his basic training at Fort Sill in Oklahoma, where he met Dave Flood from Waterville, Maine. He then went on to Officers Candidate School at Fort Benning in Georgia. At the time there were no openings for officers in the field artillery, so he trained for the infantry. Bob turned 19 in January 1945 and graduated as a Second Lieutenant on July 3, exactly one year to the day he was drafted. His first assignment was training troops at Camp Blanding in Florida.

In the fall of 1945 he was sent to Germany as part of the army of occupation. He went over on the troop ship *General Anderson* and landed in Le Havre, France. Bob remembers it being terribly devastated from all the bombing that had occurred. He and the other men in his outfit boarded a 40 & 8 train, which meant it was designed for 40 men or eight horses. Fifteen hundred troops lived in those unheated box cars for one week during the 800-mile ride to Rosenheim, Germany, which was a staging area for troops that were to be delivered to different areas of the occupation. It was so cold they had to build little fires on the floors of the box cars to try and keep warm. They eventually burnt through the bottom of the floors and they would have to build another fire in a different section of the box car. Enroute the entire train came down with diarrhea.

Bob was part of the seventh regiment and was in the third division. He was a company officer and was the platoon leader for the A company. His first duty in Germany was on the border of occupation in Obersule next to the Russian border. Bob didn't speak any Russian and the Russian soldiers didn't speak any English, but between them they

One of the jeeps Bob drove in Germany. Note the angle iron mounted on the front, used to catch piano wires Nazi youth had strung across the road as a means of sabotage.

Photographs Bob took of post-war Germany.

could both speak a little German and they soon formed a friendship. Occasionally they would have to transport someone across the border, for example a doctor, but it all went very smoothly. Every Saturday night the Russians would host a party, bringing potato schnapps and Russian vodka. Bob knew they liked American whiskey, so that was his contribution to the festivities.

The army of occupation was in place to govern the German people. Bob said they were very receptive to the Americans and at one point he even lived with a family while he was there. He started taking German lessons from a woman who was a grade school teacher in the neighborhood, and he paid her for the lessons with American candy bars. He still speaks some German to this day.

Bob soon became a Class 1 and Class 6 Supply Officer, which meant he was in charge of food and liquor for the base. He had 35 people working for him at the food depot. All but three of them were Germans and mostly they were ex-soldiers. He even had a Master Sergeant and a former Air Force Captain who he placed in charge of frozen foods. They both spoke excellent English and were reliable workers. Within six months dependents of the soldiers stationed in Germany starting coming over, and living quarters had to be set up for them. This meant that Bob's job suddenly became a much larger task.

Bob used to drive a semi-truck, armed with five guards carrying submachine guns to pick up liquor for the depot. When the truck was full its cargo was easily valued at $15,000. The armed guards were necessary to prevent raids from occurring when they passed through winding roads in the mountains. One day Bob and his men received special passes which enabled them to attend the Nuremberg War Crime Trials. The passes were good for only one day and they happened to get in on one of the days Heinrich Himmler was on the stand. He was Adolf Hitler's propaganda man during the war. They had to listen through head phones, because the trial was being translated into English by an interpreter.

Bob was able to move around the country a lot. He visited many castles while he was there and Brownfelt Lawn was one of his favorites. He was even able to spend the night in it. He remembers that the town of Heidelberg, which was a resort town, seemed untouched by the war, but other towns, such as Darmstadt and Munich, lay in ruins.

Not everyone was glad to see the Americans occupy Germany. There were still pockets of Nazi youth in some towns who would give the soldiers a hard time. One of their favorite tricks was to string piano wire across the road in the attempt to decapitate American soldiers. Bob remembers that the jeeps he drove all had an angle iron with a hook on the top attached to their front bumper. It was placed there to catch any wires the Nazi youth might have set up.

Bob went on several leaves while he was in Germany and a favorite was when he went skiing in Austria. He traveled by train to the Alps, and when he stood on top of the mountain he could see four countries around him. There were no ski lifts and you had to climb the mountain yourself to make a run down. He traveled through the town of Sonhoffen, which is where the famous training school for Hitler's SS Troops was located. Bob said all the buildings were still standing when he passed through the town.

In 1947, after almost four years in Germany, Bob traveled home on the troop ship *General Stewart*. For his service he received the European Theater of War Ribbon, American Theater of War Ribbon, The Occupation Ribbon For Germany, Good Conduct Award, and an Expert Marksmanship Award.

In the fall he was back at the University of Maine on the GI Bill studying forestry. In 1950, during his senior year of college, Bob married his girlfriend Leanne Shibles from Westbrook, Maine. It was then that he received orders to go to Korea. He was granted an extension and finished his senior year, but missed graduation. Bob reported to Camp Drum in New York and joined the 278th Tennessee National Guard as an officer. During the winter of 1951 he was promoted to First Lieutenant and trained troops headed for Korea in winter tactics and maneuvers. They set up their tents in bivouac areas in 20 degrees below zero temperatures. Leanne joined Bob in New York and lived in a farmhouse near the base.

Bob anticipated orders that would send him to Korea at any time. Finally they came in the spring of 1952, and he was sent to the Panama Canal with the 33rd Infantry Division as a line officer. His mission was to keep the canal open.

One particular duty was as vital installation guard, meaning Bob and his men were in charge of guarding Madden Dam, which held the water that supplied the whole canal.

The dam was located out in the jungle and one night around 2 A.M. Bob went out to check on his men. There was a road on top of the dam that was between a quarter and a half mile long. As Bob started walking across it to get to the guard post, something moved in the shadows and seemed to follow him. Bob pulled his 45 out and when he took a step, the figure took a counterstep. There was a 200-foot drop on one side of the dam and Bob didn't want to fall or be pushed off under any circumstances, so he watched the figure closely and soon discovered that it was a black panther lurking in the shadows. The creature eventually went off into the jungle and Bob was relieved to see it go.

Another time he was traveling down a highway in a jeep headed to a checkpoint. As he drove along he felt a bump, bump under his tires. When he looked back to see what he had run over, he saw a python start to slither away. It was about six inches thick and had been stretched across both sides of the road. It seemed unhurt by the jeep's weight as Bob watched it work its way back into the jungle.

From time to time Bob would receive intelligence reports on different ships going through the canal. If there were suspicious people on board, Bob and nine of his men would take control of the ship. A guard would be placed in the engine room, on the bridge, and in other strategic locations on board to prevent any mishaps from occurring in the canal. The Panama Canal was vital to the United States keeping its troops supplied in Korea, and there was a constant fear that sabotage would shut it down and break off the supply route.

Meanwhile, back in the States, Leanne had just given birth to their first son, Robbie. Bob didn't see him until he was six months old, when he was released from active duty in October of 1952, after serving 15 months. They later had a second son, Richard. He received an American Campaign Ribbon for his service. Bob stayed in the Reserves and joined the Maine National Guard in 1956 and 1957, where he was an Intelligence and Reconnaissance platoon leader at the headquarters in Portland, Maine.

Bob went to work for Heath Survey Consultants and traveled throughout the United States, doing natural gas leak location work. He then went to work for Hooper-Holmes, Inc., which is a commercial reporting company. He was an investigator for ten years, then became manager of their Portland, Maine, office. He retired in 1985 after 31 years. Bob currently lives in Southport with his wife of 46 years, Leanne.

SAMUEL EMERSON
Chief Machinist Mate, U.S. Navy

Sammy enlisted in the Navy on February 17, 1941, at the age of 21. He received his basic training in Newport, Rhode Island, and continued his studies at the Great Lakes Training Station in Chicago, Illinois, and at the Ford Service School in Dearborn, Michigan. On December 11, 1941, his girlfriend, Jeanette Gray of Newagen, received a card from him letting her know he was in San Diego, California, and was supposed to set sail for his new assignment

Samuel Emerson, U.S. Navy

on the *U.S.S. Nevada*, which was a battleship stationed in Pearl Harbor, Hawaii.

Keep in mind that just four days before Jeanette's letter arrived, Sunday, December 7th,1941, the Gray family had huddled around their radio listening in disbelief, like the rest of the United States, that Pearl Harbor had been attacked by the Japanese. Meanwhile, Sammy boarded the *U.S.S. Pellias* in California, and headed for Hawaii. Enroute to the islands, the *Pellias* narrowly escaped being torpedoed twice. War was at hand.

While stationed at Pearl Harbor, Sammy met up with his cousin Almond Roberts from Barter's Island, and later in 1942, was reassigned to a base in Australia that furnished supplies and made repairs on submarines. Even though the censors were strict throughout the war, Sammy always liked to think of a creative way to let Jeanette know where he was. In one letter he wrote, "I'd love to bring a little kangaroo and a koala bear home to you," which translated to, "I'm in Australia." He also stated in another letter that he was really tired of steak, because they had to eat it all the time.

Towards the end of the war, Sammy was able to come home on leave, and he and Jeanette were married on June 26, 1944. He was discharged from the Navy in San Diego, California, on September 20, 1945, after four years and seven months of service, and received the American Defense Service Medal, American Campaign Medal, Asiatic Pacific Campaign Medal, World War II Victory Medal, and the Good Conduct Award.

After the war, he and Jeanette moved to San Diego, California, and he worked as a policeman. Sammy decided it was time for a change of profession and he enrolled in a watch making school at Thacker Academy in Pittsburgh, Pennsylvania. After his graduation in 1948, he and Jeanette returned to Southport, and opened a watch repair shop in Wiscasset. As time went on, Sammy decided that he wasn't going to make a living fixing watches and decided to go back into the Navy, so he re-enlisted in 1950.

He was stationed in Newport, Rhode Island, on a destroyer tender, fixing barometers and clocks, and even taught at the war college located there. From 1963-1966 he worked on *Polaris* submarines in Norfolk, Virginia. His expertise in the field of regulating instruments and periscopes also took him to Holylock, Scotland; Rota, Spain; and Guam, Marianas Islands. He even worked on the *U.S.S. Proteus*, which was the first atomic-powered submarine in the Navy.

Sammy retired from the Navy in August of 1967, with the rank of Senior Chief Instrument Man—E9, after 21 years of service. He returned to Newagen in 1967, and worked at Samples Shipyard in Boothbay Harbor and for Ed Harding as a carpenter. Sammy passed away in April of 1979 at the age of 62.

Author's note: *Years after the war, David Warren moved to Newagen and rented a house that had belonged to Sammy and Jeanette. Their daughter Elissa later discovered that David had served on the* Sierra *with her father, and he delivered the captain's watch to Sammy every Wednesday, so he could wind it for the captain.*

FRANKLIN FARMER

Lieutenant–JG (Junior Grade),
U.S. Maritime Service

Franklin Farmer,
U.S. Maritime Service

Franklin was living in Portland, Maine, with his wife Kora and young son Franklin, when the Second World War broke out. At that time, he was working for the Lever Brothers, Co., as the manager of door-to-door advertising crews.

He then attended and graduated from the U.S. Maritime Service Officer's School at Fort Trumble, New London, Connecticut, in 1944. His war time service was primarily on Liberty ships in trans-Atlantic convoys. These ships included the *James Sullivan, Charles Dauray, Eastern Crown,* and the *Oakey L. Alexander.* On most of these ships he served as third mate, but on his second trip aboard the *Oakey L. Alexander* he served as second mate.

During one crossing the rudder on his ship became jammed while the convoy was executing evasive maneuvers. As the ship turned in circles, often just missing other ships in the convoy, it was quickly left behind with no protection from enemy submarines. Franklin was among those who went below to release the rudder, which took quite a while to accomplish. The ship was then able to safely overtake the convoy, much to the relief of everyone on board.

On another occasion a nearby tanker carrying aviation fuel was torpedoed and exploded. Flaming debris rained down on his ship, which was carrying ammunition. A noted sigh of relief was heard on board, when all the fires were put out. Franklin was discharged from the U.S. Maritime Service on August 15, 1945, and was awarded the Atlantic War Zone Bar.

After the war, he returned to his family, which by this time had an additional member, his daughter Lucinda. He then returned to work with the Lever Brothers Company, and over the next 20 years advanced from salesman to supervisor, and later became a regional sales manager. He retired from the company in 1969, and shortly thereafter, he and his wife sold their home in Falmouth and moved back to Southport. He went to work part time at Reed's Shipyard in Boothbay Harbor, and always enjoyed sailing the coast with his family and friends in his spare time. Franklin passed away on February 15, 1988, at the age of 80.

LYMAN FARMER
Lieutenant, U.S. Maritime Service

*Lyman Farmer,
U.S. Maritime Service*

During the Second World War, Lyman served on troop transports and tankers in the U.S. Maritime Service. Prior to that time he served as a quartermaster aboard the *S.S. Lewis K. Thurlow*, of which his father, Walter, was the captain. From 1923-1924 he served on the four-masted schooner, *Wm. H. Harriman*, and later in that decade was the third mate on the S.S. Ruth and the *S.S. Delfinia*. In the 1930s, he served as mate on several Bull Line steamships.

He was married to Ruth Emery of Boothbay Harbor in 1943, and when he was not at sea, they made their home in Malden, Massachusetts. After the war, he served primarily as second mate aboard crude oil tankers, bringing oil from Near East ports to Atlantic Coast ports.

Lyman retired from the sea in 1963, and built a home on Decker's Cove in Southport, and just took it easy. After the death of his first wife in 1971, he married Edith Tibbetts. After her death in 1977, he married Clella Graves of Ft. Pierce, Florida. By that time he spent his summers in Southport and winters in Ft. Pierce. Lyman passed away on December 28, 1993, at the age of 88.

WALTER FARMER
Lieutenant Commander, U.S. Navy

Walter became involved with the sea trials of navy ships built in Bath and Boothbay, soon after the United States entered World War II. He was 65 years old at the time, and wanted to serve his country. In September of 1940 he served as Assistant Navigator during the sea trails of the *U.S.S. Livermore*, DD 429, which was built at the Bath Iron Works.

From 1942 to 1946 he served as trial captain for ships built at Samples Shipyard in Boothbay Harbor. Among the vessels he cap-

Walter Farmer, U.S. Navy

tained during this period were the ATRs 11 and 12, the YMS 232, the *Robt. W. Hart, Tom Treanor, Cardinal O'Connell, Walter F. Perry,* and *Albert M. Boe.* He also served as port captain for Boothbay Harbor during the war.

Prior to this time Walter had started going to sea with his father in 1891, and had served as hand, cook, mate or pilot on coasting schooners, passenger steamers, steam tugs, and banks fishermen. In 1907 he became master of the schooner *Marion Draper,* and over the next decade was the master of several three and four masted schooners, including the Boothbay Harbor built *Anna Laura McKenney.* Most of these ships were employed in commerce with the West Indies and European nations.

By the beginning of World War I, Walter had begun a transition to steam-powered cargo ships. After serving as mate on several vessels, he became captain of the *S.S. Chelan* in early 1919. He made a trip around the world as captain of the *S.S. Deer Lodge* in 1920-1921, and was commissioned Lieutenant Commander in the Naval Reserve in 1928. With a few exceptions he continued as master of steamships until he retired and returned to his home on Southport in 1935. Between 1936-1940, he was the captain and part owner of the passenger steamer *Virginia*, which primarily ran between Bath and Boothbay Harbor.

After the Second World War, Walter continued as a trail captain for Samples Shipyard, and also began his third career as a harbor, river, and coastal pilot. His pilots' license, renewed in 1944, was for "All Steam and Motor Ships—First Class Pilot, Waters of Bays, Rivers and Harbors between Rockland, Me. and Gay Head, Mass." Most of his piloting was done on the Sheepscot River taking colliers (coal ships) and tankers up to the power plant in Wiscasset. He continued this work until 1955, when at age 80, he retired for the last time. Walter passed away on December 21, 1969, at the age of 94.

FRED FARNHAM
Cook, First Class, U.S. Navy

Fred Farnham, U.S. Navy

Fred enlisted in the Navy in June of 1941, just after his graduation from high school. He had to get his parents written permission to enlist, because he was 17 years old at the time. He and Paul Pierce traveled together from Wiscasset to Portland by train to receive their physicals. They both passed, and Fred was sent to the Great Lakes for training and later went on to Newport, Rhode Island, where he was assigned to a battleship.

Fred worked as a cook, and there were about 2,000 men on board his ship. He served in the Pacific, and after five years of service was discharged. He was awarded the Asiatic Pacific Campaign Medal, World War Two Victory Medal, and the Good Conduct Award.

Fred worked as a fisherman on Southport for many years after his discharge from the Navy, and often fished with Leslie Brewer. Fred passed away on March 31, 1996, at the age of 73.

JOE FODERA
Aviation Machinist Mate,
First Class U.S. Navy

Joe Fodera, U.S. Navy

Joe enlisted in the Navy on June 24, 1941, at the age of 18. He attended basic training at the Naval Training Station in Newport, Rhode Island. He had joined the Civilian Conservation Corps from his home in Bayonne, New Jersey, and served in Lovelock, Nevada, until 1940. Afterwards he found work at a mirror shop in the Bowery, New York.

During the war, Joe served in the South Atlantic, Africa, Europe, and the United Kingdom, as well as various bases in the United States. On a flight from North Africa to England, he had to stay overnight in Paris, France. While there he met up with his cousin, Joe Palmeri, who was with a Navy Seabee detachment. They really had a great time in the city, and wished they could have stayed longer. Later, when Joe was in London taking a train back to the base, he heard the news President Roosevelt had died. He also ran into a former high school classmate, Freddie Bayroff, while he was in England.

Joe served on two cruisers, the *U.S.S. Omaha* and the *U.S.S. Savannah*. He also served as a gunner on patrol flights. He worked and flew on PBY Catalinas, PBM, PB4Y (the Navy's version of the B-24), Dive Bombers, R6D, P2V, and S2F aircraft.

In 1943, while on a routine patrol, Joe's PBM ran out of fuel. There were ten men on board, and they usually flew 16 hour missions. Joe was taking a nap in one of the bunks, when one of the crew came up to him and said, "Get a life jacket on and get to the ditching station." Joe didn't take him seriously, and promptly fell back asleep. Shortly thereafter, he was abruptly awakened when he was told they were out of fuel. The aircraft safely landed on the Amazon River, and the crew secured her with an anchor.

Suddenly, a group of natives showed up in dugout canoes to get a better look at the plane and its crew. Joe's P.P.C (Patrol Plane Commander) told him to go with them to try and get some drinking water, because he spoke some Portuguese and thought they might be able to communicate. The P.P.C. handed Joe a pistol, just in case, and sent another crew member with him to help carry the containers for the water.

The men got into the dugout canoes and were paddled up the river to a nearby village. By the time they got there darkness had set in, so Joe turned on his flashlight. The natives had never seen one before, and were quite intrigued by it. The men were taken into a hut, where there were huge clay crocks full of water. They quickly filled their containers and were returned to their plane by canoe. Joe gave his flashlight to one of the natives to thank him for all his help. A PT boat was sent with aviation fuel, and they hand pumped 300 gallons aboard the PBM. Due to the prevailing wind conditions, the crew had to take off across the flow of the river. The PBM was towed back as close as it could get to one side of the riverbank, and the crew was soon airborne, but they just missed the tops of trees as they took off.

While in the service, Joe saw Joe E. Brown and Red Skelton perform with the USO. When Red Skelton came on to perform, he noticed that the officers had taken all the good seats near the front of the stage, so he asked the "brass" to move, saying "I'm here to entertain the troops, so please give them your seats."

In 1945, Joe was sent to Naples, Italy, where he was outfitted with infantry equipment. He and some other men were supposed to relieve troops on the front line, but plans changed at the last minute. When his ship pulled into the harbor, there were women from the Salvation Army waiting there for them with hot coffee and doughnuts. They were truly a welcome sight to see. The ships were unloaded, and their cargo was put on trucks to supply units throughout Italy. Joe remembers seeing the harbor at Naples littered with ships the Germans had sunk while they were retreating. Once the trucks loaded, they moved out and formed a convoy. There was a submachine gun mounted on top of the trucks, and one man had to ride up there for protection from roadside hijacking.

He returned to the United States, after VE Day, on the *Queen Mary*. There were 20,000 men aboard made up from the Army and Navy, and P.O.W.s that had been held in Germany. They were the first troops to return home, and the reception in New York harbor is one that Joe will never forget. He and his friend Steve from Milwaukee went up on deck, because Steve had never seen the Statue of Liberty. When the ship came into the harbor they had a clear view of the city, and were greeted by fireboats. Joe said you could see downtown, and there were people and confetti everywhere. It was really an exciting homecoming!

Joe was awarded the American Defense Service Medal, American Campaign Medal, World War II Victory Medal, Navy Occupation Service Medal with Europe Clasp, National Defense Service Medal, and the Good Conduct Medal (Five Awards) for his service. He was married to Frances Rosato, from Glen Cove, Long Island, New York, on April 12, 1947, and they had three children.

He then served on the *U.S.S. Randolph, Tarawa, Kearsage, Wasp,* and *Lake Champlain* over the next 15 years, which were all aircraft carriers. Joe was involved with the Berlin Airlift, which occurred shortly after the war, when the Russians closed the roads leading to Berlin. Food and supplies were then flown in by the United States to help keep the residents of Berlin from starving.

Joe, Lou Climo, and Dave Smith (Lou's brother-in-law, Grace's brother), were all assigned to the *U.S.S. Randolph* for a six-month

This photo is of the U.S.S. Randolph, during "Operation Pinwheel" in Malta. The harbor was too small for the aircraft carrier to turn around, so the aircraft engines were started and used to rotate the ship.

Mediterranean cruise. Lou and Joe were attached to a dive bombing squadron, and Dave was with a fighter squadron. They soon formed a fast friendship, and ran across each other at various U.S. Naval Air Stations throughout their careers.

Joe was discharged in October of 1960 from the VS 22 Squadron at Quonset Point, Rhode Island. He then went to work for the Republic Aviation Company in Farmingdale, Long Island, New York, as a service representative and a technical writer until his retirement in 1985. His wife, Frances, passed away in the early 1980s, and he was married to Grace Climo from Southport on November 1, 1986. Joe and his wife of ten years, Grace, currently live on Southport.

GERALD FULLER
Seaman First Class, U.S. Navy

Jerry enlisted in the Navy in 1945 at the age of 18. He received his basic training in Davisville, Rhode Island; Sampson, New York; and at Camp Hueneme in California. He was trained in underwater demolition, welding, and salvage diving. He was discharged in 1946 at the Fargo Building in Boston after serving in the Navy for one and a half years, and was awarded the World War II Victory Medal and the Good Conduct Award.

In the early 1950s, Jerry became the foreman of a boat yard in West Palm Beach, Florida. While there, he also

Gerald Fuller, U.S. Navy

met and married Maria Trindade Morres in 1954. He later became an engineer on a ship, and between 1979-1984, was engaged in surface testing of Trident nuclear submarines, between the Bahamas and Portsmouth, New Hampshire. Jerry became a marine surveyor in 1959, and is currently running his own surveying company in Big Pine Key, Florida, where he lives with his wife of 42 years, Maria.

MYRTLE SEAVEY FURST
Sergeant, U.S. Marine Corps,
Women's Reserves

Myrtle Seavey Furst,
U.S. Marine Corps,
Women's Reserves

In October of 1944, Myrtle enlisted in the Marine Corps Women's Reserves. She was 21 years old at the time and had been working as a clerk stenographer for the Office of Defense Transportation in Washington, D.C. She decided to sign up since there were no eligible male members in her family to help with the war effort. The Marine Corps was the last branch of the service to allow women into its ranks and the first enlisted on February 13, 1943. The slogan they used for enlistment was, "Free a Marine to fight."

Myrtle attended six weeks of boot camp at Camp LeJeune, North Carolina, and was in the 39th Training Battalion, Recruit Depot, Company B, Platoon 1, from October until December of 1944. Myrtle then served for ten months with the Engineer Division, Depot of Supplies, Islais Creek Area in the administration office in San Francisco, California. Upon her arrival she took over Sergeant Golden's duties, which enabled him to serve overseas. He was from New York City and was a really nice guy, so Myrtle hoped and prayed that he would arrive home safely and was very relieved when he did after the war. She was later transferred to the Depot Detachment, Depot of Supplies on 100 Harrison Street, also located in San Francisco, and spent 11 months working there.

Myrtle remembers VJ Day vividly as a time of great celebration, rejoicing, and thanking God for the victories. She said that in downtown San Francisco people were so happy they were hugging strangers and friends alike. On August 22, 1946, the Women's Reserves were demobilized in the San Francisco area and Myrtle received her honorable discharge that day. She served for 21 months, and was awarded the American Campaign Medal and the World War Two Victory Medal.

In 1950, Myrtle was called back to serve during the Korean War. She was affiliated with the Volunteer Training Unit, Fifth Marine Corps Reserve District in Washington, D.C., where she volunteered clerical assistance and she received her promotion to Staff Sergeant on May 2, 1949. From November 14, 1949, through July of 1950 Myrtle was a non-commissioned officer, in charge of recruiting women in the Washington, D.C. area, and was attached to the Fifth Infantry Battalion located there.

On July 19th her battalion received a warning order. On July 26th they received orders to mobilize. Only the women veterans were included, seven in all. They were given ten days to clear up their personal affairs and report to Camp LeJeune, North Carolina. Shortly thereafter they marched into Union Station and boarded the train bound for North Carolina once again.

The women's company was reactivated and they were attached to the H & S Battalion, Marine Barracks 63, Camp LeJeune. The camp adjutant stated the seven women would relieve eight men for possible combat duty. Myrtle assisted in the clerical field for special services interviewing the male Marines to either sign up or refuse their $10,000 life insurance policy before being shipped overseas. After that was accomplished she worked as a secretary to the Company Commander and First Sergeant at the supply depot.

From May of 1951 through June of 1951, Myrtle went on temporary duty to Marine Corps Schools in Quantico, Virginia, as part of the summer training program for the Women Officer's Training Detachment. She returned to Camp LeJeune on June 18, 1951, and was released from active duty on June 28th when the President declared the emergency was over.

Myrtle went back to work for the State Department in Washington, D.C., after her discharge from the Marine Corps. She later drove cross country with a friend and went to work at the Forest Lawn Memorial Park in California as a mortuary hostess. She was married in 1953 and has a son and a daughter. Myrtle currently lives in El Paso, where she works as an executive secretary for the Department of Defense at Fort Bliss in Texas.

ARTHUR GAMAGE
Shipfitter Third Class, U.S. Navy

Arthur worked at Samples Shipyard in Boothbay Harbor prior to his service in the Navy. He served in the Pacific and went to China during the war. He moved to California after the war, and died in a car accident on April 1, 1951, at the age of 25.

Arthur Gamage, U.S. Navy

EDWIN GAMAGE
Captain, U.S. Coast Guard

Ed enlisted in the Life Saving Service on October 1, 1914, at the age of 17. On April 1, 1915, it became the United States Coast Guard and Ed served as a surfman in it on Damariscove Island. When the First World War was declared more men were sent to Damariscove, as the Coast Guard served under the Navy during times of war.

During the Second World War the Coast Guard increased their vigilance around our coastal area, making nightly checks along the shoreline to

Edwin Gamage, U.S. Coast Guard

ensure blackout conditions were being met. If they were not, a quick call was made to the air raid wardens on shore, and the violation was soon rectified. Ed and his men also were on round the clock watch for any enemy ships or submarines that might venture into our waters.

Ed retired from the Coast Guard in 1945, after 30 years of service. Shortly thereafter he started doing carpentry and painting work for people on the island, along with tending a few of his own lobster traps. Ed passed away in 1980 at the age of 88.

LESLIE GAMAGE
Corporal, U.S. Army

Leslie enlisted in the Army on February 19, 1943, at the age of 21, and was in Battery A of the 733rd Field Artillery Battalion. He served as a gun crewman on medium artillery. Prior to that time, Leslie worked at Samples Shipyard in Boothbay Harbor.

He was involved in battles in Normandy, Northern France, Central Europe, and Rhineland during his service, and was discharged from the Army on January 18, 1946, after serving a little over two years and 11 months. Leslie was awarded the American Campaign Ribbon, European African Middle Eastern Campaign Ribbon, World War II Victory Medal, and the Good Conduct Medal.

He married Marsha Dolloff of Damariscotta in September of 1951 and worked as a self-employed carpenter. Leslie passed away on September 29, 1959, at the age of 37.

WESTON GAMAGE, JR.
Second Class Petty Officer
U.S. Coast Guard

Weston was 17 years old when he enlisted in the U.S. Coast Guard; the year was 1936. He served on Burnt Island off Port Clyde, at White Head, and in 1941 in Rockland, Maine.

He worked at the Port Office in Rockland, and was responsible for issuing Coast Guard Identification Cards to local fishermen and to people working on the waterfront. The card had a person's age, fingerprint, and photograph on it, and it allowed them to move freely around the waterfront.

Weston Gamage, Jr.,
U.S. Coast Guard

Weston also was responsible for all boats entering and leaving Rockland Harbor. He issued the necessary documents that authorized movement and gave military clearance in the harbor.

In 1944 Weston was transferred to Searsport, where he issued explosive handlers' permits to longshoremen who were engaged in loading bombs on ships headed overseas. His office was on a dock in Searsport, and there was a strict no smoking rule due to the nature of the cargo the men were handling. One day a small fire broke out, but fortunately it was extinguished immediately. If it had gotten out of hand, the fire could have easily set off the ammunition on the wharf and blown up the whole town.

There were often rumors of people signaling enemy ships at sea and of German submarines surfacing. Weston had to investigate these reports and was sent out in a surfboat to do so. In his own words, "The boat was really small and I had absolutely no way to defend myself if I did find something." Luckily he never did.

Weston had to go over to Vinalhaven to fingerprint the fishermen for their identification cards. He set up a temporary office next to the war rationing office and got to know the official there pretty well. Weston was really amazed one day when the official on the island showed him letters that other residents had written about their neighbors reporting they had foodstuffs, such as sugar and coffee, hoarded away.

Weston retired from the U.S. Coast Guard in 1962, after 26 years of service. He and his wife Caroline, and their two children, Gerry and Julie, then moved back to Southport. He passed away on March 20, 1996, at the age of 78.

EDWARD GAUDETTE
Private First Class,
Army Medical Corps

It was 1942 and Edward was 21 years old when he was drafted into the Army. He had been working at Pinkham's Grocery Store previously. His basic training was at Camp Pickett, Virginia.

After basic training he was sent to Palestine, just outside of Tel Aviv. While on leave he was

Edward Gaudette,
Army Medical Corps

able to go swimming in the Dead Sea. Edward said,"If you waded up to your belly in the water, your feet left the bottom and you'd be floating on your back in no time. I would get a beer and a book and float around reading." He also said, "There wasn't a living thing in the water, not even weeds. You could only dive from three feet, because the water was so hard and salty. After swimming there I would have to wash off with soap and fresh water, or else I would turn white with salt."

Edward went to Bethlehem on Christmas Eve for midnight mass at Christ's Tomb. Archbishop Spellman from New York was there and he got to talk with him after Mass. He gave Edward a set of prayer beads that he had blessed and Edward carried them with him always for luck. While there he also saw the Manger, Stations of the Cross, and the Mount of Olives.

Most of the patients in his hospital came from Italy or France. One day about 15 paratroopers were brought in with broken legs. They had jumped from what they thought was 5000 feet, but they were over a mountain and their chutes opened up just before they hit the ground. The accident happened at night and they weren't found until the next afternoon.

After serving 13 months in Palestine, they left for India near Burma during the China Burma India Theater of War. Edward was stationed with a 150-bed hospital unit where he was a food purchasing agent for three hospital kitchens. He was in charge of supplying the food for the officers, enlisted men, and for the patients.

They first lived in a brick building that had been in an earthquake and was falling apart. In this part of the country, you had to use mosquito nets and keep them tucked in all the time. Edward was sitting on his bunk reading and got up to do something and forgot to tuck in his net. When he came back and sat down, he felt something under his bottom, so he said to his buddy, "I think I'm sitting on a scorpion." Edward sat really hard so it couldn't move and his friend came over, grabbed both his hands, counted to three, and pulled. The scorpion jumped to bite and then took off. It was six inches long. The men found it and killed it with a shoe. After that Edward always tucked in his mosquito net.

It was so hot at night in India, Edward would take the sheets off his bunk, get them wet in the shower, and would put them back on the bunk. Then he would sleep with them wet. The only problem with this was that in an hour they would be dry again.

One time while Edward was swimming in the Mediterranean Sea, he swam up to a man he recognized and said "John Bird"; the man then said "Charlie Pinkham." It turned out that it was Bill Wright; he was the salesman for John Bird Wholesale Grocers out of Rockland, Maine, and frequently came to Pinkham's Store where Edward worked. He was on leave for two weeks, so they often visited together during that time.

While in India Edward got pneumonia and was in the hospital in Bombay for three weeks. After being discharged from the hospital he had to find his unit. He went to Calcutta by train, which took a week, then on to Assam, India, which took about 30 days by narrow gauge railroad. Sometimes he would have to wait a week for a train to come down the tracks before he could continue, and often the temperature would soar to 125 degrees, so he would pitch his tent in a tea patch to keep the sun off. The hospital Edward worked in had thatched roofs, which kept it from becoming too hot.

One day in December, near Christmas time, Edward received the news about his brother's death. Norman had been killed in action, in France, almost a month earlier, and it had taken that long for the information to get to India. It was a very sad and difficult time for the Gaudette family, and Edward was unable to return home, so he could be with them.

One day Edward and the other medics got a call to bring an ambulance to the landing strip. When they got there a plane was coming in with one of its four engines out. It was a great big plane and it had just dropped a bomb on Japan. The landing strip even had to be made longer so it could take off the next week. One of the bomb bays had two new engines in it. The medics were not allowed near the plane and were kept two to three hundred feet away from it, because it was a military secret. Edward never knew why until later.

Edward met a lot of nice people in Israel, but commented that there was no one to meet in India, just jungle, hundreds of monkeys, and cows. While there he also suffered from dysentery and yellow jaundice, and at one point dropped down to 134 pounds, which was a little thin for a 6' 1" man. He was sent to a rest area on top of a mountain to recuperate. It was nice, cool, and there were lots of girls there, so he thought it wasn't too bad after all.

When it was time to go home Edward went back to Calcutta, then on to Bombay, Cairo, North Africa, Morocco, the Azores, and finally New York. They flew on a mail plane that had no seats, just a cargo area. It took 22 hours flying time to come home, so the men slept on the mail bags. As they were coming into the United States, the pilot got permission to circle the Statue of Liberty. He brought the plane down to about

Edward standing on the Ruins of Jarash in Jordan.

200 feet over the water. Everyone was waving at them, because they knew it was servicemen coming home. The plane was open inside and the pilot talked with the men the whole way back. Edward stood behind him, holding onto his seat, and got to get a really good view coming into New York Harbor.

When they landed, a bus picked them up and took them to the Red Cross. They asked the men what they wanted most of all. The number one request was to use the telephone, second was apple pie or chocolate cake. Edward asked for a glass of cold milk, which promptly made him sick after he drank it.

He was sent home for 30 days on leave, then went to Lake Placid, New York, on R & R for another 30. The next stop was Fort Lewis in Washington state, where he was assigned to fight forest fires. Edward went to the camp commander and told him he was a medic, not a fire fighter, so he switched him to the dispensary where he helped with sick calls.

After being in 16 countries, including Egypt, Morocco, Jordan, and Syria to name a few and three years of service, Edward was discharged in Fort Lewis, Washington, over 3000 miles from home. He was awarded the European African Middle Eastern Service Medal, China Burma India Service Medal, the Good Conduct Medal, and two service stars for his service.

After their discharge, Edward and a friend hitchhiked from Seattle, Washington, to Tijuana, Mexico, then back to Los Angeles, California. Then he took a train back to Maine, stopping in Chicago, New York, and Boston on the way. There weren't many jobs to be found on Southport at the time, so he moved to Bangor, Maine, to try to make a better life for himself.

In July of 1947, Edward married Althea Condon, from Dixmont, Maine, and managed a shoe store in Bangor. He and his wife had a daughter, Norma. He was later transferred to Bath, then was offered the position of district manager in Nashua, New Hampshire, and was in charge of 43 stores. He retired from that position in May of 1971, and became a partner in the Nashua Saab/Subaru dealership, from which he retired in 1984. Edward currently lives in Belfast, with his wife of 49 years, Althea.

FRANCIS GAUDETTE
Seaman First Class, U.S. Coast Guard

Francis Gaudette,
U.S. Coast Guard

Francis enlisted in the Coast Guard on October 13, 1942. He was 20 years old and had been working as an electrician at Bath Iron Works prior to that time. He got on the train in Portland for the first time in his life, and rode to Boston. Francis was trained in Provincetown, Massachusetts and was later assigned to beach patrol in Cohasset, Massachusetts.

After his training was completed Francis was given a pass, which allowed him to go home for a few days. Much to his surprise he met up with fellow Southporters Walter Hart, Jr., Leon Duprey, and John Thompson on board the train. Pay at the time was $69.30 a month, with a travel allowance of $8.75 from Boston to Southport at a rate of .05 cents per mile.

Francis was later assigned to the Coast Guard cutter *Modoc*, which escorted convoys to Newfoundland. One day, while on board, he looked up on the flying bridge and saw a man wearing a jacket that had a Maine insignia on it. Francis went up to talk to him; the man said his name was Merton Leeman and that he came from a small town near Damariscotta called Round Pond. When Francis told Merton he had grown up on Southport Island, a fast friendship was formed. Enroute to Newfoundland the *Modoc* went through the Grand Banks. Francis remembers seeing fishermen hand lining out of dories and thinking they were brave to be that far offshore in such a small boats.

Duty on board the *Modoc* consisted of four hours watch on deck looking for submarines and four hours off. They never spotted any submarines, but when they shot practice depth charges off, Francis remembers seeing lots of red fish bubble up to the surface. There were 250 men on board the 250-foot *Modoc*. The men slept in very cramped quarters, in bunks stacked four high, with their clothes and life jackets on. Francis, who had grown up on the water in Southport, suffered from terrible sea-sickness while on board. The stuffiness of the cabin became unbearable and Francis began sleeping in a large coil of rope up on deck. In the morning he would wake up, slap the ice off of his jacket, and start his watch. In 30 days Francis lost 30 pounds and dropped down to a weight of 127 pounds.

While in Newfoundland the troops were treated to a U.S.O. show featuring Frank Sinatra and the comic Phil Silvers. It was a chance to get off the ship for a while and was a welcome change of pace.

Greenland was the *Modoc*'s next destination, and her assignment was to act as an escort for fuel tankers. It was summer when the Coast Guard cutter arrived there and it was fairly hot. The icebergs were magnificent and some even had waterfalls cascading off of them where the sun had melted a reservoir of water on top. Francis even recalls seeing the local people paddling by the *Modoc* in kayaks. While there, the *Modoc* was frozen into the ice pack for two days before they could get her out. The propellers were terribly bent and skin divers had to go overboard to fix them.

During the war, photographs as well as mail was censored. Francis had a camera with him while he was on the *Modoc* and shot several rolls

The Modoc in Greenland.

of film while he was in Greenland. He couldn't have the film developed or it would be confiscated by the government, so he prepared a package to send to his girlfriend back in the States and took it to the censor on board to be checked. The censor looked it over and handed it back to Francis so he could wrap the box and mail it. Francis took it back to his cabin and added the films he had shot to the box, wrapped it up, and took it to be mailed.

The films were developed stateside and were immediately confiscated. Amazingly enough, they were returned to his girlfriend after the war ended and Francis now has quite a scrapbook documenting his time in Greenland.

Mail was slow in coming to the *Modoc* and Francis often went from four to six months without any news from home. When it did arrive the news was outdated, but was greatly appreciated. From Greenland, the *Modoc* went to the Azores. It really was a rough trip. There was a wind meter on board that registered 100 m.p.h. and it was ripped off the side of the ship by the force of the wind. There were other ships in their convoy and Francis said you could look over at them and see their propellers coming out of the water. Then when you looked back the entire ship would be hidden behind the swell of a wave.

When Francis returned to Boston, he was notified that his brother Norman had been killed in action in France. He was granted leave so he could go to Southport and be with his family during this difficult time.

Francis was discharged on March 8, 1946, after serving for four years. Mustering out pay was $100. When he returned home, he decided to send to Augusta to get ration coupons. Everyone told him it would take forever to get them. Francis wrote a letter requesting the coupons and signed it "Love, Francis." Much to his surprise, the coupons he requested came back to him in the very next mail.

Francis was awarded the American Theater of War Ribbon, World War Two Victory Ribbon, European African Middle Eastern Campaign Ribbon, and the Good Conduct Award. He married Ramona Thompson, from South Bristol on January 14, 1947, and worked at Samples Shipyard in Boothbay Harbor for a while after the war. He later switched to Goudy and Steven's Shipyard in East Boothbay, where he worked for 25 years. Francis currently lives on Southport with his wife of 49 years, Ramona.

NORMAN GAUDETTE
Private, U.S. Army

Norman was drafted into the Army on April 28, 1943, at the age of 33. He received his basic training at Fort Eustis, Virginia, and later went onto Camp Crouder, Missouri. In June of 1944, he was sent overseas to Bath, England, from Camp Edwards, Massachusetts. After a brief stay there he was stationed in France. He was the owner/operator of the Shell Station and manager of the Harbor Tailor Shop in Boothbay Harbor prior to that time.

Norman Gaudette, U.S. Army

Norman was assigned to the 398th Anti-Aircraft Artillery, Automatic Weapons Battalion, Battery B. His duties included running half-tracks, which were anti-aircraft artillery guns. He was killed in action on November 11, 1944, in northeastern France by

U.S. Military Cemetery, Epinal, France

machine gun fire. He was buried at the United States Military Cemetery in Epinal, France.

Norman was Southport's second casualty of World War II, and was awarded the European African Middle Eastern Campaign Medal, Good Conduct Award, and the Purple Heart for the ultimate sacrifice he made to his country.

ELLSWORTH GRAY
Seaman First Class, U.S. Navy

Ellsworth was 17 years old when he went to Portland and enlisted in the Navy. The year was 1944. He went through boot camp and was trained as a radio operator at the Naval Air Technical Center in Memphis, Tennessee. While there he saw Bob Hope and Jerry Colonia perform with the U.S.O. After leaving the technical center, Ellsworth served on a landing craft LST#221 in the Hawaiian Islands and on various islands in the Pacific.

Ellsworth Gray, U.S. Navy

She was about 400 feet long, and 100 men plus the officers served on her.

There were three radio operators on board and they rotated on four-hour shifts. Messages were transmitted to all the ships in a certain area and the radio operator on duty had to pick out the fox identification, which was the heading that pertained to his particular ship, then he would decode it. The heading that Ellsworth listened for was WPIZ, WPIZ, WPIZ. That meant the message was intended for LST #221. Ellsworth said learning Morse Code was like learning a song. Once you got the rhythm you could decode up to 40 words a minute. While in the Hawaiian Islands, Ellsworth ran into Seldon Lewis of Boothbay Harbor and Jim Patton of Boothbay. He also met Erwin Dodge of Boothbay in Shoemaker, California.

Ellsworth was discharged from the Navy in the spring of 1946, and he went to work in the machine shop at Pratt and Whitney in Connecticut. He later drove a truck for Round Top Dairy in Damariscotta and picked up milk at local farms. He then moved to Fryeburg, where he became a parts manager for the Chevrolet dealer there. In 1953 Ellsworth moved to Clearwater, Florida, where he opened his own garage in 1958. He retired in 1986, and now lives in Hernando, Florida, with his wife of ten years, Vernina.

JOHN GRAY

Electronic Technicians Mate
Third Class, U.S. Navy

John Gray, U.S. Navy

John enlisted in the Navy in January of 1943. He had been studying electrical engineering at the University of Maine in Orono at the time. He received his basic training at Sampson Naval Training Station in New York and submarine training at the New London Shipyard in Groton, Connecticut.

Life aboard a submarine can be difficult. The quarters are very cramped and there is not much privacy. John served on both the U.S.S. Cubera and the *U.S.S. Flounder*. It took a crew of 60 men to run the battery-operated submarines, and John was one of three radar men aboard them. They worked eight hours on and 16 hours off, and since something was always wrong with the equipment, there was always something in need of repair. Early radar used vacuum tubes, which were not very reliable, so it became very challenging to keep them running. The men sometimes were all on at the same time to ensure the radar was fixed.

John's submarine headed for the Pacific on its first war patrol, but was back at Pearl Harbor within a week, because they received the news that the atomic bomb had been dropped on Japan. They then traveled through the Panama Canal enroute to Staten Island, New York. It was here that they suffered their only casualty. One of the crew members was leaning against a railing up on deck, smoking a cigar. He had just finished saying, "Boy, is my girlfriend lucky I'm coming home." Then all of a sudden the railing on the submarine broke, he fell into the canal, and drowned. All crew members on a sub are supposed to pass a swimming test, but somehow this man had gotten around it.

After the tragedy of losing a crew member, the sub encountered a ferocious hurricane. The skipper didn't want it put in the record that they submerged to avoid the storm, so they took on the tremendous seas and winds. The sub was listing 48 degrees back and forth, and everyone seemed to be sick but John, who was offering to eat everyone else's food.

The only time John was truly scared was when he went on duty and was working with the radar. He glanced over to one side and noticed that there was a solid column of water rising next to him. One of the hatches had been opened and the sea had just poured in due to the force of the storm. Much to John's relief, it was soon pumped out.

Over the Thanksgiving holiday, John was on leave and caught a train home. It was there that he met his future wife Lorraine coming home from school in Boston. He was traveling with a friend and told him: "I'm going to marry that girl." So he introduced himself to her as a friend of her brother's and proposed within the next 20 minutes. Loraine chose to ignore him at the time, but nine months later they were married.

John was discharged from the Navy in 1946 after three years, four months, and ten days of service. He returned to college on the G.I. Bill and finished his studies in electrical engineering. For the next 20 years, he worked on missiles at Cape Canaveral in Florida, and later moved to California where he was involved with similar work at Vandenberg Air Force Base. John currently lives in Southport with his wife of 50 years, Lorraine.

ROLAND GRAY
Ski Paratroopers, U.S. Army

Roland had been studying architecture at Wentworth Institute in Boston when he enlisted in the Army. He was an excellent skier and soon volunteered for the ski paratroopers. He was trained in Colorado, then sent overseas. When the infantry needed

Roland Gray, U.S. Army

men for the Battle of the Bulge, Roland was placed in the 84th Division. During the battle in Belgium, he was killed in action on December 24, 1944. He was Southport's third war casualty.

SCOTT GRAY
First Mate, Merchant Marine
....

During the Second World War, Scott served on Mobil Oil tankers and freighters for the Shepard Steamship, Co., out of Boston. He was 42 at the time, and his work took him around the world to England, Scotland, Ireland, France, Turkey, Tinian, South America, and Russia.

Prior to that time, he worked for the Eastern Steamship Company, on their line that ran between Boston and Rockland. He earned his mates license in 1919, and broadened his seafaring experience, on board ships that went to Greece, Turkey, and several other countries. In 1923-1924, he returned home and married Patience Moore from Boothbay Harbor. Scott then skippered several yachts including, the Alcyone and the *Elizabeth Ann*. He ran the general store in Newagen until he returned to the sea around 1940.

He had been sailing on the *S.S. Mobil Oil*, delivering oil from Texas to New Jersey, and decided to get off in Alabama. It was a wise decision, because the ship was torpedoed off of Florida, as she made the return

Scott Gray, Merchant Marine, pictured second from the left.

run to Texas. On board another ship, Scott watched as the ship traveling alongside of his was torpedoed and sunk off the New Jersey coastline. It was a very dangerous time to be in the Merchant Marine.

Scott was able to visit with his son Ellsworth, who was in the Navy, several times during the war, while his ship was in port in Texas, New Orleans, and out on the West Coast. He also successfully made the treacherous Murmansk run, delivering supplies to Russia, and in 1944, delivered napalm bombs to the island of Tinian in the Pacific.

The last ship Scott sailed on was the *Clarence Peck*, and he left her in 1949, after a long career in the Merchant Marine. He returned to Newagen, and resumed running the general store and post office there until 1969, when he passed away on July 22, at the age of 70.

ARTHUR HAMILTON
Army Air Corps

I have been unable to find any information on Arthur, except for a brief passage in Edith Gray's diary. It reads,

"May 1, 1942: A Mr. Hamilton coming here. Mr. Colland going to Waldoboro. Mr. Hamilton has a son in the Air Corps in Massachusetts." Mr. Hamilton was a Methodist minister, and he passed away here on the island during the war. I think it is safe to assume that his son never returned to Southport when he was discharged, and probably didn't have any ties to the island, because he didn't attend school here.

DONALD M. HARRIMAN
Corporal, U.S. Army

Donald entered the service on June 6, 1943, at the age of 21. He was trained at Indiantown Gap, Pennsylvania, and in North Carolina, and became part of the 377th Infantry Regiment. Prior to that time he had been a marine biology student at Bates College in Lewiston.

He served in the European Theater of Operations as part of the Third and Ninth Army, in England, France, Belgium, and

Donald Harriman, U.S. Army

Germany. Donald was trained as an automatic rifleman. He also had expertise using the bar M-1 rifle, pistols, rifle grenades, and in the area of individual personal concealment and camouflage. He and his outfit provided fire power support to tactical units when capturing and holding enemy positions. He was wounded in the left hand during the war, and subsequently, lost the feeling in one of his fingers.

Donald was discharged on December 12, 1945, at Fort Douglas, Utah, after serving in the Army for two years and six months. He was awarded the European Theater Medal, the Purple Heart, the World War II Victory Medal, American Theater Ribbon, and the Good Conduct Medal.

He returned to Bates College after the war, and graduated with a degree in biology in 1948. Donald started working for the Sea and Shore Fisheries Department shortly thereafter, and was married to Priscilla Morse from North Monmouth, Maine, on August 23, 1952. They had two daughters, Nancy and Elizabeth. Donald passed away on April 28, 1970, at the age of 47.

PRESTON HART
Machinist Mate
Third Class, U.S. Navy

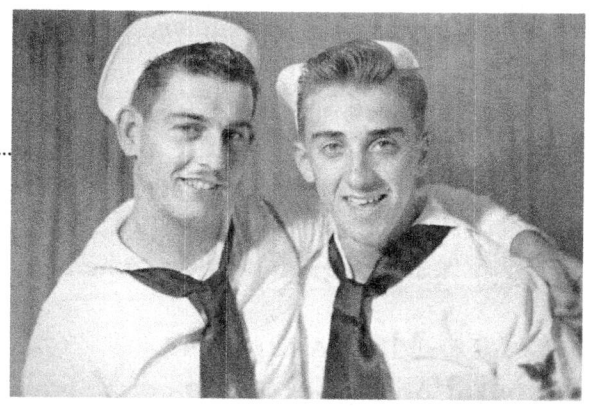

Preston enlisted in the Navy May 3, 1944, and was stationed at Hickam Field in Hawaii, where he served on patrol craft, PC-487. He had been a student at Boothbay Region High School prior to that time.

Preston Hart, U.S. Navy, pictured on the left. His friend, Leroy Harner, is shown on the right.

PC-487 was about 170 feet long and had a 30 man crew aboard. She was run by two 1800 horsepower diesel engines, which Preston worked on. The men served five days on patrol and two days on shore, and PC-487 even rode out a tidal wave during the war.

Preston had the good fortune to see several USO shows while he was stationed in Hawaii. Entertainers that preformed for the troops included: Mickey Rooney, Judy Garland, Rita Hayworth, Betty Grable, Bob Hope,

Preston kept a photo album while he was stationed in Hawaii. He was able to attend several USO shows, and collected many photographs of the performers. The above depicts a USO show in progress.

Mr. U.S.O. himself, Bob Hope.

Betty Grable   *Bette Davis*

Jerry Colona

Jerry Colona, Dorothy Lamore, Lana Turner, Nan Gray, Linda Darnell, and Ginger Rogers to name a few.

He was discharged on May 30, 1946, after two years of service, and was awarded the World War II Victory Medal, American Theater Medal, and the Asiatic Pacific Theater Medal. He married Julia Gilley from Coopers Mills on December 30, 1946, and they had three children: Preston, Susan, and Constance.

After the war, he worked for a while at the Hyde Windless in Bath, then went to work at the Brunswick Naval Air Station, as a fireman, and retired after twenty years on the job. He also worked at the Bath Iron Works on their fire department after his retirement from the B.N.A.S. Preston passed away on February 7, 1994, at the age of 67.

WALTER HART, JR.
Quartermaster Second Class,
U.S. Navy

Walter joined the Navy on October 20, 1942, at the age of 20. He had been working at the Hyde Windlass foundry in Bath prior to that time. His wife Mary was expecting their first child, and had to move in with her parents while he was gone. Walter didn't get to see his daughter Norma in person until he returned home in 1945. She was almost three years old by then.

Walter Hart, Jr., U.S. Navy

He was assigned to the Hereshoff Shipyard in Boston while his ship, U.S.S. APC 10 (Area Patrol Craft), was being built and served on her in the South Pacific. His ship was torpedoed while on patrol and he was blown overboard from the explosion that followed. Walter was rescued from the ocean and sustained injuries to his back, neck, and knee. He was discharged in Bremerton, Washington on September 25, 1945, and was awarded the Asiatic Pacific Theater Campaign Ribbon and the Purple Heart for his service. After the war Walter went to work for Bath Iron Works in the outside machinist department. He passed away on December 10, 1967, at the age of 45.

ROBERT HASCH
Petty Officer Third Class,
Navy Seabees

Buck enlisted in the Navy on June 19, 1942, at the age of 19. He was determined to get into the Navy, but had failed his first eye exam, so when he went back for the second exam, he memorized the eye chart and passed with flying colors. He was trained at Camp Perry, Virginia, and became part of the Construction Battalion, Maintenance Unit-520. He had been a student at the University of California prior to that time.

There was an outfit in the Seabees that were specially trained in under-water demolition and landing tech-

Robert Hasch, Navy Seabees

niques. This outfit is still in existence today, but now goes by the name of Navy Seals. Buck was an excellent swimmer, had competed in both high school and college events, and thought he would be a perfect candidate this type of work. He was accepted into the program, and was doing fine until he was assigned to swim across a harbor to a blue light, go ashore on the other side, pick something up, and swim back. Needless to say, Buck's eye chart high jinks finally caught up with him, because he couldn't see the blue light. He ended up swimming way off course, which alerted his instructors about his eyesight, and he was promptly reassigned to a construction outfit. Luckily he knew how to run a bulldozer.

Buck then traveled on a LST-125 (landing ship tank) from the United States through the Panama Canal, to Bora Bora, the American Samoas, and finally to Guadalcanal. They stopped along the way to make any repairs that were needed at the bases on the islands. While traveling in a convoy, one of the lead ships was torpedoed and blew up off the Fiji Islands. The order to man battle stations was quickly passed throughout the ship, and Buck took his position on the bow machine gun. There were several destroyers in the convoy and they started dropping depth charges. When the submarine finally surfaced it was strafed with machine gun fire, and eventually sank to the bottom of the ocean.

The Pacific was hot and buggy, and the men were bombed by the Japanese sporadically. One particular aviator comes to mind when Buck recalls daily life on Guadalcanal whose nickname was "Washing Machine Charlie." You never knew if he was going to drop a bomb or a kitchen sink out of his airplane when he flew over. Buck said Charlie really knew how to keep the troops guessing.

Buck ran a bulldozer and helped in the construction of Henderson Field on Guadalcanal. He was also the photographer for his outfit, and was given a Speedgraphic camera to use to document his fellow Seabees in action. He had a makeshift darkroom in a double walled tent, and really enjoyed this assignment. The natives of the island stayed up in the hills for the most part, but sometimes the men would appear and work with the Seabees for a while, then would silently disappear back into the jungle.

Bob Hope made an appearance with the USO on Guadalcanal. Buck said he brought some of the most beautiful girls he had ever seen with him to entertain the troops, and it was great to get a taste of home, even if it were just for a little while.

One day an ammunition ship blew up in the harbor. Buck said he never even heard the explosion, perhaps because it was so loud, and the next thing he knew he had been wounded in the leg by shrapnel. He was evacuated to a hospital in New Zealand, where he spent five months recuperating. Then he was sent back to Guadalcanal.

Since the Seabees ran the docks, Buck had access to all the ship's manifests. A liberty ship came in loaded with beer for the Army, but no one came to claim it for several days. Once Buck realized what the precious cargo was, he got some of his friends together, they came up with the correct paperwork, and proceeded to unload the ship of valuable cargo. It took two or three days, but they got every last case of Lucky Lager and stashed it all over the island. It was really a terrible beer, but under the circumstances, it was the best tasting beer they had ever had, and they even discovered you could cool it by placing it in a bucket of water, and spraying it with a fire extinguisher.

Buck was discharged in April of 1946 in Oklahoma City after three years and ten months of service. He was awarded the Asiatic Pacific Theater Medal with two bronze stars, American Service Medal, and the Purple Heart. After the war, he returned to college on the GI Bill, and studied cartography (mapmaking) at the University of Illinois.

Buck decided to tour around the United States in his 1935 Ford, to see where it was he wanted to live. On the fourth day he drove into Boothbay Region, and knew he had found his home. He married Jean Rogers from Illinois in 1946, and they had five children: Jayce, Marjorie, Nancy, Judy, and Jack.

There weren't many jobs around, so Buck went to work for a little over a year in Washington, D.C., as a cartographer. After that he returned to Southport and went to work at Hodgdon Brothers/Goudy and Stevens Shipyards in East Boothbay. He later became a salesman for the Carborundun Company, selling grinding wheels, but then moved on to the Raytheon Company, which at the time was developing a new product, radar domes that were made out of reinforced plastic.

Buck became interested in microwave devices, and made a career change when he became employed by the Dielectric Products, Co., in Raymond, Maine, where he worked for about four years. Then he worked for Varian and Associates, who built microwave multipliers, and made the landing radar that was used for the first moon landing. He then worked for Sylvania up until his retirement in 1971.

Buck was remarried on January 1, 1970, to Jean Swett from Southport, Maine, and they had one son, Bob. Buck currently lives on Southport with his wife of 26 years, Jean.

HELEN MARTIN HENDERSON
Yeoman Third Class, Navy WAVES

Helen enlisted in the Navy WAVES on July 8, 1943, at the age of 22. She received training at the U.S. Naval Training School in the Bronx, New York, and at the U.S. Naval Training School at Cedar Falls, Iowa. Prior to that time, she had been working for the Bethlehem-Hingham Shipyard, Inc., in Hingham, Massachusetts.

She served in New York City after completing her training, and kept track of the locations of Navy ships all over the world. Helen and the other WAVES worked eight-hour shifts using huge books of codes to

Helen Martin Henderson,
Navy WAVES

decode messages transmitted from the Navy's ships. The women made revisions from Naval districts, and updated the ships whereabouts, including what ports they were in and when they were sailing. There were six people on duty at a time, and an officer. At the end of their shift, the officer would take the code books and lock them in a huge safe.

Helen was discharged in New York on February 1, 1946, after two years and seven months of service. She was awarded the American Service Medal and the World War II Victory Medal. Then she went to work for United Airlines as a stewardess, which is where she met Ken Henderson from Springfield, Massachusetts, who was a pilot for the airline. They were married in April of 1948, and had two children, Susan and Stevie. At that time, married women were not allowed to work as stewardesses, so Helen had to give up her job. They later moved to Southport, which is where Helen still resides.

KENNETH E. HENDERSON
First Lieutenant, Army Air Corps

*Kenneth E. Henderson,
Army Air Corps*

Ken enlisted in the Air Corps on September 8, 1944, at the age of 20. He received basic training at Wittenburg College in Springfield, Ohio, then went on to advanced two engine training in Alius, Oklahoma. He also went to Instructors School at Randolph Field in Texas. Prior to that time he had been attending high school in Springfield, Massachusetts. After graduation he went to work for the Coca-Cola Company.

He was part of the 38th Bombardment Group, and was stationed in the Western Pacific, on New Guinea and Luzon, and was part of the China offensive, and air offensive over Tokyo. Ken was first pilot on a B-25, and flew 25 successful missions. On occasion he acted as flight commander, and led as many as 24 bombers on various bombing missions. He and his crew were awarded the Distinguished Flying Cross when they sank the Japanese escort carrier *Kaiyo*, on August 9, 1945. The *Kaiyo* was anchored in Boppu Bay, on the Island of Wan, off the coast of China.

Ken was discharged at Fort Devens, Massachusetts, on April 7, 1946, after one year and seven months of service. He was awarded the Philippine Liberation Medal with one Bronze Star, Air Medal with Oak Leaf Cluster, Asiatic Pacific Service Medal, American Service Medal, Distinguished Flying Cross, and the World War II Victory Medal.

He started flying for United Airlines shortly thereafter, and was married to Helen Martin from Watertown, Massachusetts, in April of 1948. In 1949, Ken went to work for the all freight company, Flying Tigers, which has since become Federal Express. He flew for them for 33 years, up until April of 1982, when he passed away at the age of 57.

DAVID HILTON
Sergeant, U.S. Army

David was drafted into the Army in February of 1945 at the age of 32. He received basic training at Fort Devens, Massachusetts, and was later assigned to Camp Gordon, Georgia. While there he met his good friend Haywood Higgins from Aroostook, Maine. Prior to that time, David had been enlisted in the State Guard in Waterville since 1942 and had worked with his brother and father at their family business, the Proctor and Bowie Company, which was a lumber and hardware business. He was married to Ann Trimble in August of 1937, and had to leave her with four children to raise when he was drafted. Luckily their families were nearby, so she received a helping hand from them.

He was later reassigned to Camp Shelby, Mississippi, for further training in preparation to go to Japan. Finally the day came, and as David prepared to board the ship in Virginia, he noticed men being taken out of line. Shortly thereafter he was asked if he had children and, if so, how many? When he replied that he had four, he was asked to step out of line, and to report back to Camp Shelby. The government had decided that men with three or more children would be sent home at this point.

David was discharged from the Army in December of 1945 after ten months of service and was awarded the World War II Victory Medal, American Defense Medal, and the Good Conduct Award. He returned to the family business, which he helped run for another 30 years until his retirement in 1975. David and his wife of 59 years, Ann currently live in Southport.

WALTER HUSKINS
Seaman First Class, U.S. Navy

Walter was drafted into the Navy in December of 1944, at the age of 25. He had been living in Gardiner, Maine, with his wife Virginia and their

*Walter Huskins,
U.S. Navy*

two children, Nancy and Gary, who were six and three months old at the time. He had been employed as a welder and steel worker at the T.W. Dick, Co., which was also located in Gardiner. He attended boot camp at Sampson, New York, and went to Aviation Metalsmith School in Norman, Oklahoma.

He was then shipped to California and was later stationed at Pearl Harbor where he worked in an office, because the Navy had trained too many men as metalsmiths and didn't have enough work for them to do. Walter was discharged from the service in January of 1946 after serving for one year and one month.

Walter went to work as a foreman at the T.W. Dick Company, in Gardiner after the war and later worked as a welder for the pipe fitters union in Maine, New Hampshire, Massachusetts, Georgia, Alabama, and Florida. He retired in 1984 and currently lives in St. Petersburg, Florida, with his wife of 56 years, Virginia.

ROBERT IRVINE
Captain, U.S. Army

Bob enlisted in the Army on July 24, 1941, at the age of 24. He had graduated from the forestry program at the University of Maine at Orono, and worked for W.T. Grant in Haverill, Massachusetts, for two weeks before he was called into the service.

He went through the R.O.T.C. program while he was at Orono, and graduated with the rank of Second Lieutenant. Bob went to Fort Devens, Massachusetts, for further training, then on to North Carolina for maneuvers. He returned to the camp the night before Pearl Harbor was attacked by the Japanese. Then he

Robert Irvine, U.S. Army, pictured on the right. His friend, Bill Hall, is shown on the left.

was sent to Camp Blanding, Florida. Bob married his girlfriend, Virgie Pfeiffer, from Framingham, Massachusetts, on April 11, 1942, and was sent overseas two months later. They didn't see each other again for over three years.

Bob went to Fort Benning, Georgia, then on to Indiantown Gap, Pennsylvania, where he boarded the *Dutchess of Bedford*, which took him to Tidworth, England. He was part of the advanced detail of the First Division, and said he had to sign for every pot, pan, and uniform that was sent over for the Army to use. The men went on maneuvers at Stonehenge. There were no fences around it, like there are now, and Bob said you could walk freely though the grounds.

After three months his outfit was moved to Firth of Clyde, Scotland, where they held practice landings in Inverness. By November of 1942, Bob had earned the rank of First Lieutenant. Once again he boarded the *Dutchess of Bedford*, but did not know where they were shipping out to. At first he thought they were going to Norway, but then changed his mind, when he saw the uniforms that were brought on board. They were lightweight, so he then knew they were going south.

Bob was in charge of Heavy Weapons Company H, including two machine gun platoons and four mortar platoons. He had to take turns standing watch on the bridge, and remembers passing by Gibraltar, which was on one side of the ship, and was totally blacked out. Morocco was on the other side, and was all lit up, because it was a free city. About halfway through the voyage the men were briefed and were told they would be the landing force at Oran, North Africa. The captain of their ship took it straight in to the shore, and the men stepped off without a scratch.

First impressions of Oran were bleak and dusty. Rommel's elite African troops were dug in up in the mountains, and it was rough going for a while. Kasserine Pass was really tough, and they almost got the best of the Allies, but then the fog cleared and the Army Air Corps came through and bombed the Germans, so they retreated.

General Montgomery and his British troops were pushing the Germans back. It was the Americans' job to push them from the other direction, which we did from Tunisia and Algeria. There were many other countries involved in this battle including England, Tunisia, and Algeria.

Bob remembers the Moroccans and Gurkhas came in at one point to replace his division. They were really tough soldiers. The Gurkhas (soldiers from Nepal, serving in the British or Indian armies) were paid for any ears they brought back from the enemy.

Meanwhile, the First Division had been told the City of Oran was off limits to them from 5 P.M. on, because they had thrown 18 M.P.s (military police) in the bay the night before. Teddy Roosevelt, Jr., was second in command, and he told his men to go into the city before the curfew, and that was how they got around it. Bob said his men may have been a little rough around the edges when they were in town, but you couldn't beat them on the battlefield.

One day, while watching a soldier try out a rifle grenade, Bob was hit in the breast bone by shrapnel. It backfired, wounding the operator, and killing the man who was standing next to Bob. He didn't even know he had been hit until his chest started to feel like it was on fire. Bob was evacuated to a nearby army hospital, and there he met a friend from Massachusetts, Bob Mayo, who lived on the street next to his at home. Because it was friendly fire, Bob was not awarded a Purple Heart. The doctor couldn't get the shrapnel out, so he decided to leave it there, and it is still in his breast bone to this day.

While in North Africa, Bob was sent back to the command post to get supplies for the men. Enroute, he and the jeep driver came upon several German soldiers. Bob threatened them with his hand clenched, as if he had a grenade, and they surrendered. Bob and the jeep driver took them prisoner, and Bob earned a Bronze Star Medal for his actions.

In the spring of 1943, Bob debarked on the *U.S.S. Chase* from Algiers for the invasion of Sicily. He and 15 other men were awarded the rank of Captain, seven out of 15, survived the invasion. Bob and his men climbed down rope ladders into Coast Guard landing crafts. When the time came to go ashore, the boat operator couldn't get the ramp to go down, so Bob yelled to his men, "Over the side!" You could see tracer bullets coming at you from every direction, and it was enough to scare you to death.

Once ashore, Bob couldn't find the battalion commander. He had a reporter and 200 men counting on him, so when the reporter asked him, "What are you going to do now?" He replied, "Keep going!" It was really rough territory, but they took it anyway. At one point, eight Italian tanks showed up, and the men had to get in foxholes. As the tanks rolled over them, Bob's men managed to put grenades in their underbellies, and five out of eight tanks were put out of commission. He was awarded a Bronze Star Medal for his actions in Sicily.

While in Sicily at the command post, Bob was hit in the head with shrapnel. He was evacuated to Palermo, but by the time they got him there, he was all right. This earned him the first of his four purple hearts. Meanwhile, his outfit pushed on and were in the northern part of Sicily by the time he was able to get back to them. It took about a month to secure Sicily, and the First Division guarded an airfield there in support of the Salerno landing. George S. Patton was the Corporal Commander at Sicily.

Bob Hope, Jerry Colona, and Frances Langford came over and performed for over 5,000 troops. Their stage was a flat bed on a truck body. Bob said it was really great to see them, and everyone thoroughly enjoyed their act. General George Patton also publicly apologized during the event. No one knew what he was talking about, then they learned that he had slapped a shell-shocked soldier in a hospital when he said he just couldn't go back to the front lines.

Once again, Bob boarded the *Dutchess of Bedford*, and returned back to England to help prepare for the landing at Normandy. Over the next seven months, he and his men were stationed in Bridgeport, England, near Dorchester, and trained on Slapton Sands in preparation for Normandy. One night during a practice, German planes came down, and 700 men were lost. Fortunately, Bob's outfit was not scheduled to train that night. Prime Minister Winston Churchill stopped by during the training, and gave words of support to the organizers of the invasion. General Omar Bradley stated he wished he could trade places with the men, and General Dwight Eisenhower, an avid football fan, often had them "huddle up" when they were discussing invasion tactics.

The Hollywood actor, Jimmy Cagney, stayed in Bob's barracks while he was in Bridgeport, England, performing "Yankee Doodle Dandy" for the troops. One evening, he and Bob had an enjoyable visit together over drinks at the little bar the men had in the barracks.

On June 6, 1943, Bob sailed from Weymouth, England, across the Channel to Normandy. Then men got into small boats around 2 A.M., and had to go around and around in them for about four hours. The invasion was scheduled for 6:30 A.M. at the break of dawn. By that time the beach was starting to look pretty inviting, because many of the men were seasick. There were 30 men, including Bob, in his boat. Three of the men left the boat with Bob, but he was the only one who made it ashore alive.

Once on the beach, Bob was machine-gunned in the leg, but he didn't stop fighting for two days, until infection set in and slowed him down. He later would be awarded the Silver Star for bravery for his actions on the beach during the invasion. He was shipped back to a British hospital in South Hampton, England, where patients were allowed a pint of beer a day, and was released after five weeks. This was how he earned his second Purple Heart.

He then traveled on a laundry truck to another hospital in Manchester, England. The doctor who saw him there said, "Well, you make the second Irvine we've admitted recently."

As it turned out, his brother, Bill, had come down with pneumonia, and was in a room just down the hall. Bob told the doctor not to tell him, and walked into his room. Bill couldn't believe his eyes! He had just been talking to a guy who had landed at Normandy with Bob, and had seen him on the beach, but then he lost track of him. Bill didn't know if he had survived the invasion or not, and nearly fell out of his bed when Bob came in. They were then able to visit for a while before Bob had to leave.

For the next two weeks, Bob waited at a replacement depot with four other officers from his outfit. They were all itching to get back to France, so they decided to send one guy to Bridgeport to see if they could get on a ship there. He called back and said an anti-tank outfit would soon be leaving, so they all headed to Bridgeport. Bob had made friends with a family there previously, when he was stationed in the town, and he stayed with them while they waited for the ship. The five officers were now technically A.W.O.L. (absent without leave), so they found a colonel and asked him if there was any chance they could get on board the ship. He asked them if they had any troops with them, and they said no, just us five officers. The colonel told Bob to write out an order for them, which he did, and they were able to return to France.

On the trip over, the ship's captain was telling everyone about the role he played in the Normandy invasion. Bob and an Air Corps officer politely listened as he told his story. Once in a while they would add in a detail or two, until finally the captain looked at them and said,

"You S.O.B.s, you were there!" Ducks (amphibious trucks) came out to get them, and it took Bob two hours to get back to his outfit. When he finally found them, his superior officer took one look at him and said, "Where the Hell have you been? I've lost three captains already. Get up there!"

The next morning, the First Division broke through German lines at the town of Saint Lo, which was flattened from the fighting. This was the beginning of the Allies pushing the Axis forces back to Germany. Within a month they crossed into Achen, the first German city they took over. Bob was wounded again between Saint Lo and Achen, which earned him his third Purple Heart. He said his companies were so spread out over the countryside it was hard not to get hit.

In Achen, he set up a command post in a butcher shop, and company headquarters were in a grocery store. Ironically enough there was a Louie Pfeiffer Department Store in Achen; Pfeiffer was his wife's maiden name. Once the area was secured, Bob got his men a clean change of clothes and they set up a makeshift bathtub that was heated by an end heater, so the men could wash up. This was the closest thing they got to R&R (rest and relaxation).

On December 1, 1944, in the town of Elendorf, Bob earned his fourth Purple Heart. He was hit in the head with shrapnel, and it took a doctor and two nurses four hours to get it out. He was evacuated to Liege, Belgium, then spent a week in Paris, France, before he was flown to Swinder, England, where he recuperated for two months. On December 24, 1944, his doctor came to him and asked him if he would be able to take a trip to the States. He said yes, and about 14 days later, via the Canary Islands, Bob was back in the United States. The trip did him a world of good, especially while they were in the Canary Islands, because he could sit up on deck in the fresh air and soak up the sunshine. He was carried aboard by stretcher, and walked off the ship when they docked in the States.

The ship arrived in Charleston, South Carolina. Bob and 5,000 other patients were unloaded, and were given the option of recuperating in Walla Walla, Washington, or Framingham, Massachusetts, because there was such an influx of wounded soldiers one hospital couldn't handle them all. Bob quickly chose Framingham. It was his hometown, and Virgie worked at the hospital for the Red Cross where he would stay. A metal plate was put in his head to help protect the wound the shrapnel had made, and it took another three months for him to recuperate.

Bob was discharged in September of 1945, after serving for four years and two months. He was awarded the European African Middle Eastern Campaign Medal with three bronze stars, American Defense Service Medal, a Silver Star Medal, two Bronze Star Medals, four Purple Hearts, and the Good Conduct Award.

Bob was going to put his degree in forestry to use after the war, but instead, he and Virgie bought a little general store in Vermont. They had a son, Robert, in 1946, and ran the store for about a year, but then sold it because it really tied them down seven days a week. Bob worked with his father-in-law as a carpenter, and got a job driving the local school bus. When he found out the fourth, fifth, and sixth grade teacher was leaving their local school, he applied for the position, which he got, and taught there for five years. Then he became the principal of another nearby school, where he stayed for 12 years.

After that he moved to East Boothbay, and was the principal and a teacher for three years at the Center School in Boothbay. When Violet Smith retired as principal at the Southport School, Emolyn Pratt and Jean Neamy urged him to apply for the position, which he did. Bob then taught the sixth, seventh, and eighth grades, and served as the school principal for the next 12 years, until his retirement in 1980. Bob currently lives in Newcastle, Maine.

Author's note: *Mr. Irvine was my principal from 1975 to 1980. Although he is not an island resident, in my heart he is a big part of Southport, and that is why I have chosen to include his story in the book.*

After completing a rough draft of Bob's story I showed it to my father, Maurice, because he had served in the same area as Bob during the war. He immediately picked up on the fact that he and Bob had been trans-ported to Oran, North Africa, on the Dutchess of Bedford *in November of 1942, but they never met each other while on board. Also, his artillery outfit, the 178th, fired in support of Bob's First Division while in North Africa.*

LEWIS C. JOHNSON
Staff Sergeant, Army Air Corps

In January of 1943, Lew was drafted into the Army Air Corps. He was 19 years old, and had been working at the shipyard in South Portland building Liberty Ships. These ships were built for England by the United States and were used to transport war supplies and cargo between the two countries. Lew went to Miami Beach in Florida for basic training, but was only there for three days, because he volunteered to fly. Then he was sent to gunnery school at Fort Meyers for about ten weeks. At eight weeks he made buck sergeant, because you had to have at least three stripes to fly.

Lewis Johnson,
Army Air Corps

Next he went to armament school in Denver, Colorado, where he studied machine guns, loading bombs, fusing bombs, cannons, and electrical turrets. In Boise, Idaho, he had flight training, and in South Dakota the men were split up into four squadrons for further training. Four years of knowledge was crammed into eight months of intensive training, because crews were needed in Europe.

Lew was now in the 455th Bombardment Group. They flew around South America, across to South Africa, and landed at Tibenham Field in Norfolk, England. In November of 1943 they started flying. Within a year Lew would fly 30 missions with his crew and would go through four B-24s. Their bombing runs included 19 over Germany, ten over France, and one in Belgium. His squadron participated in the first daylight raid over Berlin, which the British said could never be done. Lew was the youngest member of his crew; the oldest was 23.

Author's note: *The famous crew of the B-17,* Memphis Belle, *flew 25 successful missions and were sent home on a publicity tour across the United States to boost morale stateside and increase the sale of war bonds. Lew and his crew flew an additional five missions, before being sent home on rotation.*

On a New Year's Eve run over Berlin, Lew's bomber was hit and the number one port engine was lost. They had to leave the protection of the formation and come back to the base alone. It made them an easy target for the German fighters and Lew often wonders how they made it back in one piece. These planes were known as "tailend charlies" and usually were shot down. As they circled the airfield to land, the prop came off the number one engine and knocked the number two engine out. As Lew looked out the window of the bomber, he could see the prop coming down through the wing; it was at this point he remembered that the pilot's name was Winn, and figured with a name like that he couldn't possibly lose. They went in for an emergency landing and made it. Everyone said it was a miracle, and a big party was thrown in their honor. The flack from the German artillery was terrible.

After one mission, over 400 holes were counted in Lew's bomber. On another they had to ditch their plane in the English Channel. As they were going down, the crew had to throw everything out of the bomber that wasn't attached, including their parachutes and machine guns. The pilot kept the wheels down and did his best to land flat on the water. The crew then had to climb out on the wing, and get into a life raft. A British crash boat picked them up and took them ashore. The crews were equipped with flack jackets and helmets, but they usually sat on the jackets, because the flack was coming up through the bottom of the bombers.

The crew on a B-24 *Liberator* was made up of four officers and six enlisted men. Their positions included pilot, copilot, navigator, bombardier, radioman, two waist gunners, lower "ball" turret, upper turret, tail turret, and Lew's position nose turret. The bomber was equipped with ten 50 caliber machine guns. The men wore earphones and a throat mike, which allowed them to communicate with the pilot. Lew was also responsible for operating the bomb camera, located in the waist, which took surveillance photos during their missions.

The crews were thoroughly briefed before each run. Anyone not involved in the mission was sent out of the room, except the intelligence officer. A curtain would be raised, and a map showing their primary and secondary targets would be discussed. The men were also told which stalag they might be taken to if they had to bail out. They were equipped with escape kits, including a bendable file that could cut through bars, and foreign currency. Usually the man who briefed them on these matters was someone who had previously bailed out in the area they would be flying over. He had successfully escaped through enemy lines and would tell them the best escape routes to take.

If the men did have to bailout, they would have to freefall from 30,000 to 10,000 feet before they could even begin to breath. There were bailout bottles that had oxygen in them, but you had to have the time to get to them and the time to clip them onto your parachute before they could be of much help. The crews were not given practice parachuting, because the military feared they would lose too many men that way, and they needed all they could get to man the bombers.

On two separate missions, both the copilot and bombardier were killed. Lew was sent to school where he took a crash course so he could take over the bombardier's position. The crews usually participated in pattern or saturation bombing, meaning the lead aircraft would shoot flares and then the planes following would drop their bombs. On certain occasions the bombardier, whose controls were hooked onto the bomb sight, navigated the plane during the bomb run. Their targets were factories, railroad yards, and sometimes cities. The crew didn't like bombing cities.

Nose turret on a B-24, or Lew's "office," as he likes to call it.

The B-24s flew at 30,000 feet and could carry eight tons of bombs. The men had to wear heated suits, boots, and gloves, because it was about 60 below zero at that altitude and the cabins were not pressurized. The suits were heated electrically and the crew plugged them in when they got on board. They had to use oxygen all the time when they were above 10,000 feet and, by the end of the run, would look like a walrus with a big beard of ice around their mask. Their missions lasted 12 to 14 hours and they had to go without eating, drinking, or smoking. The planes had to stay on course for six to eight minutes during the bombing run.

Sometimes the radio operator could tune in Axis Sally, who played American music and was a German radio personality at the time. While maintaining radio silence, the men could hear the Germans counting their planes over the radio after they crossed enemy lines: *"Eins, Vwei, Drei, Vier."* The Germans set up smokepots to create a smoke screen over the city. The wind would carry the smoke and make it impossible to get a fix on a target. When a bomber was hit by enemy fire and was going down, you could often hear the men yelling over the radio. It was an awful sound.

Author's note: *Axis Sally's real name was Mildred Gillurs. She was born in Portland, Maine and moved to Germany in 1935, were she was employed by the Nazis and Radio Berlin.*

The radio operator was in charge of the med kit, which contained a minimum of medical supplies. Flying at such a high altitude, a man could easily bleed to death if his wounds were bad enough. Sometimes the crews had no choice but to put the injured man in a parachute, pull the rip cord, and tuck the parachute under his arm. Then they would drop him out the bomb door, hoping someone would find the wounded man and get him the medical attention he needed.

On one of their bombing runs, 40 planes went out and only two made it back; one of them was Lew's. He said it was extremely hard to go back to his barracks, because no one was there and they wouldn't be coming back. Pretty soon someone came around to clean out the men's lockers, which was really tough for Lew to watch. It finalized everything and meant new crews would be moving in shortly.

There were 500 flack batteries in Berlin, and Lew said you could see the bursting 88 shells coming up at you like snowballs. The Germans had radar sights and were well prepared to defend the city. During the war, U.S. cigarettes did not come wrapped in tin foil; instead it was used for chaff to mislead the German's radar. The waist gunner would slide the chaff (strips of tin foil) out a chute, where it hit the propeller and was spread through-out the air, giving the Germans incorrect readings on their radar.

When a German fighter was coming at you firing its machine guns, it looked like its wings were on fire to the crews in the bombers. Sometimes men in the crew would become flack happy when they returned from a mission. Their nerves and the stress of the job would get to them, and they would have to go on leave. After every ten bombing runs, the crews were automatically sent on R&R. After Lew's first ten missions, he stayed at a castle in the country. It had been turned over to the Americans by a wealthy Englishman, so their troops would have a place to relax.

The fog was awful in England. The B-24s had to circle and climb to get into a wing to wing formation. Almost as many planes were lost over England as were lost in Europe, due to collisions. Lew said his closest call occurred when he was on standby to fly a mission. He was going to fill in for a guy that was not feeling well. The crew had the engines run-ning and were waiting to get the okay to take off, when the sick man came running down the airstrip yelling, "I'm all right and I'm going." Lew got off the plane and watched it take off. Later in the day it was blown out of the sky by a direct hit from a German fighter.

Lew's B-24 after the New Year's Eve bombing mission over Berlin.

Lew's squadron commander was Jimmy Stewart, the famous Hollywood actor. While in England he flew 20 missions, then was transferred to another group. Lew often played his guitar while off duty in the officer's club, and Jimmy would sing. He later became a Brigadier General in the reserves of the Strategic Air Command.

Lew remembers England being strictly rationed. You couldn't get anything. The kids would come up to the American GIs and say, "Got any gum, chum?" Lew and his friends would go into London on the weekend. The German bombers would be flying over and the air raid sirens were going off. Everyone would run for shelter, but Lew and his friends would stand out on the street, watching them fly over with their bomb bays open. While in London Lew visited a Red Cross Club in Piccadilly Circus, and Fred Astaire's sister Adele, who was a volunteer there, offered to sew Lew's new stripes on his uniform for him.

When you went down into the Tube (subway), there were pipe bunks set up and families whose homes had been bombed were living there. Lew and the other GIs always saved fruit for the kids, and would give it to them when they rode the Tube. When the Germans were using V1 and V2 rockets, you could hear them flying overhead. They sounded like an old outboard approaching. The engines shut down on the rockets as they neared their target. Moments later you would hear the explosion when they hit. The Germans even bombed Lew's base once.

The Germans had mobile flack batteries on railroad cars. Intelligence had a hard time keeping track of them, because they moved the guns with ease from place to place, and from country to country on the rail lines. Lew remembers flying over Holland and noticing the land was flooded, where it hadn't been before. Later, when he was shipped back to the states, he found out the Germans had blown up the dikes as they retreated from the Allies.

When the bombers landed, the Red Cross met them with coffee, doughnuts, and a shot of scotch. Then the crews were debriefed by their commander. They had to tell how the run went, if they hit their target or not, types of aircraft they saw, who was missing out of the squadron, and their last known position. After a successful mission, a bomb would be painted on the side of the plane that had just flown. One of Lew's friends had a great sense of humor and came up with a decal of a full pint beer glass. The men put them on the bikes they rode into town after every successful pub mission.

In September of 1945, after three years of service, Lew was discharged. He received five Air Medals with three oak leaf clusters, the Distinguished Flying Cross for extraordinary achievement in aerial combat, the European African Middle Eastern Service Medal, and the Good Conduct Award. Lew spent 21 days on leave on Southport, and then went to a hospital in Miami, where he spent eight months of recuperation for his nerves. He was then sent to Colorado, where he ran into John J. Kelly from Boothbay, Maine. From there he went to Mississippi, Salt Lake City, and finally Fort Lewis in Washington. He got on a train, which took him to Fort Devens, and then he came home.

Lew returned to Southport after the war and married his girlfriend Franny Childs in May of 1947. They had two children, Larry and Linda. He went to work as lobsterman and currently lives in Southport with his wife of 49 years, Franny.

Author's note: *Lew sent Jimmy Stewart a card on his 80th birthday, and received a personal thank you note from him.*

Lew's Distinguished Flying Cross, awarded for extraordinary achievement in aerial combat.

One of five Air Medals Lew was awarded during his service with the 455th Bombardment Group.

RICHARD W. JOHNSON
First Lieutenant, Army Air Corps

Richard Johnson,
Army Air Corps

Dick was drafted on February 19, 1942, at the age of 23, and was sent to Fort Devens in Massachusetts for orientation. He then traveled by train to Fort Eustis, Virginia, for basic training and became part of the Coast Artillery. While there he had the opportunity to take a test for the Army Air Corps, which he passed, and was sent to the West Coast distribution center in Santa Anna, California. Once there he was assigned to primary flight school in Visalia, which lasted for two months. He then attended basic training in Merced for two months, and advanced training in Stockton, California, which took another two months. Due to bad weather, the students did most of their flying at Yuma, Arizona.

Dick graduated on January 3, 1943, at Stockton Field and was sent to Columbia, South Carolina, for training on B-25s. He was given travel time and ten days leave, which was unheard of at the time, before his training started, so he traveled to Farmington, Maine, and picked up his girlfriend, Ernestine Carver, who was working there. They returned to her parents' home on Vinalhaven Island, and were married on January 16, 1943. Dick had been working in the advertising department of Towle Silversmiths in Newburyport, Massachusetts, prior to that time.

On June 13, 1943, after more than four months of combat training, he and his crew of five men were sent to Savannah, Georgia, where they were assigned B-25G, which Dick named the Flying Caisson, because of the 75mm cannon in the nose. They had a ground crew paint crossed cannons on her nose, and then flew her overseas to North Africa out of Homestead, Florida. The crew took the southern route to Natal, Brazil, and Ascension Island, finally landing in Dakar, Africa, after 35 hours flying time. After a transition period, they flew to the Mediterranean coast and touched down in Tunis, North Africa.

The B-25Gs were medium altitude bombers, and were equipped with twin engines, a 75mm cannon in the nose, up to eight forward firing 50mm machine guns, twin 50mm machine guns in the upper turret, two 50 caliber waist guns, and a 50mm machine gun in the tail. The crew's missions usually lasted between one and a half and four hours, and consisted of sea sweeps, and low altitude bombing of shore installations and shipping. Dick flew as part of the 379th Squadron, 310 Bomb Group, 57th Bomb Wing, 12th Air Force.

The crew usually consisted of a pilot, copilot, engineer, radio man, waist gunner, and a navigator/bombardier. They were also equipped with life vests and survival kits that contained first aid equipment, pain killers, a compass, maps, and foreign money. During sea sweeps, between three and five planes flew together. On medium altitude bombing runs 18, 36, or 72 B-25s flew in formation.

Dick and his crew encountered enemy aircraft on about half of their missions, but mostly over Italy, because the Germans didn't have the resources to fly all over North Africa at that point in the war. They had air cover from P-51s and Spitfire fighters against the German Focke-Wulf and Messerschmitt ME 109s. The flack was terrible during these encounters, and Dick said you just hoped you got them before they got you.

While in North Africa, the famous P-51 fighter squadron, the Tuskegee Airmen, flew cover for Dick's outfit. For those of you who are not familiar with them, they were an all black fighter squadron who, after overcoming many obstacles both political and racial, went on to become one of the most decorated American aerial outfits of the Second World War. Dick said they were excellent airmen, and you always felt confident when you knew they would be flying cover for you.

Dick and his crew flew into Cairo occasionally for supplies. Once they picked up a troop of U.S.O. performers, and brought them back to their base in the desert. On the return flight to the base, Dick flew them in low, and they were really surprised to see how much destruction there was from previous battles. It was a wonderful change of pace and they put on a great show, considering the sandy conditions they had to work under. On another occasion Dick had a British Brigadier hitching a ride to Cairo. He wanted to fly low, so he could relive the battles he had been through.

In November of 1943, Dick left the Tunis area in North Africa and moved to an Italian Airbase in Southern Italy, near Taranto (the instep of the boot of Italy.) Although they were flying as "wingmen" on some medium altitude missions, Dick and his crew were now designated the "G" Squadron (B-25Gs, with 75mm cannons) for low altitude attacks.

It wasn't long before Dick and his crew were transferred to another group and new Command personnel, and immediately flew back to North Africa, but now further east to the Egyptian area about 200 miles from Cairo. The runway was in the desert again but near the coast, and was controlled by the British. They were flying seasweeps with Beaufighters using rockets, and were going to supplement their sea-sweeps with the 75mm cannon and 250 pound bombs. The Americans and British worked out a schedule, and the Americans were supplied rations, etc., by the British until their own U.S. supplies came overland from Cairo.

The men were now called "Hunters of the Aegean," and flew most missions "on the deck" to avoid radar pickup to the Dodeconese Islands, which are Greek. Many times while avoiding radar, they would be so close to the water that they left a spray behind. They flew in small groups of three to four airplanes, sometimes flying with the British Beaufighters as cover from enemy aircraft, but when they were attacked by Nazi fighters, the British flew under the B25s for cover by their gunners.

Whenever Dick's crew spotted a ship during sea sweep missions off the Dodeconese Islands, he fired warning shots to alert the crews, which were often Greek sailors in caiques. They were then able to get into their lifeboats and away from the ship, before a bomb was dropped. Dick's commanding officer was not pleased when he found out they had been operating in this manner, but Dick thought it was only fair to give the ships' crews a chance to get to safety, considering they didn't know what cargo the ships were carrying, and their orders were to sink all unidentified ships.

When the enemy sea activity lessened in the Dodeconese, they broke up camp in late February, and the entire unit flew to Corsica to rejoin the 310th Group. Being latecomers, the men had to set up their own tent city on the outskirts of the small town of Ghisonaccia. The main group was billeted in the town, or what was left of it. The Nazis had completely wrecked town after town as they retreated from the island. They flew low-level attacks to the Nazi-occupied harbors on the Italian Coast, but now mostly at medium altitude, 8,000 to 12,000 feet in regular B-25s, and they felt like sitting ducks way up there. The B-25Gs with the cannon had now served their usefulness.

Dick became a flight leader on the medium altitude missions, flying into the heartland of Italy with formations of 24, 48, or even more B-25s; bombing bridges, rail junctions, factories, and other targets inland. Now his group was called "The Bridgebusters."

Dick ran into a buddy from flight training school while at a field near Taranto, Italy. He flew a P-38 and took reconnaissance photos for the Air Corps. He gave Dick a piggy back ride in his P-38, and in return Dick offered to take him up and let him shoot the 75mm cannon on his B-25G, but, given immediate orders, Dick had to leave before he could return the favor.

The crews were sent to rest camps after flying a fair number of missions. From Corsica, Dick and his crew flew to Lydda, just below Jerusalem, which was then controlled by the British. They would spend a week there sightseeing before they went back to fly more missions. Another crew who had already completed their rest period flew Dick's plane back to Corsica, then in another week, when a new group arrived, Dick and his crew would fly their plane back.

Dick's B-25G on a sea sweep. Note the Flying Caisson emblem painted on the side of the aircraft.

In April of 1944, a few days before Easter, the 379th Squadron Operations, 310th Bomb Group received word to send a B25C and crew to North Africa. Dick happened to be called as pilot for this mission, but didn't fly with his usual crew. The purpose was to pick up and deliver to the 310th Group 100 practice bombs at BTC, Telergma. The secondary part of the mission was to locate and purchase fresh eggs for the entire 310th Group.

The crew's first destination was Philippeville. A few warning shots were fired at them by the Germans near Cagliari, Sardinia, as they flew over, and they later landed on the old field in Philippeville. Although the steel mating was still visible, it was surprising how overgrown it had become. They buzzed the field a couple of times to check the surface and to chase the cows away. Two men in the crew who were friendly with the local people were dropped off to deal with the egg part of the mission, and the rest flew on to Telergma, only to find there were no practice bombs there. The men there suggested looking in Tunis, so Dick and his crew flew on to El Aouina, which now seemed almost free of U.S. military. Once there they found sleeping quarters and a place to eat.

The next morning the men located and picked up the practice bombs in Jedeida. They were able to stack all 100 of them in the bomb bay section and crawl space. Then it was back to Philippeville to get on with the egg hunt. The crew landed there just in time for lunch at a farmhouse near the runway. The two crew members who had been left to locate the eggs had made arrangements with the French occupants of the house, and they graciously served the men a delicious homecooked meal. By this time the two sergeants had collected nearly 3000 eggs, but they needed closer to 5000 to serve the entire group back on Corsica.

Word spread that eggs were in demand, and the men were told a market place would be open the next morning. Fortunately they were able to borrow a weapons-carrier from the Engineering Unit on the other side of town, and drove up into the hills to a small walled village, which was where the Arabian merchants and farmers gathered to sell or barter their wares and produce. Another 2000 eggs were collected. The men carefully drove back to Phillipeville with the eggs packed between layers of straw in the body of the truck. The men rode on the fenders all the way back.

As the B-25 was loaded the tail started toward the ground, so the men had to load some of the eggs in the bombardiers area located in the nose of the plane to help compensate the weight equally. By late afternoon the men were anxious to get back to Corsica, and the plane was loaded and ready for takeoff. An emergency arose, however, and it seemed that a soldier from the Engineering Base was injured and in need of hospitalization. So the crew flew the wounded man to Telergma first, before returning to 310th Headquarters. Most of the eggs made the trip in one piece, and it was a welcomed treat from the powdered eggs they were used to.

After spending six months in North Africa, the 379th was assigned to the island of Corsica off the Italian coast. It was here during Dick's 56th mission that he was wounded. In May of 1944, while dropping bombs on Viterbo, Italy, a piece of flack caught him in the neck, but he finished the mission and flew back to Corsica safely. Dick was discharged from the hospital after a few days, and was given a "war weary" B-25 to fly back to the States so it could be modified to train new crews.

It took the men over two weeks to get back to the States, as one engine was losing too much oil to take long hops from airstrip to airstrip. They spent almost a week in Accra, which was when the invasion started on the French Coast. Dick and his crew were sure they would be called back, but they weren't. Finally they got approval to try and make it to Ascension Island, which they did, and flew the southern route home, landing in Homestead Field, Florida, one year later to the day, June 13, 1944. They then took the bomber on to San Antonio, Texas, for modification.

Dick was sent to a redistribution center in Atlantic City, New Jersey, and was later reassigned to Greenville, South Carolina, where he trained crews of B-25s and A-26s. He also worked in the Air Inspector's office inspecting property and equipment. Dick was discharged on October 15, 1945, after three years and eight months of service. He was awarded the Air Medal with two oak leaf clusters, European African Middle Eastern Campaign Medal, the Purple Heart, and the Good Conduct Medal.

After the war, Dick and Ernestine had two children, Richard and Betsy Ann. He went to work as an Art Director for the advertising agency, Sutherland-Abbott, in Boston, where he was employed for 24 years. In 1978, the Johnsons made Southport their home, which is where they presently live and where Dick works as an artist.

ROY JONES
Private, U.S. Army

Roy enlisted in the Army in 1944, at the age of 26, and received his training at Camp Clairborne, Louisiana. He had worked for the Horton, Company in Worcester, Massachusetts, prior to that time.

Roy was discharged in November of 1944, and went to work for the New England Power Company. He was married to Doris Roberts, in August of 1944. Roy and his wife of 52 years, Doris, currently live on Southport.

WELDON LAKEMAN
Chief Engineer, Merchant Marine

*Weldon Lakeman,
Merchant Marine*

Weldon was serving as a First Assistant Engineer on board ships in the Merchant Marine, when war was declared. He applied for a Navy commission and received the rank of First Lieutenant early in the spring of 1943. He also received his Chief Engineers License.

While waiting for his naval assignment, he was contacted and offered to sail on the first Liberty ship built in Portland, Maine. The ship was the *S.S. John Davenport*, and his cousin, Ray Ingalls, was also aboard. Weldon decided to take the position of First Assistant Engineer, even though he had achieved the rank of Chief, so he could stay with his cousin Ray.

He was 24 years old at the time, and he served on the *Davenport* from June 15, 1942, until May 10, 1943. The ship was assigned to convoy duty between the United States and Europe, and he made many trips back and forth on her. Weldon was later assigned to the *Robert Treat, S.S. Stephen Porter*, and the *S.S. Edward Alexander* during the war.

At one point, Weldon was issued heavy winter clothing, because they were supposed to make the Murmansk run, which was a very dangerous assignment, and many ships were lost on it, attempting to bring supplies to Russia. Luckily, the orders were later changed, and the clothing was taken back. He also served in the Pacific during the war.

He married Mary McDonald of Newton, Massachusetts, on August 2, 1944, and they had three children, Ray, Martin, and Carol. Weldon was home on leave in Southport, when he heard the news that the Japanese had surrendered. He and Mary bought a house on Southport the very next day, August 16, 1945. It had formally been Wardsworth McKown's home, and has been the Lakeman's residence ever since.

Weldon was discharged from the Merchant Marine on August 30, 1945, and was awarded the Mediterranean Middle East War Zone Bar, Pacific War Zone Bar, and the Atlantic War Zone Bar, Merchant Marine Victory Medal, and the Merchant Marine Defense Medal for his service.

After the war he continued his marine engineering career by building ships for various corporations around the world. He retired in August of 1971, and had time to enjoy his retirement years on Southport. Weldon passed away on January 27, 1982, at the age of 64.

NORMAN LEWIS
Painter First Class, U.S. Navy

Norman Lewis, U.S. Navy

Norman was drafted in December of 1943. He was 25 years old at the time, and had been working as the bridge tender for Southport and in a paint crew at Samples Shipyard. He took the first train ride of his life from Wiscasset to get to boot camp, trained at Sinica Lake, New York, and was in the E outfit. While there he met Cliff Brewer, also from Southport, who was stationed at Sinica Lake, and was in the F outfit. Norman married Mildred Marr, from Southport in March of 1940 and had to leave her to raise their two sons alone while he was in the service.

After his training, Norman went to Bayonne, New Jersey, where he worked as a Navy painter. Harold Roberts from Boothbay was stationed there with him. One evening he called his wife Mildred and said, "I'm going to be shipped out tomorrow." Mildred's heart sank at the thought of her husband being shipped overseas. The very next day the phone rang again and, when Mildred answered it, Norman told her he had been stationed at the Brooklyn Navy Yard across the river in New York.

While there Norman was asked to fill in as a dockhand at Pier 6, out on Staten Island, for a period of two weeks. One day a troop ship came in and Norman grabbed the line that was thrown to him to help secure it to the dock. As he started to tie it up, he heard a voice say "Hey! Hey!" When he looked up, he realized that Stuart Thompson, one of his neighbors from Southport, was yelling to him, and had thrown him the line. They were able to visit together for about an hour once their duties were completed.

Norman was discharged from the Navy in December of 1945 after two years of service. He returned to Southport, where he resumed his duties as bridge tender, and later retired from the job after 43 years of openings and closings. He currently lives in Southport with his wife of 56 years, Mildred.

GEORGE MARR
Private, U.S. Army

In 1940, George enlisted before the first draft in the Army. He was 17 years old at the time. He had been seining herring summers with Leland Snowman, and had been cutting wood winters with his father, Thomas, on the island.

He attended boot camp at Fort McKinley in Portland Harbor, and then was assigned to Camp Devens in Massachusetts, where he worked in the bakery. He and the other bakers supplied bread and other baked goods for the whole base.

George Marr, U.S. Army

While there he met Donald Lowery, Linwood Matthews, Donald Blackman, Morrel Colby, and Leon Cunningham, all from the Boothbay region. They were in the same outfit as George, the Coast Artillery, 240th Battery D. Due to medical reasons, George was hospitalized for a time and then was reassigned to Camp Croft in South Carolina. He also served at Camp Shelby in Mississippi, but was hospitalized again and was discharged in September of 1943.

When he returned to Southport, he worked for Elbridge Plummer on the town crew and later worked for Samples Shipyard as a ship fitter's helper. George then moved to Brunswick, where he worked for 17 years at both the Brunswick Naval Air Station and the Topsham Air Force Station. Then he moved back to the region and ran the Getty Station for ten years. George presently works at the YMCA and lives in Boothbay with his wife Marjory.

WOLCOTT MARR
Boatswain Mate Chief, U.S. Navy

Wolcott Marr, U.S. Navy

Wolcott was home recuperating from a bad fall in October of 1939, when he volunteered for the Navy in response to a call for volunteers considering the war in Europe. In 1938 he had fallen 15 feet from a tree onto frozen ground, breaking several ankle bones and causing multiple fractures. The first 20 years of his service had been spent on destroyers. World War I broke out shortly after his first enlistment and five of his 20 years were spent in China and in the Philippines. During this time he took part in the Sino-Japanese War on the Yangtze River in 1934. He retired in 1936 after serving 20 years, and married his girlfriend Elizabeth Alley.

He re-entered the service at the rank of Boatswain Mate First Class, and his first assignment was at the Newport Torpedo Station in Rhode Island where he tested torpedoes. He was later sent to Norfolk, Virginia, where he was a navigation instructor. Dom Dimaggio of baseball fame was one of Wolcott's students and was also a good friend.

His next assignment was sea duty on a sub chaser, which was operated out of Hamilton, Bermuda. Wolcott's last assignment was on the Amphibious Personnel Destroyer (APD) *Walter B. Cobb* which was enroute to Tokyo to take part in a major invasion when the message was received the war was over. The *Cobb* continued on and became part of the fleet surrounding the *U.S.S. Missouri*, where the surrender ceremony took place. In October of 1945 Wolcott retired a second time from the Navy.

He served 30 years in all, and returned to Southport after the war, where he was employed as a house painter. He later worked at Samples Shipyard in Boothbay Harbor, but returned to house painting and worked at it until he was 70 years old. Wolcott passed away in May of 1991 at the age of 92 at the Maine Veterans Home in Scarborough.

EDWIN MCKOWN
Sergeant, Army Air Corps

On December 14, 1941, Edwin enlisted in the Army Air Corps and was promptly sent to Keesler Field, Mississippi. He then went to Panama for basic training, where he trained in the mountains with the Geronimo Parachute Outfit. He had previously been a student in the National Youth Administration, where he was preparing to take his pilot's examination. By joining this program you could directly study for the exam and would not have to attend two years of college.

From Keesler Field, Edwin was sent

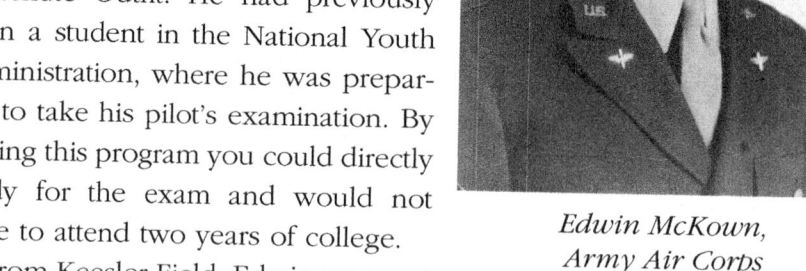

Edwin McKown,
Army Air Corps

to Howard Field, which is on the Pacific side of the Panama Canal. Enroute a German submarine was discovered following the convoy, but did not attack them. Once there he worked on aircraft and was assigned to the 72rd Observation Group and 39th Reconnaissance Squadron. He was later picked for aircraft mechanics school and the Sixth Air Force

Technicians School, which was also on the Pacific side of the isthmus. While at school, Edwin saw a friend drowning and rushed into the ocean to save him. When he got him back onto the beach, an ambulance crew took over. The American Red Cross recognized Edwin with a lifetime membership for his efforts.

Upon completion of his training, Edwin flew back to Howard Field, only to find his outfit had moved to Waller Field, Trinidad. The United States had been given this base by the British in exchange for destroyers. Edwin soon found a transport plane headed for Trinidad that needed an engineer, so he climbed aboard. In flight over the Andes Mountains, one of the magnetos (a small generator of alternating current with permanent magnets, used in the ignition systems of some internal-combustion engines) moved and one of the engines cut out.

The plane needed to gain 5000 feet of altitude to make it through the hazardous mountain pass, so they radioed they were going down, and had to throw all the freight they were carrying out to gain the needed height. They ditched the plane in a field in Barranquilla, Columbia, and lived in the embassy there for two weeks, until the necessary parts could be flown in from Panama to repair the plane. Ironically, the mayor of the city had graduated from Yale University and was thrilled to see the Americans. He personally made sure the crew was taken care of during their stay in Columbia.

Once in Trinidad Edwin was put on sub patrol, but sometime in 1942, he noticed the Air Corps was accepting applications for cadets. He was flown back to Tuscaloosa, Alabama, for a college training detachment where he attended a crash, basic training program, night and day until 1943. Edwin then studied basic flight training at the Aviation Cadet Center in San Antonio, Texas, but after graduation it was decided that there were now too many pilots, so he and the other students were put back into the ranks of the Air Corps. From Texas, Edwin was sent to Buckingham Army Air Base in Florida to train as an aerial gunner on B-25s. He then went to Columbia Army Air Base in South Carolina, where he attained 200 hours of combat flying stateside.

Next Edwin headed off for the South Pacific. First stop was the Hawaiian Islands, where his plane landed with only a few gallons of fuel left in its tank. It was not uncommon for flights to miss a refueling stop over the Pacific, and they would be forced to ditch their plane. Next stop was Johnston Island, then on to Tarawa. The island had recently been taken back from the Japanese and skirmishes continued in the surrounding Tarawa Atoll. There was a huge communications bunker on the island that was protected by six foot thick, concrete walls. A U.S. battleship offshore shot a projectile at the bunker, which put a hole in it large enough for a man to crawl through. Unbeknown to the battleship, the bunker was still occupied by the Japanese when they fired upon it.

Later, when Edwin was refueling on Los Negros, a plane from Australia landed from General Douglas MacArthur's command with 65 pregnant woman on it. They were immediately put in a compound to keep the GIs away. The Americans and Japanese had been previously at battle on Los Negros, and it was in really hard shape. There was a lot of devastation all over the island.

On Nadzab, New Guinea, Edwin was assigned to the Fifth Air Force, 345th Bomb Group, 499th Bomb Squadron Attack. They had previously engaged in middle altitude bombing, but had to remodel the planes in Australia for low altitude or skip bombing, because middle altitude bombing was ineffective in the jungle. The planes now flew so low, parachutes were useless and only took up space on board, so they were left behind to carry more bombs and equipment. They did have survival equipment in case they had to ditch the plane. Their targets were mostly shipping, anti-aircraft installations, and ground targets. Edwin occupied the top turret and was engineer on these missions, which usually lasted four hours.

Japanese submarines had become so thick, the United States could not get rations in to the GIs, so they were fed by the Australian government. Edwin is quite sure it was horse meat in those tins most of the time. His outfit was soon instructed to strip down the B-25s to their bare minimum and start flying treetop flights to Australia to get supplies from the Red Cross. These modified B-25s were known as "Fat Cats." There were 18, 50 caliber machine guns on board: two in the waist, two in the tail, 12 fixed in the nose, which were controlled by the pilot, and two in the top turret, which was Edwin's position during their various missions.

On Nadzab, Edwin's pilot suffered from a ruptured hernia and was sent back to the United States, so his crew broke up. Edwin and the rest of the crew went to Biak and got on a landing ship tank (LST) headed for Subic Bay in the Philippines. Two crew members wandered around the island, and unknowingly picked up a disease from Kunai grass, which made them deathly ill, with very high fevers. They weren't expected to live, but pulled through at the last moment. Enroute to Subic Bay, they ran into a typhoon and had to go into Palawan, Puerto Princesa. All the mechanized equipment on deck was stripped off by the force of the storm. This was the first of three typhoons Edwin encountered during his tour of duty in the Pacific.

On Palawan, opposite the Philippines, fighting was still going on between the Americans and the Japanese. There was an Allied prison camp on this island that had just been liberated. It held Americans, Australians, British, and Dutch prisoners; many of these were civilians. Several Pacific Islands were Dutch possessions. Their rich wealth of spices and other natural recourses had been exported to Europe for years.

In 1944 Edwin flew on many missions — from Clark Field in Subic Bay to northern Luzon, and Formosa, north of the Philippines, where there were many Japanese pockets that needed to be neutralized. From Ryukyu, Okinawa, and Ie Shima they flew into the Inland Sea of Japan to knock out radar installations and lighthouses, so B-29s coming in from the Marianas would have a safe passage. While on Ie Shima (located about one mile off the coast of Okinawa), Edwin ran into Herbie Smith from East Boothbay, Maine, when he was fueling up Edwin's plane.

Edwin recalls being bombed every night by hidden Japanese bases on the islands surrounding Ie Shima. After one particular bombing, he returned to his tent to find a piece of flack from a shell had come down through his tent, went through his cot, and was buried in the sand underneath. It would have wounded him for sure if he had been sleeping there. While on Ie Shima the second typhoon struck. It stripped the island, destroying airplanes, ships, and anything else in its path.

At one point while on Ie Shima, Edwin was in charge of quarters, which meant he took crews down to the planes after they had been briefed on what their next mission would be. One particular day the crew was headed for the Inland Sea of Japan and their plane was heavily loaded with fuel and ammunition. As Edwin watched the plane take off down the runway, it had a runaway prop and an engine cut out, causing it to crash. There were some large stumps at the end of the runway, which it ran into and exploded on impact. Only two members of the crew survived and they were terribly burned.

After the first and second atomic bombs were dropped, high command agreed to fly into the Inland Sea to meet Japanese emissaries. Edwin's outfit was selected to escort the emissaries to Ie Shima and then to proceed to Clark Field. The Japanese were coming to set the terms for surrender. They were instructed to paint their planes white with a red cross on the side to show they were coming in under peaceful conditions. They then proceeded to Manila to formulate the surrender agreement with General MacArthur.

Edwin had accumulated 185 points for his service overseas. The points system was created by the military, as a way of measuring your time in the service. What branch of the service you were in, where you were stationed, and what battles you took part in, all factored into the equation. The people who had earned the most points, got to go home first. Edwin was allowed to go home on the first troop ship that left the Ryukyus.

The ship was a Navy attack transport, which had recently been launched in Pennsylvania. It had just taken troops over to Europe to help keep the peace and never stopped on the way to the Pacific to get more supplies. The only food given to the GIs was lima bean soup, which wasn't going over very well with them. Edwin noticed the officers were eating well, and soon volunteered for K.P.(kitchen police) duty during the night shift. There seemed to be an awful lot of leftovers from the officers' meals, and Edwin became a very popular guy back in the GIs quarters, bringing back plates of roast beef, turkey, and ham. They also encountered a typhoon and at one point they had to call a Navy escort to help them, because a mine field had drifted in around the ship and they couldn't get rid of it by themselves. A destroyer escort soon arrived and machine gunned the floating mines, so they could proceed.

When the ship docked, Edwin found himself in Takoma, Washington, and soon was on a train headed for home. He remembers the troops taking the mattress covers off the bunks on the train and writing "Move Over God, Here Comes Doug!" When they went through cities and towns, they would hang the covers out the windows of the train and the girls would go wild. On October 30, 1945, Edwin arrived at Fort Devens in Massachusetts. He was discharged and was in Southport the next day. He had been gone for four years and eleven months and was involved in the Pacific Theater of Operations, Philippines Liberation, and the Ryukyu Liberation. The 345th Bomb Group received two Presidential Unit Citations. The first was for the Bismark Archipelago, the second for the Philippines Campaign. Edwin also received a Good Conduct Medal.

Edwin worked in local shipyards when he returned from the war, and owned his own upholstery business. He later worked for the Department of Marine Resources, but has since retired and currently lives in Boothbay Harbor, Maine.

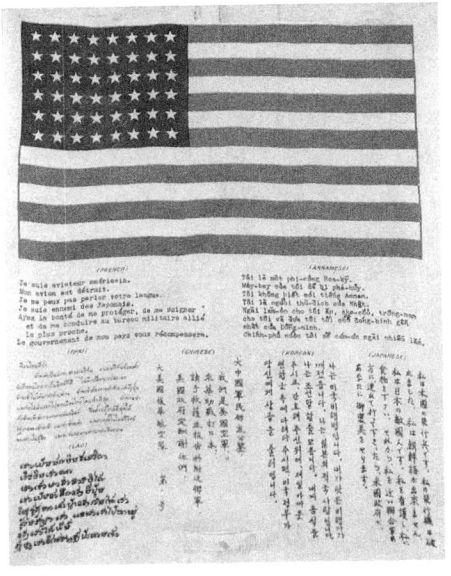

These leaflets were put in the men's Air Corps survival kits, in case they crashed or had to bail out in the Pacific.
This particular one explains in seven languages that there will be a reward for the safe return of the American aviator.

Pictured on the left: One three quarter inch, 20mm shell used on P-38s and PT Boats. Pictured on the right: One half inch, 50 caliber shell, as used on the B-25s on which Edwin flew.

CONSTANCE SHERMAN NEWCOMB
Private First Class, Army Air Corps, WACS

Connie enlisted in Portland on July 8, 1944, at the age of 24. She became part of the WACS (Women's Army Corps) Squadron D, 42 Army Air Corps. She had been teaching elementary school in Trevett prior to that time.

During her service she was stationed in Mississippi and Texas, and was trained as a classification specialist. Connie was able to visit with Linda Gray from Boothbay, while she was stationed at Kelly Field, since Linda was also in the service at that time.

Connie was discharged from the

Constance Sherman Newcomb, Army Air Corps, WACS

WACS on July 6, 1946, at Fort Dix, New Jersey, after two years of service. She was awarded the American Service Medal, World War II Victory Medal, and the Good Conduct Award. She returned home and began teaching school in Skowhegan, and then in Beverley, Massachusetts. Later she taught at the Roosevelt School in South Portland, and in August of 1962, she married Arthur Newcomb. Connie passed away on May 21, 1991, at the age of 71.

CLAYTON F. ORNE
Corporal, U.S. Army

Clayton was part of the first draft that left Southport and was called to service in March of 1941, at the age of 25. He had been working in the Civilian Conservation Corps prior to that time and helped build the road that presently goes up Cadillac Mountain in Bar Harbor. He received his training at Fort Dix, Camp Blanding, and at Fort Ord, and was in the 103rd Field Artillery Battalion.

Clayton Orne, U.S. Army

Clayton boarded the *President Coolidge* along with 5,400 other men and headed for Guadalcanal. The *Coolidge* was a former luxury liner that had been converted into a troop ship. They crossed the Pacific in 14 days and on October 26, 1942, entered the harbor of Espiritu Santo in the New Hebrides Islands, now known as Vanuatu, which was a staging base for Allied troops on Guadalcanal at the time. Unfortunately the ship missed the light flash signal that was coming from shore, which warned that she was headed straight into a U.S. mine field.

The *Coolidge* struck two mines and the captain drove her onto a reef to try and save her. The ship listed dangerously to port and soon the word spread to abandon ship. Clayton claimed he stepped off the ship without even getting his feet wet. Just one hour and 25 minutes after hitting the mines the ship slipped off the reef and sank into deeper water. Remarkably only five lives were lost. The equipment and supplies on board went down with the ship, including all the Atabrine that was available at the time, which was supposed to be delivered to Guadalcanal to help treat soldiers infected with malaria. A destroyer later picked the troops up and took them to New Zealand, where they waited a month for supplies. The 103rd Field Artillery Battalion didn't get to Guadalcanal until March of 1943, which delayed Allied operations.

Clayton was involved in many battles and invasions of the Northern Solomon Islands, Guadalcanal, Luzon, and New Guinea. He served as a heavy machine gunner and as a machine gun maintenance man. Clayton also drove trucks transporting personnel and equipment, and secured, sorted, and distributed regimental mail at one point during his service. He was hit near his heart by flack from a Japanese mortar in Luzon and was put on a plane that flew him south of Manila to a field hospital, where he slowly recuperated. In August of 1945, Clayton was discharged with malaria after four years and five months of service. He was awarded the American Defense Service Medal, Asiatic Pacific Theater Campaign Ribbon with Bronze Arrowhead, Philippine Liberation Ribbon with one Bronze Star, the Purple Heart, and the Good Conduct Medal.

Clayton worked in local shipyards for a few years and then left to work at the Portsmouth Naval Shipyard in Kittery, where he stayed for 25 years until his retirement. He then moved back to Boothbay where he lived until he passed away on September 18, 1993, at the age of 77.

KENNETH R. ORNE
Sergeant, Army Air Corps

Kenneth enlisted on December 15, 1941. He was 21 years old and had been working at Samples Shipyard building mine sweepers with Lew Yates of Boothbay Harbor. One cold December day he had been working in the bilge of a mine sweeper and kept thinking to himself, "I've got to go some place warmer than this." Later that day he met up with Edwin McKown while he was getting gas at the Esso Station. Edwin said to him, "Say Kip, let's join the Air Corp and go to Mississippi." They left on a Friday

Kenneth Orne, Army Air Corps

and on Monday were being sworn in at Fort Devens in Massachusetts. Together they boarded a troop train, which took them to Mississippi. They took their basic training at Keesler Field in Biloxi, and when the time came to be shipped out, Edwin was sent to Trinidad and Kenneth was sent to Newark, New Jersey, to train to be an airplane mechanic.

After his training, Kenneth got on a coal fired train on the west side of the Hudson river and it took him a whole day to travel 60 miles. He was then stationed at Stewart Air Force Base in Newburgh, New York, which at the time of his arrival was set up as a tent city to accommodate all the incoming soldiers. They later moved into brick barracks. The base at Stewart was used to teach West Point Cadets how to fly airplanes.

On the weekends the GIs would go into New York City on leave. They would help unload box cars during the day and then might go to a U.S.O. show in the evening. Don Cornell, who was a big name vocalist at the time, was stationed with Kenneth, and sometimes he would put on a show at the base.

In 1944, Kenneth came home on leave on a Saturday. The Reverend Forrest Littlefield married Kenneth and his long-time girlfriend, Jeannette, at her parents, Harold and Angie Dodge's home on West

Street. They then returned to the base on Sunday where they lived during the remainder of the war.

After three years, 11 months, and three weeks of service, Kenneth was discharged. He was awarded the American Theater Ribbon, Expert Rifle Award, and the Good Conduct Medal for his service. He then moved to Hartford, Connecticut, where he worked for the Silent Glow Oil Burner Company for ten years as a purchasing agent. Then he changed companies and went to work for United Technologies in the Hamilton Standard Division for ten years purchasing items for the outer space program.

About this time he and Jeannette decided it was time to move back to Maine. They purchased the former Webster's Greenhouse in Boothbay Harbor, and opened Boothbay Region Greenhouses. After 13 years in the business, they sold it to the present owners and decided to retire. Kenneth enjoys gardening and does grounds work part time for two local motels, and currently lives in Boothbay Harbor with his wife of 52 years, Jeannette.

ARTHUR PACKARD
U.S. Army

Arthur served in the Army during the Second World War. He returned to Southport after his service, and worked as a lobsterman. Arthur passed away in 1957 at the age of 49.

FRANKLIN PAYSON
Technical Sergeant, Army Air Corps

Frank enlisted in the Army Air Corps on September 11, 1942, just two weeks after his 19th birthday. He had been working as an electricians helper at B.I.W. previous to this date. He attended basic training at "Tent City," Keesler Field, Mississippi, and Aircraft Maintenance School while he was there. Later he attended Aircraft Instrument School at Chanute Field, Illinois. After this training Frank was

Franklin Payson,
Army Air Corps (left) and his
cousin, Carl Cederstrom.

stationed at Hickham Field, Pearl Harbor on Oahu in the Hawaiian Islands.

Frank's memories of war in the Pacific are described as an island to island campaign. Many of his duties included recovering personnel and equipment after each island battle, and in doing so he saw much of the destruction of the Pacific. He landed on Midway, Tarawa, and the Fiji Islands, to name a few.

His duties included calibrating instruments on board the transport planes and adjusting the compass and auto pilot. Sometimes he had to fly in a plane towing a target that other planes used for shooting practice. It was nerveracking duty to say the least. Another time Frank had to swing a compass on a plane that was being used to train new pilots. The trainees wore red eye glasses and the windshield of the airplane was green; this was done to simulate darkness. The instructor told the new pilot to take the plane straight up until it started to fade out, which he did, but when it came down it went into a spin and he had a really hard time recovering.

Many islands in the Pacific were simply bypassed by the United States Marines even though they were occupied by the Japanese, because they held no significant value. On one transport flight Frank and the crew of the plane opened the cargo door and dropped a bomb out on one of the occupied islands. They didn't usually do this, but wanted to be able to say they had bombed a target.

Every month the men had to have eight hours of flight time to meet the requirements of flying status. There weren't always instruments that needed calibrating, so sometimes the men would hop on a cargo flight to earn their time. One day Frank had been assigned to a B-24 that had just had the fuel in its tanks changed, but at the last minute a friend of his, who worked in the operations office, told him a general's plane was just about to go up, so why not wait and go on it instead to earn the time. Frank agreed and watched the B-24 take off towards Honolulu. All of a sudden he noticed the airplane coming back towards the field; as it flew over the runway, it blew up and all hands were lost.

Frank's base was offered some planes that were stationed on the other end of Oahu. Five or six crew chiefs and Frank got on the DC-3 to go check them out and got ready for take off. There were six wooden interlocks on the outside of the plane marked with red ribbons. They hold the plane in place on the runway and it is the crew chief's duty to remove them. Also the pilot is supposed to move his controls around to make sure they have been removed. Meanwhile at the other end of the runway there was a band playing because a military review was taking place. Back in the DC-3, the pilot had decided to let his navigator take the plane, who forgot to check his controls, and one of the interlocks was still in place. As they headed down the runway Frank vividly remembers the tail end starting to come up, the brakes coming on screeching terribly, and the band disbanding in front of them, as the airplane rapidly approached the review field.

One of his most memorable and probably most enjoyable duties during the war was when he helped bring in the U.S.O. shows to the GIs after the battles were over. Celebrities in these shows included Bob Hope, Betty Grable, Jack Dempsey, and many talented others.

While overseas Frank had the opportunity to see not one, but two people from home. One was his cousin Carl Cederstrom, while he was passing through Pearl Harbor with the Navy, and the other was Norma Clifford, who was stationed on Oahu at the Naval Hospital.

Frank served three years and three months in the Army Air Corps before returning to Southport. He received the Asiatic/Pacific Ribbon, Silver Wings, and the Good Conduct Medal for his service. He recalls that his parents' home seemed like a dollhouse to him for the first few days, because he had been living in wide open barracks for so long. Also all the young children on the island he remembered seemed to have all grown up.

Frank attended the University of Maine at Orono on the GI Bill and studied mechanical engineering. He worked at the Portsmouth Naval Shipyard for 29 years, and currently lives in York with his wife of 45 years, Charlene.

LEWIS DANA PAYSON
Aviation Cadette, U.S. Navy

During the summer of 1942, Dana registered with the Coast Guard, and got an identification card, so he could run boats for Mrs. Righter. He attended the University of Maine at Orono, and was enrolled in the mechanical engineering program. All male students were required to take Army R.O.T.C. training the first two years of their schooling, and classes were held twice a week, and on every Saturday the students met to drill and have further instruction.

In December of that same year, Dana decided to join the Navy, and enlisted in the Naval Aviation Cadet-V5 program, in Boston, Massachusetts. Now he had been connected to three different military services in less than a year. New recruits were trained at Williams College, and then went on to Chapel Hill, North Carolina, for physical training. Afterwards, they could attend any flight school in the country. During a physical, doctors discovered Dana had a problem with his back. He was unable to further his training, and returned to Southport to recuperate on medical leave until January of 1945, when he received an honorable discharge.

After the war, Dana returned to UMO and graduated in February of 1950, with a B.S. in mechanical engineering. He enlisted in the Air Force for flight training, and was stationed at Perrin Air Force Base in Texas for one year. Then he returned to Boston and worked as a design engineer at the Stone & Webster Engineering Corporation for two and a half years.

Dana married Muriel Logan of Attleboro, Massachusetts, in November of 1952, and went to work for the Chance Vought Aircraft Company, also located in Boston, where he helped to designed an early type of pilot-less aircraft. Ironically enough, the company was located in the same

Dana Payson, U.S. Navy

building, where he enlisted in the Navy in 1942. In 1954, he changed employers, and worked for Pratt and Whitney Aircraft Company, for about a year.

In 1955, he went to work for the Raytheon Company in Bedford, where he worked as a design engineer on the early Sparrow Missiles, and in later years on the ground control equipment for Hawk and Patriot Guided Missiles, which were used in the Gulf War. Dana retired in 1988, after 32 years on the job, and currently lives in Burlington, Massachusetts, with his wife of 44 years, Muriel.

CARL PIERCE
Apprentice Seaman, U.S. Navy

On June 1, 1945, just two weeks before graduation, Carl joined the Navy. He was 18 years old at the time, and had begged his parents to let him join when he was 17, but his mother refused to sign the document that would allow him to enlist. A few days later the principal, Mr. Abbott, called Carl's sister Evelyn down to the office and gave her his diploma.

He was trained in Sampson, New York, was sent to school in Bayonne, New Jersey, for further training, and was later assigned to the new aircraft

Carl Pierce, U.S. Navy

carrier *U.S.S. Princeton.* He was on her when she was commissioned in Philadelphia and received a Plank Owners Certificate for his participation. The war came to an end shortly thereafter. The ship was commanded by Captain John Hoskins, who lost a leg during the war and thought his career was over. Instead he was given the command of the *U.S.S. Princeton,* and Carl said he could use the ship's ladders without any trouble. A movie was later made about his life, and Sterling Hayden played his part.

He spent much of his time at sea during the early years of his career and traveled all over the world to many countries, including Scotland,

Portugal, Spain, Italy, France. He found that he enjoyed running the ship's store and became the Master Chief Ship's Serviceman, a duty which he held for 30 years. Master Chief was a new rating and Carl was the first in the Navy to make that rank. He later was stationed in Argentina, Newfoundland, and in New York City. He returned to Southport after his retirement from the Navy, and owned and operated The Maine Made Shop here on the island for many years. He sold local crafts and was well-known for the products he made out of wood, including clam hods and tables. He was also the town clerk and tax collector. Carl passed away on February 8, 1993, at the age of 65.

NORMAN PIERCE
Seaman First Class, U.S. Navy

Norman was drafted into the Navy on December 23, 1943, at the age of 32. He received his basic training at Sampson Naval Training Station in Sampson, New York, and was then transferred to Fort Pierce in Florida as part of an amphibious outfit. He was soon sent to Newport, Rhode Island, where he ran into Southport resident Wolcott Marr, who was there waiting for his transfer orders. He also met Freeman Rand, a Southport summer resident, while getting a cup of coffee at a U.S.O. Club in Norfolk, Virginia.

Norman Pierce, U.S. Navy

He then served upon the *U.S.S. Montour*, which traveled between New York and New Orleans transporting troops, and on the *U.S.S. Blakely*, Destroyer Escort-140, which took him from South Carolina to Panama patrolling for enemy submarines. His duties on board both ships included postal clerk and assisting the officer on deck.

Prior to being drafted Norman had worked on the bending floor of the harding plant at the Bath Iron Works, but was later transferred to the South Portland Shipyard's pneumatic department as part of the air crew for drilling and chipping. This work was directly involved with the building of Liberty Ships for the war effort. He was married to Martha Black of Brunswick, Maine on March 1, 1940, and was only able to return home twice on leave during his three years in the Navy.

Norman was discharged in 1946 and was awarded the American Theater Ribbon for his service. After the war he worked for the Maine Department of Transportation until his retirement in 1975. He currently lives in Freeport with his wife of 56 years, Martha.

PAUL PIERCE
Ships Cook First Class, U.S. Navy

Paul Pierce, U.S. Navy

Paul enlisted in the summer of 1941 with his friend from Southport, Fred Farnham. He was 24 years old at the time. He and Fred were eating lobster rolls at his aunt's house when Fred said, "Let's join the Navy." Paul agreed, they finished their lunch, and hitchhiked to Boothbay Harbor, where they caught a ride to the train in Wiscasset. Fred had never ridden on a train and was a little nervous, and Paul asked him if he wanted to go home. He said no and they continued onto Portland and got their physicals. On the way home, they stopped at the Oxhorn Dance Hall in Wiscasset and met Wes Gamage from Southport there. Paul had been fishing with Leslie Brewer prior to this time.

Paul became a Cook Second Class and worked for two months at the Charleston Navy Yard. Then he was assigned to a seagoing tug boat in Port Arthur, Texas, where he stayed for three months. He came back up the coast to a dry dock in Norfolk, Virginia, and continued back to the Charleston Navy Yard around Thanksgiving time.

Paul was home on leave visiting his parents when the news about Pearl Harbor reached him. He caught up with Leon Duprey, who was driving Maynard Robinson's lobster pound truck between Southport and

Boston, and caught a ride back to the Navy Yard. Upon his return he went back out to sea on the 160 foot seagoing tug. The weather was unusually calm and before he knew it, they were in the middle of a horrible storm, and a Coast Guard Cutter had to come out and rescue them.

They then headed for Argentia, Newfoundland, and Paul remembers seeing a shipwreck close to shore enroute. The locals were hauling men up over the rocks with a rope. They had fuel oil that was floating in the water in their eyes and, when the rope began to chafe, finally breaking, a wave swept the blinded men back into the ocean.

While in Argentia, Paul met celebrities Victor Mature on the Coast Guard cutter U.S.S. Bean, and Douglas Fairbanks on a cargo ship that was docked there. When Paul went to the dance halls, there was usually someone playing a small accordion, and he would bring a couple of oranges with him for the girls. There was no fruit available in Newfoundland or milk, because some of the cows had developed TB (tuberculosis) due to improper breeding, and had to be destroyed.

Paul hurt his hand in Newfoundland in 1942 and was told to go back to Boston to have it operated on there. On the way back, the Coast Guard cutter Paul's tug was tied to caught on fire and five men lost their lives. Paul sometimes stayed in an old sea captain's house in Boston. The owner told him where the key was kept and he could let himself in when he wanted to. Her son had been killed when a German submarine machine gunned him off the rocks in the Virginia Cape. Paul slept in what had once been his room, when he stayed there. One night he heard someone moving about in the house. Paul knew he was the only one there that evening, so he jumped up, grabbed his things, and dashed out, dropping the house key in the mailbox. He never stayed there again after that incident, it was just too creepy.

After recuperating, Paul was assigned to the destroyer Barneget and was in charge of the galley feeding 3000 men a day. Once back in Newfoundland he met Kenneth Piltz from Southport, who was serving on a net tender there. He also ran into Gene Williams from Boothbay Harbor. One of his duties including weeding out the men from his ship from the men who came off other ships. Rations were limited and he didn't have enough to feed everyone.

On one trip back to Newfoundland in 1943, Paul went on an Army Transport. Near Halifax, Nova Scotia, it was struck by an English Tanker.

Paul was asleep in his bunk at the time and the collision knocked him out of it. He immediately knew what had happened and raced to get topside to the life rafts. The men on board didn't have to abandon ship, but, by the time they got into Halifax Harbor, they were over half full of water. Paul then cooked at the Royal Canadian Air Force Barracks for about a month until he could get on another ship bound for Newfoundland.

Paul was also part of task force 21, which escorted ships from the North Atlantic to England. He didn't spend much time in England, because they usually turned around and came right back. In 1944, Paul's asthma sent him back to Boston to the Charleston Naval Hospital, where he was discharged after serving two and a half years. He received the European Theater of War Ribbon, American Theater of War Ribbon, World War Two Victory Medal, and the Good Conduct Award.

Paul worked as a cook at Bowdoin College at the Beta House for a while, then at the Brunswick Naval Air Station, which was being used for the returning GIs as a freshman campus for the University of Maine at Orono. He then was hired at the Burnham and Morrill Bean Factory, where he baked beans. He later went to work at the Bath Iron Works as a security guard, which he retired from after 22 years. Paul currently lives in Brunswick with his wife of 48 years, Myrna.

KENNETH PILTZ
Chief Boatswain's Mate, U.S. Navy

On October 9, 1941, Ken enlisted in the Navy. He was 23 years old and had been working as a bank teller at Manufacturers Trust on Wall Street in New York City prior to that time. Bob Marr, who summered on Southport, went to enlist with him. He was at Fargo Barracks in Boston, Massachusetts, awaiting transfer to boot camp when Pearl Harbor was attacked by the Japanese, and was never sent to basic training. Instead he was assigned duty on the *U.S.S.*

Kenneth Piltz, U.S. Navy

Guntree AN-13, which was a net tender. The ship was sent to Argentia, Newfoundland, to tend the anti-sub nets there, and did so for the next year and a half until she returned to Portland, Maine, in the spring of 1943 and was based there.

Ken returned on leave in October of 1942 to Southport to attend the wedding of his sister Priscilla to Bob Marr at the Cove Cottage Inn. After the festivities he traveled to North Sydney, Nova Scotia, and boarded a civilian ferry named the *Caribou*, to return to Argentia, Newfoundland. Enroute the ferry was torpedoed by a German submarine, in Cabot Strait, on October 14th. Canadian naval craft saved 101 passengers and crew members from the water, but 137 others lost their lives due to the attack. It was reported at the time that the submarine surfaced and watched her go down while her victims struggled in the water and, in doing so, capsized several lifeboats from the sinking ferry. Survivors told their rescuers that the captain of the *Caribou* steered her towards the U-boat's hull, when he noticed the surfaced submarine, in an apparent effort to ram the attacker with her icebreaker's prow, but the U-boat slid under before he could do so.

Ken had 50 dollars with him at the time, but it was lost when the ferry sank, so when he was rescued and brought ashore to the Salvation Army, he wired his mother to send him some money out of his bank account at home. He couldn't tell her what had happened to him in the telegram, due to censoring, and an account of the sinking did not appear in the newspaper for at least a month after the event, so when she received his telegram she thought he had lost his money playing poker on the ferry, and she didn't send him any. A few weeks later the story was disclosed in the local newspaper and, when his mother realized what had really happened to him, she felt terrible that she hadn't sent him the money right away.

His next duty station was at the U.S. Naval Net Depot in South Portland. Ken advanced to the rank of Chief Boatswain's Mate after passing the tests for Seaman Second Class, Seaman First Class, Boatswains Mate Third Class, Boatswains Mate Second Class, and Boatswains Mate First Class, three and a half years after his enlistment in 1941. He also married his girlfriend Jane Smith on October 9, 1943, while he was stationed there. He was discharged in September of 1945 and was awarded the National Defense Service Ribbon, European African Middle Eastern

Area Campaign Medal, American Defense Medal, Good Conduct Medal, and the American Theater Service Medal.

Ken remained in the reserves after the war and was called back to serve in the Korean War in 1950. He was sent to San Francisco, California, to help recommission the *U.S.S. Rockwall* APA-230 and was later transferred to Norfolk, Virginia, where his next duty station was with a Sea Bee unit at the Amphibious Construction Battalion #2, in Little Creek, Virginia. Ken traveled to Japan and Hong Kong on a sea going tug, bringing disabled destroyers, submarines, etc., back to the United States to be repaired. He was awarded the Asiatic Pacific Area Campaign Medal for his service.

After Ken's tour of duty there he was transferred to Boston, Massachusetts, on the *U.S.S. Atka* AGB-3, which was an ice breaker. His duties now included keeping the shipping lanes free of ice block over the northern route and transporting Danish diplomatic groups to Greenland for routine checks of the health and welfare of the Eskimos living there.

Ken was then sent to the Service Craft Naval Station in San Diego, California. He was assigned to the *U.S.S. Burton Island* AGB-1, which was another ice breaker whose home port was Seattle, Washington. While aboard the *Burton Island* he was sent to the South Pole to explore and map uncharted area. He and his crew discovered a mountain range while on this mission. Ken was in the vicinity of both poles during his duty on the two ice breakers.

He was later transferred to the *U.S.S. Tawasa* ATF-92, which was a sea-going tug home ported in San Diego, California. Her purpose was to tow submarines, destroyers, etc., needing repair to the U.S. shipyards located there. Ken's next duty station was at Service School Command, U.S. Naval Training Center, San Diego, California. His last tour was at the Naval Station also in San Diego, where he was discharged after 22 years of service. During his service Ken was awarded a Silver Star for good conduct, a Bronze Star for Second Award National Defense Service Medal, and a Navy Unit Citation for his service aboard the *U.S.S. Burton Island* AGB-1.

After his discharge Ken worked for the Post Office as a letter carrier for 15 years, before retiring to Pahrump, Nevada, where he lived with his wife of 51½ years, Jane. Ken passed away on January 5, 1995.

KENNETH PINKHAM
Seaman First Class, U.S. Navy

Ken was drafted into the Navy at the age of 22, on October 13, 1944. He received his training in Sampson, New York, and was later reassigned to Norman, Oklahoma. The troops were moved by train, but when they got to Buffalo, New York, it was snowed in and they soon found themselves shoveling. In fact they spent three weeks there shoveling out, until the trains could get through. He married Idalene Leeman from Boothbay Harbor on November 15, 1941, and had been working at the Bath Iron Works as a tin smith prior to that time.

Kenneth Pinkham, U.S. Navy

He worked as a sheet metal worker for the Navy during the war and was also stationed in El Sentro, California. While in Oklahoma, he met John "Dinney" Brackett from Boothbay Harbor. He and his wife had an apartment off base with their two girls, and they often invited Ken over to visit.

While Ken was in the Navy, he and his wife had a daughter. He was only able to get home twice on leave to see his family, but luckily Idalene had a lot of family support to help her while he was gone, because now she had a son and a newborn to take care of.

He was discharged on April 11, 1946, after one year, five months, and 28 days of service, and was awarded the World War II Victory Medal and the American Theater Medal. Ken returned to work at Bath Iron Works after the war, and he and Idalene had another son. He retired from B.I.W. in 1983 after 33 years of service. Ken passed away on January 25, 1984, at the age of 61.

ELBRIDGE PLUMMER
Sergeant, U.S. Army

Elbridge was drafted into the Army on May 5, 1942, at the age of 31. He was in the 350th Infantry Regiment, Company B, and attended truck driving school at Fort Knox, Kentucky. Prior to that time he worked for the Civilian Conservation Corps, as an Assistant Leader, in the 158th Company at Southwest Harbor, Great Pond, and Acadia National Park. The C.C.C. was created by President Roosevelt to help provide jobs for young men during the depression. He served in North Africa and in Italy

Elbridge Plummer, U.S. Army

while in the Army, first in the infantry and later in a tank division.

Malaria almost took his life while he was in North Africa, and continued to plague him, as it reoccurred several times after the war. While in Italy, he was in line in a truck convoy helping supply the front line units at the Anzio Beach Head with ammunition. The trucks were brought in on LSTs and then formed into a convoy on the shore. Another truck driver pushed ahead of Elbridge's vehicle and a shell landed on it, killing the man and wounding Elbridge in the leg, arm, and back. His daughter Faye remembers asking him, before she knew this story, why he let people in store lines push ahead of him. He just said "If they are in that much of a hurry, let them go." Perhaps the above account sheds some light on his casual attitude. Elbridge served in battles in North Appenines, the Po Valley, Naples-Foggia, and Rome-Arno.

On May 31, 1945, Elbridge wrote the following from Pisa, Italy, to his fiancee, Hazel, back in the states:

> Dearest Hazel Louise,
> We moved into a small town in early winter on about the damnedest front I've ever seen. We stood guard at night in holes on the mountain side and when not our turn at guard we slept

in houses in this small town. Four of us had one room in a small house.

At first the people seemed doubtful of us, as if they did not wish us there, but did not dare to say we could not stay. A young fellow of about twenty five, his mother who was sick in bed, the boys girlfriend, who keeps house in the day time, and the father. As time went on we got on better. (I am glad the other three were pretty good fellers) We gave him some cigarettes, and he set us up a small stove in the room, and they got us some mattresses to sleep on. We gave them things from our Christmas packages, soap, (which they could not get), coke, candy, and so on.

Now the mother was sick, the heavy black bread did not agree with her, so we saved pieces of white bread from our meals, before we left she was out of bed and downstairs by the fire quite a bit, as we gave them quite a bit they wished us to eat with them at times, which I did not like to do, they had but very little, and it did not taste very good anyway.

We used to bring back some of our food to them. Well, when it came time for us to leave they were very sorry for us to leave, they were going to have a big Christmas dinner for us, things they had been saving but we moved out two days before Christmas. The old lady had to kiss us good bye (two of us).

Time marched on, the war was over, and a few days ago I called in a few hours to see them, and talk about being glad to see me. They made me eat as much as I could, they have more food now, the mother saw me first on the street, and you would think I was her own son by the way she grabbed me, She was very well and the son said it was the white bread that done it.

The fellow and the girl was married last month, they waited for the war to end. The fellow did not want to get married now because there is not much money to be made. The name of the town is Pracchia. The fellow hunted all over town to get me some cards of the place. Which I will send or bring to you. The girls mother who lives across the way got a bunch of roses for me when I left.

The young fellow has learned some English from us. He had a book to set down words in. They asked for the other fellers, two were wounded. I plan if possible to send them back a package when I get home and it gets so one can send things, soap, blades, maybe coffee.

Bye. Love,
Elbridge

At the end of the war, Elbridge was offered a position in the Army as a mathematician, but told them he'd had enough of the service. Somehow the paper work related to his service had been lost in the shuffle coming from North Africa to Italy, so he was discharged as a Private First Class on October 7, 1945, at the separation center at Camp Edwards, Massachusetts, even though he had earned the rank of a Sergeant. After three years and five months of service in the Army, Elbridge was awarded the European African Middle Eastern Campaign Ribbon with four bronze stars, the Purple Heart, American Defense Service Medal, World War II Victory Medal, and the Good Conduct Medal.

He married Hazel Adams of Houlton, Maine, in New York City on October 14, 1945, and they had four children: Gail, Faye, Glenn, and Blaine. They returned to Southport and he talked about working for a new company called Central Maine Power, but decided not to take their offer, as he didn't think the company would last. Instead he lobstered some and worked on the town roads, later becoming the town road commissioner. Elbridge passed away in March of 1990 at the age of 79.

Hazel Adams Plummer, U.S. Naval Reserves, Nurses Corps

Hazel Adams Plummer
Lieutenant – JG (Junior Grade),
Nurses Corps, U.S. Naval Reserves

Hazel enlisted on February 16, 1944, at the age of 23. She received nursing training at Houlton-Aroostook General Hospital, then after taking the state nursing boards, she moved to

New Jersey in 1942. She worked at Middlesex General Hospital for a year, then transferred to Wyandotte, Michigan, to work at the General Hospital as an operating, psychiatric, and obstetrics nurse. Michigan was nice, but the humidity was draining her, and she lost a lot of weight. The hospital refused to transfer her or let her go, so she signed up in the Nurses Corps, and when she was called in, they had to let her go. Hazel was then assigned to a hospital in Portsmouth, New Hampshire, where she served as ward supervisor.

When Hazel was nine, she met a handsome man named Elbridge Plummer, who came to Houlton picking potatoes almost every year, during the Depression. He was ten years her senior and came from a little island called Southport in the southern part of the state. After their first meeting, she informed her mother, "I'm going to marry that man." Her mother brushed it off as a silly, school girl crush, but Hazel knew what she was talking about, even at that early age.

Elbridge and Hazel corresponded throughout the war and he even sent her roses and an engagement ring through the mail, while he was serving in Italy. One day, a short while after the ring arrived, another letter from Elbridge came for her, with the following poem included in it:

As I sit by the bank of a river trying to forget for a moment the war,
my thoughts wander back very fondly to my sweetheart,
> *across on the other shore.*
The night is dark and so dreary, not a star in the sky above,
but I don't even notice the kind of night,
> *as I think of the girl that I love.*
As I think of the happiness of ours, before we came to part.
Softly I touch her picture that I carry so close to my heart.
I stare at the trees and water, but really I don't see a thing,
for my thoughts are still of the girl I love,
> *the girl who is wearing my ring.*
But at last this bliss is broken, as my mind comes back to my task,
but I am happy and proud that she loves me,
> *for darling that is all that I ask.*
So I rise from my place by the river, and still my thoughts of the past,
and only try to think of the future of our love that I know will last.

At the war's end Hazel was reassigned to U.S.N.R. Midshipmen's School at Columbia University in New York, where she cared for midshipmen and V-12 trainees. She knew Elbridge was going to be discharged at any time, and was supposed to come to New York, but she was not sure when. One day, as she was walking down a busy city street she heard a man's voice call out, "Hazel!" She knew it was Elbridge without even turning around, because the people who knew her in the city addressed her as Lieutenant Adams.

The newly reunited couple planned to marry, but when Hazel asked her superiors for their permission, they informed her that she couldn't be discharged for that reason. It was at this point, after being separated for over three years from Elbridge, that Hazel informed them she would go A.W.O.L.(absent without leave) if they wouldn't let her get married. Her superiors finally gave in, noting her determination, and a short leave was granted. Hazel then went directly to Saks 5th Avenue and purchased a wedding dress, fancy robe, and a nightgown with matching slippers. They were wed in New York City, at the Little Chapel Around the Corner on October 14, 1945.

Hazel was discharged on December 16, 1945, after one year and ten months of service. She and Elbridge returned to Southport where they raised a family and she later continued her nursing career. Hazel currently lives in Gardiner, Maine.

GEORGE POOR
Harbor Pilot

George was a self taught man. He was born and raised on Southport, and never attended high school. Over the years, he successfully rose through the ranks, to become a Harbor Pilot in Boston Harbor. He passed away about 25 years ago. I tried to contact his family to learn more about his service, but was unsuccessful in my efforts. I think we can surmise that George's position must have fallen under military jurisdiction during the war, and for that reason, I have decided to list him with the veterans.

GORDON J. POTTLE
Private First Class, U.S. Army

Gordon entered the Army on May 16, 1944, at the age of 18. He received basic training at Fort Devens, Massachusetts, and became part of the 26th Division. He had worked with his father, Theodore, at his general contractors business, driving trucks, and had also been employed at Samples Shipyard prior to that time.

He was sent to Central Europe, including Czechoslovakia and Germany, where he served as an automatic rifleman and drove transport trucks for military personnel and supplies. Gordon hauled rations and gasoline from the depot to the squadron area, and provided mechanical maintenance for the two ton trucks he drove. He spent 15 months in the European Theater of Operations, and was discharged at Fort Dix, New Jersey, on, May 13, 1947, after two years and one month of service. He was awarded the European African Middle Eastern Campaign Medal, World War II Victory Medal, and the Good Conduct Award.

Gordon married Marlene Parmenter from Boothbay Harbor, on May 13, 1947. They had two children, Sally and Clayton, and he returned to the general contracting business, including construction, trucking, and mechanical work. He later took a caretakers job on Southport, where he worked for many years. Gordon passed away in May of 1986, at the age of 60.

EARL PRATT, JR.
Buck Sergeant, Army Air Corps

Earl was 24 years old when he was drafted. The year was 1942. He had been helping run the Alley at Cozy Harbor with his father Earl prior to that time. He traveled to the Recruit Reception Center at Fort Devens in Massachusetts, where he was run through the usual series of tests and examinations. When the time came to get shots, Earl found himself standing behind one of the biggest men he had

Earl Pratt, Army Air Corps

ever seen in his life. He was the kind of guy you want in your corner during a fight. Every time a doctor would get a needle out to inoculate him, he would pass out. The staff would revive him and the line would move on to the next medication station, and it would promptly happen all over again. Earl couldn't believe that a fellow that big would be so terrified of needles.

Earl soon found out they didn't have a uniform big enough to fit him and he would have to wait until one came in. He was assigned to tend the boilers and hot water heaters in five of the barracks on the base. They were fired by hard coal, and he performed this task for ten days while he waited for his uniform. He also had KP (kitchen police) duty. Somewhere along the line it had been decided that it would help the war effort if bakeries stopped slicing loaves of bread, which really translated into someone else having to perform the task later. Earl said he worked in a huge kitchen and, as soon as they got through slicing one truck load of bread, another one would show up. It seemed like a never ending job.

While there Earl ran into Earl Widden from Southport. He was Dorothy Marr's brother and was also stationed at Fort Devens. Finally his uniform arrived and he was sent to Westover Field in Springfield, Massachusetts, for basic training. Earl remembers being on guard duty around the perimeter of the air field early in the morning when the dawn patrol, made up of B-25s, would leave to check the coast for submarines. Fire would come out of the engines' exhaust as they took off, making it quite an impressive sight.

The base had its own barber shop that was manned by civilians. They had received a 4F rating, which meant they didn't pass the physical requirements to join the service. Hair cuts were .15 cents at the time. You could go to the PX and buy 3.2% beer. Schlitz and Budweiser were .15 cents a bottle, and Old Milwaukee and Piels were .10 cents.

Earl took an IQ test while at the base, and they determined from it that he would be assigned to a ground crew in the Air Force. He was shipped to Richmond Army Air Base on one of two troop cars that were attached to a regular passenger train. Usually troop trains had between ten and fifteen cars in line, with the middle car being a baggage car, which served as a kitchen with a stovepipe coming out the sidedoor. The cooks burned soft coal in their stoves to cook with. The troops then ate in shifts and took turns bringing their mess kits to the kitchen car and returning to their seats to eat. In Earl's case the troops were coupled to a regular passenger train and had a dining car assigned just for the troops. There were even black waiters on board to serve them their meals. Earl ate his meal on Hellgate Bridge going over the East River in New York.

When his train came into Washington's Union Station, Earl noticed that they were using every kind of engine they could get their hands on. The railroad had borrowed them from all over the country to help keep up with the troops passing through. There was even a ten wheeler from the Chicago and Northwestern Railroad, which eased the process of switching cars. The train then proceeded on the Richmond Fredricksburg and Potomac Railroad, which took him through Quantico, Virginia. When he looked out of the train he remembers being quite surprised by seeing several black men on the platform dressed up in zoot suits. (A popular men's suit from the 1940s, characterized by full-legged, tight-cuffed trousers and a long coat with wide lapels and wide, heavily padded shoulders.) It was really quite a contrast to everyday dress and especially to his uniform.

One hundred and sixty men got off the train with Earl at the Broadstreet Station in Richmond and soon discovered that there was no one waiting for them with transportation to the air base. There was a grassy lawn in front of the station, so they went over and all fell asleep. Around daylight, someone at the base remembered the men, and trucks were sent out to pick them up. They moved into brand new barracks, which were filled with cockroaches within the week. Earl thought great, now we'll get some sleep, but much to his chagrin, they were ordered out on the field and went straight into calisthenics at sun up.

The base was located near Chesapeake Bay and the men were often served oysters for supper. You would come into the mess hall and there would be raw oysters in a GI dish pan, fried oysters in another, and then french fried potatoes. It was really quite a treat. On the other hand, at breakfast, they used bacon that had been baked, not fried, and when you brought your tray to the table you had to pick the baked cockroaches from it, then you could commence to eat your breakfast. While there an Army cook told Earl the secret ingredient to S.O.S. (s___ on a shingle). It was a dish that was often served and consisted of crumbled hamburger, some said dried chipped beef, and cream sauce, with a touch of dry mustard, the secret ingredient, for flavoring.

Earl was assigned to an aviation engineering supply company and was in the 390th Airbase Squadron. It was their job to supply the engineers with the tools they would need overseas. This included everything from tractors to shovels. The engineering supply depot was located south of Richmond, and to get to it you had to pass by the Lucky Strike Factory on the Petersburg Pike. The men would load 20 or 30 trucks with supplies and then would head back to the base. Earl was on the lead truck and would stand on the running board to give his convoy orders. A fist raised in the air, moved up and down, meant go. It was a powerful feeling to know your signals controlled the movement of the whole convoy.

There was a camouflage battalion on the base. The men in it were colorblind and could detect camouflage with the naked eye. There were also black units stationed at the base. One day Earl realized a man in his unit was missing. He looked all over the base for him to no avail. Earl later discovered that the man had been sent to one of the black barracks. His skin was very light and his ethnic background had gone undetected up until that point.

Equipment had to be shipped out by train to the various ports so it could be sent overseas. Earl's job was to load equipment on flatcars and

Earl acting as engineer on the yard switcher at Richmond Army Air Base. His friend, Johnny Johnson, is pictured on the right.

secure it. Six by six wedges of wood had to be cut to block it in, and that was the first time Earl saw a two-man chainsaw work. It was an air powered saw made by Disten. The wedges were spiked down to the floors of the flatcars and then everything had to be wired in tight. Once the train was loaded, railroad inspectors would come and inspect the cargo.

While at the base there was a shortage of potatoes. Everyone was craving them and when a freight car full of them appeared outside the main gate, it became Earl's duty to fire up the Davenport Locomotive they used on base to move supplies around. He coupled the gas-powered, four-cylinder engine onto the car of potatoes, but it wouldn't budge, so he yelled out to his friend, "Release the brakes!" When he did, it easily rolled into the base and everyone was really happy at supper that night.

Pay was $30.00 a month and, to earn a little extra money, Earl worked for special services after hours. There were two movie theaters on base and he sold tickets at one of them. The two theaters were two miles apart, but were run with the same film. Movie times were staggered and, when the first reel was over at Earl's theater, a jeep would pick it up and run it over to the second theater to start the movie there. They ran three shows a night between the two theaters and only once ran late, when the jeep shuttling the films back and forth got a flat tire. Fred Astaire, Bob Hope, Jerry Colona, and Francis Langford also performed on the base thanks to the U.S.O.

One day Earl picked up a copy of the Richmond News Leader and there on the front page was the headline, "Les Brewer Has Biggest Herring Catch in Southport, Maine." Earl couldn't believe it, Les was his neighbor back in Southport, and here he was in Richmond, Virginia, reading about him on the front page.

Earl also had bomb loading details on various days. The bombs were put on trains and taken to ships that were waiting to go overseas. Many of the B-25 bomb bay doors were opened and huge gas tanks were fitted in where the bombs usually went. Then the pilots flew them to England and ditched the extra fuel tanks in the ocean when they were empty.

Mail was sent free for anyone in the service. All they had to do was put their rank, name, and serial number in the left corner and write free in the right corner and it would be delivered. There was also another form of correspondence called V-Mail. The writer filled out a form with the appropriate information and wrote their letter on it. Then the form was photographed on microfilm along with hundreds of others and was flown overseas where it was developed and distributed to the troops. This saved transporting multitudes of bulky mail bags back and forth. Earl had a friend named Dan McBride from Malden, Massachusetts, who had been shot down and taken prisoner in a German P.O.W. camp. Earl often wrote to Dan on V-Mail. Dan was one of eight children, seven of them boys, who all served and all made it home safely after the war.

Earl was engaged to Emolyn Smith before he went into the service and returned home on leave to marry her at the Southport Yacht Club on December 25th, 1942. Reverend Arthur Hamilton presided over the ceremony, it was open invitation, and most everyone on the island was there. Jerry, Emolyn's brother, was even home on leave and attended in his uniform. The newlyweds briefly honeymooned in Waterville, Maine, where they heard Bing Crosby sing "White Christmas" for the first time, and then Earl had to return back to his base in Virginia.

Earl served in the Air Corps for two years. He then worked for General Electric in Lynn, Massachusetts, for a year and a half, testing steam turbines. While living in Malden, he and Em had a son, Wayne. They returned to Southport to run the Alley at Cozy Harbor, which he still does to this day with his wife of 54 years, Emolyn.

Engineer Property Office, Earl sitting at the desk at the far right.
Author's note: *The office equipment came from the Civilian Conservation Corps when the war broke out.*

BODO RICHTER

Private, U.S. Army

Bodo enlisted in the Army in Boston, Massachusetts on June 23, 1942, at the age of 27. He received basic training at Camp Lee, Virginia, and then went on to Camp Forrest, Tennessee, for further training, where he became part of the Headquarters Detachment, 4th Service Command. He had been a student at Harvard University, studying romance languages and literature prior to that time.

Ludwig Richter, Bodo's father, was a Doctor of Chemistry for the I.G. Farben Company in Leverkusen, Germany, near Cologne. They are the

Bodo Richter, U.S. Army

manufacturers of Bayer Aspirin. His mother, Martha, was a German Jew, and her family had disowned her for marrying Ludwig, because he was a Christian.

In March of 1933, Hitler was coming to power in Germany. At the same time, Bodo and his brother, Bruno, were graduating from the Gymnasium (high school, plus two years in Europe). Ludwig took them aside and told them, because he was Chairman of the Democratic Party of the Rhineland, he would surely be on Hitler's "hit list" of people to get rid of because his political views conflicted with the Nazis. Also, the I.G. Farben Company had offered him a quick divorce from Martha, because they valued his work at their company, and didn't want to lose him because of his association with a Jew. When he flatly declined their offer, they counteroffered with a position in the United States, which he promptly accepted, because he foresaw what was going to happen in Germany with Hitler in power, and wanted to get his family out before anything could happen to them.

Ludwig came over on a ship by himself, and was not allowed to bring any German currency into the country, so he had to start from scratch in the United States. He found a small room at a boarding house, in

Rensselaer, New York, and saved all his money, so he could send for his family in Germany. Bodo and Bruno came over first, on the *S.S. Hansa*, in June of 1938. Ludwig wanted them to continue their education in America, so they enrolled in college; Bodo at Harvard, and Bruno at Boston University, where he studied business.

Meanwhile, Martha and her youngest son Arno, age 13, were back in Germany, packing the family's belongings. They left in 1939, on the last boat that was allowed into the United States from Germany. The immigrant quotas were now full, and any ships that came after theirs were turned back.

Bodo had only been in the United States for two weeks when he was approached by an unidentified man on the street, who asked him to join the Bund, which was an underground Nazi organization in the United States. By this time, Hitler's power was strong and his grasp was far reaching, even on American soil. Bodo quickly declined the offer, but had the presence of mind, after the shock wore off, to go directly to the F.B.I. and tell them what happened. They thanked him profusely, and told him he was a model citizen. About two weeks later, the headlines in all the newspapers read, "F.B.I. Cracks Nazi Spy Ring on the East Coast."

When war broke out on December 7, 1941, Ludwig came to his two oldest sons and said, "I'm so grateful to be in the United States with my family. I want my sons to serve in the Army." Bodo and Bruno both enlisted right away, and because of their German background were trained by the Central Intelligence Corps (C.I.C.) to infiltrate the enemy, and work as spies for the U.S. Army. Bruno was sent to occupied France and Germany during the war, and stayed in the Army until 1952, as part of the Army of Occupation in Germany, and helped reorganize the country.

Bodo completed his training, but injured his leg and developed a stomach ulcer, which wasn't helped any by Army food. He received an honorable medical discharge on January 30, 1943, after serving for seven months and seven days. Younger brother Arno graduated from high school in 1942, and was drafted into the Army. He, too was sent to Europe, and ironically enough, bumped into his brother, Bruno, in Verdun, France, on March 25, 1945.

After the war, Bodo became a university professor at the University of Pennsylvania in Philadelphia, teaching Renaissance Literature. He taught there for 15 years, then went to the State University of New York at Buffalo, where he stayed until his retirement in 1985. He married Gail Norton, a life-long summer resident of Southport, on December 31, 1965, and they had three children, Andrew, Claude, and Michelle. They made Southport their home in 1988. Bodo passed away on February 2, 1990, at the age of 74.

HAROLD ROBERTS
Seaman First Class, Navy Seabees

Harold enlisted on April 4, 1943, at the age of 18. He received his basic training at Sampson Naval Training Center in New York, and became part of the 144th Naval Construction Battalion. He was then stationed in New Jersey for about six months. Harold had worked for Clayton Dodge at his lumber mill prior to that time.

He received orders to report to Port Hoeneme in California, where he stayed a short time before leaving for the Pacific. Harold's battalion went to

Harold Roberts, Navy Seabees

work rebuilding the islands of Guam, Sai Pan, Tinian, Truk, and Japan, which had all suffered devastating destruction during the war.

On one of the islands in the Pacific, Harold remembers seeing the company cook throw some turkeys out that had spoiled. Before they had time to lie on the garbage pile, some of the natives grabbed them and soaked them overboard in the salt water, later using them to feed their starving families. Also, in the Pacific, Harold met up with Edgar Lewis, who was in the Marine Corps and was from Hodgdon's Island in Boothbay. It was really great to visit with someone from home when you were so far away.

While on Guam, Harold and some of his friends discovered that there was a stockpile of beer in a quonset hut on the island. They climbed up on it, and took off a section of the metal roofing, allowing them to lower themselves inside and grab about 40 cases of beer. There was quite a party on the island of Guam that night, to say the least!

On May 24th, 1946, Harold was discharged from the Navy, after three years and one month of service. He received the Asiatic Pacific Area Medal, American Area Ribbon, and the World War II Victory Medal. He then returned to Maine to finish his education. He completed four years of high school in three at the Boothbay Region High School, and decided to go back into the service.

In 1951, after graduation, he joined the Air Force, and earned a rank of Airman First Class. He was trained in Cape Cod for 12 weeks, and was later assigned to Camp Elmenderth in Anchorage, Alaska, where he served as Military Police on the base. His last assignment was at Bolling Air Force Base in Washington, D.C. It was there that he married Marion Huskins of Southport, Maine, on November 17, 1953. Harold was discharged from the Air Force on February 12, 1955, after four years of service.

He and Marion moved back to Southport and he went to work at Samples Shipyard in Boothbay Harbor. He was later employed as a carpenter with various builders in the region, and finally, worked at the Newagen Inn doing maintenance, up until his retirement in 1986. Harold passed away on April 16, 1996, at the age of 71.

GEORGE LINCOLN ROCKWELL
Commander, U.S. Navy

Lincoln Rockwell, U.S. Navy

Lincoln summered in his youth on Southport, with his brother and father, "Doc" Rockwell, the well-known Vaudevillian comedian and writer. He was an exceptional student, artist, and musician, and was the leader of the Phantoms of Swing, a band comprised of local talent. He also created a map with his brother, depicting all the homes in the Boothbay Region. Lincoln attended high school at Hebron Academy here in Maine, then continued his education at Brown University until his junior year, when he enlisted in the Navy and won the wings of a navy pilot. He flew fighter planes off the carrier *Wasp* in the Pacific, and earned the three gold stripes of a commander.

After the war he operated advertising, sign, and photography studios both in Portland and Boothbay Harbor and was married, later having three children. In 1948, he won a $1,000 first prize in a national illustrator's competition for an illustration which was later used in a National Cancer Society Advertisement.

Lincoln returned to active duty during the Korean War and became an air combat instructor. He also became exposed to right-wing, anti-Semetic literature in California, and started to believe Adolf Hitler was the greatest mind produced in the last 2000 years of civilization. In 1952, Lincoln was transferred to Iceland where he commanded a unit. He divorced his first wife and married an Icelandic woman, with whom he had four more children. She later left him and returned to her native country.

In 1955 Lincoln was discharged from the Navy after serving his country for 19 years. He became the publisher of a magazine written for the wives of servicemen called *U.S. Lady*. It was designed and marketed as a magazine that gave up-to-date information on the living conditions in military installations around the world, homemaking information to service wives, and to help rebuild the morale of wives whose discouragement and loneliness impaired their husbands' service careers.

After the magazine's failure in 1958, Lincoln seemed to break down, and he became more involved with the fascist right wing of politics. He collected money from a dozen or so followers and founded the American Nazi Party in 1959, and self appointed himself Fuhrer of the organization. The party believed in white supremacy for the world. Its expressed policy was to deport Negroes to Africa, liquidate Jews, and hang traitors. Many top ranking U.S. politicians were singled out by the party as traitors during this time period. His naval reserve commander's commission was revoked in 1960, because of his activities with the Nazi Party. Lincoln predicted he would be elected President of the United States on the Nazi party ticket during the upcoming 1972 elections. Instead he was assassinated, at the age of 49, by a sniper's bullets. The hit took place in front of a laundromat in Arlington, Virginia, located across the street from the American Nazi Party headquarters, on August 25, 1967. Minutes later, John Patler, a former Marine, and recently ousted fourth ranking officer within the Nazi Party, was arrested for the murder.

Matt Koehl, second in command of the organization, announced shortly after Lincoln's death, "The party will carry on without Rockwell. Anyone who thinks you can kill an idea or a movement with a bomb or bullet is crazy. We will continue to fight for white power."

Author's note: It is a tragedy that a life that held so much promise was diverted to such evil and hatred, when it could have been used for good. I also find it very disturbing that an organization based on nothing more than hate can thrive within the confines of our country. After writing this story, I am all the more convinced and determined that we as a nation must do everything within our means to educate the masses as to the destructive power of the American Nazi Party and other organizations like it. Knowledge is power, and I believe the history of the last 50 years especially must be taught in depth in our schools, not skimmed over, or we are doomed to repeat it.

ELBRIDGE SHERMAN
Chief Petty Officer, U.S. Coast Guard

Elbridge enlisted in the U.S. Lifesaving Service in 1938, at the age of 22. Prior to that time he had worked in an out-of-state factory making batteries, after he graduated from Boothbay Region High School. When the war broke out he was stationed at various lifeboat stations on the East Coast and served on a troop ship in the North Atlantic. In 1943, he married Irma Forte, while he was stationed at the Nahant Lifeboat Station in Nahant, Massachusetts. They later had two sons, Earl and Alan.

Elbridge Sherman,
U.S. Coast Guard

Sometime toward the later part of the war he served as Chief Engineer on the *U.S. Army M/V FS-528*, which was a small freighter manned by the Coast Guard, used to supply military units on various South Pacific Islands. During the war he attained the rank of Chief Petty Officer, and was authorized to wear the rating insignia of Chief Motor Machinist Mate, Chief Machinist Mate, and Chief Engineman. He received the Asiatic Pacific Campaign Ribbon, World War II Victory Medal, and the Good Conduct Award for his service.

After the war Elbridge was reassigned to the Nahant Lifeboat Station and was later transferred to the Annasquam River Light in Gloucester, Massachusetts, where he served as the lighthouse keeper. His final tour of duty was at the Rockport Lifeboat Station in Rockport, Massachusetts. He was discharged in 1955 after serving 16 years in the Coast Guard.

Elbridge then worked for the Boston and Maine Railroad in Boston, Massachusetts; Graves Boatyard in Marblehead, Massachusetts; Lynn Tool and Dye Manufacturing Company in Lynn, Massachusetts; and finally for General Electric, also located in Lynn. He later retired from G.E. and moved back to Boothbay Harbor. Elbridge passed away on November 7, 1993, at the age of 78.

MAURICE SHERMAN
Buck Sergeant, U.S. Army

Maurice Sherman,
U.S. Army

Maurice was 24 years old when he was drafted into the Army. He had been working in Boothbay Harbor at Samples Shipyard, building mine sweepers with his father Chester, when he received his draft card in the mail. The year was 1941.

He was sent to Fort Devens where he took a written test, and then went on to Fort Bragg in North Carolina for 13 weeks of basic training. While there he was transferred to the 178th Field Artillery. The men were not issued live ammunition while on guard duty and often an officer would jump out at a soldier to make sure he was paying attention. After the bombing of Pearl Harbor in December live ammo was issued, and the officers ceased their training techniques. Now they made sure they identified themselves clearly as they approached the guards.

Maurice's unit trained on 155mm Howitzers. They have a short barrel, but can shoot over a mountain and land on the other side, up to eight miles away. Each battery had four guns and were identified by the letters A,B,C,D,E,F. Maurice was later sent to Camp Blanding in Jacksonville, Florida, for further training. He joined a Forward Observers Group which consisted of an officer, radio man with a field telephone, and Maurice driving the jeep with the glasses used for observing the field of fire. They had to go wherever the best location was to observe, and it varied from the top of a building to the top of a mountain.

While at Camp Blanding, Maurice decided to take a four-hour test, which when passed enabled you to train to fly B-24 bombers. He had guard duty that day, but found someone who was willing to take his stint. The only problem was his First Sergeant wouldn't let them trade. Maurice took the test anyway, but only had two hours to work on it before he had to go on guard duty. He got a 70 on the test and is sure he would have easily passed it, had he been able to work on it for the full four hours. Looking back on it now he is glad he didn't get into the program, because so many men didn't come home from those bombing missions.

Maurice's outfit then went on maneuvers in two or three states and ended up in Indian Town Gap Reservation, Pennsylvania, where they boarded a train which took them to the *U.S.S. Wakefield* in New York. She had been the biggest ocean liner in the United States, but had recently been converted over into a troop ship. It was now August 5, 1942. The troops were supposed to rotate from their quarters to being on deck every 12 hours. Maurice stayed up on deck as much as possible, because the rooms were overcrowded and many of the men were seasick. During the voyage Maurice was up on deck with hundreds of other men, and happened to look up at the bridge. One of the men looked familiar and when he stepped forward, Maurice realized it was Richard Alley, who was his next door neighbor from Southport, so he started waving his arms and yelling, "Richard!" at the top of his lungs. Finally Richard noticed him and came down. They arranged a place to meet and talk later when he was off duty. There were over 10,000 troops on board the ship, and Maurice and Richard never saw each other again until after the war.

The troop ship landed in Greenock, Scotland, on August 20th. The men went on by train to Salisbury Plains in Southern England, where they continued to train in preparation for combat. They received British rations, which consisted of corned beef from Argentina, brown bread, and tea that had the milk and sugar already in it. Maurice preferred the American rations. While in England Maurice saw one U.S.O. show. Al Jolson and Myrle Oberon were the guest performers.

On November 24 they received orders to embark to North Africa. They boarded the *Dutchess of Bedford* in Liverpool on November 27th, and traveled in a convoy, passing Casablanca, which at that time was French Morocco. Blackout conditions were not enforced, because it was a free city, and the lights really stood out, illuminated the night sky, as Maurice's ship passed by. He arrived in Oran, Algeria, eight days later. Enroute Maurice heard Bing Crosby sing "White Christmas" for the first time when it was broadcast by the BBC over the ship's radio.

The men moved into a bivouac area and set up tents. They were now 18 miles south of Sidi Bel Abbes, which is home of the French Foreign Legion. Maurice ran into soldiers from their compound once when he was in a bar with some of his friends. The French soldiers were issued money made out of aluminum, which was rectangular in shape, had a V inscribed in it, and was only worth a beer or a glass of wine. Maurice noticed all the French soldiers were leaving at the same time, and asked one of them why they were going so early. The man told Maurice that if they weren't back at their compound on time, their heads would be shaved, and that the second offense for being late was even worse.

Maurice also saw many Moroccan soldiers while in North Africa. He said they were really tough — the rumor at the time was they could easily sneak through German lines at night and identify German soldiers by the feeling of their boots, then the Moroccans would silently kill the soldiers and escape back to their base undetected.

Conditions in North Africa were challenging to say the least. In the morning, ice had to be removed that had formed in the water containers over night and anti-freeze was put in the jeeps to keep them running. During the day the temperatures were up around 85 degrees. At night the men would dig a shallow pit in the sand to put their tents over. The sand retained the heat of the sun and helped to keep them warm as they slept. The men had to take the drug Atabrine during the summer months to help prevent them from catching malaria. There were also huge fields full of brightly colored poppies, which brightened up the landscape.

Once, while on assignment in North Africa, Maurice and the rest of his forward observer group were driving in a jeep across the desert, when an American soldier stopped them. He told them they had driven into no man's land and would be captured by the Germans if they proceeded much further. The men quickly changed their route and returned to the Infantry Command Post.

In March of 1943 the men went on a 700-mile convoy by truck to Haidra, Tunisia, in support of the 34th division. The convoy was over 100 miles long, and the dust cloud it produced went on for as far as the eye could see. The U.S. troops were strafed by fighters and frequently fired on by German artillery. On March 30th two Howitzers in Maurice's D-Battery were hit by shell fire, and were put out of commission. On April 19th the batteries moved on to Beja, Tunisia, where they fired in support of the First Divisions attack. After the hill fell, they moved to support the 34th division on hill 609.

If an incoming shell landed close enough to you, the concussion from it was strong enough to rip the seam wide open up the back of your

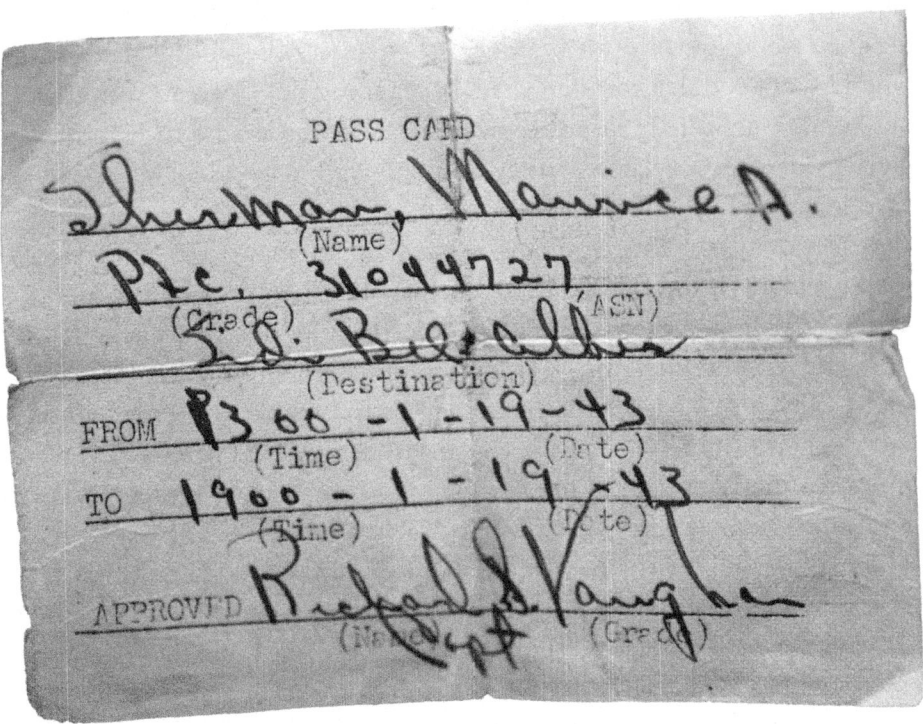

Maurice's six hour pass for Sidi Bel Abbes in Algeria.

jacket. Maurice was an eyewitness to this while in North Africa, under direct fire from the Germans.

On May 3rd Mateur fell and the following day the U.S. battalions moved into position. The infantry was very strong at this point and on May 8th the American forces broke through the German's southwest defense in Bizerte. British armored units also broke through their lines and occupied Tunis. This action later resulted in the unconditional surrender of General Rommel, known as the Desert Fox, and his Axis troops in North Africa. The 178th battalions fired 8,765 rounds in support of the infantry during the African Campaign. After the German surrender, they stayed in North Africa and trained until it was time to board LSTs (landing ship tanks) in Bizerte to sail for Salerno, Italy. Once there, they attached to the Sixth corps, under the 13th field artillery brigade, and moved into a position South of Venafro during November as support fire to the Second corps on Mt. Lungo and in San Pietro.

During the winter of 1943, Maurice's battalion moved in to support the Third division for the crossing of the Volturno River. Assigned to a mountain nicknamed the Million Dollar Hill, due to the dollar amount of shells that had been fired off of it, Maurice began to observe the field of fire when he noticed that the sky was a brilliant red color. There were blackout conditions in Italy just like the rest of Europe, so he thought it was quite odd. Maurice later learned that he had witnessed Mt. Vesuvius erupting.

While on duty, the Germans started counterattacking with smoke shells, making it impossible to see. When the attack subsided, Maurice started walking back to the infantry command post, but was hit by incoming enemy shell fire. Several fragments caught him in the left ankle, but he managed to hobble back to the Command Post. He then had to spend the night there because the Germans kept dumping shell fire down the back side of the mountain, which is were he had to go to get to the hospital.

The next day two of his friends helped him down a mule trail and took him to the tent hospital, where he was operated on. He was then sent to a hospital in Naples. The building it was housed in had been built especially for Mussolini, because he wanted to host the next Olympics in Italy. Its walls were painted with beautiful murals depicting Olympic events. It was the first time Maurice had slept in a bed with clean sheets for a very long time, and he said when he woke up, he thought he'd died and gone to heaven.

While there he met a Japanese-American soldier who was suffering from severe sinus infection. The man was from Hawaii and was used to a different climate than the one he had encountered in Italy during the winter. He had been an eyewitness to the bombing of Pearl Harbor and had signed up to fight for his country after that. He and the men in his unit had to work twice as hard to prove their loyalty to America, because of their ethnic background. They soon gained a reputation as one of the toughest outfits in the service and were often sent in to take care of difficult situations. An example of this would be during the war, a division from Texas was surrounded by the Germans, and this man's unit was sent in to get them out, and successfully did.

After ten days, all seriously wounded patients were flown on C-47s back to Bizerte in North Africa. Maurice noticed German P.O.Ws working as orderlies there. While staying in the 50-bed tent hospital, Maurice came down with malaria. He also met a man there named D.T. Rogers from Brownsville, Texas. The two soon stuck up a friendship, but after three months Maurice was shipped back to Italy and lost track of D.T. Ironically 52 years later their paths would cross again. (See the epilogue at the end of the veterans section for further details.)

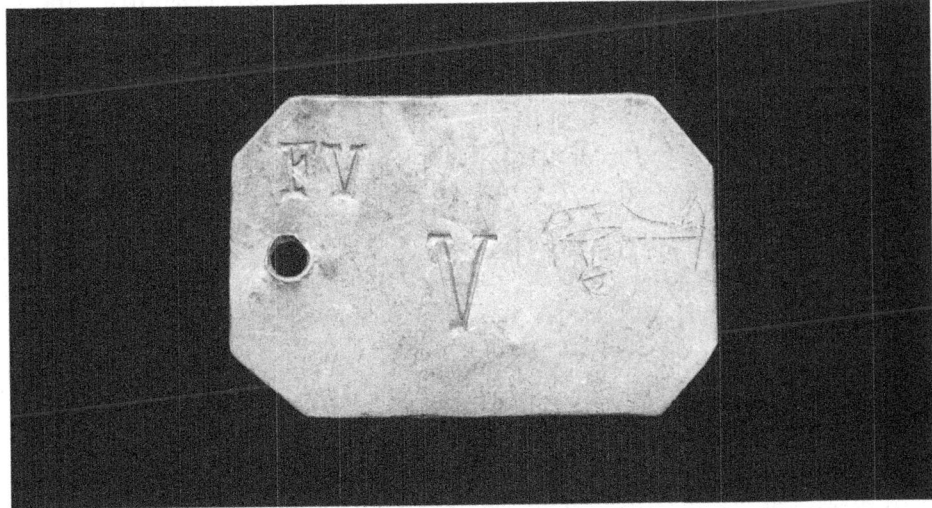

The aluminum coin a soldier in the French Foreign Legion gave
Maurice in Sidi Bel Abbes, in November of 1942,
worth one beer or a glass of wine.

By this time Italy had capitulated and Maurice boarded an Italian cruiser in North Africa, which took him back to Italy, where he found his outfit in a valley looking up at the Cassino Monastery. On board the ship, Maurice noticed the Italian sailors wore wooden clogs, which were really noisy on the iron deck. Also their main meal seemed to be sardines. The Germans had taken possession of the monastery during the war and still occupied the building. They had the valley under close observation and fired their artillery on any trucks or soldiers trying to pass through it. Maurice's outfit suffered many casualties here, and when the losses became so severe, the Army's engineers were brought in to construct a new main supply route.

The 178th set up their base seven miles away from the Cassino Monastery. Maurice vividly remembers wave after wave of American bombers flying in overhead to bomb it. The walls of the monastery were said to be 14 feet thick and the concussion of the exploding bombs fiercely shook the sides of the men's pup tents. An Australian unit was set up near Maurice's. There was a crater from a bomb explosion separating them, and an Australian soldier with a sense of humor put a sign up in it that read, "Another fine example of American Precision Bombing."

Author's note: *While on a recent trip to Italy, I was able to visit Cassino Monastery. It has been completely rebuilt since the end of the war.*

Maurice's position changed from Forward Observer to Instrument Operator at this point. When the battalions moved forward to a new position during the night, the captain would tell Maurice where he wanted the first gun and then the second, third, and fourth guns would have to line up precisely. Maurice and the Sergeant of the #1 gun would have to work together setting it up, then they would call a position to the next gun and so on. This is not the easiest task when you have to work in the dark. Once the four guns were lined up, a smoke shell was fired and the forward observer would radio in new coordinates. If the guns were lined up correctly, they could commence firing on a target.

The outfit reorganized in February of 1944 and changed to the 248th Field and Artillery Battalion. Maurice was now part of the A Battery. They then moved into position for an attack on the Gustav Line. It was said that artillery spread for 60 miles or more across Italy for this battle. Once there they started an artillery barrage in support of the French Infantry, First Motorized Infantry, Second Moroccan Infantry, Third

Algerian Infantry, and the Fourth Moroccan Mountain Division. An average of 1,000 rounds of ammunition were fired per day. Every day the same order came down through the ranks...Attack!

Maurice ran into a British officer during one particularly strong Allied artillery attack and said to him as the British let a round go, "Boy, they're really putting on quite a barrage." The British Officer simply replied as if it were nothing more than a fist fight, "A bit of a due." The concussions from the explosions were tremendous. Maurice said all you could do was stand there and absorb them.

The soldiers pushed the Germans back through Ausonia, Esperia, San Oliva, Pico, Castro dei Volsci, Cassino, Patrica, Gavignano, and Rome. The Germans were now in a full retreat. Somewhere before they came into Rome, the men set up camp in a vineyard. In the evening Maurice and his friends would visit the farmer and his wife who owned the land. They lived in a stone house and only had a fireplace to heat it. There was one light bulb hanging from the ceiling, but they hadn't had any electricity for a very long time. Maurice and his friends would give them sugar, soap, or whatever they had extra of, and the farmer would boil chestnuts in a kettle for them to eat. They were raising their grandchild and Maurice made a two-wheeled cart for him to pull around out of some scrap wood.

About this same time, Maurice was visited by a man from Maine who was a relative of the Gaudettes on Southport. The Germans started shelling shortly after he arrived and the men had to duck behind a stone wall to visit.

Maurice remembers advancing into Rome and being met by enthusiastic Italians waving American and Italian flags yelling "Paisano!" which translates in English to "Good friend!" He also remembers a lot of dead German soldiers and horses. The Germans were using anything they could find to pull their artillery and many of the animals became casualties of the war. Later, while on leave in Rome, Maurice discovered that the only thing you could get to eat was spaghetti with no sauce and no cheese. After watching the Italians eat for a while, Maurice caught on to their technique and ordered some spaghetti for himself.

One day, Maurice found out Elbridge Plummer, a good friend from Southport, was in the area. He got a jeep, and tried to get to his outfit, but the roads were too muddy, and he had to turn around.

July was hot in Italy. There were beautiful shade trees, planted every 20 feet, lining many of the streets. As the American soldiers advanced towards Rome, the Germans had placed explosives at head level on most of the trees. When detonated, it would snap the tree so it would fall precisely across the street, to slow the progression of the advancing Allies. Maurice discovered how they had done it, because some of the explosives did not go off and were still on the trees. Crews of engineers were brought in to clean the trees out of the way, and this was the first time Maurice had seen a two-man chainsaw work. Also many bridges had been destroyed as the Germans retreated, and the engineers had to build replacements so the Allied troops could keep pushing them back.

One day while traveling in a convoy, orders came through to pull over and stop. Maurice started to wonder why they had to wait so long, but his question was soon answered when Generals Eisenhower and Clark drove by him in their jeeps.

October brought the rainy season to Italy. There was mud everywhere. The engineers even had a hard time keeping pontoon bridges in place, because the current was so strong. The soldiers were issued one half of a tent and, when it was time to make camp, you had to find someone else to button yours with to make a complete tent. When the torrential rains hit, it was impossible to sleep on the ground, so at one point Maurice found a small unoccupied building and moved his gear into it.

One day a box arrived for him from home, which he opened immediately. The next day he was quite surprised to find a scorpion in it, who had apparently taken up residence in the box during the night. At this point Maurice made sure the uninvited guest would not return again.

Maurice received orders to go home on rotation while he was in Florence. It was there he also met up with his cousin, Roger Gray, from Edgecomb. They were almost to the winter line, which was located in the mountains. There was six feet of snow in some places, and neither the Americans or the Germans could move. It was the first time Maurice was home for Christmas in over two and a half years. When he arrived in the United States, he noticed Italian P.O.Ws were unloading ships on the dock.

After a two-week leave, he was sent to Lake Placid, New York, for Rest and Relaxation (R&R). Then it was on to Keesler Field, Mississippi. During the Battle of the Bulge men were needed badly, so they took them out of the Air Corps and put them on the line. Now ground forces were being sent to replace the men in the Air Corps. Maurice took a Basic Airplane Mechanics course while he was there, but then was told they badly needed cadre for the airfield and against his objections he was put in the medics. One day while on leave, Maurice went to Biloxi, Mississippi, to look at the shrimp boats. As he walked around the wharf he noticed a man who looked familiar, working on a crash boat. The man turned out to be Butch Brewer from Boothbay Harbor, Maine.

After two weeks he was shipped to Sheppard Field in Texas, where he worked on the maintenance crew for the rifle range until the war ended. Maurice's outfit was involved in 585 days of combat, in 80 different firing positions. His battalion occupied 26 different bivouacs in Tunisia and Italy, and fired 153,242 rounds of ammunition from 155mm Howitzers. They supported American, British, Canadian, French, Moroccan, Algerian, Indian, South African, and Brazilian Infantry Divisions throughout the war.

On September 8, 1945, Maurice left Wichita Falls, Texas, and arrived in Indiantown Gap, Pennsylvania, by train. The compartments were so full, he and many other soldiers had to stand for 200 miles while other

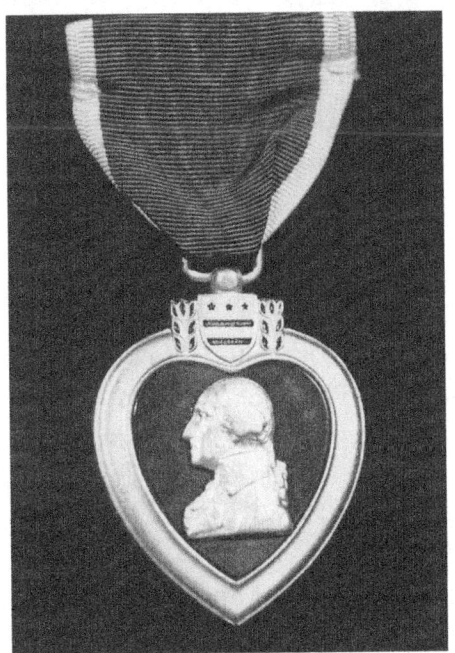

Maurice's Purple Heart, earned during the Italian Campaign.

Howitzers under cover in the Italian mountains.

soldiers sat three to a seat. Maurice was discharged after four years, one month, and eight days of service in the Army. He received the European African Middle Eastern Campaign Medal with four bronze stars, the Purple Heart, the American Defense Service Medal, and the Good Conduct Medal.

Maurice went to Wentworth Institute in Boston after the war on the GI Bill, and studied building construction. He married Evelyn Pratt of Malden, Massachusetts and Southport, on October 8, 1950, and they raised three children: Susan, Bill, and Sarah. He has worked as a self-employed builder on Southport Island for many years, and currently lives with his wife of 46 years, Evelyn.

SIDNEY SHERMAN
Staff Sergeant, Army Air Corps

Sid enlisted in the Army on March 12, 1945, at the age of 19. He received basic training in Biloxi, Mississippi, and was trained as an airplane mechanic and as a demolition specialist for unexploded ordinances. Prior to that time he had been a student at Boothbay Region High School.

Sid was stationed in Italy and was able to see quite a bit of the country while he was there, including the Isle of Capri, Naples, Venice, and

Sidney Sherman, Army Air Corps

Florence. He also traded cigarettes and candy bars with German prisoners of war for paintings they had made of Florence, the gondolas of Venice, and the Swiss Alps. Sid was discharged in July of 1947 after two years and four months of service, and was awarded the European African Middle Eastern Campaign Ribbon, World War II Victory Medal, and the Good Conduct Award.

In 1949 he was called back during the Korean War and was stationed at Bedford Air Force Base in Massachusetts and Mitchell Air Force Base in New York. He was discharged as a Technical Sergeant after a little over a year. He worked several odd jobs when he returned home and later went to work for Central Maine Power in 1954, from which he retired after over 30 years on the job. Sid passed away on September 13, 1992, at the age of 66.

ALLAN SMITH

Radio Operator, Petty Officer
First Class, U.S. Navy

Allan Smith was 17 years old when he enlisted in the Navy. He had just graduated from high school in June of that year, and signed up in July of 1942. He was called up for active duty on October 25, as an apprentice seaman.

He spent three weeks in boot camp at Newport, Rhode Island, and three months in naval radio school in Noroton Heights, Connecticut. He finished radio school with a rate of radioman, Petty Officer Third Class, and was assigned to the *USS Rocky*

Allan Smith, U.S. Navy

Mount AGG 3, a communications ship. Allan and the crew would later receive a Presidential Citation for their service on her. It was a new ship that had just been launched from a shipyard in Hoboken, New Jersey, in March of 1943. It left New Jersey for San Diego, California, by way of the Panama Canal, then on to Pearl Harbor, Hawaii, to join the Pacific Fleet as the flag ship of Admiral Chester W. Nimitz.

The *USS Rocky Mount* left Pearl Harbor and participated in nine major operations. These included Kwajalein and Enewetok in the Marshall Islands Atoll; Saipan, Tinian, Guam, Leyte, Luzon, and Mindanao in the Philippines; Iwo Jima, the Battle of the Coral Sea, and the Battle of Leyte Gulf.

Allan's brother Gerald, who enlisted in the Navy, was trained for the amphibious forces and was sent to North Africa and Italy about the same time Allan left for the South Pacific. The mail situation was not very good, and Allan often waited up to three months to receive news from home.

Early in 1945 Allan's ship was anchored in the Philippine Islands preparing for the invasion of Okinawa. He was in the radio room copying code when one of his shipmates called over to him and said "Hey Smitty, your brother is here." He thought someone was trying to be funny and turned around to see who the joker was, and there was Gerald standing in front of him. During one of the periods when no mail had arrived from home, Gerald had been transferred from Italy, back to the States for leave and then was reassigned to the Pacific Fleet. It turned out his ship was anchored beside Allan's. They were there for three days and, thanks to the officers on both ships, they were allowed to be together all of the three days on either ship. Allan commented when interviewed that it was just about the best three days of his life. When both ships left the Philippines, Gerald's ship went to Okinawa and Allan's went to Borneo.

Allan's ship was in the South China Sea on VJ Day in August 1945. They had received orders to proceed to China and arrived in Shanghai on August 25, 1945. With his three years of service, and most of it overseas duty, he had enough points for discharge, but he had to wait until there was a troop ship from China to the United States. Finally on October 1, 1945, he left Shanghai on the *USS General Rose*. Twenty one days later they arrived in Seattle, Washington, and boarded a troop train for Boston, Massachusetts, arriving there on the second day of November.

He was discharged as a Radio Operator, Petty Officer First Class, on November 4, 1945, and arrived back in Southport on November 5th, having served for 37 months with 31 of those overseas, and received the Asiatic Pacific Theater Ribbon and the Good Conduct Award.

When asked how Southport had changed when he returned, Allan replied he really didn't see that much change in Southport at the time, but now realizes that he had changed considerably. Allan moved to Connecticut after the war and found work driving a bus. While there he met and later married Gloria D'Amico on October 29, 1949. They later had a son, Gary. He worked in heavy construction for a while but found that he really enjoyed commercial real estate, so for the past 37 years has worked for the Jarvis Realty Company in Manchester, Connecticut, where he is the general manager. Allan currently lives in Guilford, Connecticut, with his wife of 47 years, Gloria.

GERALD SMITH
Coxswain, U.S. Navy

It was October 27 and the year was 1942 when Jerry was sworn into the U. S. Navy. He attended boot camp in Newport, Rhode Island, and was there three and a half weeks, which was just long enough to get his uniform and gear, see the dentist, and get all his shots.

Jerry reported to North Station in Boston where he attended radio school, but he didn't really like it. After a few weeks, he requested to go back to general detail so he could go to sea, which was what he had

Gerald Smith, U.S. Navy

enlisted for originally. While at North Station, he ran into Walter Hart, Jr., from Southport, and had dinner with him and his future wife and her family.

After waiting a week Jerry was assigned to a draft with the code name Dumb 29. He then sailed for North Africa. The ship went through the straits of Gibraltar enroute and was on constant alert for German submarines sailing by Spain. Spain was a neutral country and did not have mandatory blackouts, so German submarines would lie and wait to catch ships silhouetted against the Spanish shoreline, and try to torpedo them. The destroyer's screen was kept busy dropping depth charges all night, so no one on board got much sleep.

The purpose of Dumb 29 was to establish a base at Tenes, North Africa, which is located a few miles from Algiers. While involved in this endeavor, Jerry heard his cousin Sewall Smith, Jr., had been killed in a German air raid in Algiers. Sewall had been a mate in the merchant marines and was manning an anti-aircraft gun when his ship got hit.

Sometime in June of 1943 some seamen, including Jerry, were transferred from Tenes to Arzew, North Africa, where they joined the Fourth Naval Beach Battalion. While there they did a bit of training, hiking, and shooting. Then in August they went to Oran, North Africa, and boarded an assault ship for the invasion of Salerno, Italy. Jerry's outfit consisted of radiomen, signal men, a boat repair group, and what they called the hydrographic group, which was Jerry's.

On September 9th his group hit the beach in the first wave with the 36th infantry. It was then that Jerry learned the full extent of what the hydrographic group did. Their job was to wade out into the water, check for obstacles and sand bars, and then choose the best channels the boats should use to bring the troops ashore. The rest of his group set up and ran the beachhead. It was touch and go for a while, but finally with the ships shelling and the Air Corps bombing, they were able to maintain their hold on the beachhead and the Army moved on inland.

After three and a half weeks on the beach, part of Jerry's outfit went back to Arzew, North Africa, and about a week later the rest sailed back. Jerry said his outfit was pretty lucky, because they only collected a few Purple Hearts for that battle and fortunately he wasn't a recipient of one.

In February they left Arzew and went aboard the *H.M.S. Glengyle* for transportation back to the town of Salerno, Italy, where they set up a base in the town arena. The volcano Vesuvius had recently erupted and they got ashes from it on the ship while they were at sea. They later had to clean the ashes out of the arena before they could set up their tents. While there they had the chance to see Naples, Pompeii, and Rome, and even had an audience with Pope Pius.

They then went into bivouac north of Naples with the U.S. Army 40th Engineers and trained for what turned out to be the invasion of southern France, which took place in August. Jerry turned 21 on that beachhead and was a Coxswain, having recently been promoted in Salerno.

After the invasion, Jerry's unit went back to Oran and boarded a ship headed for the U.S. They had been in the Mediterranean for 19 months. After a short leave at home, Jerry was transferred to the West Coast and reported aboard the *U.S.S. Gosselin*. They left San Diego, California, and headed west, stopping at Pearl Harbor to refuel, re-provision, and rearm.

The ship later stopped at Ulithi Island and they had a couple of hours recreation on the beach on the island of MogMog. Then it went on to join the escort of the troop ships for the invasion of Okinawa. On the way they picked up a submarine on their sonar. After an hour or so of hunting, and a few deep and shallow patterns of depth charges, they hit the sub. Evidence of the hit soon came to the surface, including oil and wreckage.

After escorting the troop ships in, they went on Picket Line Duty to guard against air raids and submarines. Jerry said a lot of ships and men were hurt on that Picket Line due to Kamikaze pilots. At one point they picked up survivors of an auxiliary personnel destroyer. Two bombs and a suicide dive bomber got her. Jerry believes her number was 47. Jerry's ship hit a Japanese plane with its single five inch mount gun. It knocked the wing off the plane and the pilot tried to hit their ship as he was going down, but he missed. After things calmed down and were under control, Jerry's ship joined several destroyers that were pretty well shot up, and headed for Subic Bay in the Philippines for repairs. His ship had a hole in her side that had to be fixed, and luckily there were some repair ships in Subic Bay by this time that could do the job.

When they sailed into Subic Bay the first ship Jerry saw was the *U.S.S. Rocky Mount*, on which his brother Allan was a radioman. As soon as they dropped the hook, Jerry went to the officer on duty and got a boat to take him over to his brother's ship. Needless to say, Allan was really surprised to see Jerry walk into the radio shack. With the cooperation of their officers, the brothers were able to spend three days together. Jerry had not seen his brother for over two and a half years. Jerry said, "The one thing about having your brother's ship and yours in the same place is how you feel in an air raid, and we had one there one night. You worry more about his ship then you do your own."

After repairs they returned to Okinawa, and were there when the atomic bombs were dropped. When the Japanese surrendered, they were part of the escorting vessels for the *Iowa, Missouri*, and *H.M.S. Duke of York*. Going into Sagamiwan, Japan, they anchored overnight and then went on to Yokosuka and Tokyo. It was August 27th when they went into Sagamiwan, and even though Jerry was at general quarters (ready for combat) all day, he thought it was a great way to celebrate his 22nd birthday.

After the surrender was signed, Jerry's ship was chosen to go around to the Japanese P.O.W. camps to pick up prisoners. They picked up everyone from Hong Kong Volunteers and Philippinos to U.S. Army, Navy, and Marines. When Jerry saw how they had been treated by the Japanese he thought the U.S. should have dropped an atomic bomb on the Imperial Palace. While on this detail, everyone but Jerry was counting their points to go home. Instead he went to see the doctor for a physical and shipped over. He figured someone had to make sure we kept the peace.

After the prisoner detail, they were released from Western Pacific and sailed into San Francisco, California. Jerry then left the ship for leave and reassignment. He felt fortunate to have had the chance to help put both the Germans and Japanese out of business.

Jerry entered the Navy as an Apprentice Seaman and after duty on the *U.S.S. Cavalier* (twice), the *U.S.S. Juneau* with two tours of duty in Korea during the police action, the *U.S.S. Chittendon County*, the *U.S.S. Carter Hall*, and *U.S.S. Walke*, Jerry retired as a Chief Boatswains Mate. During the Second World War, he was awarded three area ribbons for the Atlantic, North Africa Middle Eastern Mediterranean, and Adriatic Pacific, a Victory Medal, and an Occupation Medal for Japan.

In June of 1948, Jerry was ordered to shore duty in San Diego, California, and in July of that year, Isabel Reed of Boothbay, Maine, joined him and they were married in the Naval Chapel on North Island. Rear Admiral Bieri gave the bride away and his wife was matron-of-honor. The Admiral's aide and his wife were also there. Jerry and Isabel later had two children, David and Jeri Lynn.

Jerry later received the China Service Medal for his service after the Second World War. During the Korean War he received the United Nations Medal, Korean Medal, and a Korean Presidential Unit Citation, and during the Vietnam War was awarded the National Defense Medal.

He retired from the Navy in 1962 after 20 years of service and went on to work for Sears Roebuck in Torrance, California, where he worked as a building engineer for 21 years. After 32 years of marriage, he lost Isabel to cancer, but was married again in July of 1981 to a California native named Janice Merit. Jerry currently lives on his ranch in Delano, California, near Bakersfield, with his wife of 15 years, Janice.

Norma Clifford Smith
Pharmacist Mate Third Class,
Navy WAVES

In 1944, with her parents' permission, Norma enlisted in the Navy WAVES. She was 20 years old at the time and had just graduated from pre-nursing at Westbrook College. A Navy WAVE officer spoke at her graduation ceremony and Norma said her speech was so inspiring, most of the girls in her class enlisted right away.

She went through boot camp at Hunter College in New York and had further training in Bethesda, Maryland, which you could call a crash course.

Norma Clifford Smith,
Navy WAVES

The women were promised a rate (particular rank) if they scored over 90 on their test and Norma studied hard to achieve that score.

Her first assignment was at the U.S. Naval Hospital in Key West, Florida. Then she worked at the Miami Dispensary. The nurses were on 12-hour shifts Monday through Thursday and worked 15-hour shifts on Fridays. Norma and her friends would sleep on the beach during the day and would go to work at night.

From Florida, Norma was reassigned to U.S. Navy Ten in Oahu, Hawaii, and it was the first time the WAVES were sent over seas. Alaska was the other choice given at that time, but Norma decided to follow the sun. Her new assignment was a 5,000-patient hospital that was the first stop for U.S. soldiers who had been Japanese prisoners of war in the Pacific. The men were screened there for 24 hours and then depending on their various conditions, both physical and mental, were assigned to hospitals stateside.

Norma was terribly seasick four of the five days that it took to get to Hawaii. She can remember being so sick that when an abandon ship drill was held, she couldn't even get out of her bunk, and she didn't care if they were going to court-martial her or not for refusing to participate. On the fifth day at sea she managed to become instantly well for the big dance that was going to be held on board that night, and looking back on it now credits her speedy recovery to a determination not to miss that dance for anything in the world.

Her first patients were both 19 years old and both were paraplegics. They had horrible bedsores and Norma always turned them so they didn't have to see each other's back. She said they were very courageous, and never complained or felt sorry for themselves. In fact Norma said it was a common sight to see a man on crutches pushing a man in wheelchair around the hospital. They all looked out for each other.

There were 105 men in a ward and Norma's duties included taking TPR (temperature, pulse, and respiration), serving meals, giving shots, baths, dressings, and whatever else needed to be done. Due to the excellent training these nurses had received, they were allowed to perform more duties than expected normally back at home. Many of the men had been involved in the Battles of Iwo Jima and Okinawa. Most of them were only 17, 18, and 19, younger than Norma.

While in Hawaii Norma met her future husband, Edgar "Smitty" Smith. She was in line at chow hall and Smitty got a friend of his who worked with Norma to introduce them. He was also a Pharmacist Mate stationed at the hospital. They dated until the end of the war, were engaged back in the States, and were married in 1948. Norma and Edgar had three children: Barry, Bonnie, and Robin.

Bob Hope and his USO show performed for the patients and the hospital staff on Oahu. Norma can remember helping bring every patient who was able out of the hospital to see the show. It was a great change of pace for the patients and for the staff. Norma met Carl Cederstrom while she was stationed in Oahu. He looked her up and they were able to visit for a while when she was off duty. Norma also met John Druce, who was Charlotte Harold's boyfriend. Charlotte summered on Pratt's Island and she and Norma were best friends.

Norma came down with a sore throat one morning and was put in the WAVES' ward for a few days of observation. The mentally disturbed ward was located next to hers and she remembers it was very difficult to try to fall asleep. The men in it kept calling out in their sleep and yelling. One man in particular kept repeating "Where's Genevieve?" over and over, finally another man on the ward, who hadn't spoken a word since he arrived at the hospital, yelled out, "She's out on liberty!"

When VE Day was announced, everyone at the hospital was ecstatic, but when VJ Day was announced the place went wild and a street dance soon occurred. Norma had signed up for the duration of the war plus six months, which was customary at the time. She was discharged in 1946, just short of serving two years in the Navy WAVES. She returned to the States on board a hospital ship and was assigned a cabin on the D-deck, which is located way below, and in turn was equally as seasick coming home as she was on the voyage going over.

Norma was an LPN for 27 years, working at both St. Andrews Hospital in Boothbay Harbor and H.D. Goodall Hospital in Sanford. She also ran the summer sailing program at the Southport Yacht Club for 30 years. She currently divides her time between Southport and her cottage on David's Island.

LESLIE EARL SNOWMAN
Private, U.S. Army

Earl was drafted into the Army on December 27, 1941, at the age of 21. He attended basic training at Fort Dix, New Jersey, and was part of the headquarters company, Plotting Battalion, 501st Signal Air, Warning Regiment. He had worked as a lobsterman prior to that time.

He had only been in the service a short time when he was hospitalized at the Walter Reed Hospital in Washington, D.C., for nerves. Earl was discharged on June 29, 1942, after six months and three days of service. He returned to Southport and worked at Bath Iron Works, welding for about a

Leslie Earl Snowman, U.S. Army

year, and then went to work at Samples Shipyard in Boothbay Harbor. He later went back to fishing and did so for the remainder of his life. Earl passed away on February 16, 1994, at the age of 74.

EUGENE STOVER, JR.
Third Class Pharmacist Mate, U.S. Navy

On March 15, 1946, Eugene was notified that he would be drafted in the Spring. He was 17½ at the time and was attending Boothbay Region High School. John Abbott was the principal at the time, and he told Eugene if he did some extra work during the school year, he would be given his diploma before he left for the service. Robert Goodspeed, Robert Perkins, Harry Pinkham, and Leo Barter from Boothbay were all drafted at the same time with Eugene. Mary Kenniston was a teacher at the school during this time and she was really upset when Eugene and his friends left, because it meant there would only be three boys left to participate in the graduation ceremonies she organized.

Eugene went to Bainbridge, Maryland, for eight weeks of training at the Naval Training Center located there. He met Jimmy McGlauflin from Boothbay Harbor going into boot camp as he was going out. Much to his chagrin it was discovered that he was 35% color blind, and he was given three options of duties he could perform in the Navy. They were cook, truck driver, or medic. Once they took a look at his Navy test scores his options were slimmed down to medic. He then spent three months training at the Portsmouth Naval Hospital in Virginia.

Eugene was assigned to the sea/air rescue in Virginia in the Fifth Naval District at Norfolk Naval. He spent three or four months there

Pictured from left to right: Eugene, Jr., Eugene, Sr., Joe, and Jack Stover.
Photo was taken in the early 1950s.

helping discharge men off aircraft carriers and destroyers. Everyone had to have a physical before they could go home. While there he met up and visited with Alan Cederstrom, who was from Southport. He was on a Maine Maritime ship headed for South America when the boilers started taking on salt water and they had to come into Norfolk Naval for repairs. He also met up with Bob Goodspeed and Robert Perkins of Boothbay Harbor when their ship came into the base.

He was discharged in July of 1948 and was awarded the American Theater of War Ribbon and the Good Conduct Award. He then went to the University of Maine at Orono on the GI Bill and studied history and government and physical education. He discovered his training in the Navy had more than prepared him for the classes associated with the physical education program and that is why he took on a double major. He joined the reserves in July of 1948 with the idea that he might like to go back into the service after college and was discharged in July of 1953.

In 1950, Eugene received a notice informing him to report for service in Korea at the Fargo Building in Boston. At the time the United States Government had passed a regulation stating that the upper quarter of college classes would be exempt from service, so when Eugene reported they told him to go on home, because he was in the upper quarter of his class. He boarded the next train back to Wiscasset, his father picked him up at the station, and he was back in Orono after missing only two days of classes.

Eugene married Ethel McKarthey of Bristol, Connecticut, in May of 1951. He finished college and took a job teaching physical education at Camden High School. After a year he was offered a job at Wiscasset High School, where he has taught for 42 years. He has handled every position, from history teacher to physical education, from assistant principal to his current position as athletic director. Eugene currently lives in Wiscasset with his wife of 45 years, Ethel.

EUGENE STOVER, SR.
Chief Boatswains Mate, U.S. Coast Guard

As a young man Eugene joined the Lifesaving Service, which later became the Coast Guard in 1915, and was stationed on Damariscove Island. When the Second World War broke out his duties changed slightly. They now included submarine patrol and spotting lights along the coast, because blackout conditions were now in place along the eastern seaboard. He had worked in a shipyard in Bath prior to that time.

Eugene was awarded the American Theater of War Ribbon for his service and he later retired in 1945 after serving 20 years in the U.S. Coast Guard. Upon his retirement he worked with his brother-in-law, Manley Reed, during the winter months and summers he piloted private boats. He moved to Orlando, Florida, in 1968 and summered in Boothbay Harbor every year thereafter until he passed away in 1988 at the age of 87.

OLIVE STRATTON
Captain, U.S. Army, WAAC

Olive Stratton,
U.S. Army, WAAC

Olive joined the WAACs (Women's Army Auxiliary Corp.) on October 17, 1942, at the age of 41. It was the first military group established for women, and a national call was issued for those interested in applying. There were two categories open for service, one to qualify for officer candidate school, or two, to become an enlisted person. Prior to this time, Olive had wanted to attend college like her three brothers, but her father didn't believe in educating women. Instead she worked for him as a secretary, bookkeeper, and manager at his car dealership in Malden, Massachusetts, H.C. Stratton Mercedes Benz, and became one of the first automobile saleswomen in the Northeast.

In September of 1942, Olive reported to North Station in Boston and boarded a train to Des Moines, Iowa, as part of the 2d Co. Officer Training Company, 6th Class. Olive was older then the rest of the women on the train, and was put in charge of the New England group. Upon their arrival they lived in barracks at the old cavalry post. Olive had a bunk next to Priscilla Emery, now Bissell, from Portsmouth, New Hampshire, and they soon became lifelong friends.

While at Ft. Des Moines, the weather was very rainy. One day the women were told the uniform of the day would be raincoats, but Olive did not go along with that, so she wore something else when they went to stand in formation. She was promptly pulled out of line by their officer in charge, who was a very young man, and was given extra duties that day for not obeying his orders. The rest of the women thought it was hilarious, but tried to hide their amusement, so they wouldn't get assigned extra duties as well.

The women were given time off from their WAAC training on Saturday afternoons and Sundays. Many of the girls would grab the first train or trolley car to get into town, and would head off to the nearest cocktail lounge. Often times, male officers would be there, also out of uniform, and one of them would call out, "Attention!" The whole room would immediately fall dead silent, as the women's training had taught them to do, and then they would hear one of the men say, "See, I told you they were all WAACs," and the entire room would explode with laughter.

After six weeks of rigorous training, the women were graduated with commissions as second lieutenants, gold bars and all. They then were granted two weeks leave and everyone returned home to visit their families. The women soon became commanding officers of the new training companies that were being formed out of new arrivals, who were arriving as enlisted volunteers by the hundreds daily. It was a very hectic time to say the least. The task of trying to supply the girls with uniforms and train them proved to be a difficult one. Women's uniforms were almost nonexistent, so they were often issued men's gear. It was bitter cold on the prairie, and the training grounds were always covered with ice.

Towards the end of the war Olive was assigned as a guardian to transport ships that were bringing troops home, both male and female. She was discharged from Fort Dix, New Jersey, on July 23, 1946, after three years and eight months of service, and was awarded the American Campaign Medal, European African Middle Eastern Campaign Medal, World War II Victory Medal, and the WAAC Medal.

After the war, Olive returned to Southport, and went to work for Blenn Perkins, who was an attorney in Boothbay Harbor. She later worked for Samples Shipyard for a brief period before starting her own real estate business in 1957. She retired in 1982. Olive passed away on May 4, 1991, at the age of 90.

JOHN SWETT
Private First Class, U.S. Army

John enlisted in the army in 1946, at the age of 17. He had been attending Richmond High School prior to that time. He received his basic training at Fort Belvoir, Virginia, and became part of the Combat Engineers, who specialized in dismantling explosives and building bridges. He received specialized training for two months while there to learn how to work safely with explosives.

He served with the Combat Engineers in Gorizia and Trieste, Italy. While he was there, he became part of an elite group of troops known as the "T.R.U.S.T.," which stands for Trieste – U.S. Troops. The group was made up from American, British, French, and Italian forces, and was 20,000 men strong. Their job was to dismantle explosives that were left over from the war and to rebuild bridges that had been destroyed during the fighting.

There were camps of German prisoners set up all over the areas John served in. They were used as workers in post-war Italy cleaning the soldiers' clothes and serving their food. They were later returned to Germany. John was sent back to Fort Wadsworth in New York after one year's time in Italy. He was later reassigned to Fort Dix, New Jersey, where he served in the ambulance corps.

John served for 18 months and was discharged in March of 1948. He received the European Theater of War Medal and the World War II Victory Medal for his service. After the war he went fishing with his father Leon from 1948 to 1950. He then made his living as a truck driver and married his girlfriend Lois Rathbun from Cranston, Rhode Island, in 1953. In 1958, he went to work at the Mystic Seaport in Mystic, Connecticut. He became the supervisor in 1965 and retired from that position in September of 1994. John currently lives in Mystic with his wife of 43 years, Lois.

LESLIE SWETT
Private, Army Air Corps

Leslie enlisted in the Army Air Corps on September 19, 1940, at the age of 27, and served with the 19th Airbase Squadron at Nichols Field in Manila. He had been a lobsterman prior to that time.

The base where he was stationed was later overrun by the Japanese, and Leslie, along with the other men, was taken prisoner. He was reported missing May 7, 1942, and no further word was received by his family until 1945, when the Americans recaptured the islands. It was then confirmed by the War Department in Washington, D.C.,

Leslie Swett, Army Air Corps

that Leslie had survived the Bataan Death March. (The Japanese marched the captured prisoners in early April of 1942 from Mariveles 55 miles to the railhead at San Fernando under the most inhumane conditions. During the march 2,300 Americans and between 7–10,000 Filipinos died.) Leslie later died of dysentery in a prison camp located in the northern part of the island. Leslie was Southport's first war casualty.

Below you will find excerpts from letters written to Minnie Hart of Southport from Leslie Swett in Manila. As the letters progress, note the feeling that things are starting to build up around him. More men are coming and no one is being sent home on rotation. Apparently the last mail Leslie sent was Christmas cards to everyone back home. Minnie's never arrived.

March 28, 1941

Have traveled around the world half way, when one reaches here. Had a stop in Panama, San Francisco, Hawaii, Guam and on to the Philippine Islands. Stationed at Hicham Field for four days while in Hawaii. Manila very beautiful. Had to sleep in tents until barracks are completed. Both bombers and pursuit planes are stationed here. A great thrill is to wake up at daylight and see them all on the line ready to take off at dawn. Several of the boys are from Maine and Massachusetts. A regular down east crew as the sergeant puts it.

Love, Leslie

April 20, 1941

Really appreciate you sending the *Boothbay Register*. You can't imagine how much one can enjoy reading about the local news when one is so far away from home. I have been put on guard duty, one night on and one night off. Looks like I will stay on for a couple of months at the least, until new recruits arrive from the states. We are now on our way to the hot and rainy season, several days the temperature has been up to 99 degrees. Don't get to town very often as only half the personnel can leave the post at one time, guess they call it an emergency as we always used to leave about any time when not on duty. I have seen several plane crashes lately. Seems as if it gets to be a habit, when one crashes there is always a couple more to follow. Have a lot of young pilots just came over from the states and do not have much flying time, maybe that is the reason.

Love, Leslie

July 19, 1941

Have been getting around the country slow but sure, there are several interesting places that I hope to visit before we return, which is a long time yet. Perhaps you noticed that our time has been extended for the duration of our enlistmen. Which means three years of foreign service then again they say it might be for the duration of the war, whatever that might be. Have acquired me a portable radio which is very pleasant to have. Much of my spare time is spent reading and with the company of the radio. Am in hopes to buy a camera soon. Many good pictures to be had.

P.S. Please excuse writing, am writing when on guard on a small board, also have an eye for the D.D.

Love, Leslie

September 24, 1941

Have had a couple of blackouts this month, they were all quite successful and interesting to be a part of. Maybe they soon will have to be more real, but at present the war situation is very quiet. There are a large number of troops still arriving from the United States and no one is being discharged or sent back to the U.S. from here. How is Amby making out in the Army? What are the rest of the boys doing? Be sure and write and tell me all the news from there. Not much good at writing myself, but will try and answer them all.

Best wishes to all.

Love, Leslie

Raymond Swett

Motor Machinist's Mate Third Class, U.S. Navy

Raymond Swett, U.S. Navy

Raymond enlisted in the Navy on February 24, 1944, at the age of 34. He received his basic training at Sampson Naval Training Station in New York. He served on the *U.S.S. Neunzer* D.E. 150 (destroyer escort), and was stationed in South Hampton, England, and Belfast, Northern Ireland. He had been employed as a machinist at the Bath Iron Works prior to that time.

The crew of the *U.S.S. Neunzer* witnessed their sister destroyer escort, the *Frederick C. Davis*, torpedoed and sunk with almost all aboard, and in the following action, helped destroy the German submarine, U-546. Raymond was discharged on November 7, 1945, in Boston, Massachusetts, after one year and nine months in the Navy. He was awarded the European African Middle Eastern Campaign Ribbon, World War II Victory Medal, and the Good Conduct Award for his service.

Raymond was married to Charlotte Parker from Gardiner, Maine, in December of 1945. Together they raised four children: Raymond, Jean,

Pamela, and Bobby. He returned to B.I.W. as an outside machinist, and retired from that position in the late 1960s after working for over 30 years in the shipyard. Raymond passed away in June of 1969 at the age of 59.

MAURICE TAYLOR
Chief Petty Officer, Navy Seabees

*Maurice Taylor,
Navy Seabees*

Maurice was 33 years old when he enlisted in the Navy Seabees. The year was 1943 and he had been working as a ships carpenter on mine sweepers at Samples Shipyard in Boothbay Harbor, Maine. He married Alvina Webber from Southport in August of 1935, and they were expecting their first child when he went into the service.

When he boarded the train to go to boot camp an officer singled him out, handed him all the train tickets and papers for the troops, and said, "You're in charge." Maurice met up with Norman Gaudette from Southport while on board. He had been on leave and was going back on duty. It was Norman's last visit to Southport, because he was later killed in action while in northeastern France.

He also met Howard Brewer of Boothbay Harbor when he went up to see the draft board in Wiscasset. Later, when Maurice was standing in a chow line in Davisville, Rhode Island, he heard someone call out "Hey Boothbay!" It was Howard again and they continued to see each other throughout Europe because they were both assigned to the same outfit. Howard was always telling his friends stories about home — like the time he told his friends that people in Maine ate hot minced pie for breakfast — and when they wouldn't believe him, he would find Maurice to confirm them for him.

Maurice went through basic training at Camp Allen in Norfolk, Virginia, then was sent to Camp Perry in Williamsburg as replacements for outfits that were being sent overseas. This is where his battalion, the 69th, was formed. Seabees received military training just like the infantry. He later went to Camp Endicott in Davisville, Rhode Island, for advanced training.

While at Camp Allen, an entire barracks on the base was quarantined. Maurice heard the reason was because someone had caught meningitis. Many years later, when Ed Fenderson came to Southport as its new Methodist minister, Maurice found out that it was Ed who had caused the quarantine. During the summer of 1944 the 69th battalion split up. Maurice's section went to Europe and Ed's went to the Pacific.

Before shipping off to Europe, Maurice's outfit spent six months in Argentia, Newfoundland, working on a base for the Navy, Air Corps, and Army. It had been started by civilian workers and the 14th battalion. Maurice worked finishing the Navy's portion of the base. While there, one of Maurice's friends asked a native, "When does summer start?" The man replied, "It came one Sunday last year, and when it started to warm up I took a nap, but when I woke up summer was over." The land was not very good for farming where Maurice was, but they could raise some potatoes, cabbage, carrots and beets. The locals made a liquor out of the potatoes which was called "Newfie Screech."

The fog was very thick in Newfoundland, and for a two-week period the mail plane couldn't even land. There was a terminal for the Newfoundland Narrow Gauge Railroad in Argentia, so when Maurice received a pass to go on leave, he decided to go to St. John, which was about 60 miles away. He boarded the "Newfie Express" as it was fondly referred to, and after riding all day arrived in St. John. He later found out that it would have only taken a few hours to get there if he had used the local taxi service.

The 69th battalion received orders to return to Davisville, Rhode Island. Maurice boarded an old passenger ship that had been made over into a troop ship. The ship was escorted by two destroyers. It was a very rough, and Maurice had been out on deck during the crossing, until an officer made him go inside. Later, as he watched the destroyers, the waves were breaking over their smokestacks. During the night the transport ship rolled to 40 degrees, which was the hardest they had ever recorded. It was so rough even one lifeboat washed off deck.

The next morning, when Maurice woke up, he kept hearing a loud banging noise. After some investigation, he discovered some steel lockers on board had broken loose and were sliding back and forth as the ship rolled from side to side. The men had to eat standing up that next morning, which was a real challenge. The tables on board had two heights they could be set at, so you could eat either sitting down or standing. Also you had to keep one hand on your tray or it would easily slide off the table onto the floor.

The men went through further training in Rhode Island just before the June 7th invasion of France. They went to Brooklyn, New York, by train and got on the transport ship S.S. *General William Mitchell*. The crossing took ten days and they landed in Liverpool, England. On board Maurice met up with Donald Boyd from Boothbay Harbor. There were lots of bombed out buildings and the remains of several smaller ships that had been sunk were still in the harbor. The 69th battalion then boarded a train which took them to Plymouth, England, where they started building pontoon wharves and docks that would be towed across the channel to France. During the summer of 1944 the Seabees ran two work shifts daily in England. Maurice created a carpenter shop in a bomb shelter and stayed there until he received orders to go to France.

The 69th battalion arrived at Omaha Beach to relieve a battalion that had been there since D-Day. They spent six weeks there, and Maurice said that there wasn't a lot left standing on the coast, and the mud was awful. The men lived in tents, and Maurice's first duty was to set up oil burners in all the tents. He and his friend Benjamin Deane, who was from California, set up the carpenter's shop off to one side of the tents, and were kept busy there until they were sent back to England for the winter.

Maurice vividly remembers picking up an issue of *Stars and Stripes* in England and reading the headline, "Les Brewer has record breaking herring catch in Southport, Maine." It was really a nice surprise. Later, in France, he read about the fire that destroyed the Newagen Inn.

The 69th was transferred to Belgium by troop ship. Once there they were issued ammunition and went by convoy through Holland to Bremen, Germany. At one point they were held up for two or three days in Holland while the British were in the process of taking over the city of Bremen. The men were put up at Nempcel Kazarne on the Brunneweg Strasse in Verden, which had once been a German cavalry school. Maurice's first assignment in Bremen was to go to the submarine yard and take all the plans and blueprints he and his detachment could find, crate them up, and send them back to the United States. They then set the yard up for U.S. Navy submarines.

When the 69th battalion first moved into Bremen, they had to post a guard at the old school because the regular Navy had not arrived yet with MPs (military police). One night a friend of Maurice's was on guard duty and it was really dark. The man kept hearing something walking towards him so he hollered, "Halt!" Whatever it was didn't stop walking and he wondered if he should shoot. Pretty soon an old horse wandered into sight. It hadn't been fed well and was really thin, so he let it in the entrance gate. A guy in the battalion was from the west and immediately adopted the horse. In three or four weeks, with some tender loving care, he had that horse looking great and even managed to find a bridle and rode it around the compound.

Maurice heard a rumor two days before it was officially confirmed that the Germans had surrendered. That would mean that the older men in the battalion would be discharged and Maurice got his hopes up that he would soon be going home. Whenever there was an empty plane, men from the battalion were being flown back to England. A detachment was assigned to go to Frankfurt-am-Main, Germany, to set up Naval Headquarters. After checking the roster, Maurice discovered his name was on the list to go to Germany.

Maurice's workshop at Omaha Beach. His friend, Ben Deane, is pictured on the right.

Maurice set up his carpenter shop in the basement of a barracks. It was in really hard shape and he had to replace most of the windows in it. The barracks was located at the end of a street. There was a gas station that still worked on one side and on the other side was a building that had been bombed. As Maurice looked up at it he noticed that one side of it had been torn off by the blast. On the second floor he could see what was left of a bathroom. The tub and mirror were still there, but everything else was gone.

There were German carpenters from the town that helped work on the barracks. Maurice shared his tools with them and one man in particular used to visit Maurice quite often. Maurice finally caught on that the man didn't really have that many questions to ask, he just liked the George Washington Tobacco Maurice smoked in his pipe, and wanted to fill his on every visit.

The Germans built an arena near Hamburg for the Olympic Games before the war, but never had used it. It had a large swimming pool and stadium. The Americans took it over as a recreational place for the troops, and Maurice was able to swim there one night a week, because it wasn't that far away from his workshop.

One day the Chief Carpenters Mate, who really didn't know much about carpentry, appeared with a slip of paper that had specific dimensions on it for a double door with glass panes for the recreational hall. Navy personnel had converted an unused garage into a recreation hall for the men to use while they were in Bremen. The dimensions for the glass were backwards on the slip of paper. The height was written down as the width and vice versa. One of the men in Maurice's crew, who had been employed by Sears and Roebuck in Portland, Maine, noticed the mistake right away and brought the paper to Maurice.

The man asked him, "What do you want to do?" Maurice replied, "You were told to follow orders, so make the door even if the orders are wrong, and whatever you do don't lose that slip!" It was quite a job to complete, but the men made a really nice door, and when it was finished Maurice told them to send word to the recreation hall. Two guys came over to pick it up and said, "That isn't right." Maurice said smiling, "Well, it's made according to the specifications we received." With the original order in his pocket Maurice walked over to the recreation hall, where he met the officer in charge. The man asked him, "What's going on?"

Maurice explained the situation and told him who had designed the door. The Chief Carpenters Mate really got chewed out, and the doors were hung just the same, with the panes of glass going horizontally instead of vertically.

Maurice left Germany on a convoy of trucks, which took him to Le Havre, France, where he waited for a transport ship to come and take him home. There were a lot of soldiers that had been waiting there longer than the Seabees and they got to go home first. Ship after ship left loaded with soldiers and the Seabees were getting a little impatient. When the Seabee's Officers discovered that the troop ships had empty quarters on board, designated for armed guards that had originally been on board to defend the ship from submarine attack, they decided to start sending their own men home a few at a time in these facilities. The armed guards had been left in the U.S. after Germany surrendered. Unfortunately the Army caught on and put a stop to it.

Finally the rest of the 69th battalion was told they were definitely going home. They were put on a Liberty Ship, which took them to Boston Harbor. Maurice immediately found a telephone when they landed and called his wife Alvina for the first time in well over a year and a half. Maurice was sent to Davisville, Rhode Island, for a week, then he came home on leave for 30 days. His daughter Kathryn had been born on September 30, 1944, while he was in England. Maurice received a letter from his wife Alvina telling him he had a new baby daughter, just before he went across the Channel to Omaha Beach, in France. Maurice arrived in Southport just before Kathryn's first birthday.

At the end of his leave, Maurice returned to Boston and was discharged on October 25, 1945. He had served two years, ten months, and 25 days in the Navy Seabees and was awarded the European Theater of War Medal. He returned to Southport after the war, and worked as a self-employed builder for many years. Maurice currently lives on Southport, with his wife of 61 years, Alvina.

JOHN THOMPSON
Coxswain, U.S. Navy

John enlisted in the Navy on August 17, 1942, at the age of 24. He married Marcia Wright of Portland in April of 1945, and had been working for W.L. Blake, a plumbing company in Portland, prior to that time. He served in Boston; Little Creek, Virginia; and Aragonite, Newfoundland. While there he bumped into Marcia's cousin, Merritt Wright from South Portland, who was in the Coast Guard. He also saw the Eddie Douchin Orchestra play as part of a USO show.

Pictured on the left, John Thompson, U.S. Navy. His brother, Stuart, appears on the right.

The Coconut Grove fire occurred while John was stationed in Boston. He along with other servicemen in the area were called upon to help clean it up. It was a terrible tragedy, because many lives were lost needlessly. The fire exits had been blocked by tables, as the management tried to fit more people into the nightclub.

John ran a shuttle boat between his ship and the shore while he was in the Navy. He was discharged in Williamsburg, Virginia, on October 3, 1945, and was awarded the American Theater Ribbon, World War II Victory Medal, and the Good Conduct Award for his service. After the war he worked for the J.E. Goold Company, in Portland, which is a wholesale drug business. John passed away on December 27, 1980, at the age of 62.

ntia?

ROSS STUART THOMPSON
Boatswains Mate First Class,
U.S. Coast Guard

Stuart enlisted in the Coast Guard on July 22, 1942, at the age of 22. He received his basic training at Manhattan Beach, New York, and was later stationed on Faulkner Island Light Station, North Dumpling Light, and at Fishers Island, all located in the Long Island Sound. He had been employed as a ships' carpenter at Hodgdon Brothers Shipyard in East Boothbay prior to that time.

Stuart Thompson,
U.S. Coast Guard

He was later assigned to the Army Transport, *General W.P. Richardson* AP 118. She was manned by the Coast Guard, but was under the control of the Navy. Stuart helped put the ship into commission, for which he was awarded a plank owner's certificate and also decommissioned the ship at the war's end.

One day while Stuart was standing watch on North Dumpling Light Station in the Long Island Sound, he saw a fishing boat foundering nearby. He launched a lifeboat singlehandedly and, as he approached the boat, he could see a man overboard, so he rowed toward him and pulled him into the lifeboat. It was a stormy, winter day and the sea had quite a swell going, so it wasn't the easiest thing to do alone. Stuart learned the man's name was Joseph Dolan when he got him aboard, and that he lived nearby, so he took him to his house once they were ashore. Mrs. Dolan was rather surprised when the men came to her door, completely encased in ice, but she quickly regained her composure and started running hot baths in her two bathtubs — fortunately she had two bathrooms! Once they were full, she ordered the men in with the hopes of thawing them out.

Stuart made over eight round trip crossings of the Atlantic during his service. At first his ship was painted in camouflage and was assigned to convoy duty. She was so new and fast, she easily outran the other ships

Army Transport, General W.P. Richardson AP 118.
Shown above painted gray, and below painted with a
camouflage pattern, to help disguise her during convoy duty.

in the convoy as well as enemy submarines. The *Richardson* soon received new orders to be repainted gray and to travel the North Atlantic alone. She often departed from New York, New York; Boston, Massachusetts; Hampton Road, Portsmouth; and Newport News, Virginia.

Her destinations included: Southhampton, England; Marseilles and Le Havre, France; Trinidad, Spain; Port Said and Suez, Egypt; Karachi, India; Khorramshahr, Iran; Casablanca, French Morocco, and Naples, Italy. When she traveled through the Suez Canal, men pulled the *Richardson* through by hand, on ropes.

Stuart's ship always entered a port in the Mediterranean Sea under the cover of darkness, because it was safer that way. When they arrived in Naples, the ship's captain held back entering the port, due to the amount of light coming from it. The crew soon learned that the light was coming from the eruption of the volcano on Mt. Vesuvius. Morocco, on the other hand, was a free city, meaning it was neutral, and didn't have blackout conditions, which was dangerous to the ship. Stuart recalled entering the sea, and seeing the city ablaze with light and activity. Blackout conditions were very important during the war, because light would silhouette a ship, making it an easy target for enemy submarines.

Stuart ran into many people he knew from home, including Norman Lewis of Southport at Staten Island, New York; Ed Clifford of East Boothbay as he transported him across the Atlantic; Lawrence Boyd of Southport, bringing him back from France; and Merle Hyson of Boothbay, who Stuart transported to Europe and back. The one thing Stuart never got used to during his numerous voyages during the war was bringing the wounded soldiers back. It was very difficult to see so many men suffering.

Stuart was discharged on February 20, 1946, after three years and seven months of service, due to his eligibility under the points system. He was awarded the American Area Medal, European African Middle Eastern Campaign Medal, World War II Victory Medal, and the Good Conduct Award. After the war he worked with Leon Duprey buying and selling lobsters for Maynard Robinson up and down the Maine coast. He was married to his long-time girlfriend, Jean Luther, on June 21, 1947, and later had two daughters, Mary Lou and Anne. In 1951, Stuart took over his father's position as superintendent of the Southport Water Supply, which he ran for 21 years. He also worked with Maurice Sherman as a self- employed builder over the years, and owned and operated the town school bus. Stuart passed away on September 9, 1988, at the age of 67.

EDWARD TIBBETTS
Corporal, U.S. Army

Edward was drafted into the army at the age of 18 in 1944. He went to Camp Blanding in Florida for his basic training and later went to Camp Ruker in Alabama, where he joined the 66th Infantry Division . He had been lobstering and seining with his father, Walter, Sr., on Southport prior to that time.

From Camp Shanks in New York he boarded the troop ship *U.S.S. George Washington*, which was headed for Dorchester, England. Austin Snowman from Southport had served on this same ship when he was in the Merchant Marine. It originally belonged to the Germans, but had been captured during the First World War.

On December 24, 1944, Edward boarded a Belgian ship, the *Leopoleville*, which was transporting troops to France. Around eight o'clock at night the ship was torpedoed by a German submarine. The torpedo hit in the hold, just below Edward's quarters, and between 800 to 1000 men were lost. Another ship came up alongside them and the

Edward Tibbetts, U.S. Army

men were instructed to swing over to it on a knotted rope. It was cold, dark, and really rough. There were 20 to 25 foot seas, and all Edward could think of was that he really didn't want to fall into that water under any circumstances. With his life jacket on, Edward grabbed the rope and successfully swung across to the other ship, which took the men to Le Havre, France. The torpedoed ship sank in less than four hours.

Edward met Parker Reed from Boothbay Harbor while he was training in Florida. They were in the same outfit, but were in different companies. Parker was washed off the *Leopoleville* when it was torpedoed and was picked up by a rescue boat, which took him ashore. Edward and Parker saw each other from time to time after that, while they were stationed in Europe.

Edward's division regrouped and they stayed in France for the rest of the war. It was very cold and they slept in sleeping bags on the ground. He said one morning he woke up and it had snowed about 12 inches the night before. Everyone was covered in snow and couldn't find their boots, which they had taken off before they went to sleep.

The men guarded two German pockets; one was St. Nazant and the other was Lorient. They had bunkers to live in which had small stoves, but you had to be careful that they didn't smoke too much. Also, when it rained, you had to bail them out. Edward was in St. Nazant when VE Day was announced.

Then he was part of the Army of Occupation that went into Germany. He really saw a lot of destruction there, especially bombed out buildings. Edward found out his brother Walter was in a nearby town and got a pass to go and see him. By the time he got there Walter's unit had shipped out. It was the closest Edward ever got to seeing him during the war.

Later he was sent back to Marseille in southern France, to help run a camp for U.S. troops who were coming back from Germany. He got a pass to go to Paris while he was there and took advantage of it, by going to see the Eiffel Tower, Tomb of the Unknown Soldier, and other famous attractions. Even though Paris had been liberated, there were still signs of the German occupation around. Next he was transferred to the 11th Engineers company and went to Salzburg, Austria, where he worked in the mountains.

Edward was sent to Linz, Austria, as part of the Army of Occupation and stayed there until he came home. While there one of his duties was to guard one end of a bridge. Russian soldiers guarded the other end. Often they would meet in the middle of the bridge and would try to talk to each other. The Russian soldiers always wanted to know if Edward had a Mickey Mouse watch, because they wanted to trade with him for it. It apparently was a popular item with them.

At one point Edward drove a ration truck while he was in Austria and he was responsible for picking up bread, eggs, and other boxed goods. It was then that he witnessed a Displaced Persons Camp. Men and women from Yugoslavia, Hungary, Romania, and Czechoslovakia had been taken from their homes by the Germans and were forced to work in their factories as slave labor. Some were as young as 15. Now they had no way to get back and didn't even know if they had a home waiting for them. The U.S. military offered them shelter and food, and they occupied several barracks on the base.

Edward also helped guard German P.O.W.s and supervised them while they were on work details. Most of them were just ordinary soldiers who went to war when their country called. They were willing to work and didn't cause any problems. On the other hand, there were some German SS who felt they were superior, even over their own infantry soldiers. They didn't want to be held in the same barracks with them and they didn't want to work. Edward and the other guards would always find an infantry soldier who could speak English and they would put him in charge of the work detail. It really made the German SS angry and it delighted the men from the infantry. I guess you would call it a morale builder.

Edward was finally sent back to the United States by ship. The trip took ten days and it was really rough. When they landed in New York, the longshoremen and tugboats were on strike and refused to help dock the ship. The captain waited for a while, but then decided that he would go in without them. He radioed ahead and said "You'd better tell those strikers to move, because I've got a ship full of sick soldiers and I'm coming in." It ended up that Red Cross volunteers helped take the lines and secured the troop ship. Edward thought it was quite ironic at the time that, instead of receiving a hero's welcome as he and the other soldiers came ashore, they were met by strikers picketing the docks.

Edward went on to Fort Dix, New Jersey, where he was discharged. He then caught the train from New York to Boston, and in Boston switched trains and headed for Portland. Then he got on a bus that brought him to Wiscasset. At the time his parents didn't have a telephone, so he had to hitchhike back to Southport. It was now June of 1946 and he had been gone for two years and one month. Edward was awarded the European African Middle Eastern Campaign Ribbon with one bronze star, and the Good Conduct Medal for his service. He currently lives on Southport, where he makes his living as a lobsterman.

GEORGE TIBBETTS
Private First Class, U.S. Army

George was drafted into the Army in February of 1943, at the age of 18. He had been a lobsterman on Southport at the time, and lobsters were then selling for .18 cents a pound. He went to boot camp at Camp Swift in Texas and later went on maneuvers in Louisiana, Missouri, and Norfolk, Virginia.

While training at Camp Swift, George noticed that the black and white soldiers were segregated from each other. They had separate barracks, mess halls, and even drinking fountains. One day George got on a

George Tibbetts, U.S. Army

bus to go into town. The seats in the front of the bus were full, so he found an empty one in the back. During this time period in America, the back of the bus was where black people were "expected" to sit. George noticed the bus was not moving and pretty soon the bus driver called out to him. "Hey soldier, I'm not moving this bus until you come and sit down front, we don't do that here." George was really stunned. He hadn't encountered prejudice like this before in the North.

He left Norfolk on a troop ship headed for India. The voyage took 33 days. It was hot and rough, and George was seasick the entire voyage. The men were fed an orange in the morning and a sandwich at night, and were not allowed up on deck. They sailed over the Equator twice enroute and made a stop in South Africa, where they were allowed 12 hours shore leave. When the ship prepared to leave the port, word spread around that several men had deserted. George later found out nearly 30 men were gone and to this day has always wondered what happened to them.

The next stop was Bombay, India. George boarded a train and was on it for three or four days. The heat was almost unbearable and the trip was extremely slow. When the train made stops, people would come up to it looking for food. The GIs had corned beef and rice, which was eagerly accepted by the local people. It didn't seem to George that these people even had houses to live in. They just made a camp wherever they were and did their best to survive the obvious poverty they lived in.

George and about 20 other men then got on a plane heading to North Burma. It was flown into the combat zone near Myitkyina in the mountains. The airfield was crude and incoming airplanes could land, but they couldn't fly out, so they had to remain there until further construction was completed. Crews worked nonstop to expand the airstrip, which they eventually did while George was there. George and the other men were coming in as replacements for Merrill's Marauders. They were an outfit that was specially trained to go in over the mountains to get the Japanese out.

There were British troops on the mountain and at one point the U.S. Army ran out of K and C rations, which were the soldiers' food supply that came in a box about the size of a VCR tape. Each box contained a can of meat, some crackers, a chocolate bar, cigarettes, etc. Due to the American's ration shortage, the British air dropped some of their rations to them in five gallon square cans. British rations consisted of a biscuit and tea, and each can was supposed to feed 25 men for the whole day. It was not what George would call a meal. There was no field kitchen on the mountain and the troops had to make do with what they had.

Nearly 200 of the men in George's unit were killed in their first skirmish with the Japanese. The high command had misjudged the position and strength of the Japanese troops and sent the American GIs into a nearby valley, where they became sitting ducks for the Japanese, who were dug in the surrounding hills. George said, "If it weren't for the courage and leadership of the Captain in my unit, none of us would have made it out of that valley alive." Many of the men, including

George, wondered what real significance this mountain held. The jungle was thick and it rained all the time. The bugs were innumerable and the food was scarce. While on duty, George was severely wounded. He had been in Burma for only a month.

George had been shot in the head and was immediately taken back to a field hospital, where he was unconscious for over three weeks. When he came to, he thought it was the next day. George was later transferred to a hospital in India, where it was discovered he was suffering from malaria in addition to his head wound.

At one point near the end of his stay in the hospital in India, one of the nurses helping to put his boots on noticed one wasn't going on very well. When she pulled it off his foot, the largest spider George had ever seen crawled out of it. The spider had made a nest inside his boot while he'd been unconscious, and no one had noticed it.

Once George was well enough to travel, the doctors decided to fly him back to the United States. On the way home he passed through Egypt, where he was able to see the great pyramids. George spent a year's time in three different hospitals after arriving back in the U.S. He recuperated in Miami, New York, and finally in Framingham, Massachusetts. President Truman had started integrating the military hospitals at this time. Sometimes George would have black nurses check in on him. He remembers they were always very cautious about taking his pulse. He thinks they must have thought he would react badly to having a black nurse take care of him.

George was discharged in May of 1945 after two years and three months of service, and earned the China Burma India Campaign Ribbon, and the Purple Heart for his sacrifices. He returned to Southport, started lobstering again, and married Barbara Rand on February 3, 1946. George thought it had been hard to make a living on Southport when he left to go in the Army, but now there seemed to be more money around. George is still lobstering, and currently lives on Southport with his wife of 50 years, Barbara.

WALTER TIBBETTS, JR.
Corporal T5, U.S. Army

Walter was drafted into the Army on November 17, 1942. He received his training in Texas at Camp Maxi and Camp Swift, and was part of the 327th Engineering Battalion. Prior to that time he had been lobstering and seining for herring. Due to his experience on the water, Walter was assigned to the Army Engineers and operated a motor boat for them. His duties included hauling troops, ammunition, and equipment across rivers.

Walter Tibbetts, Jr., U.S. Army

Walter served in Rhineland and in Central Europe. He was responsible for the safety of the cargo he carried while crossing rivers and frequently was under enemy fire while performing his duties. He participated in the crossing of the Rhine River and helped with the building of a bridge across it as the Allies pushed Hitler's Army further back into Germany. He was assigned to boat #13, but no one in his outfit wanted to get in it, because they figured it was jinxed, and they wouldn't make it across. The boat soon proved them wrong, and made many successful trips back and forth carrying supplies.

Walter was discharged on February 9, 1946, at Fort Devens, Massachusetts, after three years and three months of service. He was awarded the American Theater Campaign Ribbon, the European African Middle Eastern Theater Ribbon, the World War Two Victory Medal, and the Good Conduct Medal. He returned to Southport and married Eleanor Thibodeau from Friendship on December 11, 1965. Walter made his living as a fisherman on Southport. He passed away on November 16, 1976.

HAROLD WEBBER
Staff Sergeant, U.S. Army

Harold Webber, U.S. Army

Harold and his wife Phyllis purchased a small cape style house in Bath, Maine. They moved in on December 7, 1941, only to turn on their radio and hear the news that Pearl Harbor had been bombed by the Japanese. Harold turned to Phyllis and said, "I won't be here long." He and his wife were wed just about a year prior to this time, on December 28, 1940, so he was not called into service until 1944, at the age of 25. As a rule, the Army called up unwed men first, and when Harold left, his daughter Judy was only three years old. Prior to that time, Harold worked for four years as a welder at the Bath Iron Works.

He went to Camp Croft in South Carolina for three months of boot camp, but it was cut short because the Army needed men in Europe, so they shipped him over. While at Camp Croft he met Henry Dixon, who had been a classmate of his at Boothbay Region High School. Henry was the company clerk and would always check the new names on the roster. When he saw Harold on the list, he kept an eye out for him and made sure he found him when he arrived.

Harold sailed from New York on the *Queen Mary* to Glasgow, Scotland. Then he traveled through England by train to South Hampton, where he picked up a ferry to Le Havre, France. He was in the machine gun squad of the 87th Division, 345 Regiment, First Battalion Charlie Company. They arrived in Germany just after the Battle of the Bulge. Harold and three or four other men were replacements in the division. He said it was really hard going in that way, because you didn't know any one there. Within a few days one of the men he came in with was dead. It almost became easier to not make close friends, because you never knew when you were going to lose them.

Sometime in March, Harold and his squad were paddling across the Rhine River south of Koblenz in assault boats. The boats were made out of plywood and looked like a square-ended punt. Each man had a paddle and they encountered light rifle fire from some Germans as they were crossing.

Harold met three Russians while he was in Germany. They had recently been held as P.O.W.s, but had been released when the Germans surrendered. They tried to talk with each other, but the language barrier got in the way. Harold also saw a lot of B-7 bombers flying overhead in Germany. When they returned from their missions, they flew in the same formation, and you could count how many were missing.

On April 15, 1945, Harold and two men from his squad were guarding a town at one end of a road. Their post consisted of a rifleman and two men

Harold's Bronze Star Medal, which was awarded in Germany when his squad of three men held their ground and captured 28 German soldiers.

on a machine gun. Some German soldiers started firing on them, but the men held their ground and pretty soon the Germans ran out of ammo. A white flag of surrender was raised on a rifle so Harold and his two friends captured the men. There were 28 German soldiers in all and Harold and his squad were awarded the Bronze Star.

On VE Day (Victory in Europe), Harold's regiment was ten miles inside the Czechoslovakian border. It was beautiful country filled with hills and rolling valleys. One day a U.S. P-38 twin engine fighter came up behind his unit. As they watched it glided through the valley from side to side. The pilot was having great fun and it looked like a good time to Harold. Later he watched as a P-51 chased a German fighter behind a mountain, machine gun fire was heard, and the P-51 came out from behind the mountain, but the German aircraft did not. Coming back from Czechoslovakia, they passed through Plauen, Germany. The British had extensively bombed the city and it smelled horrible, because there were many bodies left in the rubble that hadn't been taken care of.

Harold made a big mistake as the Army was withdrawing, on its way back to France. He was offered a pass to go to Paris on leave and didn't accept it. He really wishes he had now. At this point the men were slowly being shipped back to the Atlantic coast. When Harold returned, he was told that he would be part of an invasion of Japan. He was sent home on a one month furlough and during this time VJ Day (Victory in Japan) was announced.

When his leave was over Harold went to Fort Benning in Georgia where his regiment was broken up. He was sent to Fort Devens, where he was a typist in the office of one of the motor pools. The first Staff Sergeant got appendicitis and there were no other Sergeants available, so they gave Harold Buck Sergeant stripes and sent him to the Staff Sergeant's desk. Finally a real first Sergeant showed up and Harold was put in charge of a work detail that started closing up the camp. It was here that he made Staff Sergeant. He got a military drivers license and drove a dump truck around the base cleaning barracks up so they could be closed.

Harold was discharged in September of 1946 after two years of service and was awarded the Bronze Star, Combat Infantry Badge, European Theater of War ribbon, Good Conduct Medal, and the World War Two Victory Medal. He joined the Army reserves at this time and in September of 1950 was called back to serve in the Korean War.

When the men were shipping out, Harold's name was cut off the bottom of the assignment roster and, instead of going to Korea, he boarded a plane headed for Frankfurt, Germany. Harold served in Trieste, Italy, which is on the border of Yugoslavia, for one year. At the time it was thought that it would become another hot spot like Korea and there was a regiment of U.S., British, and French troops stationed on the border. Sometime before September Harold was shipped to Fort Benning in Georgia, was discharged at Fort Devens, and finally was sent home to Southport.

Harold went to work as a carpenter for Bill Luther and Maurice Taylor, on Southport after the war. Then he worked for Cliff Brewer, at his boatyard in Boothbay Harbor, which later moved on to Southport. Harold also worked for Norman Hodgdon in Boothbay Harbor, until Norman passed away, and Bob Fish took over his operation. Harold retired in 1981, and currently lives on Southport, where he is a caretaker for several cottages on the island.

ELIOT WINSLOW
Lieutenant, U.S. Navy
and Coast Guard

Eliot enlisted in the Navy in November of 1939, at the age of 32. At the time, President Roosevelt had declared all single men in the United States, 32 and under, must serve their country for one year. Eliot met both criteria and soon found himself training on a fishing dragger that had been converted into a mine sweeper in Boston Harbor. He had been selling

Eliot Winslow, U.S. Navy
and Coast Guard

paint at Hancock Paint and Varnish Company in Quincy, Massachusetts, prior to that time.

There were still two dories on the converted dragger and they were used whenever work needed to be done to its exterior. Eliot could easily scull a dory, which both fascinated and infuriated the Chief Boatswain's Mate, and he told Eliot, "I don't want to see you rowing standing up, we look stupid enough now as it is."

One day Eliot had the choice of scraping paint or rowing across the harbor to get the mail for the mine sweeper in East Boston. He of course chose the latter, eyeing the opportunity to row the dory for a while and hating scraping paint with a passion. He rowed all the way over only to discover there was no mail that day. Eliot could hear that paint scraper calling his name, and when he found out a movie was being shown on one of the Navy ships that was anchored in the harbor, he decided to take it in.

Night had fallen by the time the movie was over and Eliot saw this as a perfect opportunity to row back standing up. He hadn't gone very far when a search light was placed on him and he couldn't see to row. It was the harbor police and they asked him, "Where are you going sailor?" Eliot replied, "Back to my ship, the *Puffin* at Pier 1." They said, "Throw us your painter and we'll give you a tow." Eliot did, and then he went to sit in the stern of the dory, to enjoy the ride. When the harbor police took off in the opposite direction of Pier 1, it occurred to Eliot that this might not have been such a good idea.

Back at the police station it was discovered that Eliot had no identification, no liberty card, and no dog tags. When he tried to explain that he had simply rowed ashore for the mail, the police soon found that he didn't have that either. Things were not looking too good for Eliot at this point. The police even went as far as to say, "How do we know you're not a spy, and you stole that uniform off of a clothesline somewhere?" At this point, Eliot knew he was in hot water, so out of desperation he said, "Call the *Puffin* and ask for the Chief." The police took him up on the offer and the conversation Eliot overheard went something like this.

"We picked up a guy claiming to be Eliot Winslow. He's got no identification and he was rowing a dory standing up when we apprehended him." At this point the Chief blew his stack and said, "That's the S.O.B., keep him there!" Which is exactly what the harbor police did, and Eliot ended up spending the night in jail. When he returned to the *Puffin* the next morning he knew he was in the doghouse when he saw the Chief waiting for him to board. As soon as he was on deck the Chief gave him Hell and said, "I told you so!"

In 1941, Eliot transferred to the U.S. Coast Guard. He was then assigned to a weather patrol off Greenland on the *Menemsha*. She was an old coal burning ship with no guns, and Eliot soon came to the conclusion that if they ever encountered the enemy, they could neither fight nor run, so he decided then and there that it was time for a transfer.

The Navy and Coast Guard buildings were located next to each other in Boston. Even so, his transfer took three months to go through. His new assignment was anti-submarine warfare on the Coast Guard cutter *Argo*. He ran convoy duty from New York to Key West, Florida. On one run they picked up an echo off the bottom which they thought was an enemy submarine. Depth charges were quickly released and oil soon surfaced. The men thought they had a sure hit, only to discover their target was an old sunken ship.

During this same period the Germans started using aspirin as a means of deception. They discovered that they could release large quantities of the substance in the water and, as they dissolved, Allied ships would pick up an echo on their sonars from the disturbance instead of the submarine, and it could make its escape. This method went undetected by the Allies until a captured crew member from a German sub slipped up and said the word *pillenwerfer*, which in German means pill that effervesces. It was then that the Allies caught on to what they were doing.

On each trip out of New York the *Argo* took new recruits on board to break them in. They were referred to as 90-day wonders at the time. Eliot bumped into a man from Augusta named Richard Sandborne on one particular trip. They got to talking and soon found out the man's father had a summer cottage on Grand View Road in Southport. Eliot and Richard kept in touch after the war and Richard later went on to become the Mayor of Augusta.

Just after VE Day was announced, three German submarines were intercepted off the gulf of Maine enroute to Japan. They had received a message on board telling them that the war was over, but they thought the code had been broken and it was a hoax. When they realized it was true, they surrendered. Eliot was assigned to escort them into Portsmouth. Using armed Marine guards, the submarines were boarded and the crews were separated. There were about 75 men in each crew and they were put aboard the *Argo*, where they were held in the chain locker and in the lazarette.

General Kessler, who led the blitz on Poland in 1939, was also captured on board one of the subs. Eliot said his demeanor was calm, cool, and collected. On the other hand, Captain Fenler, who was one of the skippers, came to Eliot and said, "My men have been treated like gangsters!" Eliot's response was, "That's what they are! Get the Hell off!" as he pointed his finger towards the door. A photographer was on board and captured the whole scene on film. Eliot's photo and a description of the encounter with the skipper was soon seen in newspapers all over the country.

The crews were transported to the prison in Portsmouth, New Hampshire, where they were held until they could be returned to Germany. While imprisoned there one of the captains committed suicide by slitting his wrists using the crystal from his watch. It was later discovered that one of the submarines had a false keel and tons of mercury were stored inside of it. The secret cargo was worth a small fortune and was intended to help perfect buzz bombs that were being used on England at the time.

The head of the New England district of the Navy contacted Eliot and asked him, "What would you like as a reward for this task you performed?" Eliot thought for a moment, then said he would like the chance to bring his ship to Southport. The request was granted and early one morning in 1945 the Coast Guard cutter *Argo* wound up in Ebenecook Harbor. A conversation overheard by the captain between two crew members went something like this, "Where are we?" "I don't know, but there's a spruce limb in every porthole."

Meanwhile Navy Headquarters was going out of its mind trying to pinpoint the location of the *Argo*. They had a long magnetic chart of the world set up showing the position of several ships out on various maneuvers. Apparently this chart didn't have Love's Cove on it and, even though the *Argo* was reporting her latitude and longitude, Navy Headquarters couldn't seem to find it. Needless to say, there were several radio messages sent back and forth to clarify their position.

At the time, Wardy McKown was overheard saying, "Only a damn fool or Eliot Winslow would bring a ship like that in here!" Eliot's parents, Charles and Alice, boarded the *Argo* and he took them for a cruise just off the end of Southport, near the Cuckhold's Light. His mother got very seasick during the trip and his father said, "If I ever marry again the first thing she'll be is a sailor." They eventually took mercy on Alice and put her off at the Gulf Dock in Boothbay Harbor.

The U-805, first submarine to surrender, is escorted by Coast Guard cutter Argo to Portsmouth, New Hampshire. Ten prisoners were stowed in the forward anchor chain locker, 20 aft over the screws, with five officers below decks, all under heavy guard.

Shortly after the war's end, Eliot received a package from the Navy. Inside the box was General Kessler's Iron Cross and one of the skipper's watches. Also enclosed was a letter that read, "In recognition of our verbal battle in Portsmouth."

Eliot's next assignment was also in the Gulf of Maine. As the military started bringing men home from Europe by plane, the Coast Guard and the Navy positioned their ships 100 or more miles apart all along the coast. The idea was if one of the planes had to ditch into the ocean, a ship would be nearby to pick its crew and passengers up.

Eliot was involved in three rescues during his service in both the Navy and Coast Guard. The first was off Greenland and he picked up four survivors in a lifeboat. The second was off North Carolina where a ship had sunk during a hurricane and they were able to rescue eight or ten men from the water. The third occurred on January 6th, 1944, when Barbara Hutton's yacht (she was an American socialite), the St. Augustine, was rammed and sunk by a new U.S. merchant ship coming out of Philadelphia. There were 26 survivors and the rest froze to death in the icy water. Eliot was awarded a Navy medal for his participation in the rescue effort.

Eliot was discharged on March 1, 1945, in Boston after serving for five years and four months. He was awarded the American Theater Ribbon and the Good Conduct Medal for his service. He came back to Southport and Maynard Robinson got him started in the cruise boat business. He also later started a tugboat business called Winslow Marine. Eliot and his wife of 35 years, Marjorie, live in Southport. They have one son, David, and they currently own and operate their tugboat business and Robinson's Wharf.

*Lieutenant General Ulric Kessler of the Luftwaffe,
captured aboard one of the three submarines intercepted off the
Gulf of Maine in May of 1945. He is pictured passing time aboard
the Argo. Note the timely topic he is reading.*

MAURICE SHERMAN: EPILOGUE TO STORY

The year was 1943, and Maurice found himself in Bizerte, North Africa, lying wounded in a drafty tent hospital. He soon struck up a friendship with a fellow from Brownsville, Texas, named D.T. Rogers, and they often told each other stories about their native states to help pass the time.

Maurice vividly remembers D.T. telling him about a six-foot rattlesnake he once found in his garden in Texas. The snake was coiled and ready to strike, so D.T. got a hoe and killed it. Maurice replied at the end of the story, "I think I would have used a shotgun." D.T. just laughed and said, "I skun the snake and pinned it up on the side of my barn."

Another large point of discussion formed when Maurice found out that D.T. grew watermelons on his farm and sold them for about ten cents a piece. When Maurice told him how much they sold for in Maine, they quickly devised a plan to buy a refrigerated airplane after the war and ship watermelons to Maine.

After three months of recuperation in Bizerte, Maurice received orders to return to Italy and find his outfit. He never saw D.T. after that and always wondered what happened to his good friend from Texas.

In February of 1995, my father, Maurice, and I were driving to Lewiston. He started telling me about D.T. and I began wondering if it would be possible to find this man after all these years. When we returned home I called information in Brownsville, Texas, and asked if there were a D.T. Rogers listed in their directory. The operator said no, so I asked for the number of the town office, hoping someone there might remember D.T. The clerk was very helpful and even checked records on his computer, but still no D.T.

I sat and thought for a moment and then it came to me. D.T. was wounded during the war, so the Veterans Administration must have a record of him. I got the number for the VA Hospital closest to Brownsville, Texas, and talked with an administrator there. The woman said she couldn't give out personal information, but she did have a telephone number for a VA Regional Office if it would be of help. I thanked her and jotted the number down.

I dialed the number, and much to my surprise the voice on the other end said, "Togus, how may I help you?" I couldn't believe it — the woman in Texas had given me an Augusta, Maine, phone number. I quickly recovered, and asked to speak to someone who could help me find my father's friend. I was transferred to Chuck Pervier in the Veterans' Services Division. Chuck then told me that there was a way we could try to locate D.T. I excitedly took down the information which included writing a letter and raced up to my parents' house.

When I told my Dad what I had done, he was pretty amazed and said, "Well, let's go write that letter." We sent it out the next day and anxiously awaited a response. We figured it would take months to locate D.T., but much to our surprise, when I called Chuck at the VA a week later, he said he had already forwarded the letter. At three o'clock that afternoon my Dad came through the front door of his house. The phone was ringing and my mother Evelyn picked it up. The voice on the other end identified himself as D.T.'s brother-in-law and asked if Maurice was there, because D.T. would like to speak with him.

D.T. was really surprised to hear from Dad and said that he too had always wondered what had happened to him after the war. He also said, "Remember how drafty that tent hospital was in Bizerte?" After 52 years some memories never fade away. D.T. had moved to Arizona when he returned from the war, which is why I couldn't find any record of him in Brownsville, Texas. He worked as a barber there for many years, but has since retired, and now lives with his sister and brother-in-law. My mother told me when my Dad got off the phone he was grinning from ear to ear, and said "I've got to call Sarah and tell her." When I picked up the phone, my Dad said "Guess who I just talked to?" I was so excited I almost dropped the phone. I told Dad it was ten times better than watching an episode of "Unsolved Mysteries."

If you would like to try to locate a friend of yours from the service, either call Chuck at 1-207-623-8411, ext. 5551, or write him at the following address: Chuck Pervier, VA Regional Office, Veterans Services Division, Togus, Maine 04330.

Author's note: It is also possible to get copies of your discharge papers that you may have misplaced over the years, and to apply for medals or ribbons you were entitled to, but never received during the war.

E. Gray and Sons, Newagen, Maine.

Pinkham's Store, West Southport, Maine.

E.W. Pratt General Merchandise, West Southport, Maine.
Also known as The Pavilion or The Alley.

BACK ON THE HOMEFRONT

Author's note: The following remembrances and stories were collected after I came to the realization that the veterans I was interviewing really didn't know that much about what life was like here on the island while they were gone.

I remember December 7, 1941, very well. It was the day the Japanese bombed Pearl Harbor. I was 10 years old at the time, and was walking to Sunday School with my oldest brother, Eugene. I asked him if this meant the world would be coming to an end. — *Jack Stover*

My father, Walter, had the tallest flagpole on the west side of Southport. When the Second World War broke out, he received a letter from the United States government asking him to lower the top section of his flagpole, because German U-boats were using it as a reference guide for navigation. — *Bob Eaton*

I had been working as a waitress for five dollars a week at the Fullerton Hotel in Boothbay Harbor. When the war broke out, the Coast Guard took over the hotel and I was out of a job. I then tended my small farm on Southport, where I had sheep, ducks, chickens, cows, and a pig. — *Winona Taylor Rand*

As children, we were probably totally unaware of what war or war machine really meant. I do remember that patriotism was in, and we were encouraged to do our share for the war effort. Purchasing defense stamps at school, for 10 or 25 cents, was one way we could help. When you saved 18 dollars and 75 cents in stamps, you could trade them in for a 25 dollar war bond. There were posters on the walls at school, showing how many bonds it would take to purchase a tank or airplane. — *Katie Rand Copland*

The coastal patrol came down from the Fisk Hotel in Damariscotta, and made the rounds, checking all the shore roads on the island. The patrol was comprised of army soldiers, and they drove a weapons carrier, which is like an elongated jeep. My mother, Louise, always had lemonade for them in the summertime, and hot cocoa for them in the winter. My Grandfather Pardy, Royal Luther, loved seeing them come up over the hill, and he always managed to tell the soldiers a few of his lighthouse stories, and sometimes, my mother would even cook them a hot meal.

— *Jean Luther Thompson*

During the war, the trains were packed wherever you went. One time I had to sit on the table of a dining car all the way back from Boston to Wiscasset, so I could get home to Southport.   — *Emolyn Smith Pratt*

One winter I went to work at Reed's and Samples Shipyards on mine sweepers. I sawed timbers for the boats. Charlie Reed and I also built a building at Samples. Charlie was careless about the staging, and I really didn't want to get up on it.   — *Leslie Brewer*

I was home the day a telegram arrived stating my brother, Maurice, had been wounded. It is a day I will never forget. My mother, Ruth, received it and all it said was that Maurice had been wounded. It didn't say how badly he was wounded and it didn't say where. The next few weeks were very worrisome for everyone at the Sherman household, until a letter came from Maurice, and we knew he was alright.   — *Marilyn Sherman Spinney*

I was teaching school in West Harbor during the war. My mother, Violet, sister Thelma, and I had rented the house next to the Lawnmeer Inn on Southport. It was there in the evening that we first heard Maurice Sherman had been wounded. It was an awful, nerve-racking time, because all you could do was wait for more details. No one knew how badly he was injured or if he would be coming home. My family was very friendly with the Shermans, and we often walked to the Strand Theater in Boothbay Harbor to see a movie with Ruth, Connie, and Marilyn.   — *Emolyn Smith Pratt*

When my older brother, Eugene, went into the service, a star was hung in the window to show our family had a child serving in the military.

— *Joe Stover*

At night, the bus that transported Bath Iron Works workers to Bath was parked next to George Webber's house. Some of the kids in the neighborhood and I used to get on it in the evenings and collect bottles for returns. On occasion, we also helped ourselves to the grapes on George's grapevines.   — *Katie Rand Copland*

★

My mother, Doris Brewer Farnham, had a 1941 black Studebaker during the war. When I came home on leave, she always gave me a ride back to Union Station in Portland to catch the train. She never drove by a soldier or sailor without offering him a ride, so by the time we got to Union Station, the car was always full.   — *Fred Farnham*

★

My youngest daughter, Becky, was born on the day of the Newagen Inn fire. There was an outbreak of scarlet fever at St. Andrews Hospital, and my husband, Roscoe, refused to let me have the baby there, so Dr. Phil Gregory was called and he came over to Wilma Marr's home on Dogfish Head (now Stranahan's cottage) and delivered the child that afternoon.   — *Winona Taylor Rand*

★

One night I was up rocking my newborn daughter, Linda, in the livingroom. (Now Ted and Linda Dowling's home.) Suddenly, I noticed that the sky was bright red, so bright you could read from the illumination. I called to my husband, Leland, who came rushing out into the room. The Newagen Inn was on fire!   — *Lucy Alley Snowman*

★

I left the house, when Lucy called my attention to the fire, and headed for the Inn, but when I got to a telephone, the lines had been cut. I turned around and went over to the Post Office, and used their phone. The fire department had been alerted, but with so many men gone to war, there weren't many left on the island to help fight the fire. The Coast Guard was called in, and they brought a portable pump. It was obvious at this point that they would need more help, so one of the men drove to the nearest telephone, and called the Boothbay Fire Department. The Inn, which was a four-story building at that time, burned flat before they could get there. The fire had been set, that was obvious, and many rumors started to circulate, even to the extent that the Germans had done it to signal their offshore fleet. It was quite a feat during the war to get anything, due to the rationing, so when it was announced the Inn would be rebuilt, the rumors really started to fly around the island. A crew of 40 men worked day and night, and the Inn was rebuilt in no time. — *Leland Snowman*

Franklyn Payson had a Model A convertible, with a rumble seat. When he went into the service, it was stored under our parents porch for safe-keeping. All the kids in the neighborhood envied that car, and when the coast was clear, we often found ourselves taking imaginary trips all over the island, without ever moving an inch. — *Joe and Jack Stover*

On Sunday evenings, the Epworth League met at the Methodist Church on Southport. It was the equivalent of youth fellowship as we know it today. — *Marilyn Sherman Spinney*

Pompadours, a woman's hair style that was created when you swept the hair straight up from your forehead, were all the rage during the war. Women also wore their hair long and covered it with a netting, which was called a snood. — *Emolyn Smith Pratt*

There was no one left to mow around the monument in front of Pinkham's Store, so my siblings and I would put our sheep over the fence and that is how the town kept the grass under control during the war years. — *Barbara Rand Tibbetts*

In January of 1945, there was a terrible snowstorm, and the town snow plow was broken, so no one could move on the island. They did have another plow, but it needed chains for traction. Cecil Pierce, Leland Snowman, and my husband, Cliff, were the town selectmen at that time, and they walked to Boothbay Center to get the chains, and then walked home in that bitter cold weather to assemble them.— *Katherine Thompson Buck*

One summer during the war, Arthur Fiedler, the famous conductor of the Boston Pops, visited Southport, and came into my grandparents store. Lizzy Snowman, who was a German war bride from the First World War, walked into Pinkham's and recognized him immediately. She went right up to him and said, "I know you. I saw you conduct in Germany." Apparently, Mr. Fiedler didn't wish to be recognized, and he politely backed out of the store. — *Ronald Orchard*

During the war servicemen and women didn't need to buy stamps. Instead they marked the word "free" in the right corner of any letter they wanted to mail, and put their name and serial number in the left corner. This process was known as "Franking." There also was a method of letter writing known as V-Mail. You picked up an 8¼" x 10¼" form at the post office or military base, and wrote you letter on it. The form was then photographed, which saved it on microfilm, and the reels of film were shipped overseas to be developed. Once the film was developed on the other end, you letter was printed on a piece of 4¼" x 5¼" paper, and the original was destroyed after it was determined the corresponding film had safely been delivered to its destination. This saved sending bags and bags of mail by sea and air, and on paper usage during the Second World War. *— Earl Pratt, Jr.*

★

Grange was held every Thursday night at the Town Hall. It started off with a meeting, then refreshments were served. Ruth Sherman or Violet Smith would play the piano for dancing and musical entertainment afterwards. Sometimes there was a cake walk or we played seven in, seven out, which is a musical game. *— Marilyn Sherman Spinney*

A letter sent home by Sergeant Earl Pratt, Jr., to his mother, Evelyn, while he was in the service. Notice the word "Free" is marked in the upper right corner. Servicemen and women didn't have to pay for postage during the war.

If you belonged to Grange, you could go to a meeting in any town, and quite often my friends and I would walk over from Boothbay Harbor to attend. Once in a while a local band played that consisted of Carl Pierce on drums, Chet Fossett on saxophone, Roscoe Pinkham on clarinet, George Hodgdon on drums, and Ralph Knapp on the trumpet. They were really good and also played at the high school dances.

— Ralph Spinney

I remember going to Grange square dances, up at the Town Hall. They were a lot of fun, and all the kids turned out for them.

— Neil Payson

When my daughter, Kathryn, was born, I took her over to Irene's in Boothbay Harbor, so we could have a photograph taken, to send to Maurice in Europe. He built a frame for the picture when he received it, and carried it all over Europe, until he came home to us in October of 1945. That photograph now hangs on my kitchen wall.

— Alvina Webber Taylor

During the winter, when we were back in Malden, Massachusetts, my parents, Earl and Evelyn, were Air Raid Wardens in our neighborhood. They had to wear helmets and an arm band, which identified them as Civil Defense volunteers. When they were out on patrol, it was my job to answer the telephone, and I was instructed to do it in the following way, "Pratt Precinct One. Can I take a message?"

One night an oil truck came down our street with all its lights on during an air raid drill. Things got pretty exciting there for a while, until the wardens got to the driver, and told him to turn his lights off. Another night one of our neighbors came around and said, "I think this is the real thing! I heard they spotted an enemy plane over Boston!" Rumors like that were always running rampant during the war.   *— Evelyn Pratt Sherman*

One afternoon while I was visiting in Malden, Massachusetts, I received a call from Stuart, telling me that he was on leave in Boston, and would I meet him at the North Station. I agreed, and hurriedly got ready to go. As I sat waiting on a bench at the station, I felt a tap on my shoulder, which caused me to turn my head. There behind me was

Stuart and two of his friends. They didn't say a word, instead they lifted up their Coast Guard caps, and much to my surprise, they were all bald as cue balls. Their ship was supposed to pass over the equator, and in anticipation of the event, the whole crew shaved their heads to celebrate, but at the last minute, they received new orders, which changed their course, and brought them to Boston.   — *Jean Luther Thompson*

★

It was awful when the news arrived that Norman Gaudette had been killed in France. The island was such a close knit place, it really effected everyone as if Norman was one of their own.   — *Emolyn Smith Pratt*

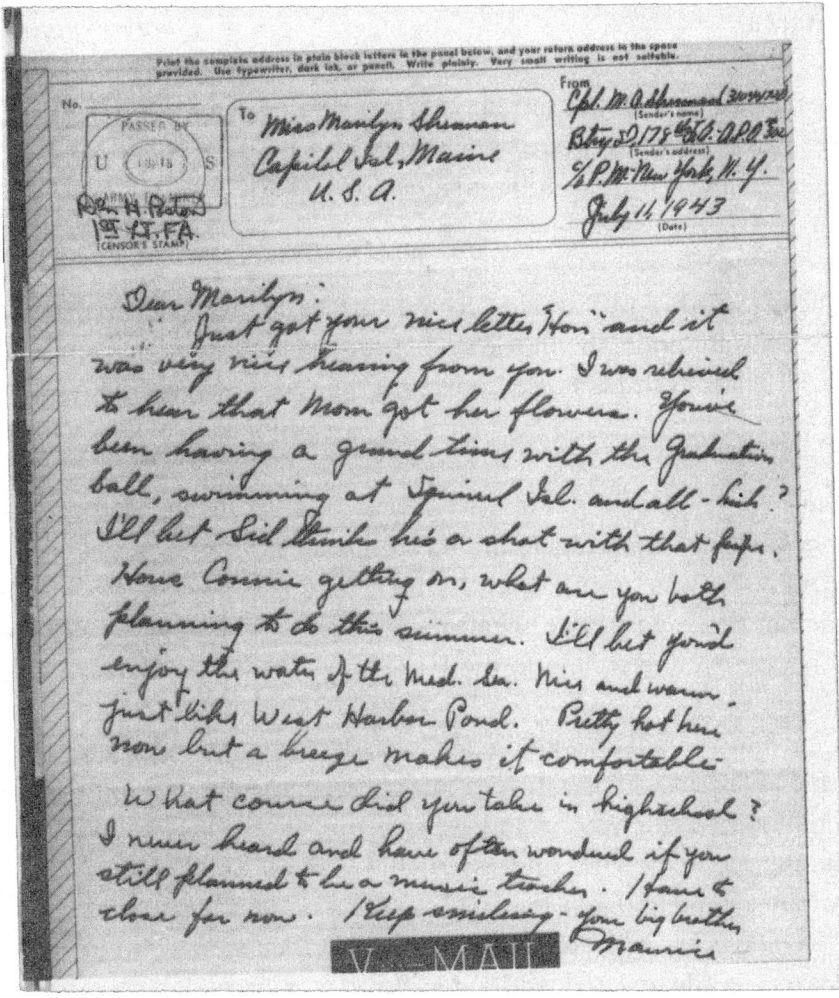

A V-Mail letter sent to Marilyn Sherman from her brother Maurice.

I took a list of the groceries I wanted into Pinkham's Store and gave it to Charlie or Izetta, who were the proprietors of the store. The items would later be delivered to my home. This was a very handy way to shop, especially when the twins, John and Bill, were born.

— *Katherine Thompson Buck*

★

Servicemen and women could get a furlough ticket, which entitled them to pay half of the fare on a bus or a train.   — *Earl Pratt, Jr.*

★

Bob Hope had a popular radio show, which came on at ten o'clock at night on Tuesday evenings. We always gathered around the radio to listen to it.   — *Emolyn Smith Pratt*

★

I especially remember the Christmas of 1945, because the Battle of the Bulge was raging in Europe, and somehow it didn't seem like we should be celebrating, but I had four small children at the time, and couldn't let them down.   — *Winona Taylor Rand*

★

Thelma Smith and I walked to the movies in Boothbay Harbor quite often. One afternoon, the movie actor Tom Mix made an appearance at the Strand Theater with his horse Tony, and I got his autograph.

— *Marilyn Sherman Spinney*

★

Saul Hayes ran the Strand Theater in Boothbay Harbor. Every Wednesday was bank night, and there was a drawing for a cash jackpot. Sometimes it was as much as 100 or 150 dollars, which was a lot of money in those days. The theater was so full, all the seats were taken, and people were standing in the back.   — *Ronald Orchard*

★

One Sunday while waiting for church to commence, I remember Connie Sherman walking in with her parents, Chester and Ruth. She had recently joined the WACS, and was wearing her uniform. All the girls, including me, were very impressed, and wanted to join too.

Another Sunday, I got into my mother's bureau and found a pair of silk stockings to wear to church. When I walked into church all the ladies got really excited and said, "Evelyn, where did you get those stockings?" I simply replied, "They're Mom's."   — *Evelyn Pierce Blake*

The Alley was open in the evening, until nine or ten o'clock, and people used to walk down after supper for an ice cream, to bowl, or just to visit. The jukebox had all the latest hits, and the kids used to dance in the dance hall. There were war time posters up all along the bowling alley wall. The one that sticks out in my mind the most was one with a hand coming up out of the water and a sailor's hat floating nearby. The caption read, "Loose Lips Sink Ships."   — *Evelyn Pratt Sherman*

★

You could buy an Oldsmobile Business Coupe for 852 dollars or a Willis Americar for 595 dollars in 1941. The cost of a Firestone new tread tire was four dollars and forty four cents. Wooden tires were seriously being considered, if the war was going to last much longer, due to a shortage of rubber.   — *Merle Farnham*

★

When the veterans started coming home to Southport, my parents, Charlie and Izetta Pinkham, started getting some exotic requests for different kinds of food at the store. The men and women weren't necessarily looking to buy the old standbys anymore, like salt fish or meat and potatoes, now they were asking for strange items like pasta and fruits that came from all the corners of the world. My parents soon found they had to start stocking different types of foods on their shelves, to keep their newly returned customers happy, because the veterans diets and taste buds had changed while they'd been gone.   — *Phyllis Pinkham Cook*

A service star. Courtesy of the Southport Historical Society.

MASON BRITTON, SR.

Dollar-a-Year Man

In 1940, the United States government approached American heads of industry to help Washington get organized for war. The men were asked to work for a limited period of time on a W.O.C. basis (without compensation), but then it was discovered there was an old law on the books forbidding that practice. A compromise was made, and it was decided to pay the men a dollar a year, which then coined the phrase "Dollar-a-Year Man."

England and France were flooding the United States with orders for airplanes, ammunition, and other supplies, and quite frankly, we weren't prepared to handle their requests. This program got United States production going, built and converted factories for the manufacturing of war related products, and in the end helped the Allied forces win the war against the Axis powers.

Mason Britton, Sr., a long-time Southport summer resident, ran a machine tool business. He was asked to head the Tools Division for the government, which he did from 1940 to 1941. Many ships full of tools were sunk enroute to Europe, and it proved to be a challenging task to keep the Allied countries supplied during the war. In 1944, he was sent to Europe to see what would have to be done to help rebuild its countries after the war. In 1945, he became the Director of Surplus Properties.

In 1947, President Truman awarded Mason the President's Medal of Merit for all his help during the war. It is the highest civilian award a President can bestow on an American citizen. Mason continued serving his country in this capacity during the Korean War as well.

Mason Britton, Sr.'s, check, signed by President Roosevelt. Mason worked as a Dollar-a-Year Man in Washington, D.C., during the war.

THE WAR EFFORT AND WOMEN

I saw the need for a marine engines repair shop, and opened one called Marine Service, Inc., in a building that had been Al Eames blacksmith shop. In present day that would be located near the Tugboat Inn in Boothbay Harbor. When the Second World War broke out, the U.S. government needed parts badly. Working with a go between man, I started getting substantial orders for aircraft turnbuckles, and in turn I started hiring and training local housewives to do the work. Wendell Rand of Southport was the foreman of the turnbuckle shop.

The demand for the product kept increasing, and before I knew it, I had 30 women working for me. They included: Agnes Dunton, Bessie Emerson, Muriel Giles, Grace Gaudette, Peggy Giles, Wanneta Greenleaf, Anna Hart, Muriel Greenleaf Howard, Rena Holmes, Doris Hutchins, Stella Hodgdon, Franny Childs Johnson, Carolyn Lewis, Etta Lewis, Geraldine Mahoney, Madelyn Mudge, Elsie Poole, Anna Perkins, Leona Pinkham, Doris Page, Aura Perkins, Bessie Rust, Violet Smith, Rebecca Seavey, Barbara Sturtevant, Lillian Tucker, Beverley Winslow, Carolene Warren, and Shirley Williams. My daughter Evelyn even worked on Saturdays and during school vacation to lend a hand. The women worked eight hour shifts. Two shifts ran per day, and I oversaw the second shift.

At the same time, I also had a small machine shop in the building, and Cliff Buck and Lyman Fisher of Southport worked there for me during the day. They did light machine work for Hodgdon Brothers and Goudy and Stevens Shipyard of East Boothbay, who were building mine sweepers at the time.

I was allotted more ration coupons to get gas for my truck, because I was a civilian defense worker and my business was producing products for the war effort. In turn I also had to keep close track of my mileage and document where I had traveled.

Reed Brothers of Boothbay Harbor had a contract with the government to build 30 plane re-arming boats, which would be used to deliver ammunition to seaplanes. I sub-contracted with them to install the engines and electronics systems in the boats, and hired local lobsterman Kenneth Holmes to help me with the work. — *Cecil Pierce*

Author's note: *The women's names were compiled from Cecil's 1945 ledger and from the memories of the women who worked in the machine shop.*

I worked Saturdays and during school vacations to lend a hand at Dad's shop. The women worked eight hour days, and I remember one day when it was nearing the end of work, I was so tired, I could just barely stand on my feet, so I decided to sit down for a minute. Pretty soon Dad came along and said, "What are you doing?" so I replied, "Dad, my legs are tired." He quickly pointed out that no one else was taking a break and I'd better get back to work. It was the longest 15 minutes of my life.

— *Evelyn Pierce Blake*

The airplane turnbuckles my father produced for the war effort had to be very precise. I can remember him bringing home boxes and boxes of defective ones, and burying them in the old cellar hole out in the field. I can only imagine what people will say in a couple of hundred years when they are unexpectedly discovered. They'll probably think they've made a real archaeological find, and they'll wonder what we used them for here on Southport Island.   — *Evelyn Pierce Blake*

One day I was helping Harriet Orchard deliver groceries to Christmas Cove. As we neared our destination smoke was in the air, and we could both see fire starting to spread across the lawn. Harriet quickly turned the car around and we headed back to the firehouse to grab some Indian tanks, so we could fight the fire ourselves. Normally we would have turned this situation over to the fire department, but most of the men had either gone to war, were out fishing, or were working for the war effort locally, so the responsibility fell on the two of us.   — *Marjorie Childs Collins*

I used to help the ladies roll bandages at the Town Hall for the Red Cross.   — *Jean Luther Thompson*

I can remember my mother, Winona, sewing uniforms for British children. I believe it was through the Red Cross. The fabric was dark and had pin stripes on it. I thought they were really ugly at the time.

— *Katie Rand Copland*

I knit sweaters for the Red Cross to help the war effort. One pattern was used, and we passed it around the island from house to house.

— *Dorothy Alley Brewer*

My husband Carl worked as an airplane engineer for General Electric, in Lynn, Massachusetts. I also worked for G.E., running a machine that produced airplane parts for the war effort.   — *Evelyn Stratton*

I worked in Washington, D.C., at the War Department Office during the war, and was a secretary to the Chief Signal Officer in the Warplane Section. Lists of outfits that were being shipped overseas often came through the office I worked in. Therefore I was fully aware when my eldest brother Harold, or "Bud" as I called him, was being shipped out, but was unable to share that information with my family or even with him when he came to visit me. I knew I was saying goodbye to him and it was a very difficult secret to keep.   — *Doris Boyd Arnold*

When my husband, Norman, was drafted in December of 1943, I was left with two small sons to raise by myself. I rented the Bridge House for six dollars a month from Ralph Thompson, and soon went to work on the Southport Bridge for eleven dollars a week. This was enough for me to pay the rent, pay my sister-in-law five dollars a week for watching the boys while I worked, and I even saved enough money to buy a washing machine.   — *Mildred Marr Lewis*

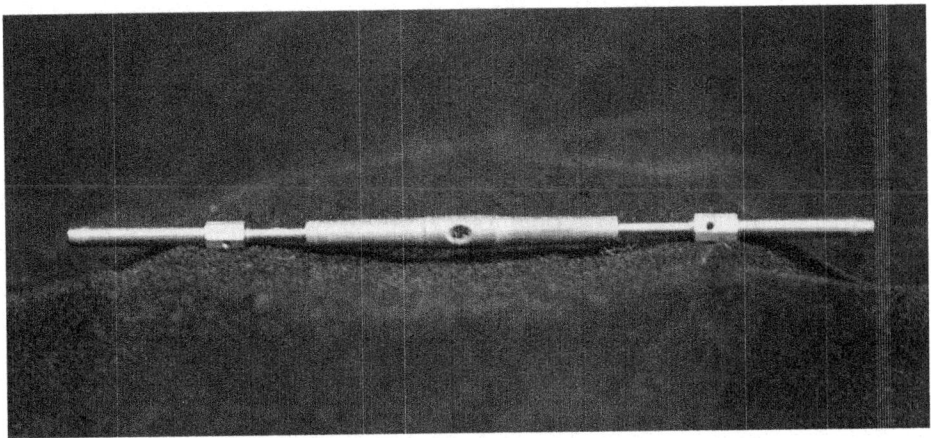

One of the airplane turnbuckles Cecil Pierce produced for the war effort.

CIVIL DEFENSE AND BLACKOUTS

In the spring of 1942, there was a flurry of activity on the island that was war related including: Air raid wardens, airplane spotting, first aid, etc. People were so used to the Depression they were glad to have work, and help the war effort. I can remember walking at nine o'clock at night and there wasn't a light to be seen anywhere due to the blackout. My father, Cliff, was out almost every night helping to enforce the blackout conditions on the island with the other air raid wardens.   *— Robert Buck*

I was one of Southport's selectmen and volunteered to be the Chief Air Raid Warden for the town. I had several men working with me, including Edgar Huskins, Douglas Pinkham, Albert Seavey, John Swett, Ralph Gray, Cliff Buck, and Roscoe Rand. Every night it was our duty to ride around the island, with dimmed lights, making sure everyone had their blackout curtains drawn, so no light would shine from their houses. If there were lights showing, we would stop at the house, knock at the door, and ask the occupant to blind that light.

At night the glow of lights would silhouette a town or a ship on the water, giving enemy submarines a clear target to torpedo. Only after many ships were lost in U.S. waters did blackout conditions become mandatory across the Atlantic seaboard. Street lights, porch and garage lights were hooded, and car headlights were blocked, allowing only a minimum of light to shine through them.   *— Cecil Pierce*

My uncle, Ney Brewer, owned a 1927 Apperson Jack Rabbit, which was a touring car. When it was mandated that car headlights had to be blackened, Ney refused, and said there was no way he was going to paint his headlights. When he was informed that he wouldn't be able to drive his car if he didn't, he promptly went to the local sail loft and had two canvas covers made, which he tied under each light, like bonnets on a baby's head.   *— Merle Farnham*

Beula Harding and I walked over to Fisher's Hill in Boothbay Harbor, to stand a watch at the airplane spotting tower. After a while,, I could see something in the sky, and I got really excited and said, "Beula, look, it's an airplane!" Beula glanced up in the sky and said, "Katherine, that's not an airplane, that's a seagull!"   — *Katherine Thompson Buck*

Sometimes there were emergency blackouts. If one occurred and you were driving, you were supposed to pull over immediately, and shut off your lights. Cigarettes were supposed to be extinguished as well.

— *Merle Farnham*

When I was 13 years old, I used to help man the plane-spotting tower in the Town Hall parking lot. I even called two planes in, but they turned out to be friendly aircraft.   — *Joe Stover*

Automobile headlights had to be partially covered during the war. At first we had to cover them with tape, so a space one inch wide and three inches long was visible. Then we were supposed to use black paint to cover them, instead of tape. Finally, a plastic shield was developed, and it covered the top half of the headlight. I drove up to Brunswick one evening, and nearly got arrested, because of my regulation blackout headlights. The town was far enough away from the coast that it wasn't necessary to shield the lights on automobiles, so when I drove into town, the police noticed me right away, and pulled me over.

— *Alfred Huskins*

Stuart Thompson, while home on leave, posing with two cars that have regulation blackout headlights.

Air raid drills were standard practice. At night the siren would sound and all the wardens would go around the island, making sure no lights were visible. Street lights were painted black on the side facing the ocean, and everyone had black paper over their windows. One night the siren went off. It woke me up and kept on screaming. (We were living where the present Southport school is now.) I thought for sure the Germans had landed. As it turned out, the Newagen Inn was on fire.

At school we were taught to push all our desks to one corner of the room, and get under them. I suppose the idea was that they would protect you from falling debris if we were ever bombed. — *Katie Rand Copland*

Famous for its yachting

TOWN OF SOUTHPORT
LINCOLN COUNTY, MAINE
Office of the Selectmen

CLIFFORD H. BUCK   CECIL E. PIERCE   THOMAS P. MARR

—; *Blackout Permit* ;—

Southport March 16, 1942

To Roscoe Rand Warden

This entitles you to drive your auto during Blackouts in the town of Southport

Southport Police Force
T.P. Marr Lieutenant

Courtesy of Winona Taylor Rand.

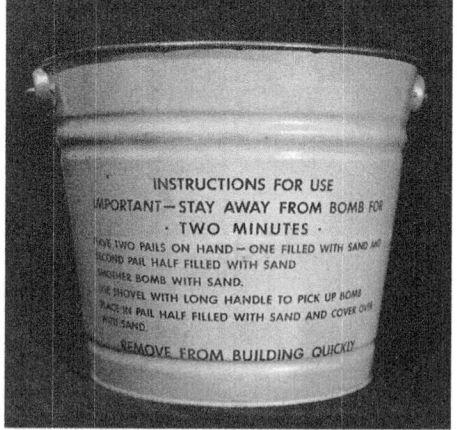

Incendiary bomb bucket from Don and Jill Hansen's Southport cottage.

Instructions for use were printed on the back, in case there was an air raid.

As a teenager, I helped man the airplane spotting tower that was located in the parking lot of the Southport Town Hall. I remember that there was a poster on the wall of the building that showed different types of planes, and it was supposed to help you identify any that might fly overhead. Shifts at the tower lasted for two hours at a time. An airplane log was kept that indicated the type of plane, when and where it was spotted, and who spotted it. Also, there was a telephone hooked up inside and it was my duty to report any airplane sightings to a higher command, located out of town. I thought it was very exciting when I had a plane to report, and I recall hoping I had said everything just right to the authorities, when I called it in.   — *Evelyn Pierce Blake*

On June 21, 1943, my mother Violet and I were living in the Thompson homestead beside the Lawnmeer Inn, which was closed during the war years. One Sunday morning at dawn, I awoke to the roar of an airplane diving low above our house, then climbing to dive again. I ran to my mother and shouted excitedly, "Mum, Mum, planes are attacking us! Wake up and crawl under the bed! That's what we're supposed to do!" My poor mother was so weary and lame from working at Cecil

Evelyn Pierce posing on her parents' car. Note only half of the headlights are covered.

Pierce's machine shop, making airplane turnbuckles, she was slow to respond, so I scrambled under her bed for protection while the plane continued to climb and dive.

With each successive dive, I soon realized that no bombs were exploding, but as the roar finally subsided, the town fire whistle began to wail. I was convinced it was an air raid. Then all of a sudden the town fire truck came speeding by our door. Mustering up my courage, I stepped outside, and stood on a big rock by the Cove Cottage annex. It was then that I saw smoke and flames shooting from Bill Alley's house, located just over the bridge that goes to Newagen.

Later that morning at church, I learned that many people had been as frightened as I was. The plane was on a routine patrol of the coast and the pilot, after spotting the fire, feared everyone was still asleep and the fire would go undetected. He alerted the residents the only way he knew how. The pilot was successful in his efforts, but many of the volunteer firemen admitted they almost sought shelter instead of venturing outside, because they too thought it was an air raid.

— Thelma Smith Blake

Doris Brewer Farnham's car with hooded headlights.

Taken out of the May 1, 1942, issue of the *Boothbay Register*

Clothing Prices

- Ladies and Misses Coats: $10.98 -$14.98 -$19.50
- Pumps and Oxfords: $2.98 – $3.98
- Cottage and Tailored Curtains:.79 -.98 – $1.25 – $1.35
- Young Men's Sport Coats: $8.95 – $10.98 – $12.50
- Men's and Young Men's Wool Suits: $18.75 – $22.50 – $24.00
- Men's Dungarees: $1.00

Food Prices

Roast Beef	.29/lb	Chicken	.27/lb
Top of the Round	.39/lb	Coffee	.23/lb
Sirloin Steak	.35/lb	Large Eggs	.39/doz
Pork Loin	.27/lb	Apple Sauce	.13/can
Hamburg	.27/lb	Peas	.18/can
Haddock	.23/lb	Crisco	.68/can
Mackerel	.08/lb	Soup	3 for.27/can

Popular Comic Strips During the 1940s

Buck Rogers in the 21st Century	Terry and the Pirates
Mutt and Jeff	Gasoline Alley
Lil' Abner	The Katsinjama Kids
Little Orphan Annie	Toonerville Trolley
Moon Mullins	Blondie
Polly Pippin	Major Hoople
The Gumps	*Up Front by Bill Mauldin

* (This cartoon ran in the military newspaper "Stars and Stripes." It featured Willie and Joe, two typical soldiers.)

SOME OF THE POPULAR MOVIES AT THE STRAND THEATER IN BOOTHBAY HARBOR DURING THE 1940s

My Favorite Blonde, with Bob Hope and Madeline Carroll.
Till We Meet Again, with Ray Milland and Barbara Britton.
The Memphis Bell, in Technicolor, photographed by the 8th Air Force.
Bowery To Broadway, with Maria Montez, Susanna Foster, and Jack Oakie.
Tonight and Everynight, Rita Hayworth, Janet Blair, and Lee Bowman.
Thunderhead, with Roddy McDowell, Preston Foster, and Rita Johnson.
National Velvet, with Elizabeth Taylor, Donald Crisp, and Mickey Rooney.
Little Old New York, with Alice Faye, Fred McMurray, and Richard Green.
Heaven Can Wait, with Jean Tierney, Don Ameche, and Charles Colburn.
The Fleets In, with Dorothy Lamour and William Holden.
Mrs. Miniver, with Greer Garson and Walter Pidgeon.
Pardon My Sarong, with Abbott and Costello.
The Maltese Falcon, with Humphrey Bogart.
Bahama Passage, with Sterling Hayden and Madeline Carroll.
Adventure of Warden Eden, with Glen Ford.
Fantasia, an animated film released by Walt Disney.
How Green Was My Valley, with Roddy McDowell.
Casablanca, with Humphrey Bogart and Ingrid Bergman.

ERNIE PYLE: AMERICAN WAR CORRESPONDENT

Armed with a portable Underwood typewriter, Ernie Pyle eloquently covered the Second World War like no other correspondent before or after him has been able to do. His devotion to the men in combat, especially infantry soldiers, was one of the greatest morale boosters of the war, and earned him the admiration and respect of the common soldier. His style was simple, yet descriptive, and he always used individual names and hometowns of everyone he quoted. This technique left the soldiers feeling represented and personalized the war for the people back home, reminding them of the sacrifices the GIs were making on their behalf.

Ernie covered the war in Tunisia, Sicily, Italy and France. He reached the Pacific in January of 1945, and started convering the Okinawa operation, landing on Ie Shima in the Ryukyus. On April 18th, near Tegusngu, he took two bullets in the temple from a Japanese machine gun, and died instantly in a ditch. President Harry S. Truman paid him the ultimate tribute, "No man in this war has so well told the story of the American fighting man as American fighting men wanted it told."

Popular Radio Programs of the 1940s

- Major Bowes Amateur Hour
- Stage Door Canteen
- The Kate Smith Hour
- Burns and Allen
- Helen Trent (soap opera)
- Our Gal Sunday (soap opera)
- Young Doctor Malone (soap opera)
- Bob Hope's Pepsodent Show
- Fibber Megee and Molly (and their closet)
- Sammy Kaye and His College of Musical Knowledge
- Shep Fields and his Rippling Rhythms
- Buck Rogers in the 21st Century
- Sergeant Preston of the Yukon
- Lux Radio Theater
- Jack Armstrong, The All American Boy
- Edward R. Murrow (news broadcaster)
- H.V. Kaltenborn (news broadcaster)
- Lowell Thomas (news broadcaster)
- Gabriel Heater (news broadcaster)
- Walter Winchell (news broadcaster; his signature line was "Good Evening Mr. and Mrs. North America and All the Ships at Sea.")
- The Jack Benny Show
- The Fred Allen Show
- The Green Hornet
- Amos and Andy
- Snow Village
- The Kay Kaiser Show
- The Shadow
- The Lone Ranger

POP SONGS

Give Me Five Minutes More
My Devotion
Serenade in Blue
Deep Purple
That Old Feeling
You'd Be So Nice to Come Home To
That Old Black Magic
Dancing In The Dark
Miss You
Marie
I Think of You
My Buddy
Lili Marlene
Something to Remember You By
The White Cliffs of Dover
As Time Goes By
I Can't Begin to Tell You
Sleepy Time Gal
Auf Wiedersehn, Sweetheart
By The Light Of The Silv'ry Moon
Tangerine

The Gypsy
Seems Like Old Times
To Each His Own
My Prayer
Peg O' My Heart
Maria Elena
Mexicali Rose
La Vie En Rose
Where or When
Linda
Moonlight Becomes You
Harbor Lights
We'll Meet Again
Now is the Hour
It Had to Be You
Always
Sleepy Lagoon
Love Letters
Embraceable You
I'll Be Seeing You
White Christmas

This infamous character seemed to appear wherever there were GIs.

RATIONING

Store owners couldn't have the gasoline they sold replaced without turning in the ration stamps their customers had used to buy it. There were four kinds of stamps, A, B, C, and E. A allotted a very small amount of gasoline, B a little bit more, and C was considered a good fill up. E was specifically issued for commercial fishing boats.

My father, Earl, was always short on gasoline stamps and could never figure out why. The local fishermen would always come to the rescue, and turn in some stamps, so he could get his gas tanks refilled. They had unlimited use of gasoline, and always had extra stamps, because their work was vital to the war effort. At the end of the war he took the Alley cash register in to be serviced, and discovered when the cash register drawer opened and closed, it had created a suction, and all the missing stamps were in a pile under the drawer. He'd had them the whole time, and didn't realize it.   — *Earl Pratt, Jr.*

My grandfather, Charlie, looked to the future, and started stocking up on supplies in advance, when it looked like there might be another war. I can remember people coming from all over the region to shop at the store. He opened at 6 A.M., and his customers would be lined up all the way around the monument, waiting for the store to open. Sometimes the store stayed open as late as midnight or one o'clock in the morning. He made a deal with a farmer in Edgecomb, and was able to get fresh meat, when no one else in the region could.   — *Ronald Orchard*

Women's silk stockings were very hard to come by during the Second World War. Cosmetic companies, such as Revlon, introduced a product called "leg paint," which was used by women to produce the illusion of stockings. An eyebrow pencil was used after the application of the paint to draw in a seam going up the back of the leg. Many years after the war, my good friend, Flo Walker, wrote to the Revlon Company, inquiring if they had any leg paint left. The company searched their warehouse, and shortly there after, Flo received a case of leg paint in the mail.

— *Evelyn Stratton*

I couldn't get a doll carriage for my daughter, Sandra, so her grandfather Brewer, made one out of a wooden box for her.

— *Dorothy Alley Brewer*

My father, Fred, rode to work at BIW with several other men on a regular basis. During the war, he had the opportunity to buy a 1941 Studebaker Champion, but first had to go to the ration board to get permission to do so. He sometimes worked nights or on Saturdays or Sundays, and the other men didn't, so he had no way to get to work.

Permission was granted by the board, after he explained why he needed the vehicle, and he went right out and bought it.

— *Merle Farnham*

I drove to Desler's Market in Gardiner once a week for meat during the war. They butchered their own cattle, so they had meat when other places couldn't get it. There was always a long waiting line, but it was well worth it. I was issued more gasoline ration stamps, because I drove a truck for the lobster pound, so I always had enough gas to get there and back.

— *Alfred Huskins*

Teachers were in charge of signing up people for ration coupons in the towns where they worked. We determined how much sugar each family needed, depending on the number of people living at home, and issued the coupons for it.

— *Emolyn Smith Pratt*

We use to have scrap metal drives for iron on the island. When the Japanese cut off the United States rubber supply from certain islands in the Pacific, tires became scarce, and the kids used to round up old tires on Southport to be recycled. We earned a penny a pound for our efforts.

— *Robert Buck*

Earl Pratt, Sr., brought Cains mayonnaise back to Southport from Malden, Massachusetts. He got a case of it from Ed Babb, who knew Mr. Cains personally. You couldn't get mayonnaise anywhere during the war, and it was really appreciated by his neighbors in Cozy Harbor.

— *Dorothy Alley Brewer*

*These ration stamps were used to purchase gasoline,
the tokens were for meat.*

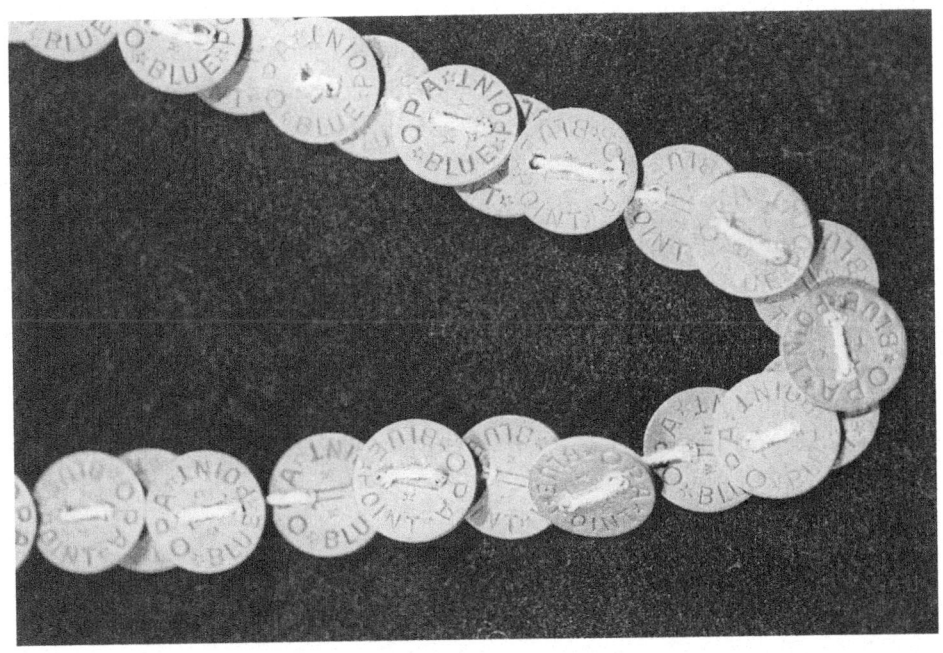

I found a whole case of Rinso powdered detergent in Pinkham's barn during the war. Everyone was really excited, because they hadn't been able to get any for about a year.   — *Janet Elderkin Azzoni*

★

During the war you weren't allowed to have a camera on the Bath bridge, or anywhere around the Bath Iron Works. If you were caught with one, the camera would be confiscated, and you would be taken into custody by the authorities.   — *Merle Farnham*

★

Shoes were rationed, and leather shoes were extremely hard to come by, but you could get dress shoes made out of cloth.

— *Jean Luther Thompson*

★

During the war my husband, Carl, and I were unable to come to Southport very often from our home in Malden, Massachusetts, due to gasoline rationing.   — *Evelyn Stratton*

★

We all did our part for the war effort, saving tin cans, turning in our empty toothpaste tubes in exchange for a new one, collecting scrap metal and rubber. Gas was rationed, so if someone had to make a trip to the harbor, it was a joint shopping effort. At school we had saving stamp drives and the classes competed against each other, and later turned them in for war bonds. Each day, Mrs. Smith, would conduct the current events session, and everyone was encouraged to bring in a news item, which usually turned out to be about the war.   — *Jack Stover*

★

Oleo came in a plastic bag. It was white, and a yellow dye tablet had to be added to it to give it color. I mixed it together with a little salt, then formed it into a block, like the oleo we're used to now. I also had to can vegetables, because there were no freezers. My husband, Leslie, had a big garden in the field across the street (formally Dave and Betty Pierce's), which helped provide the family with fresh vegetables. He also salted hake and mackerel in barrels in the cellar, to help us get through the winter.   — *Dorothy Alley Brewer*

★

No new license plates were issued during the war, so when the plates on my mother's car started to look faded, I took them off and repainted them. Many of our neighbors noticed the freshly painted plates and said, with a twinge of jealousy, "Hey, how'd you get new license plates?"

— *Merle Farnham*

Author's note: *The next four stories are all about some old coffee that was found in Charlie Pinkham's barn during the war. Everyone I interviewed about it seemed to remember the event differently, and the coffee soon went from the best I ever tasted to a substitute for sand on the ice.*

My grandfather, Charlie, found some 35 year old coffee in the top of his barn. Everyone was really excited about the discovery, and when it was opened, it seemed to be good, after all those years.   — *Ronald Orchard*

I remember Charlie Pinkham finding a case of coffee in his barn. It had been there for a really long time, and didn't exactly taste like coffee, but it tasted pretty good.   — *Winona Taylor Rand*

I remember the day Charlie Pinkham found some old coffee he had stockpiled in the top of the barn. It was a real treasure, because coffee was hard to come by. There were also a lot of shoes and boots, but they had been there so long, the rubber had turned hard on them. A large carton of matches was opened that same day, and Charlie discovered it had started to burn from the inside of the carton. It's a real wonder the whole barn didn't go up in smoke.   — *Leslie Brewer*

I remember when Charlie Pinkham got his winter supply of beans for baking and the big wheels of cheese. We heard these items would be rationed, so we got a good supply of them, before the coupons took effect. I can still smell the cheese! The supply of new items also gave him the chance to clean out the top of his barn. Some very old cans of coffee were discovered up there, which some people tried, but it wasn't very good. I think they finally used the old coffee on the ice, instead of sand, so you wouldn't slip. I believe Charlie's find was also reported in either the Portland or Boston newspaper.   — *Jack Stover*

As the war progressed we collected paper, lead foil from cigarette packs, rendered fat, and scrap metal, which was turned in for the war effort. I can remember seeing large balls of foil and an old washing machine someone had turned in at the school house.

— Katie Rand Copland

Meat came into Pinkham's once a week. It was first come first serve, and my mother, Louise, and the other ladies would walk up to the store to wait in line for it.   *— Jean Luther Thompson*

Lucky Strike cigarettes had a dark green package, which used the same green coloring the military did for camouflage. When the war broke out, they changed their package color to white, and their new slogan was, "Lucky Strikes green has gone to war."   *— Ronald Orchard*

We had to sign up at the Town Hall for ration coupons, which were allotted by the number of members in your family. We had coupons for coffee, gas, and sugar. Everyone was eating Spam, as a substitute for meat, which wasn't always available. We soon grew quite tired of Spam.

—Dorothy Alley Brewer

We had coupons for meat during the war. If Charlie didn't have meat at the time, your name would be listed in his book, and that put you in line for meat when he did get some in. Often times, Pinkham's Store was the only place in the region with fresh meat, and I can remember seeing people line up all the way around the monument waiting to get some. Customers even came over from Boothbay Harbor for it. One time I sent my children up to the store for stew meat and they came home with a rack of lamb chops. It was all Charlie had, so I made a lamb chop stew and it was really good.   *—Winona Taylor Rand*

During the war, I had chickens and a rooster with an ugly disposition. Whenever I opened the hen house door the rooster would jump on my back and scratch me all up. I finally said to myself, enough's enough, and we ate him for supper.   *—Leslie Brewer*

I used to go to a place in Harpswell during the rationing, where you could buy meat. Sometimes it was horse meat, but that was all you could get.   *—Leland Snowman*

I remember having to eat a lot of scrapple during the war, which was a ham substitute. You also had to be very thrifty with butter and gasoline, because they were rationed.   —*Marilyn Sherman Spinney*

☆

My grandfather always enjoyed a good gimmick at the store. One time he tied a salt pollack up next to the soda cabinet. His theory was, when his customers came into the store, they would grab a piece of salt fish, which in turn would make them extremely thirsty, so they would buy at

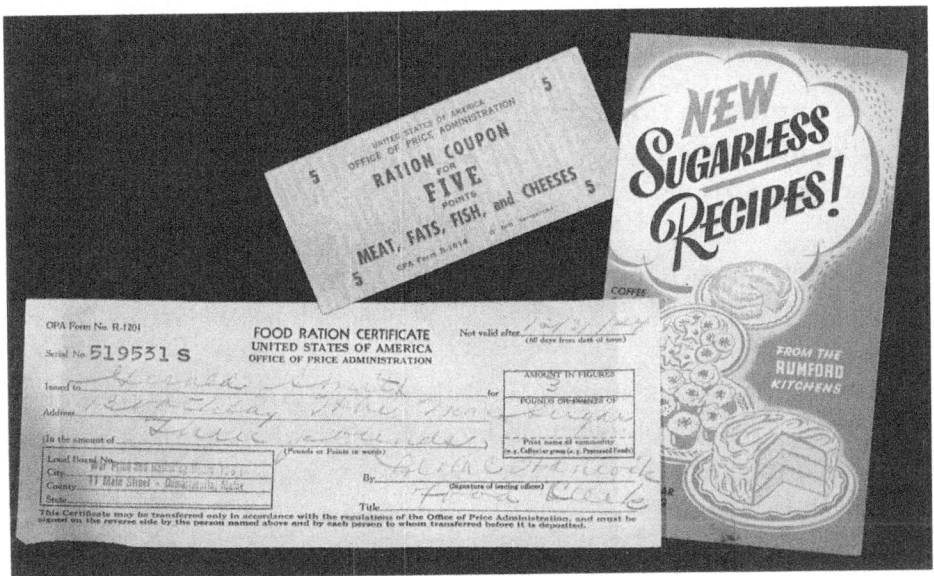

Gerald and Allan Smith's ration coupons.

least two sodas. Another time he brought a whole barrel of pickles into the store and put a sign on it that said, "Spear a pickle for a nickel." He straightened a cod fish hook out for this promotion, which was used as a spear. His customers then strategically tried to spear the largest pickle, so they would get the most for their money.   *—Ronald Orchard*

Several times, I put my name on a waiting list for stockings, at a store overtown. There were two or three other Dorothy Brewers at that time in the Boothbay Region, and they always got to the stockings before I did.   *—Dorothy Alley Brewer*

I often walked to Howard McKown's store on the Landing Road to get groceries during the war, so my father, Chester, wouldn't have to use the car and waste gasoline.   *—Marilyn Sherman Spinney*

We often used honey in place of sugar, when there was strict rationing.   *—Marion Huskins Roberts*

I had to torch eggs at my grandfather's store. He had a box with a small hole in it, and a bright light bulb shining underneath it. It was my job to hold each egg over the hole and look for a shadow, which is how you check for baby chickens. If the egg was not good, I set it aside and put it to good use later in neighborhood egg fights with my friends.

—Ronald Orchard

We ate a lot of fish and Spam during the war. Sometimes the only meat we were able to get was horse meat. It was red and coarse grained, but it tasted okay.   *—Leslie Brewer*

I was working in Melrose, Massachusetts, one winter at the Clear Weave Department Store. The store sold silk stockings when they could get them. Usually they were very hard to come by, because silk was being used to make parachutes during the war. Every morning the clerks would line up by the counter before the store opened in preparation for the customers who were already waiting outside. When the door opened, there was a rush of women into the store, all hoping to purchase stockings. Sometimes after the stockings were all sold out and things had calmed down, the clerks would find just one left, which meant someone had walked off with three stockings.   —*Franny Childs Johnson*

Cigarettes were rationed during the war. When you could get them, they cost 12, 15, and even 20 cents a pack. When the salesman would come to Pinkham's Store, he would slip everyone sample packs, which contained four cigarettes, because he knew we all smoked, and it was difficult to get them.   —*Marion Huskins Roberts*

A meat substitute came out during the war, which was made out of soy. It came in a powder form, and after you added some water to it, you could make little patties, the size of hamburgers. We called them "Bean Burgers," and I thought they were really pretty good. —*Ronald Orchard*

When I graduated from the eighth grade, I didn't have a dressy pair of shoes to wear to the ceremony that was held at the Southport Town Hall. My sister, Becky, was just a baby at the time, and didn't wear shoes, so my mother, Winona, used her ration coupon to buy me a new pair of shoes.   —*Barbara Rand Tibbetts*

I was able to get a case of evaporated milk for my youngest child, Peter, during the rationing, because he was a baby and needed the added nutrition.   —*Dorothy Alley Brewer*

I had to sell my Ford Roadster, because I couldn't get gas for both it and my husband Roscoe's truck. He was the Town Road Commissioner, Constable, and also helped to enforce blackout conditions on the island. Roscoe was given extra gasoline ration coupons, so he could perform his town duties.   —*Winona Taylor Rand*

During the Second World War, sneakers weren't produced, because the rubber that would have normally been used for the soles was being used in the war effort. Ringling Brother's Circus was looking for sneakers, and someone told them that they might know where they could get a few pairs. Sure enough, when they contacted my grandfather, Charlie, a deal was made, and they purchased every sneaker he had in his barn.
          —*Ronald Orchard*

Christmas was terrible during the war years. There wasn't very much in the shops, and I had to hunt and hunt just to find something I could use as stocking stuffers for my children. One year, I ended up with some pencils, and that was the best I could do.   —*Dorothy Alley Brewer*

Warren Payson had an automobile during the war years. The Paysons and the Stovers saved their gasoline ration stamps, and every once in a while, they would pool them together and make a trip to Bath or Portland. It was really something special if you got to go out of town. Sometimes a bunch of red bananas would be purchased, if they were available in the stores. Each child got to have just one, and boy what a treat that was!   —*Joe Stover*

SOUTHPORT FIRE DEPARTMENT

Author's note: These excerpts were taken directly from the Southport Fire Department's log book, which at the time was kept by Charlie Pinkham, who was the fire chief. They represent the three biggest fires fought during the war.

April 27, 1942: Porter Block

The Southport Fire Department was called in to assist the Boothbay Harbor Fire Department. The lower Porter's Drug Store, J. Edward Knight, a chiropractor's office, and Carbone's Fruit, Co. were lost. There was at least $100,000 damage done by the fire.

April 13, 1943: Newagen Inn, 3:00 A.M.

This was the largest and most expensive fire in Southport, with over $250,000 damage. The log annex caught in the south end; the cause could not be determined. It was all ablaze when discovered, and annex was doomed as well as the main hotel which was attached. The log structure made a very hot fire.

We set our engine at the ice pond, just north of the recreation hall, and immediately burned out a bearing. Called Boothbay Harbor and the Coast Guard. When the wind veered to the southwest and then the west it looked bad for the Newagen settlement, but the wind changed again so the cinders were not heading for the houses. The Harrington cottage, which was very close to the annex, had to go as we could not get any-where near.

This was a big loss to Joshua Brooks and at a time when material was very scarce for rebuilding. As bad as this was it had its good side. Joshua Brooks was ailing and seemed to be losing interest in life, but being a man of action and always surmounting a business challenge, and although getting on in years, he received this blow as a prize fighter would accept the first blow from an opponent. His spirit was up, his old vim and punch came back. He rebuilt a new hotel as best he could with the material at hand, and saw the hotel business back on its feet, living several more years to enjoy the spot which he had so much love for.

January 7, 1945: Boothbay Harbor Waterfront

Loss of Pool's Market, Bowling Alley, Register Building, Scott's Boatyard, Sail Loft, Harris Shop, and The Red Dragon Gift Shop. We set our pumper on the Yacht Club wharf, which used to be located in down-town Boothbay Harbor, and started pumping at once. The temperature was below zero and very disagreeable to be fighting fire, we kept our pump going long after the need of water for the reason if we shut down our hose would freeze. We finally got word to stop and return home. The neighbors nearby made coffee and provided a lunch which we took in relays. This was much appreciated, and very helpful to the men on this early zero morning. Our hose was a mess, and took a long time to thaw out and clean.

Author's note: A rumor was passed on to me, that I found very inter-esting during my research, so I thought I would share it with my readers. I have no way of proving this, but I was told this actually took place a few summers ago. Apparently a tourist walked up to the front desk at Fishermen's Wharf Motel in Boothbay Harbor, and asked if there had been a large fire here in 1945. The person behind the desk said, "Yes, a lot of the waterfront burned down." The man then replied, "I thought so. I served on a German submarine during the Second World War, and we surfaced just outside the harbor in January of 1945, near a small island. While our batteries charged, we watched the fire burn."

THE SHEEPSCOT

The day before I was supposed to go into the service, I was notified by the fish commissioner that my draft notice had been deferred because I was a fisherman. My occupation was considered vital to help feed the troops and the country. Many captains were deferred, but their crews were drafted, so it was impossible to get a good crew to go fishing during the war.   *—Leslie Brewer*

Fisherman were issued identification cards, by the Coast Guard, during the war. A photograph and a fingerprint were required to get one. Many of the fishermen had been seining for herring, and their fingerprints had worn off from handling nets, so it was hard to get a good print.   *—Leland Snowman*

My father, Edgar, and I ran the lobster pound in Ebenecook Harbor, for H.O. Atwood. During the war lobsters cost between 15 and 18 cents a pound and it cost us 40 cents a bushel for the bait we used to feed them. Willis Brewer and Lincoln Webber kept their lobsters crated during the week, then when they got enough together, they would bring them over and sell them to us.   *—Alfred Huskins*

The Coast Guard was in charge of patrolling Southport's waters. One night I was out looking for herring and found a Coast Guard patrol tied up to the Cedarbush Buoy, sleeping instead of keeping an eye on the river. I cut them adrift and have often wondered where they ended up, and what their response was when they finally woke up. *—Leslie Brewer*

Many auxiliary boats and yachts were taken over by the government to help patrol coastal waters during the war.   *—Leland Snowman*

The sailing program had just started at the Southport Yacht Club, and I had one of the five SYC class sailboats Herbert Decker built. Janet Elderkin and the Coletti brothers had one too. During the war, we had to fly signal flags, identifying our boats, when we sailed up and down the river. My dog Spike always went with me, and I can remember see-

ing the crash boats, *Rough Rider* and the *Eight Ball* on patrol in the
Sheepscot. *—Evelyn Pratt Sherman*

My uncle, Ney Brewer, took Bath Iron Works destroyers on trial trips,
and brought tankers up and down the Sheepscot River during the war
years. *—Merle Farnham*

During the war, my father, Joseph, was stationed on Burnt Island
Light, in Boothbay Harbor. Due to blackout conditions, many offshore
lighthouses up and down the coast of Maine were not lighted including
Monhegan, Matinicus, and Mt. Desert. The inshore lighthouses such as
Burnt Island, the Cuckholds, and Hendrick's Head light were in operation, but special curtains were hung in the windows, which cut down on
the amount of light they could produce. Also, fog horns were not used
because they could potentially help the enemy. *—Willard Muise*

At Mile Beach, located on the southern end of Georgetown, practice
bombing took place during the war. The United States government even
trained some British pilots there. They had a crash boat that must have
gone 40 knots, which was used to rescue downed pilots. It was kept at
the Five Islands wharf, and I saw several planes go down, while I was
out fishing. All the practicing was done in a restricted area, so I could-
n't get very close to see what was going on. Everyday it was very noisy,
as airplanes flew over from the airbase in Brunswick on their practice
missions. My second cousin, Charlie Davis, from Five Islands was towed
out of the restricted area while fishing for cod. *—Leslie Brewer*

One day, late in the afternoon, I heard an airplane motor stopping and
starting. Pretty soon, someone came into my grandfather's store and said
an airplane had crashed in Boothbay. We all went over to take a look at
it, and arrived before the military could get to it. The plane was a F4U
Corsair, which was American built, but was being used to train British
pilots. It crashed in a field at the White Farm, which is located across the
street from the present day Knights of Pythias Hall. The pilot was alright,
and when the military people started to show up, we were told no photographs could be taken of the aircraft. *—Ronald Orchard*

Around 1942, a 50 to 55 foot yacht moved into Cozy Harbor. There were several men on board, and they always went up river in the direction of Barter's Island. One day, when the men came ashore, Eddie Childs, the town sheriff at the time, rowed out to peek inside the yacht, because there had been several reports of suspicious activity on it. When he looked inside, he discovered that the yacht was full of electronics. It was then surmised that the men were spying on Bath Iron Works, and were reporting the information they gathered about the ships back to the Germans. The crew returned unexpectedly, and spotted Eddie rowing away from their yacht. They promptly boarded, and left Cozy Harbor, later scuttling the yacht somewhere off Powder Horn. It is presumed that they were picked up by boat by other German sympathizers operating in this area.   —*Leland Snowman*

I remember that fancy yacht well. When the crew realized their secret operation had been discovered, they took her off Powder Horn and sank her in about 20 fathoms of water, leaving a rope from the yacht to the surface, with a life preserver tied to it to mark the spot. The water was much too deep to recover the yacht or its equipment, and the life preserver was cut adrift a short time later.   —*Leslie Brewer*

All the kids used to go down to the beach and look for submarines. We were certain we saw periscopes emerging out in the river, but looking back on it now, I'm sure it was only our overactive imaginations.

—*Katie Rand Copland*

There was a district nurse, of foreign extraction, living in the little house that faces Lighthouse Beach. The men enforcing the blackout conditions on the island always had problems with her, because she refused to keep her shades drawn, and often times they were found in various stages of being up, down, or somewhere in between, as if she were signaling someone. It was rumored that a submarine had gone up the Sheepscot River, and picked up supplies on Westport Island. Shortly thereafter, the district nurse was moved to a new assignment inland.   —*Ronald Orchard*

It was a warm summer's night in 1942 or 1943, when Lee Lanning and I decided to sleep out in sleeping bags on the front porch of Lee's parents house. (Now the West's home on Salt Pond Road.) Later in the dark we heard depth charges going off out towards Seguin. It was easy to recognize them, because they made the ground shake tremendously. Suddenly, the sky lit up with the red glow of flares and it soon became easy to see all around us. We watched the flares drift down into the sea and then all was quiet again. —*Leanne Shibles Eaton*

John Gray's father, Gilbert, spotted a submarine somewhere off Newagen, and reported it to the authorities. The Coast Guard showed up, asked for a description, and questioned Gilbert about what he had seen. —*Ellsworth Gray*

Two Navy crash boats, the *Rough Rider* and the *Eight Ball*, were kept tied up in Boothbay Harbor (what is now known as Wotton's Lobster). They were summoned by blowing the town fire siren, one long blast. If the crews were downtown, you would see sailors in their white uniforms scrambling to get back to the boats. Shortly thereafter you would hear the engines start and the boats would leave the wharf full bore.

—*Merle Farnham*

During the war, there were plenty of tuna fish, but no new hooks to hold them. The metal that was normally used to make the hooks was going toward the war effort. —*Leslie Brewer*

Fishing boats were not allowed to have radios on board during the Second World War, so I carried homing pigeons with me while I was fishing. When I had a good set, I would write a note to Manela, telling her to call the Juliano Brothers, affix it to the bird's leg, and release it. When the military put in a radar station on Morse's Mountain in Sebasco, it interfered with the pigeon's minds. After that, all they could do was fly around and around in circles. They could no longer find their way home, and I lost my source of communication with the mainland. —*Alvin Brewer*

I kept my eye on the pigeon coop throughout the day. When I noticed a bird had returned, I would go out and get the message from Alvin. Then I would call the Juliano Brothers, and let them know how many barrels they needed to bring for Alvin's catch. —*Manela Brewer*

A lot of Criss Crafts were confiscated during the war, and were used as patrol boats in the river. Lieutenant Ernest Hale and local crew member, Bob Marr, used to let the neighborhood kids go on patrol with them once in a while. It was a great treat!   —*Ronald Orchard*

I was jigging for cod on Great Ledge in the first *Sandra Ann*, when I heard a noise behind me, and saw a submarine and its periscope surfacing. I got the hell out of there, just as fast as I could, and reported the incident to the Coast Guard. That night the depth charges started going off in the river, and the concussions from them cracked the plaster in the ceiling of my house. A day or two later, I returned to the same spot, and saw a lot of oil floating on the surface of the water.   —*Leslie Brewer*

I was east of Seguin in my lobsterboat, when I saw a German submarine surface, apparently to recharge its batteries. I reported it, and was questioned in depth by the Coast Guard about what I had seen.

—*Leland Snowman*

One night when Stuart was home on leave, he and I decided to take a walk to Pratt's Island. Blackout conditions were in full swing, and we could hardly see a thing, but we could hear a heavy motor running. We quickened our pace, following the noise, and the closer we got to Pratt's Island the louder the sound became. Once we were over the bridge, we walked straight through the four corners, and out onto the rocks. We couldn't see a thing, but Stuart figured it was a submarine surfaced nearby, recharging its batteries.   —*Jean Luther Thompson*

I got up one winter morning and walked down to Pratt's Island. On my way there I began to notice one set of men's footprints in the snow, coming off the island. When I got to the beach, I realized the footprints came out of the water, up the beach, and down the road. Someone had been put ashore on the beach. I quickly started following the footprints back off the island, but by the time I got to the main road, the snow plow had gone by, and erased all traces of the prints.   —*Leslie Brewer*

During the war years, my father was stationed on Damariscove Island. He was always very tight lipped about any of the activities around our surrounding area. My brothers and I questioned him often, but he would tell us very little. I do remember the Coast Guard taking over many of the beautiful, local, pleasure boats, painting over the fine varnish with their flat, gray paint, and using them to patrol our coastline. I also recall an incident that took place, after we had moved to Boothbay Harbor. Dad brought home a large, black bundle, and would not let us touch it. Shortly thereafter, a Coast Guard truck stopped at our house, and picked it up. We later learned it was a German liferaft, and it was thought that some spies had used it to make a landing somewhere in our coastal area.

—Jack Stover

Dana Payson's Coast Guard identification card.
They were required for anyone operating a boat during the war.
Dana ran a boat for a summer resident, before he went into the service.

During the war, boat owners had to apply for a license to operate their vessel in the territorial waters of the United States. The Coast Guard reviewed your application and had the power to grant or deny your license. The actual form was pretty basic, and I will replicate the one my grandfather, Earl Pratt, Sr., filed on July 18, 1943 below:

Vessel: *Evelyn III*; **Nationality:** U.S.; **Length:** 13.6
Owner/Operator: Earl W. Pratt, Sr.; **Citizenship:** U.S.
Address: 478 Fellsway East, Malden, Mass.
Purpose for which vessel will be employed: Pleasure
Waters in which vessel will be employed: Sheepscot River,
    Southport, Maine
A license is hereby requested to operate the vessel described above for the purpose and on the waters specified. I certify that the statements made in this application are true, to the best of my knowledge and belief.
Date: July 18, 1943
Signature of Applicant: Earl W. Pratt, Sr.

LICENSE NOT VALID WITHOUT OFFICIAL SEAL.

The vessel described above is hereby authorized to operate for the purpose and on the waters described in the application from the date indicated below until: Change of ownership or Revoked, with the following exceptions.
DO NOT allow enemy aliens, cameras, or firearms on board.
DO NOT allow persons aboard without Coast Guard identification card, unless the Master will personally vouch for itinerant guests.
DO NOT leave inland waters of the United States without a permit from the Captain of the Port for each trip.
DO NOT operate within 100 feet of any Naval or Military establishment, shipbuilding plant, power plant, oil or freight dock, except on legitimate business.
DO NOT operate at night except when absolutely necessary on legitimate business.
Date: July 19, 1943 Signature of the Captain of the Port
Place: Portland, Maine
C.G. Identification card no.: 01-1-78064

PRE-WAR NEWS FROM EDITH GRAY'S DIARIES

Edith Gray

Author's note: I would like to thank Marge Barter, Edith's daughter, for allowing me to use her mother's diaries, so we could take a quick glimpse into the past through Edith's eyes. After reading excerpts from them, I have developed a great respect for Edith's knowledge of world events. She really was on top of all the latest news, and quite often foresaw what the Axis powers next move would be. Please keep in mind that because these are diary entries, the dates may not always correspond with the date of the actual event. Sometimes Edith didn't write it down until the next day. Also, they may not always be in sentence form, and there may be abbreviations.

1940

January 5, 1940. Germany is making threats, as tho she'll have to fight Finland if England lends Finland any money. Also, she might attack Sweden if Russia can't beat Finland, on account of Germany having to get raw supplies from Sweden. Guess she's afraid England might fight with Finland against Russia and so blockade around them so that she can't get her supplies from Sweden. Why doesn't she tell Russia to lay off Finland as she and Russia are supposed to be such good friends. Poor Finland! Perhaps poor Sweden! As if its their fault!

January 11. In Finland the other day they repulsed a division of Russians, the second time they have done it and driven back 17 or 18 thousand men and killed thousands. In this battle the Finns, lost a lot, too, but not as many as the Russians. Wish it could end before spring, when the weather is good. It will be horrible then more than now. There are so many more Russians than there are Finns. Russia's invasion of Finland is having an awful effect on the whole world. Anything may happen!

January 26. Russia got her "crack troops" sent back by the Finish. Of course they can't keep going.

February 2. Poor little Romania is now trying to please both England and Germany, fighting for her life. So far she seems to be repulsing Russia everytime, but what will probably happen later, England may send bombing planes to drive Russia back.

February 6. On the radio they are talking about sending money to Finland for them to use for anything they like, not just for food,etc., but war supplies if they are to exist. Russia will annihilate them soon as the snow goes. They are doing wonderfully, tho, at repulsing them.

February 17. An English destroyer took 300 or more prisoners off a German ship in Norwegian waters. I think she did just right, but Norway is demanding she give them back!

February 23: Poor Rumania is between the devil and the deep blue sea. England and France told her if she sold her oil to Germany or if she agreed to, they would not send her the cotton and iron, etc. that she has to have from them as the poor little country is getting together her fighting forces, so as to be ready. I supposed Germany will start to take oil by force and she probably will.

February 24. Hitler talked on the radio, he told how they surely would win over England.

February 28. Roosevelt sent Sumner Wells to the foreign countries on a "peace mission." Not really a peace, that is I don't mean to cause the war to end, but to talk things over, and try to find out about everything. They want to have the right kind of peace, want to prepare for it, beforehand while the war is still on.

March 7. The new English ship, Queen Elizabeth, the largest in the world, reached the U.S. today, eluded submarines, no one knew it was coming. It came over here to be safe until it is finished.

March 14. Finland and Russia have signed a peace treaty, but poor Finland had to give in to Russia. All the men and money she had lost, and all for nothing. That awful Russia!

March 18. They say they are trying to talk over peace some. Sumner Wells comes home Wednesday. Hitler and Mussolini had a conference today. Poor little Finland had to give into Russia. Little countries have no rights over there.

April 11. Terrible fighting off the coast of Norway.

April 12. There is the most terrible sea battle raging off the coast of Norway in several places. Easily the worst naval engagement in the world's history. Been going on for several days. Germany invaded Norway, also Denmark. England must have guessed that she was about to because she planted mines off Norway's coast. Norway felt bound to protest to England for help, being afraid of Germany. Next day Germany put armor in Norway and took over Oslo, the capital and other cities. It will be something terrible. England will fight to try to take Norway back for the Norwegians. They are holding Germany back in places. What will all this horror come to in the end?

April 13. Terrible fighting off Norway and on the coast, too. I guess Germany is occupying Norwegian cities. I don't see how she can get a great many troops over there. She will try Sweden probably. She's so cruel!

April 14. We've been talking about the war and the terrible fighting off Norway. Really don't know what is going on. They aren't giving the particulars out.

April 19. Fighting on three fronts in Norway. Poor Norway! They think Italy may go into the war on Germany's side. I don't see why. Doesn't she know she'll be much worse off than she is now. What a terrible mess!

April 20. If Italy knows what is good for her she won't go into this war. People better tell Mussolini they won't fight.

April 22. They think that there was some kind of spy work going on in Norway, or the Nazis couldn't have gotten in there so easily all of a sudden.

May 3. The Germans are driving the Allies right out of Norway. Oh, it's terrible!

May 10. Germany has invaded Belgium and Holland! Chamberland resigned as the Prime Minister of England and Winston Churchill is now PM. How will it all end?

May 13. The fighting in Belgium and Holland is terrible! The worse the world has ever known! This is going to be the most horrible war. I hope Germany won't win it. I don't see how she can, but I suppose anything can happen. It seems like it.

May 16. There is a fearful battle going on in Belgium and France. Over 50 miles of front. Two million men invaded, thousands of planes in the air, and the tanks and infantry, etc. One can't imagine how it is!

May 17. The war is terrible! The Germans have taken Brussels. The fighting is awful! Roosevelt spoke yesterday very plainly, a speech before the United States Congress asking for 896,000,000 dollars for defense, and he certainly told them plenty about where we stand in this war, and that we will fight with something to fight with if our way of life if threatened. Wants to make 50,000 airplanes a year. Italian papers made fun of his speech and said he was just inciting the American people to war against Germany. They can't understand.

May 18. The war is terrible. Germans are driving back the Allies in Belgium and France. Took Antwerp where they had moved the government. Within 120 miles of Paris. England is sending men and supplies in.

May 20. Terrible fighting is still going on. They say that French have stopped them in one place. They have a new man at the head of the armies. I hope it will help.

May 21. The war news is terribly discouraging. Germany seems to be having her way. Reaching the channel ports. The French Premier said a bridge that should have been blown up was not, either thought oversight or treachery.

May 28. Something terrible happened in the war. King Leopold of Belgium surrendered with an army of 200,000 men to the Nazis, making it easier for the Germans.

May 29. The Allied armies in Belgium and France are trapped. Over half a million are in a pocket. It is terrible. The killing is beyond imagination.

May 31. The Allied armies are retreating from the pocket. About half of them got across to England, but they were bombed in the water and in the boats from the air. A terrible nightmare!

June 1. The British soldiers say that the Germans bomb and machine gun the refugees, women and children. It must be true. Also, run the tanks right over them as they retreat. Hundreds of thousands of British, French, and Belgian troops have reached England. Boats of all kinds were used to get them over, while the Germans bombed them from the air. Of course there are hundreds, thousands more to get out. Situation is a little better. They are going to try to hold the town of Dunkirk.

June 2. Germans are bombing French southern cities with droves of planes.

June 6. Germany is trying to drive the French back toward Paris. Terrible fighting. Lot's of talk of "National Defense" in our country.

June 8. The Allies bombed Berlin. Military parts. Germany ought to get a taste of her own medicine. The U.S. is planning a big defense program. Talking about ways of training men. Ford says give him six months and he can be ready to put out 1000 planes a day!

June 9. Germans seem to be driving the French still tho there is no panic on the part of the French. I wish they would stop them.

June 10. Italy declared war on the Allies. Mussolini made a speech. It was broadcast. "A war for peace, justice, etc." He thinks Germany is winning. If the Allies seemed to be having things their way he would have gone in on their side. Ralph said he is a vulture. Now that is what they are calling him. He wants to get in on the spoils. If Germany doesn't win, he won't get much.

June 11. Mussolini certainly knows what we think of him after hearing Roosevelt's speech last night. Roosevelt said, "He stabbed a neighbor in the back." Secretary Hull said, "One of the worst catastrophes that ever happened to humanity." The Germans are within 35 miles of Paris. The government is leaving and people are evacuating the city. They will fight tho instead of giving up their city. The crown Princess of Holland and her daughter have arrived in Halifax, Nova Scotia. Mussolini said in his speech, "The war was because of those who had control of the wealth and gold of the world." The French say they will defend Paris every foot until they die. Paris is nearly surrounded by the Germans. They are only 12 miles from the city. American ambassador has not left yet.

June 13. The Germans are taking Paris over by this time. French decided to make it an "open city." They decided to hand it over after the Germans fought through their fortifications so as not to destroy the city. American ambassador, Mr. Bullitt stayed. He informed the German government of the French decision. Premier Reynand of France asked Roosevelt to give every material aid possible to the Allies, because they are fighting a war on behalf of all free people. Roosevelt had already promised all aid possible.

Everyone is now talking about the war. Having coffee and dough-nuts and talking about the war news. Nine tenths of the time it is uppermost in all our minds. Anything can happen now at anytime. We shall have to fight in all probability. They will take England on next.

June 15. The battle of France is very serious. They will probably have to give up to Germany. What an awful thing when they fought so bravely, too.

June 17. France is giving up to Germany. Hitler and Mussolini are talking and France is getting Spain to negotiate with Hitler to see about peace and demands. He'll demand plenty for Germany and Italy. It's too awful!

June 18. The peace hasn't been put thru yet. They are still fighting. Germans are driving French back. Probably Hitler terms will be unacceptable. In that case they will probably keep on fighting and he'll take the whole country.

June 19. Germany hasn't made her demands yet, but it is rumored that she wants everything, all her recourses, her fleet, and arms. They say some think the fleet has joined with the British.

June 23. The peace terms have been made public. Germany is taking everything France has. Occupying all the East and northwest of France. Keeping the prisoners, but making France pay for their keep and making France give up the prisoners she has. Making her give up all her resources, ammunitions, stores, war ships, all war implements for them to use against England. Parts of the Army say they won't give up. The British have control of the French fleet, but Germany has demanded they be returned.

June 24. France has not published the German terms yet. It was London that told what we have heard so far. News said France and Italy make terms today, Italy only been in the war two weeks. Don't see how she can have so much to say. They say the French fleet will be interned. Germans promised not to use them in war against England. I wouldn't believe Hitler under oath. Terrible things certainly taking place in this poor world.

June 26. It surely seems as tho poor France is ruined. Her government that signed the peace terms was a new one. The other government did not want to do it. Hard to tell what will happen from one day to the next.

June 28. Russia has grabbed part of Romania in a bloodless invasion.

July 1. Saw war pictures at the movies. They were taken from a fighting plane in the air over the English Channel when the boats were taking the troops from Flanders.

July 2. Germany and Italy have got together on Rumania. They are scared for fear the Russians would go to far.

July 4. Thrilling and terrible news from Europe. Air raids over England and also over Germany and Holland, etc. Churchill cried while talking to Parliament telling them of the fight between English Navy and French naval vessels. He said the British Commander asked the French to either give the boats to Britain or scuttle them. He wouldn't give consent as their was a battle. He (Churchill) said that there must have been a good many French casualties. It seemed to all those who had been such close Allies, but Hitler is very mad because of the taking of French boats to England. Hitler's word to not use the fleet cannot be believed and of course they couldn't allow the French fleet to be used to help conquer England. Some difference between the way those nations live and the way we live. Been talking of it all day on the radio, it being our 4th of July!

July 6. Germany has forced France to break off diplomatic relations with England because of the British having the battle, attacking the French fleet and not letting those ships in English ports go back to France. I suspect that made Germany very mad. It must have, and of course they can boss France now.

July 7. They say the British have ships watching off the Island of Martinique (French possession) in the Caribbean Sea. Hope it won't cause any trouble with us. There really seems to be hard feelings between England and France over England taking the French fleet. I don't see why, should think they'd want them to have it. It may be that Germany wants to make trouble between France and England. It is probably her doing.

July 8. Germany is dictating to France just what kind of a government she shall have and it certainly will not be a Republic or Democracy. It had been decided what will happen to the few ships in Alexandria, Egypt, left from the French fleet. English are lying in wait. She has asked them to surrender, because England doesn't want to fight them, but they can't let them turn those ships against England.

July 9. There was a terrible air raid over England today.

July 11. News reports say the bombings over England and France are becoming terrible. Worse yesterday and today than before.

August 1. Boys between 21 and 31 will be drafted for peace time service. Air fights over England and Ireland. They think it may not be long now before the Germans attack England.

August 4. England is bombing vital spots in Germany and doing quite a lot of damage. I hope she breaks the morale of those gullible Germans.

August 5. England and the world think that Germany is getting ready for her offensive on England, troops, etc. on the Channel or near the Channel ports in France and Belgium. England and United States are "on the outs" with Japan, especially England right now.

August 6. They fought awfully off Channel coast of England yesterday. Three attacks on English convoy ships by German bombers and torpedo boats. Terrible! England claims to have brought down 70 German planes.

August 10. Air battle over England everyday. Also, England retaliated over Germany. Where will it all end?

August 13. Germany has started her "blitzkrieg" on England, they think as she is sending bombers by the hundreds. Terrible fighting. They also think the southeast is being shelled by the big guns from the French coast.

August 15. Terrible air battle involving 5,000 planes over Britain.

August 19. Our ambassador to France, Bullit, said in a speech that we are now in as much danger from Hitler as France was a year ago. It is causing some discussion.

August 20. United States and England are going to get together and decided on a base for United States on one or more of England's territories. It is pleasing to them and I guess to us.

August 24. The Germans are shelling England and France.

August 31. Terrible fighting in England. 1,000 planes over London and other towns. Yesterday 1,000 Nazi planes!

September 3. Still terrible fighting over England.

September 9. Germans are sending droves of planes over London and other parts of England and bombing and setting fires something terrible. Saturday night 400 were killed and 1300 hurt in the raids.

September 17. Both Germany and England bombing something terrible.

September 26. Terrible bombing over Berlin. Trouble in French Indo China with Japan. We have put an embargo on scrap iron to Japan. She isn't going to like that.

September 27. There was an agreement made in Berlin between Japan, Germany, and Italy armies directed at the Untied States. It sounds very serious, say they will unite in war against any nation that joins Britain. We have repeatedly told Japan hands off the Dutch East Indies. It seems as tho that is just what she contemplates doing, attacking them.

October 4. Mussolini and Hitler met at the Brenner Pass for a conference today. More deviltry I suppose.

October 9. The Italian newspapers said if United States didn't recognize what the Axis powers are doing then it would be war for us. Mussolini is quite outspoken.

October 14. England is doing as much damage to Germany and the coast that she is occupying as they are doing to England now. Good to give them the same and see how they like it. They thought England would give in to them and it would be easy because the British couldn't bomb them but guess they found out differently. They have to stand it too, not much fun!

October 16. They say that Germany was already to invade England and the British Air force bombed the ships and did so much damage that the soldiers had to be taken off and the idea abandoned.

October 17. The Germans are bombing England in waves of 1,000s. England is very brave and the morale is fine. England has also bombed Germany, too. Germany says they bomb only military objectives while the British bombed hospitals and civilians. Oh, yeah!

October 22. The Axis powers are bringing pressure to bear on France and Spain to join them in fighting Britain. Isn't that something! They want Gibraltar, heard they're going to attack Egypt in earnest.

October 25. They say 17,000,000 men registered and that they plan a peace time army of 800,000 by June. The boys don't know their numbers yet. Next Tuesday the Secretary of State will draw the first number from the gold fish bowl they used in the First World War.

October 26. France has given into Germany, of course she had to. Don't know just what they'll have to do to help the Germans.

October 28. Italy has invaded Greece and England has sent ships and men there to help Greece. Italy is fighting Greece from Albanian border. She occupied Albania year or so ago.

November 1. The paper said only 80 boys would be chosen from the State of Maine for Service.

November 4. Greece is doing pretty well for herself against Italy. I hope it continues.

November 8. United States is going to make planes for U.S. and England, 50/50 everyday, just as many for one country as the other.

November 11. Greece is getting the best of Italy so far.

November 15. Last night the Germans entirely destroyed the English city of Coventry. 500 planes dropped every kind of bomb and killed thousands.

November 20. Germany has lined up some of those Balkans on her side today and putting pressure on others I guess. It looks as tho Turkey will have to fight. I hope Russia will not help Germany, but I suppose she will. Both England and Germany are bombing cities terribly.

November 22. Greece is driving the Italians back but I suppose Germany will do something to help Italy. Of course she will win in the end because she's more powerful.

November 29. Rumania is having a revolution!

December 1. Greeks still have the Italians on the run. Germany is taking the food from the countries she dominates and starving them purposely so she can blame it on the British blockade and so turn them from being pro-England to pro-German. Such fiendish schemes!

December 6. Hitler will interfere in Albania where the Greeks are driving the Italians.

December 7. No airplane activity over England to speak of today. They don't know the reason why. Having an upset in the Italian Army offensive. England wants credit from us.

December 9. Italy is being beaten on all fronts they say. Good enough. London had almost the worse bombing of the war last night.

December 11. The British won back that territory they lost to the Italians in Egypt. Wonder what Mussolini will think now?

December 12. England asking for money. They will have to reverse the Johnson Act (refusing to lend money to any country that defaulted on First World War debts). Of course England did, but we will have to help her all we can. It is as much for ourselves as for her. If we can help with ships, airplanes, money, etc., we may not have to send our men to war.

December 13. The British have the Italians on the run. They say Italy is really upset, but no real news comes out of the country. Both the Greeks and British are giving them plenty. England has taken thousands of Italian prisoners in Egypt.

December 27. England and Germany did not bomb each other on Christmas day, but have started to again.

December 29. Roosevelt is going to speak on the radio tonight. We will want to hear that. We will certainly be in this war the whole way. We must sent the armaments and we must train the men because we must help England, that might be all that we will have to do. If we can help her win short of sending our men, that will be all to the good. Germany bombed London terribly tonight, as bad as she ever has before. Roosevelt gave a talk on our position in the world, and in relation to the warring countries. We must help England or it means the end of Democracy in the world. It is our own defense of our way of life. Spoke very plain. Hitler is not going to like it. The German papers made no comment this morning. Of course England was pleased.

December 31. Hitler says the Democracies are "war mongers." The last day of the year – I wish this war could end before we have to send our boys.

1941

January 1, 1941. Germany is sending troops down through the Balkans. Supposedly to help keep Italy in Egypt. They are some mad over Roosevelt's Sunday speech. Some of our boys are receiving their numbers for the draft.

January 3. Germany demanded so much from the government of France that Marshal Petain will not comply. Probably Germany will take over completely now. They think that (Count Von Luckinar) is operating in the South Pacific, now as he did in the other World War. He's the one that Lowell Thomas wrote a book about.

January 7. Germans are moving down into the Balkans, have been for some time, they are getting ready to do something. Roosevelt message to Congress was about raising money for our own defense, 17½ billion. That isn't counting the amount for England's defense. Sales taxes on everything – it can't be helped.

January 9. The British and Americans have got together and are allowing us to send Red Cross mercy ships through to France from the U.S., to feed the French children and the Red Cross is going to see that they get it. If it works O.K., they will see about sending some food to Spain. Herbert Hoover wanted us to feed the starving people in the occupied countries for a long time, because Germany had taken their food, to feed their own people.

January 12. Lots of discussion in Congress over the defense program and aid to Britain.

January 17. Still a lot of discussion among the congressmen over our aid to Britain program – don't know what will happen to the world this year.

January 19. Some think the President is asking for too much power. They are divided in this "all aid to Britain." The opposition is as earnest as the other. It seems so it is hard to know just what is the right thing to do.

January 24. Lots of people think if the "Lend Lease" Bill is passed will be right in the war and will be sending ships and men in no time.

January 26. There are riots in Italy between Nazi soldiers and Italian soldiers. Probably Nazis taking over Italy to "protect" her, then going to invade Africa.

February 1. They say Hitler has thousands of planes and will use poison gas just as soon as the weather permits, and will start a terrible drive in England.

February 2. They expect the "Lend Lease" Bill to pass the House this week and in two weeks in the Senate.

February 6. They passed the Lend Lease Bill so the time is limited to two years. They had a time, but I guess it will pass now.

February 8. The Lend Lease Bill passed the House. They changed it allowing only 1/10 of output to go to England in 1941. Awful large number of thinking people are against it. I wish we could all know for sure what is really the best for us to do, if we could look into the future. British are taking one city after another from Italians in Africa. France will not give in to Hitler, so I suppose he will take over the Vichy government, certainly it must make him some mad that he doesn't have more power there. Of course he would control the French fleet and French Africa so to stop the British in Africa.

February 10. British broke off relations with Rumania. Shelled Genoa, Italy. There is talk about Bulgaria. Germany is putting troops in those Balkan states by the thousands. Probably to help the Italians in Greece.

February 18. Hitler is taking over Bulgaria, his specialty, taking over little countries. Turkey acts as tho she will not do anything about it.

Hitler wants to get Greece, because she is getting the best of Italy. They think Germany is pushing Japan into the war to take over French Indo China and Dutch East Indies. Today was the day that they call the boys for Army service, so they said.

February 19. Hitler is telling France she will have to get food supplies from her African colonies or she'll suffer and they say that means war between France and England because she would have to use her fleet against the English fleet to get across the Mediterranean Sea. Also, she is expected to bring pressure to bear on Greece (she had large forces down there in the Balkans) to force her to stop fighting Italy, and Italy was the one that started it as she attacked Greece.

February 20. Hitler bringing pressure to bear on Greece and France. Controversy on Lend Lease Bill in Senate!

February 23. Hitler had most of the Balkans under control. Germany on shortwave asked America what kind of Germany program they would like to hear from Germany. A telegram went to Germany worded in "American slang, poor German, and excellent Yiddish." Made Hitler mad because what the telegram said was not complimentary.

February 28. In Congress the Senate is debating the Lend Lease Bill and having real fights on the floor. Those against it say Roosevelt will be a dictator and will be in the war when there is no need of it. Both sides very bitter. Senator Wheeler of Montana said very hard things about those that head the opposition.

March 1. Bulgaria joined the Axis powers. Going to be something doing down there. Congress still debating the Led Lease Bill to England!

March 6. They think Yugoslavia is going to join the Axis powers!

March 8. Lend Lease Bill has finally passed the Senate!

April 21. The Balkans and the Nazis are pushing into Greece, pushing English and Greeks back. The Yugoslavs fought for a while to hold them back but they gave up.

April 22. Hitler offered French government all kinds of territory if they would fight England. Hope they won't have to, but he usually gets his way.

April 23. Turkey expects Hitler to attack in about ten days. I don't see why Turkey and Russia don't get together and with the Greeks and British, attack the Nazis all at once. They can't do anything one at a time!

April 24. The Greek King George and government fled to the island of Crete and his armies are retreating.

May 18. Everyday we are creeping nearer war. They will convoy the ships to Britain with our navy probably. Germany will sink any ship no matter whose. She said so, and of course you know she would. Some Senators want us to enter the war now. Someone was saying the other day that we should take different islands and Dakar, a French port in Africa, and the Azores, etc. That would be an act of war all right! We are going to have two large air bases in Greenland by permission of the Danish government.

May 13. We have been very excited over the news. Hitler's #1 Nazi, Rudolf Hess, 2nd or 3rd in line after Hitler himself, flew to England, and is a prisoner of war! All kinds of guesses why and what for, etc. He intended to go there, had pictures of himself for identification, bailed out of the plane, and broke his ankle. He is now in a hospital. People are wondering if he will tell any military secrets. He could tell plenty. Churchill didn't talk about him, until the Nazis gave out the information he was missing, said he was insane, and probably committed suicide, etc. He had been in England for two days by then!

May 15. There are all sorts of stories going around in both Germany and England about Rudolf Hess, but the truth is not out yet about his flight to England.

September 11. Roosevelt is to speak tonight. Important! There had been three boats sunk by Germans. One just going to Iceland with supplies and I suppose Roosevelt will say that we must insist on freedom on the seas. We will be having battles probably from now on.

October 28. Roosevelt talked in his speech as tho we are really in the war, guess we will be if we arm the ships. He said a secret paper they got said Hitler planned to carve up South America and abolish religion.

November 11. It is quite serious, the trouble between Japan and United States. There is a Japanese envoy on way to Washington now, to talk it over. If Japan could be sure Hitler would win the war they wouldn't hesitate to make war on us, but they can't be sure and they need our trade. Churchill gave a speech yesterday and said if we would declare war with Japan that Britain would declare war within the hour on them too.

November 17. Roosevelt and a Japanese envoy are talking over conditions between our countries. It seems like a serious situation.

November 24. Our government is arming our merchant ships and our navy is going to convoy ships to England and they are looking for German U-boats. United States is sending troops to Trinidad, because of the terrible fighting in North Africa. May mean that Germany will get control of the French fleet and incidentally French Guiana and most of our aluminum supply comes from down there. Germany forced the Vichy government of France to oust the French general because he was friendly with England and they put in Darlan, who has been more pro-German.

November 26. It wasn't Trinidad where our forces went, it was Dutch Guiana. They are going to hold a conference. Hitler and all his "enforced friends" to decide about, "The new order in Europe."

December 7. Terrible news on the radio this afternoon. Ralph (Edith's husband) turned on Kaltenborn, and he had astounding news Pearl Harbor had been bombed. We all looked at each other in astonishment. Ralph said, "Japan has signed her death warrant!" Lots of rumors the first day. 300 service men dead and 104 civilians, the next day said 3,000 were killed.

December 9. Rumor that Germany, Italy, and Japan are going to make a simultaneous attack on the United States. Rumor Japanese airplanes over San Francisco last night.

December 12. Hitler made a speech and put the blame on Roosevelt.

December 13. David Blake joined the U.S. Marines. He wanted to join the Army Air Corp with Kenneth Orne and Eddie McKown, but he was too young. They say the entire eastern coast of the United States may have to be blacked out.

December 14. Glendon Ayer joined the Naval Reserve. Walter Winchell on radio talking about F.B.I. arresting Japanese in California as enemy aliens.

December 20. Congress passed the bill yesterday, that all men from 18 to 64 will register. Those 20 to 44 will be subject to draft.

1942

January 6, 1942. Roosevelt addressed Congress. We have to go all out for war. 56 billion this year for arms, etc. Civilians will have to do without tin, rubber, aluminum, etc.

January 14. The news said U-boats are getting more and more active off the Atlantic coast.

January 19. A third tanker has been sunk off this coast by German subs, off North Carolina. This time 23 lost, also one in Connecticut and one in New York.

January 25. German sub sank another tanker off North Carolina. 22 lost.

January 30. Hitler made a one hour and 55 minute speech. He said more and more subs would be sinking American ships. But he didn't say that Germans would win the war within the year, as he always does.

February 2. Some maneuvering off here in the water. Ralph looked through his glasses and saw 14 or 16 planes and what looked like and aircraft carrier. Before that we saw boats off there and puffs of smoke.

February 7. There have been 17 boats torpedoed on this coast.

February 15. Singapore had fallen!

March 22. MacArthur's gone to Australia to take charge of the defense.

April 18. There was a loud explosion in the night last night. Just one shook the house. The Americans have bombed Japan, news on the radio today.

April 29. The U.S. forces seem to be keeping the Japanese off the Solomons, sunk 18 ships. In Russia the fighting is terrible. Germans are slowly pushing the Russians back. Oh, dear!

May 22. The Germans and English are fighting on the Island of Crete. Germans parachutists and men by gliders dropped down from the air. Not much news getting out but the battle is fierce. It will be bad if Germany gets the Island, as it will control the whole eastern Mediterranean Sea.

May 27. The British got the *Bismark* after she got the British battle ship *Hood* with a hit that exploded her magazines and her with 1,340 men, but the English followed her and got her. She had 1,500 men. Guess they don't know whether many of her men could be saved. It is horrible! I know the British would got her after what she did to the *Hood*.

June 22. Germany invaded Russia this morning. Never declared war or delivered any message or said anything. Just marched right in with tanks, and bombers. Russia should have known — trying to be friends with Hitler!

September 1. MacArthur's forces are holding their own.

September 15. Terrible fighting in Russia. Hand to hand combat in the city. Russians said they will all die before they will give up the city, and they cut off their retreat by burning the bridges.

September 18. Stalingrad is still holding, terrible fighting, worst in history.

October 2. They are driving the Japanese on New Guinea.

October 13. Fierce fighting again on Solomon Islands. Guadalcanal is where David Blake is. Destroyed several Japanese ships. We lost a destroyer. The Marines holding a point and keeping Japanese off with help of Air Corps. The Russian winter is coming on so German activities are halting in Russia. Probably can't take Stalingrad in Russia with their cold winter.

October 15. Awful fighting down at Solomon Islands. Japanese landing reinforcement and so are we. Poor Babe (David Blake's mother) must feel awful. I bet that is where Sammy (Emerson) is, too.

October 16. Letter from Sammy saying it was winter, but not very cold. He may be in the Pacific. We have forces there and are sending more. Had battles last week and drove the Japanese out of the parts they held.

November 6. They have the Germans on the run in Africa. Hope it continues this time.

November 8. Very good news last evening. Ralph pounded on the floor upstairs. A very big Allied force has landed in French North Africa. Roosevelt made a speech in French by shortwave to the French people telling them not to think we want any conquest or territory or anything. We came as friends to liberate them from the heel of Germany and Italy. It was a very good speech. He spoke good French. We don't know yet just how much fighting there was. Roosevelt said it was done before Germany knew it. The British have General Rommel on the run and captured half of his forces over near Egypt where they have been fighting so hard and now this invasion will make it hard for him to get reinforcements. Italy will be pretty scared we will invade her next. Germany will probably have to take some forces from her front in Russia so that will weaken her there. That this is the "second front," that was needed, can't be doubted.

November 8. The Vichy government of France (sympathetic to Hitler) broke off relations with the United States this afternoon.

November 9. Lot of talk over radio about the invasion into Africa. The Vichy French are resisting and there is fighting. Algeria gave up yesterday. Relations were not broken off yesterday as first stated, but they were today. Italy is scared, said they can look for trouble anywhere and it is all the fault of the United States. Imagine!

November 10. Our forces have taken Oran and Casablanca from the darn foolish French. The idea of fighting us for the Germans the way the Nazis have been murdering the French. I simply can't understand that!

November 19. The Free French have joined our forces in North Africa. Petain asked to resist the Americans and English but they rallied around the French leader who is against the Vichy government. We are still successful in Guadalcanal in the Solomons.

November 27. The French have blown up the whole French fleet based at Toulon, France. The Germans were going to take it over. Over 60 ships lost. So, the French are not going to work with the Nazis.

November 28. In Russia they are driving the Nazis every way they wish. There are thousands bottled up. The British fleet are in Mediterranean Sea, at least some of it, waiting to see if any of the French fleet escaped form the explosions when the French blew the ships up yesterday. Want to get at them so Germany can't. A submarine escaped into Barcelona, Spain.

November 29. Our Marines and other forces holding their own in the Solomons.

December 12. They are fighting pretty hard in North Africa with the Germans. We hear Glendon (Ayer) is sailing home from there.

1943

January 17, 1943. A tanker went by, it was convoyed by two planes. Guess there aren't any submarines off here.

February 15. Several French ships, battleships, and cruisers, etc., left Dakar, and came across the Atlantic, one is in New York, one in Philadelphia, and two are going to Boston. No U boats got them. They are then expected to go to Casablanca. The Russians still have Nazis on the run. Gaining back the cities the Nazis took last summer and winter.

February 26. The Americans and British have driven the Germans back some more.

March 3. Terrible fighting in North Africa, and plenty everywhere else.

March 4. General MacArthur sent word that our bombers destroyed a Japanese convoy of 22 ships and at the same time dropped bombs on one of their air drones (a pilotless aircraft operated by remote control) in the East Indies. The biggest demolition of a convoy in the war.

June 1. The Allies are bombing Germany and Italy plenty. They asked for it! China is doing good for herself. We must be getting stuff to her somehow or she couldn't have so much to fight with. Sammy said in a letter to Jeanette that he is "going north" from where he was (Australia) and it is terribly hot. Sweat was pouring off of him. Have to have the engineroom door shut so no light gets out, and it was awful. Ralph says he is probably going to India. Churchhill and Roosevelt had a conference in Washington and have planned something.

July 19. The Allies bombed Rome today. Had orders not to bomb St. Peters or anything like it, just military objectives, but Rome told about them bombing school houses, etc., as they and the Germans always say! The Allies have got about half of Sicily now and have about demolished Naples.

September 9. There has been a number of developments in the war situation. Mussolini has resigned or been kicked out, or killed, nobody knows. Yesterday Italy surrendered unconditionally. There is still plenty of fighting. The Allies took Sicily a while ago and have invaded Italy. They are bombing Germany, occupied France, Holland, and other places unmercifully. Russia is pushing them out with terrible fighting. MacArthur is pushing back the Japanese on the Solomons and surrounding them in Lae on New Guinea.

September 17. Yanks landed in Italy! There had been dreadful fighting at Salerno. Finally drove Germans and have a foothold. Germans took away divisions from Russians front as Russians have their second front. They've been wanting all kinds of fronts and guns for us. The British were on the west of Italy and have marched through and joined us now. Germans had to retreat. Fighting was fierce and lots of men lost on both sides. War is in real earnest now. Germans tried to drive us into the sea, over and over again – dreadful! MacArthur has taken Lae, New Guinea, so the Japanese aren't having things all their way either. Germany has heavily fortified northern Italy, so to save Germany from being fought on, and to keep the Allies out. They say they took Mussolini out of prison and took over the city of Rome and the Pope is really a prisoner!

October 16. Awful fighting in Italy, Russia, and also in India. They are doing better than was expected so soon with the Japanese. Awful fighting in Italy near Rome. They are destroying paintings, sculpture, arts, etc. They killed men, women, and children in the streets in Naples and burned the city. Doesn't seem so anyone human could do such things. It isn't war. It is murder!

August 24. The war is going very good. Two invasions of France. Horrible fighting – Hitler can't hold out much longer. The Russians are on the way to invading Germany itself. We have taken several islands south of Philippines.

Author's note: Edith's diary stopped here in late August, and she didn't pick it up again, for reasons known only to her.

On the Homefront With Edith Gray

The following excerpts were taken from Edith Gray's diaries. They reflect everyday life here on Southport during the war. Her entries include prices, movies, and observations.

1941

December 28, 1941. We're going to put an oil burner in the kitchen as Ralph can't get his wood out and to buy it would cost 17 dollars a cord! The new oil burner costs 30 dollars and a new Bulova watch costs 35 dollars.

December 29. No new cars will be made after early 1942.

December 30. Saw Spencer Tracy in *Dr. Jekyll and Mr. Hyde* at the movies.

December 31. Bought four retreads. It is going to be very hard to get tires. They say they won't be sold to private cars.

1942

January 6, 1942. They are saying there is a run on sugar. I don't think that is right, but I'd hate to go without sugar in the winter for cooking. The air raid wardens met at Frances Gray's. Cecil Pierce came down to see Ralph about going to Damariscotta to learn about air raid work.

January 8. Earl Snowman is in New Jersey in the Army Air Corp and Glendon Ayer is in the Naval Reserve.

January 11. Guns firing somewhere, funny time of night for guns, must be in Portland. Ralph was asked to be an air raid warden, and went to the meeting in Damariscotta. Ed Huskins, Roscoe Rand, John Swett, and Cecil Pierce is the head of it.

January 14. Jeanette has gone to a first air raid meeting with Frances Gray.

January 15. Airmail to the boys in service is six and a half cents instead of 20 cents, as it was before. Fifty people were at the first air raid meeting Jeanette attended. Couldn't buy any large safety pins. Will see if Charlie Pinkham has any. He has everything. Jeanette went to Dr. Phil at the hospital to have a small growth removed on her arm. It cost five dollars.

January 17. Airplane with 22 aboard smashed into a mountain in Arizona. All killed, one was Carol Lombard, wife of Clark Gable. They were on a U.S. bond drive. There was a queer thing happened this afternoon about four o'clock. We heard a plane for just a few seconds and then a big explosion, but couldn't see anything. Ralph went down to the shore and there was not anything there. After the explosion we didn't hear the plane anymore. Ralph said it sounded like one might have exploded in the air. It was rough, if anyone or thing was in the water, it couldn't have been seen.

January 24. Got some cloth. Four different pieces for a blouse and dress. The man was down today and raised the price from 25 cents to 27 cents on the same goods. He's getting two cents more profit on a yard! Over town Anne Kendrich said her next lot would be 35 or 39 cents. Ralph goes to air raid meetings all the time.

January 26. A sweetheart valentine was 25 cents. Ralph got the radio fixed for three dollars.

January 27. Both hot water bottles need new washers and I can't buy them anywhere. Jeanette is studying her first aid course.

January 30. Just paid the last payment on my sewing machine. Two and a half years cost 103 dollars.

January 31. Bought a mirror. It was 15 cents, and was quite a large one.

February 3. Eddie Gaudette delivered our groceries. He said I could have five pounds of sugar Friday if I ordered it on Wednesday.

February 4. Got some things at the A&P store, but they are more expensive than at Charlie Pinkham's. They say there is a shortage of tea. You can only have one pound at a time.

February 8. On the Red Cross drive people gave 50 cents. One gave two dollars. Ralph gave one dollar.

February 14. Bought Valentine gift for Marjorie. Raised $13.20 on the Cape for the Red Cross. Marion Swett headed it for Southport Island. I did for Newagen.

February 15. Bought a new hot water bottle for 98 cents.

February 16. Jeanette went with Hazel Dow and Francis Gray to a air raid meeting.

February 18: No new oil burner being sold and maybe no oil.

February 20. It said on the radio that we may not have the 12 ounces of sugar a week we have been getting, only eight ounces a week. I won't be doing much cooking I guess.

February 21. Stopped at the A&P store. Things have gone up in price. A shortage in toilet paper. Isn't that something!

February 22. Going to the harbor, we met Margaret Stover and Joe walking over to see Jackie, who is in the hospital with a bad case of appendicitis, and he had bronchitis when they operated on him. Margaret said she had a ride back with Jenny Boyd who was visiting Lawrence, who had his appendix out too. That means that young Lawrence, Buddy, and their father, Lawrence, all had their appendix out inside of four months!

February 23. Lester Barter couldn't find any men to dig a grave. The men are all working at Samples Shipyard and Ralph was helping Charlie Gray. He finally got Jim Parrish. Eleazer Giles hauled out our wood and ate dinner with us and he fed his horses. The kids loved that. Big basket of flowers of pink and white carnations and snaps was seven dollars.

February 28. There is going to be a shortage of electric irons. I'm going to get one as mine is old. Old-fashioned measles going around, most everywhere on the island. Katherine Buck said Sidney Sherman has them and her little boy is taking something for them. Katherine is expecting a new baby in three weeks. They say there will be a short-age of men's garters, imagine! There is no toilet paper in the A&P store and I couldn't get any at Charlie Pinkhams!

March 1. Saw the movie, *How Green was My Valley*. Very good.

March 2. Made an apple pie for town meeting. We had an eclipse of the moon. A lot of guns going off. They are very loud. Maybe coming from Portland.

March 3. Katherine Buck had twin boys!

March 4. Ralph sent two tires away to be retreaded and couldn't get them back. I call that stealing, government or no government. Ralph bought a used tire and paid eight dollars for it. Ralph is making out the income tax. He thought of going to a lawyer to get it done this year, but it costs four dollars!

March 11. Jeanette went to a first aid meeting, so I rode up with Ralph and Chester Sherman. We dropped him off and brought Ruth Sherman back with Jeanette from their first aid meeting. Jeanette practiced first aid on me this afternoon. Bandages and artificial respiration, etc. She nearly killed me!!!

March 17. Men went to see a launching at Samples. I priced electric irons over town, and they were nine dollars. At Sears they are seven.

March 19. Ralph took Jeanette and Francis Gray and Ruth Sherman to a first aid meeting.

March 22. We are going to have a trial blackout soon.

March 26. We went to see *Bahama Passage* with Sterling Hayden, who Ralph has met, and Madeline Carroll. Very pretty scenery, but not much of a story. Sterling Hayden came on board the *Tyrone* and wanted to buy it. Ralph told Mr. Tener and he said, "Who is he?" Have to go around for cancer control, Bernice Pinkham asked me. Bought a new little radio at Sears for ten dollars.

April 6. Ralph has gone to Portland to find out about yacht regulations. The government may take over private yachts. Maybe the Yacht Ralph is on, the *Tyrone*. Jeanette and Frances Gray passed their air raid wardens test!

April 11. Dr. Phil made a house call.

April 13. Ralph went to a first aid meeting at the town hall.

April 18. Ralph has to stand watch from 12 to 2 A.M. starting tonight at the observation post. Harold Powers is to stand watch with him. Two men or two women have to be there day and night. It is up by the town hall.

April 21. Sent for several flower seeds $1.30. Now they are up to 15 cents a package.

April 22. Went to the movie, *Adventure of Warden Eden*, a Jack London book, with Glen Ford. A good show. Ralph bought a tire for five dollars. A Mr. Hall brought it down from Damariscotta. He had two blowouts with the tires Mr. Hall sold him. Ralph told Maynard Robinson he was going to, "Turn the heat on," so when they saw Mr. Hall coming with that tire, Maynard said, "Guess you lit a torch under that fellow!"

April 23. Another flat tire and Ralph had to have it fixed. Ralph had watch from 12 to 2 A.M.

April 26. Air raid meeting and Boothbay Harbor has a blackout tomorrow night, so I guess we will too. Ralph will find out.

April 27. Well, we had a blackout, our first! Just turned out the lights for half an hour. The school house bell rang for the beginning and the ending. I have all curtains pulled down, as Cecil Pierce came down and told Ralph that from now on all houses with windows facing the ocean would have to be blacked out. Guess all the guns we have heard mean something. Scott Gray and Lester Barter saw what they thought was a submarine one day. U-boats have done, and are doing plenty.

April 27. A bad fire at Boothbay Harbor last night, early morning. The lower drug store, Hartungs, and fruit store burned. All the upper parts where the lawyer's office is and Dr. Barrows. D.A.R. hall burned as well. A terrible loss! Took up for the cancer fund, $11.71.

May 1. A Mr. Hamilton coming here. Mr. Collind going to Waldoboro. Mr. Hamilton has a son in the Air Corps in Massachusetts. Heavy firing offshore somewhere three different times.

May 2. Some of the women are getting 45 cents an hour for cleaning cottages. The job of rationing the sugar has been given to the school teachers, as if they didn't have enough to do. Some of the women will help them. You have to tell even the color of your eyes and your weight to sign up!

May 4. Today began the sugar rationing. If you have more than six pounds to a person in a family, you can't get a card until it is used up. I think I have six or seven pounds. I'll have to look and see. Paper said dim out three miles inland from the coast. Now selling blackout curtains all over town. Ralph talks about the government taking the *Tyrone* over and putting it in commission for the Coast Guard. The *Tyrone* is tied up at Robinson's Wharf along side of the *Bowdoin*.

May 8. Had a blackout. Whistles blew up to West Southport and the school house bell rang.

May 10. Ralph and Harold stood watch at the observation post from 12 to 2 A.M., but the other party didn't come, so they didn't get home until 4:30 A.M.!

May 11. Sammy is in the Navy as a First Class Machinist Mate. He made 64 dollars a month.

May 12. The men got their gas rationing cards. They will be allowed enough to go to harbor once a day to work. Boats can have three gallons a week. The selectmen have charge of this.

May 14. Ralph filled up the gas tank at Pinkham's. Tomorrow they start rationing. I bought Marjorie a pair of pajamas, $1.98.

May 18. Today Ralph attended the last air raid meeting for the study of gases. Bought a cotton dress and paid five dollars for it. That was too much!

May 21. Bought a pajama pattern for 35 cents. I have to go around for the federal government to ask people to sign up for defense bonds or stamps. Katherine Buck is heading the drive on Southport.

May 28. Girls waiting on tables at the Boothbay House get seven dollars a week, plus tips.

May 29. Bought a clothes brush for one dollar and a change purse with a zipper. It has places to fit change in it for $1.50, for the kids.

May 31. David Blake was home on leave and then he will sail to some foreign country. He has had five months of training.

June 1. The fishermen were told by the Coast Guard to put 12 inch high letters on their boats. *Press Herald* has gone up to five cents, *Boston Post* is still two or three cents.

June 2. Jeanette bought a party dress $8.95.

June 3. Went to a foolish movie, *The Great Mans Lady*, with Barbara Stanwick and Joel McCrea.

June 5. Graduation ball cost 50 cents.

June 6. Glendon Ayer was home on leave, been to Trinidad. They have sunk five submarines and once just cleared their own mine fields that they had just laid.

June 9. Blackout between 9:00 and 9:30 P.M., lasts 20 minutes. Most everyone will be at the movies or coming home. We won't, as Ralph is at an air raid wardens meeting tonight. Two fisherman out of Gloucester were sunk by a German U-boat. No lives lost, but in the boats rowing for about 36 hours.

June 12. Saw the movie, *Tortilla Flat*. We've been looking at cars. Can get a good second hand one for 175 dollars.

June 15. We had an air raid warning, because two unidentified planes went over.

June 16. They say there will be an invasion of Europe before 1942 is out.

June 22. I sent for material for a skirt. They sent my money back and said they can't get anymore.

June 28. Eddie Gaudette told us Friday he is called for the draft. We don't know who will take his place. The F.B.I. have found eight German spies that landed in this country from U-boats. They had plans, maps, and guns, etc. No real details. Isn't that nerve?

June 30. Cost five dollars to have a car inspected. It is a new war time law to raise money. Actually not really an inspection it's just because you own a car. All car owners.

July 4. No fire crackers or fire works. A very quiet 4th of July. Not like the 4th we know.

July 7. Eddie Gaudette was drafted. They have a new 21 year old summer boy named Hayes delivering groceries for Pinkham's now. U-boats still at it. Ralph has an awful time, because they don't get those swift mosquito boats going after them. He would like to command one.

July 9. The "submarine menace," as they call it and all the spies the F.B.I. is finding are terrible!

July 17. Bought an electric plate and oven for 15 dollars.

July 20. No library sale this summer as no one has the sugar to cook with. We will just ask for donations of money.

July 21. Ralph is making out an application for gas for boat and another one for the car.

July 23. Ralph got a card from Portland saying the Merchant Marine needs licensed officers and asking questions for him to answer. I hope they won't take him.

July 24. I bought a dress from Sears. It has two imperfections, right on the front, so I'll have to send it back. Went to see the movie, *Fantasia*. Lovely music!

August 2. We were driving thru Edgecomb when there was an air raid alarm. We had to stop at the side of the road until the all clear whistle blew.

August 26. We saw the movie, *Woman of the Year*. Got my oven for $1.75 at Marsons, they were three dollars at Hartungs. (These were ovens that sat on top of oil stoves.)

August 9. Not many people coming to the library, so we open only on Saturday afternoons now. No gas, I guess.

August 11. Butter is 11 cents a pound.

August 21. The house across from the library at Newagen was rented for 20 dollars a month.

August 24. I put up blueberries. We can get extra sugar for canning. Got 21 pounds for two dozen jars of blueberries, two dozen jars of huckleberries, and two dozen jars of cranberries. They allow one quarter of a pound to a quart jar. They allow three pounds of sugar for pickles, jams, jellies, and also tomatoes.

August 26. Saw the movie, *Mrs. Minerva*, with Greer Garson. A war movie and very sad.

August 28. Ralph has been picking blueberries – a lot! We have 13 quarts of blueberries put up and three more to put up. Blackout at three in the morning. School house bell rang. Ralph jumped out of bed. They said the noise over town was awful, and scared everyone to death.

August 31. Newagen can't find a place to board the new school teacher. Bought a slacks suit for Marjorie at Senters for $2.98.

September 1. Ralph picked eight quarts of blueberries. Now we have 40 quarts put up. Plus we have pie about everyday.

September 7. Roosevelt's Labor Day speech on the radio this evening. Wants to stabilize prices and wages, so we won't have inflation.

September 8. The Navy is taking over the Fullerton Hotel over town for its sailors.

September 11. I had an eye exam. It cost $4.50. Rumor that the Army may take over Newagen Inn. If they do everyone at Newagen will have to move as they will use all of Newagen for maneuvers.

September 12. Harriet Orchard can't come down to deliver the groceries anymore. No one can, and they can't find anyone. It will be hard to get along without Pinkham's! Two sailors stationed on Cuckolds Light come from inland Massachusetts. They came to the library, and they don't seem to know anything about the water.

September 16. *U.S. News* has gone up from two dollars a year to four dollars.

September 24. Night before last there were queer explosions and the southern sky lighted with flairs, like fireworks, only not colored. Was also told to send the Christmas packages to servicemen by November 1.

September 25. I bought a 25 cent war stamp towards a war bond. Getting *Readers Digest* for Sammy for Christmas. Usually three dollars a year, but they reduced it for the servicemen. Went to see a crazy movie, Abbott and Costello, *Pardon My Sarong*. I didn't like it.

September 29. The Coast Guard visited the *Tyrone* yesterday and told Ralph not to take the sails off her. They may take her and asked Ralph if he would go with her. He said he didn't know.

September 30. Ralph bought a pair of shoes as they are talking of rationing mens' shoes and rubber boots.

October 1. The lights on cars have fog lights now, half of the lights are blotted out.

October 3. A jeep came down again in the yard with two soldiers, don't know what they were looking for.

October 7. Went to the movies to see *The Maltese Falcon*, with Humphrey Bogart – awful picture.

October 10. Babe got a letter from David. He is on Guadalcanal in the Solomons. He said they spent the night in a foxhole and they were seeing plenty. The letter was censored, but they didn't cut any out.

October 14. Went to the movie, *Major Barbara*, a George Bernard Shaw play with Wendy Hilley. Very witty. (The Gray's almost always went to the movies on Wednesday nights, because it was bank night, and there was a cash prize awarded to a lucky ticket holder.) Ralph won't let me pick cranberries because there is a bull moose on the island!

October 15. Only five tires are allowed, any more than that have to be turned in. Awful fighting on Solomon Islands. Japanese have landed reinforcements. Poor Babe feels awful.

October 25. They are having the fuel rationing tomorrow and the next day. By the Register it looks like Mrs. Smith will have all of Southport. I have to look up all my old receipts. I suppose to see what I used last year.

November 3. Burned 62 gallons of oil last year.

November 8. Very good news last evening. A big Allied force has landed on French North Africa. They have Rommel on the run and have captured half his force over near Egypt.

November 17. We bought a platform rocker for 24 dollars.

November 18. Awful naval battle off Solomon Islands. We lost two cruisers and four destroyers, but Japan lost 23 ships and in all thousands of men. They asked for it!

November 19. The men working at the shipyards are making 75 to 85 cents an hour.

November 20. I'm going around with petitions for money to buy new hymn books. They want at least 20. Ralph gave enough for two.

November 23. Ralph saw Eddie Gaudette over town today. He said he made a nice looking soldier on leave.

November 29. Our new minister, Reverend Hamilton, said his son has joined the Army Air Corps and wants to be a pilot.

November 30. The house across from the school house sold for $1,700!

November 31. We stopped at Pinkham's to get groceries. We couldn't get any steak at the Harbor.

December 5. We have to turn in the old toothpaste tubes, before we can get a new one.

December 8. A taxi from the Harbor to Southport costs 75 cents. Twelve dollars to go to Portland.

December 16. Bought a billfold for a Christmas gift. It was three dollars.

December 17. They may cut the garden supply down lower still, also our meat supply. Meat isn't rationed yet, but can't find it half the time.

December 21. Ralph has no spare tire. Guy Leavett's is expecting 12. The mail is very slow coming thru. Everything has to take a back seat for the service, which is okay. There must be a terrible lot of mail of all kinds right now.

December 24. They say there are warehouses full of packages that can't be delivered, because of lack of help.

December 27. There is a new income tax of five percent on all income that has to go to the government! Ralph went to work at Reed's Shipyard for 85 cents an hour.

1943

January 1, 1943. New store, Poole's, opened on Commercial Street. Bought two and a half pounds of haddock at 85 cents. Awful price!

January 8. A new rule out today. No unnecessary driving, no amusement or parties, etc.

January 9. No condensed milk at the Harbor. Awful cold at the library and only enough wood for two more Saturdays. Guess we'll have to close up. Emolyn Smith and Junior Pratt got married on Christmas Day. She teaches school at West Boothbay Harbor and he is in the service.

January 27. Sammy is a Machinist Mate First Class. Now he gets 136 dollars a month in the Navy.

February 8. Bought a leg of lamb at the First National for $2.13.

February 19. Beginning tomorrow we cannot buy any more canned stuff until March! When rationing starts, everyone is allowed five cans. They will have 48 points for the month of March.

February 26. We can get ice cream at Pinkham's, but at the Harbor you can only have a pint at a time.

March 1. A 1941 Studebaker costs 500 dollars. Can't find any film for my camera, and only three can be sent to the drug store at time. Was able to get Ralph a thermos at Pinkham's. There were none at the Harbor.

March 9. No more metal lunch boxes, now they're made of fiber.

March 11. I bought two cans of stuff, and used up 14 points on a can of raspberries, and 14 points on a can of waxed beans.

March 18. You can rent a room at the Boothbay House for five dollars a week.

March 25. The ban on pleasure driving has been somewhat lifted. Rationing began on butter, oleo, fats, and cheese. Jeanette started working at the diner for 80 dollars a month.

April 13. Newagen Inn burned to the ground. Started about 2:30 A.M. The whole Cape was lit up. If it hadn't been raining, the Cape would have burned. The Coast Guard helped fight the fire.

April 17. Bought two plants. Geraniums are 40 cents and azaleas are two dollars.

June 5. John Gray goes to Troy, New York for the Navy. He thinks he will have a year's study and training. He gets 50 dollars a month, plus his uniform, and he has to do his own laundry.

June 10. Hard to get gas or tires. Some gas tanks have a "no gas" sign out. More heavy gunfire today.

June 19. No gas in Boothbay Harbor, but Ralph got a new tire of synthetic rubber. Mr. Leavitt said it was the first one in the district.

June 20. Ralph has a victory garden in the swamp. He just planted 21 pole beans.

July 5. The library is only going to be open on Saturdays instead of every afternoon. Guess people don't have the gas or tires.

July 11. John passed his exam. He finished tenth in a class of 250. Very good I'd say! Rensselaer College, Troy, New York.

July 13. Ralph couldn't get any meat or butter at the Harbor and up to Pinkham's he could not get waited on. Should think the summer people would go in the day time and give the men who work all day a chance at night.

July 19. We have been talking about buying the Lundy house for 2,500 dollars (now Prisilla Harriman's). Sent to Sears for two cheap dresses, $1.98 each. You now have to have code flags on your boat, even a skiff!

July 22. Ralph trying to start building a house, but can only get 500 dollars worth of lumber a year.

August 24. I'm trying to raise money for church repairs. Water runs in around the furnace. Several people have given me one dollar at the library towards the fund. They need 500 dollars.

September 9. Got 24 dollars for the church fund. Glendon Ayer was home on leave. He had been in Trinidad again.

September 22. Miss Susan Zebriski died at their cottage on Bayberry Lane while her sister Miss Rebecca sang, "Jerusalem the Golden." Mr. Hamilton had the service for her and he preached a lovely funeral. He ended with a poem about a tree by the sea withstanding the storm. Just right for Miss Susie. She did so much for Newagen. We will miss her dearly.

September 23. To have a picture enlarged cost one dollar, after making a negative. It used to be 25 cents.

October 12. I got 1000 dollars pledged for the bond drive and that was just from the natives. Our quota is 20,000 dollars. 8,500 more pledged from some of the summer people. It was really too large a quota for Southport. Newagen gave almost 10,000 for the bond drive. Very good! Collected 800 dollars for church repair. A pair of glasses with exam in Waterville for Marjorie from Dr. Howard Hill was 17 dollars.

November 9. Ralph is having a awful time getting tires. It's been a month since he ordered one.

December 3. Shall go to the library tomorrow. Will be the last time I can go until we get wood. Can't get any.

December 30. Can't find a flannel nightgown anywhere. I got a black dress in Waterville for Marjorie and paid $13.98 for it. A gray tweed skirt was six dollars.

1944

January 5, 1944. No coal in the harbor.

January 24. We had the worse storm in 25 years, a week or so ago. There was one foot of snow, and Boothbay Harbor and Southport were isolated. No mail, no groceries, bread, or anything came through. Our plow did great work, but at the Harbor their's couldn't get the snow out at all. This was the trouble. The snow was wet and then it got cold and froze.

February 12. Ralph finally got a little coal. 500 pounds brought it down himself, little by little in his car, so we have been warm enough over this cold spell.

July 16. Another war bond drive. It's the fifth one I have been on. The last one we went over the top. It said so in the newspaper.

August 24. The war is going very good. Two invasions of France, horrible fighting. Hitler can't hold out much longer. The Russians are on the way to invading Germany itself. We haven't had any fairs or anything to raise money for the library this summer.

Author's note: Edith's diaries ended here, for reasons known only to her.

VE and VJ Day

There was a big bonfire in the Alley parking lot when the Japanese surrendered, and everyone came down to celebrate.   —*Leslie Brewer*

I was attending the latest movie with my friends, at the Strand Theater in Boothbay Harbor, when all of a sudden we heard car horns honking, and people yelling and screaming. Everyone ran out of the theater to see what was going on, and much to our surprise we found the streets filled with cars and people. The Japanese had surrendered,

and the war was over. Everyone had turned out to celebrate the victory.
—Evelyn Pierce Blake

VJ Day in Boston was wild! The town just exploded, and there were
soldiers and sailors everywhere. We were riding on the elevated train at
City Square, when the announcement was made that the war was over.
Later that evening, we went into Boston, to the hotel on the corner of
Tremont and Boyleston Streets, to meet up with my sister, Thelma, and
her husband, Carl. The restaurant on the first floor was so full, we could-
n't get in, so we had to talk with them through a window. When Thelma
and Carl decided to come out, they couldn't get through the crowd, so
they climbed out the window.   *—Emolyn and Earl Pratt*

I remember when VE Day was announced. There was a lot of noise
coming from the bowling alley (E.W. Pratt's Store). I started walking my
youngest daughter, Becky, toward the store, but she was frightened by
all the noise, and we had to turn around and go home.
—Winona Taylor Rand

I was fishing in a skiff out in the Sheepscot River with one of my
friends, when all of a sudden, we started to hear church bells ringing and
gunfire. We both decided we'd better row ashore to see what was going
on. When we reached Cozy Harbor Pavilion, there were people everywhere, and someone told us the war was over. Japan had surrendered.
—Ronald Orchard

On VJ Day, I vividly remember getting on the town school bus, with
my parents to ride around the island. We stopped and picked people up
as we went along. I tapped out Morse code on the horn for the letter V,
which symbolized victory, as my father, Cliff, drove the bus. The Lincoln
School closed in 1945, but someone went up, and rang the bell to celebrate the end of the war. (It was formally located on the hill behind
Ronnie and Nancy Spinney's house.) Also, one of the old ships in Mill
Cove was set on fire to celebrate the end of the war, and it smoldered
for several days afterwards.   *—Robert Buck*

MAINE P.O.W. CAMPS

Few people today are aware of the deep concern that was expressed by the military and Department of Justice in Washington in regard to the vulnerability of the forests of Maine against sabotage during the First and Second World War. Enemy agents were suspected of plotting the destruction of one of the nation's chief resources, and for this reason forestry wardens were issued revolvers and ammunition.

During the First World War, two German spies were caught red handed in the Maine woods, with the intent to do harm to the forest. Luckily the weather conditions were not appropriate for forest fires, and they were apprehended before they could complete their mission.

During the Second World War, our forests were once again considered vulnerable to sabotage by subversive agents working within the country. The forests were not considered to be a primary target, but their burning could serve as a diversionary action, so they were watched over carefully during the war. The Maine Forestry Department was very short-handed due to enlistment in the military and the draft, but still played an important role in the national defense effort of World War II.

The burning of blueberry barrens along the coast was also prohibited during this time period, because the glow from their fires might silhouette the shoreline and give aid to enemy submarines that were lurking nearby.

There were four main prisoner of war camps in Maine during the Second World War. They were located in Houlton; Hobbstown, near Jackman; Princeton; and in Soboomok, near Greenville. Also, at various points during the war, there were several smaller camps around the state, including camps in Augusta, Bangor, and Presque Isle. They held Germans, Austrians, and some Russians. Most of the German prisoners were from General Rommel's Elite African Corps.

Author's note: *Isn't it ironic that my father, Maurice, was sent to North Africa to fight against Rommel's men, and in the end, they were sent to Maine as P.O.W.s.*

The war effort called for a great increase in paper products, which meant greater wood production. At that time, several representatives from Maine served on the War Production Board, and they were all well aware of the potential paper shortage that was at hand. In particular Hollingsworth and Whitney, now Scott Paper, was the only company in the world making tabulating card stock, which was an item that was very much in demand by the U.S. Army. For this reason, the P.O.W. camps were assigned to Maine in an attempt to alleviate the critical manpower shortage the war had created in the woods.

A great family friend, Duluth Wing of Eustis, Maine, was an eyewitness to life in the camp at Hobbstown. He was not old enough to join the service, but was employed by the Kennebec Pulp and Paper Company out of Augusta. He drove a truck through the camp everyday between 1943 and 1944. The compound had four watch towers, several buildings, and was encircled in barbed wire. Duluth's company had camps on Spencer Lake beyond the P.O.W. camp, and was also involved in the cutting of timber for the pulp wood effort.

The P.O.W.s were transported from overseas by ship, then were transferred by railroad all over the United States. Their clothing was marked in large letters with "PW" on the back, indicating prisoner of war. The men who came to Maine were required to cut eight tenths of a cord of wood a day, and were paid 80 cents for their efforts. Also some of the prisoners were put to work planting and digging potatoes, or they worked in canning factories throughout the state. From 1944-1946, 34,000 cords of pulp wood were cut by P.O.W.s.

During the early stages of their imprisonment, many P.O.W.s deliberately broke the tools they were given to work with as a means of sabotage. This problem soon was overcome when the prisoners discovered the camps had a crew fixing the tools each evening, therefore a large supply of tools was ready for them every single morning. Also, the men discovered that they would rather work with new well-cared-for tools than do an equal amount of work with a broken one.

Although prisoners had ample opportunity to escape, there really was nowhere to go, because the camps were located deep in the Maine woods many miles from the nearest town. Three enterprising young Germans did make a break from the Hobbstown camp where they were imprisoned. They even made makeshift snowshoes for their escape, and traveled about 30 miles in four nights before they were apprehended near the West Forks village. Two wardens picked up their trail near Spencer Stream, and followed it to a deserted logging camp. The men put up no resistance, and disclosed their plan had been to get to the coast, board a ship, and go to Argentina, where there was a large German population. They had a total of 11 cents between them.

Generally the P.O.W.s were well behaved, hard working, and very intelligent; some even spoke three or four languages. Once in a while there were some Nazi hardliners within the Maine groups. Once identified, they were shipped off to higher security camps in the midwest. There were more than 500 camps scattered across the United States, which were run under the strict guidelines of the Geneva Convention.

During one trip from the midwest to Maine, it was discovered that many of the young soldiers had been brainwashed into believing the German Luftwaffe had destroyed New York City's entire skyline. One of the men even boasted to the guards on the train, "We will win the war because our leaders' air force is destroying your country." The word quickly spread from the guards to their superiors, so enroute to Maine the War Department arranged to route the train over tracks that gave the young German soldiers an uninterrupted view of the still intact New York skyline. As the train passed by, the soldiers stared out the windows in disbelief, only then realizing they had been lied to all along.

Another trainload of prisoners got a special treat upon their arrival in Portland. A Deering Ice Cream truck dropped off hundreds of double-dipped ice cream cones that were passed throughout the cars. Within a few minutes the entire mood had changed on the troop train.

About 100 one-time seminarians made a brief stop in Maine in 1944. Apparently their studies had been interrupted by the war, because Germany did not exempt divinity students from combat service. They represented several denominations, Catholic, Lutheran, etc. Even before the Second World War ended, the State Department took a long look at German's postwar future and decided that religion could be a powerful force in restoring the country. The War Department ordered prisoner staging areas in Europe to screen out seminarians to be sent to the United States, where they were placed in divinity schools to complete their education.

The P.O.W.s were also offered the opportunity to take correspondence courses through the University of Maine. The most popular course was English, but they could also study political science, preliminary medicine, math, and philosophy.

When the war ended in 1945, the P.O.W.s were not immediately shipped home from Maine. The U.S. Army feared a sudden influx of such a large group of people might not be the best thing for war-ravaged Germany, so many of the P.O.W.s were detained for up to a year following the war, and even then, many were transferred first to English and French camps before being sent home. Some prisoners even applied for jobs at several Maine papermaking companies, but there is no record if their applications were accepted. The last boatload of prisoners left the United States for Europe in the summer of 1946, but there were still 26 German and 15 Italian escapees who had not been found.

Author's note: I would like to take this opportunity to thank Austin Wilkins from Augusta, Maine. He was the former Maine Forest Commissioner in our state from 1958-1972, and it was with his permission, that I was able to use his book, Ten Million Acres of Timber, *as a reference for this story. He also provided me with many newspaper articles and correspondence he had received on the subject of P.O.W. camps in Maine. They were an invaluable aid to my research, and this story wouldn't have been possible without his help.*

INTERNATIONAL STORIES

Author's note: These stories were collected for two reasons. One, to help my generation grasp a better understanding of the Second World War and why the United States became involved in it, and two, to preserve them for future generations. The following stories reflect the personal memories and viewpoints of the people I interviewed.

ENID JOHNSON
England

Enid was three years old living in Birmingham, England, when the British declared war against Germany in 1939. She remembers there were no street signs posted in the southern part of the country, because invasion by Germany was a real possibility and they didn't want to give the enemy any advantage. She also recalls her family listened to the evening news, first in English, then in Welsh, on the radio.

Cars were up on blocks everywhere, because there was no petrol available, and they often had to sleep in air raid shelters, which were made out of cement and were very damp. Earwigs were a constant companion in the shelters.

Rationing was very strict in England. Eggs, butter, milk, flour, sugar, and meats were all on the list. Families with children were given a few extras, but it didn't amount to very much. When you went to the market, you expected to stand in line for a very long time. Also, you brought your own bag for your groceries and newspaper to wrap the food in.

Enid and her siblings were brought to America in 1947. On their first night here they stayed at a boarding house. Their mother was downstairs talking to the owner when a fire truck went by with its sirens on. Enid's mother and the owner soon heard several thumps from upstairs, so they went up to investigate. The children were all under their beds. In England they had been trained to roll out of bed, hit the floor, and roll under the bed if they heard a siren, because it meant an air raid was coming. They didn't think it would be any different in America, so they all practiced what they had been taught.

Enid and her husband Bruce currently divide their time between South Pasadena, Florida, and Southport.

CARY LAINE
Finland

During the Second World War, Cary was a small boy living in Vaasa, Finland. His father, Aarne, fought in the Winter War and the Continuation War for the Finnish Army against the Russians. There weren't many resources or uniforms for the soldiers, so they had to wear their own clothes. The government confiscated all the cars and trucks in the country for the Army. If your vehicle survived the war, it was returned at the war's end.

Finland had been a part of Russia, but gained its independence in 1918. Prior to that time, the Russians were concerned about the strong feelings of national-

Aarne Laine, Finnish Army (left), and a friend and fellow soldier. Uniforms were scarce during the war for the Finns. Note Aarne's only piece of clothing that is part of a uniform is his hat.

ism that were running throughout the country, so they disbanded the Finnish Army in 1902. This move did not squelch the patriotism of the Finnish people, and many of her college students started sneaking into Germany to be trained by the German Army. In fact 1700 young men were trained, and they formed the 27th Light Infantry Battalion. In three or four months, with the help of the Germans, the newly trained Finnish Army drove the Russians out of their country. Cary said when you visit graveyards in Finland, you will see a 27 on the gravestones of any of the men who formed the original battalion, and have since passed away. This outfit returned to Vaasa, Finland, in January of 1918, and became the cadre of the Finnish Army, organizing and training the rest of the Finns.

In November of 1939, there was a dispute over Karelia, and when negotiations failed, the Russians attacked Finland. This was known as the Winter War, and fighting continued until mid March of 1940, when an armistice was signed because the Finns had run out of ammunition. The Russians had suffered large amounts of casualties during the war, but that fact was not mentioned at the time of the armistice. It was later revealed in Nikita Khrushchev's memoirs that Russian casualty figures were around 1.5 million during the four months of the Winter War. Aarne returned home in March of 1940, and resumed his job as a salesman of fine glass and china. The Finnish Army didn't pay its soldiers, so the companies they worked for tried to keep a paycheck coming to their families while they were gone.

The town of Vaasa is located on the western coast of Finland. Cary was only five years old when the war broke out, but he can remember missing his father terribly when he left to rejoin the army. Cary slept with his father's pajamas for the first few nights, because they still smelled like him, and it was comforting.

During the Winter War, the Russians started bombing the town of Vaasa at night. Cary's mother, Ingrid, took him and his sister, Raili, to the basement, but was terrified that their house would be hit and collapse on them. The next night at bedtime, she dressed the children in their overcoats, boots, hats, and mittens. When the bombing started, she took the children outside, and they hid in the woods. Cary remembers thinking it was great fun. After Christmas, Ingrid decided to move her family to her sister's home in the country, where bombing wasn't a threat. The Laine family stayed there until the middle of March, then returned to their home in Vaasa.

There was peace for about a year, then in mid June of 1941, the Germans came into Finland, and together with the Finnish Army, attacked the Russians. This is what was known as the Continuation War to the Finns. Aarne, aged 34, fought in the area of the Isthmus of Karelia near Lake Lagoda. He served his country until the summer of 1944, and was able to return home on leave several times. The Finns were accustomed to the winter weather, and were experts on skis, which they used to their advantage. Aarne told his son many years later that the German troops that were sent to Finland were ill prepared and many of them froze to death in the harsh winter environment.

The German Army moved into Vaasa, but their presence soon became an inconvenience to the town, expecially to the children. There were no barracks to house the soldiers, so they took over the school, and the children were moved to an old schoolhouse located on the edge of town. Cary remembers there was a very distinctive smell of body odor and wool when the German soldiers were in town. In fact, he used to watch them march through the town square, practicing their goose step.

The Laine family had six immediate relatives in the war. There was no age limit, so everyone that was able went to help fight. One of Cary's cousins was killed by a Russian hand grenade during the fighting, and he can remember attending his funeral, as well as many of his neighbors.

There is a huge cove in Vaasa, and when it froze over, the German planes would land on it. One day one of the planes flipped over on the ice, and all the kids in town went out to see it, but the German soldiers chased them away. There was also a Russian P.O.W. camp on the outskirts of town, which the kids sometimes sneaked out to, so they could look at the prisoners.

During the war, there was rationing, and it was very hard to get butter, milk, meat, sugar, and coffee. Ingrid had relatives in the United States, and they often sent the family care packages, which helped them get through the tough times.

Gasoline was not available in Finland, so the buses ran on one-inch square blocks of wood. They carried bags and bags of the blocks on top of the buses, and every so often the bus would stop, and more wood would have to be dumped into the tank. The wood smoldered and created a gas, which was filtered and ran into the engine. Cary remembers the buses really smelled, and the backs of them were covered in creosote.

Adolf Hitler tried to force General Mannerheim of the Finnish Army to round up the Jews in his country and transport them out of Finland into Germany. The General refused and told Hitler, "If you try to force us, we will fight you." He also refused to make Finnish Jews wear a yellow arm band with the Star of David on it, which would identify them to the Nazis.

Cary said there was a lot of ammunition and trash left behind by the German Army, so the older local kids started making bombs out of it, then they taught the younger kids how to do it. None of the children were ever hurt in Vaasa from this highly creative and dangerous activity, but they easily could have been.

One of Cary's friends had a hand grenade his older brother had brought back from the army. One day all the kids in the neighborhood came over to get a better look at it. Cary's friend was telling them how it worked, and pulled the pin on the grenade. The fuse started to hiss, so the boy threw it on the floor of the livingroom, and all the kids stood there motionless, staring at it. They didn't know it, but the boy's brother had taken the explosives out of the grenade before he gave it to him. When the fuse burnt out and nothing happened, all the kids were really stunned, and decided they'd better go home. Looking back on it now, Cary says it's a miracle they all weren't killed.

Early in 1944, it was obvious the Germans were beginning to loose the war, so the Russians gave the Finns an ultimatum. If you don't tell the Germans to get out of your country, we will take it over again. There were some Communist Finns in the country who thought that would be alright, and in fact, many of them joined and fought with the Russian Army during the Winter and Continuation War.

The Finnish government decided they would rather keep their independence, so they told the Germans to leave. The Germans didn't like their options very much, so as they fled to the north of Finland, to get into German occupied Norway, they destroyed and burnt everything down in their path. They even took the locks and hinges off the doors to salvage the metal for their army.

In the summer of 1944, Aarne, returned home safely to Vaasa. He earned the rank of Corporal and was awarded three medals for his service. He thought the Russians would try to take Finland back, so in 1948 the Laine family immigrated to the United States. Ingrid had been born in the United States, so her children had dual citizenship, and the family was not held up by immigration quotas. Aarne became an American citizen in 1952, and worked as a salesman for an import/export company. He later became a cabinet maker. Aarne worked at this job until he passed away in 1968, at the age of 62. Cary and his wife Suzanne currently make their home in Southport.

RAGNHILD SPIEGEL BAADE
Poland, East and West Germany

Ragnhild lived in Glisnica, Poland, during the Second World War with her maternal grandmother, Elise Reutt, mother Karin, and sister Astrid. Her village was small and was far from any city, so there were no bomber attacks that she can remember. Her father, Gunnar, was a forester who had been studying to teach forestry at a college level. He was drafted by the German Army in 1941, and because he spoke fluent Russian, he was sent to translator school. He was able to come home on leave once in a while at the beginning of the war, but those visits became fewer and fewer as the war progressed. He was later assigned to parachute behind Russian lines and radio information out for the German Army. Near the end of the war he escaped into Estonia and boarded a ship that took him to Schleswig Holstein, Germany. He was then arrested by the British, and put in a P.O.W. camp. Later he was transferred to an American P.O.W. camp, from which he was released in August of 1945.

The Spiegel family took refugees into their home throughout the war. Ragnhild's mother and grandmother always tried to lend a helping hand to those in need, and towards the end of the war they had a third cousin living with them and a Latvian woman and her daughter. One day German soldiers appeared in their village and notified everyone that Russian forces were approaching rapidly and they should evacuate as soon as possible. Grandmother decided the best way to leave Poland was by wagon, so she traded goods with local Polish farmers for one.

When she returned there was quite an uproar in the house as everyone was trying to decide what they should take. Each person packed as quickly as they could and Ragnhild, four and a half at the time, and her younger sister, Astrid, had to make the excruciating decision as to which one toy they would bring with them on the wagon. As they left their house and started out on what would become a long, cold journey, there was a line of people fleeing as far as the eye could see.

People carried their belongings in everything from sleds to baby carriages, and as the Spiegel family progressed they noticed dead horses and cars that had been abandoned along the roadside. Since the roads north and south were jammed with trucks and people, their trek leader decided to travel west. Grandmother was the only one who could keep the horses moving, so she and Karin and the other adults walked beside the wagon while the girls rode on it.

Their town was located about 150 miles outside of Germany proper, which was the border as it was, in 1918. Along the way they stayed in abandoned schools and factories. Ragnhild remembers trying to sleep, but the lights were kept on all night long so people could come and go without stepping on each other. Their progress was slow, to say the least, and their horses were weak because there was little to feed them.

One day, shortly after crossing into Germany proper, grandmother stopped to help someone by the roadside and lost sight of the wagon. She and her family were soon separated and the wagon was later abandoned because no one could make the horses move. Some German soldiers gave Karin and the children a ride to the nearest railway station, and they were able to get on one of the last trains that went west. It took them to Halle, where they lived for the remainder of the war. Karin registered with the Red Cross, and was reunited with her mother, who died of pneumonia a few days later. The city was industrial and air raids soon became a common occurrence, unlike the quiet life they had lead in Poland.

This photo was taken in Glisnica, Poland in 1945.
Ragnhild, age four, is shown with her grandmother, Elise Reutt.

There was a bomb shelter across the road, but sometimes the raids came so suddenly you didn't even have time to get out of bed, and the cellar of the house was the only protection available. Much of March and April was spent in air raid shelters. Towards the end of April the Americans advanced into Halle and the occupants breathed a sigh of relief, because they knew the war would be over soon.

The Spiegel family was forced to leave the room they lived in, along with everyone else in the apartment house, and move into the attic because the Americans needed living quarters. The German occupants were not allowed to have any bedding or cooking utensils, so during the day while the Americans were gone, and only one or two guards were left on duty, the women instructed the children to play hide and seek with them. While the guards were occupied, the women climbed in the back windows of the buildings and gathered bedding and cooking pots, so they could cook for their families and keep them warm.

The Americans only stayed for a short time, because General Patton had gone too far east and was ordered to withdraw. Then more fighting occurred, before the Russians marched into Halle. The German Army kept up a resistance as best they could, allowing civilians time to flee towards the West.

During the fighting the Spiegel family and their neighbors sought protection in a small air raid shelter, located in front of their house. After waiting in it for hours, it was decided by the group that Karin should be the one to go out to find out if it was safe to leave the shelter, because she spoke Russian. Ragnhild was right behind her mother as she opened the door to step outside. Much to Karin's dismay, they came face to face with a Russian soldier pointing his gun at them. He ordered her to tell everyone inside to leave the shelter immediately, which they all did. For a while it seemed that the Russian Army had free reign of the city, and then all of a sudden, it stopped. A strict 7 P.M. curfew was set up and many areas of Halle became restricted to civilians.

On May 8th it was announced that the war was over. There were no communications available in the country and they had no idea where Gunnar was or the rest of their family. The Red Cross set up registration centers throughout Europe for displaced persons. It was hoped that by creating lists of people's names and their whereabouts, families might be reunited. Ragnhild remembers her grandmother drilling her endlessly on her first and last name, where she was born and her sister's name. Both girls wore name tags throughout the war, as most children did, in case they were ever separated from their family. Years after the war, even up into the late 1950s, photos appeared in magazines as families tried to locate loved ones through various publications. After his release from the P.O.W. camp, Gunnar saw his wife's and childrens' names on a Red Cross list, and the Spiegel family was reunited in Halle in August of 1945.

There was no work available after the war and Gunnar was forced to look in other towns for a job. He found one in Stolberg, but there was no housing left to rent due to bombing. He transferred to a school of forestry in Jena, which was located in the Harz Mountains, and was located in a castle. The whole family was able to live together for about a year, and were given several rooms in the castle for living quarters.

Gunnar lost his job at the school, because he let his students sing a song the Communists didn't approve of. He was forced to transfer a few weeks before his son Raoul was born in 1946, and the family again waited for a place to live. They were forced to live apart for two years until an apartment opened up in Schwarzburg-Thuringen, East Germany, in December.

Astrid, Raoul, and Ragnhild Spiegel
in Schwarzburg, East Germany, in 1949.

Food was rationed throughout the country. Ragnhild remembers always being hungry and, at the time, it seemed there was not enough to live on and not enough to die for. Her mother would have the children collect acorns, then she would grind the bitter nuts, adding the substance to the small amount of flour she had in order to stretch it out. Stinging nettle was also collected, boiled, and eaten as soup, and beechnut seeds were gathered and pressed to make oil. Blueberries were cooked and put in bottles, which were stopped with newspaper and covered in wax to seal them. Keep in mind that there was no sugar to preserve the berries and the bottles often exploded in the winter under pressure. There were some apple trees in their new neighborhood and Gunnar was in charge of dividing the apples among eight of the nearby families, so everyone would get equal amounts of the fruit.

Gunnar settled in to teaching forestry at the new school, and enjoyed it very much, but it wasn't long before the Communist Party was pressuring him to join them and to spy on his forestry students. For the most part, they had been German soldiers during the war, and the government suspected they were dissatisfied with the Communist party. At first there had been a military government in East Germany, run by the Russians, but in 1949 rule was handed over to the German Communist government.

Finally, Gunnar was given an ultimatum by the Communists, either report on his students or he would be arrested and sent to Siberia. Then his family would be returned to their birth places. This meant his wife Karin would be sent to Russia, Ragnhild and Astrid to Poland, and baby Raoul would stay in Germany. Family separation was a tactic commonly used by the Communists during this period. Gunnar was placed under house arrest at this point and was only allowed to walk from his house to the school where he taught. He couldn't even take his students out into the forest unless they were accompanied by a "real Communist."

At this point the Spiegel family decided to escape to the West. Their plans became all the more urgent when Gunnar began disappearing for two or three days at a time, while the Communists would interrogate him on his political views and those of his students. They sought help through the underground, and as fate would have it, one of Gunnar's students was their contact person, who arranged for a guide to take them across the border.

Karin made arrangements with their minister to store a few of their personal items with him and some of the sympathetic members of their congregation. They couldn't easily carry many of their belongings across the border, so many things had to be left behind. In the fall of 1951 Ragnhild made several trips carrying the family's possessions to neighbors' homes for safe keeping. Her younger brother and sister weren't told about the family's plans to escape for fear they might accidentally let the information slip to the wrong person. In December Karin fell ill with pneumonia. There was no medicine available in their town, so all she could do was rest and hope for the best.

One day Karin's doctor, who knew about their plans for escape, dropped by to let them know codeine could be purchased at the pharmacy in a neighboring town. He thought that if she could take a dose of it before they attempted to cross the border, it would at least stop her from coughing, and perhaps prevent giving the family away to the border patrol. Ragnhild, being the oldest of the children, was instructed to board a train to the next town to get the medicine for her mother. Gunnar would have gone, but he was still under house arrest. She did as she was instructed, but missed the last train back, and had to walk home alone. It was a terrifying journey for an 11-year-old to make by herself at night.

Christmas was bleak to say the least. All the Spiegels' money had gone towards their escape and there wasn't any left to buy presents for the children. Nor would they have wanted to give presents, since they would only have to be left behind. They did have a tree, but the younger children, eight and five years old, didn't understand why there weren't any gifts under the tree for them.

The family waited day after day, hoping Karin's health would improve, but it didn't and they were running out of time. December 31st was the date set for their guide to take them over the border. January 3rd was the beginning of the new semester at school, also the day Gunnar had to give the authorities his answer. Despite all this confusion, he managed to leave his term papers corrected, so the person taking his place wouldn't have to do it.

At four o'clock in the morning, on New Year's Eve, the children were told to put on as many clothes as they could wear. While they were dressing, Ragnhild packed a bag of food for the trip. Astrid and Raoul were told their mother was ill, and they were taking her to a sanitarium near the border, thus providing the perfect cover story for the Spiegel family.

Karin packed a small bag with clothes and some personal documents, including the family's birth certificates. Ragnhild remembers the oddest sensation coming over her as they left the house. Dishes were still in the sink and plates were on the table; it didn't seem like they should leave until these things were put in their proper place.

The Spiegels met a few people on the road as they walked out of town and Gunnar worried that people might recognize them and think it was suspicious they were on the road that early. They had to walk up a mountain to get to the train station, which was very difficult for Karin, who was coughing most of the time at this point. She and Ragnhild purchased the tickets for everyone and they boarded the train. They changed trains several times before arriving in Saalfeld.

Here they boarded another train, which would take them directly to the border town Sonneburg. Once the Spiegels were in the train seated, the border police started making their way through the train checking everyone's documents. They stopped at the Spiegels' compartment and asked for their papers, which they looked at quickly, before handing them back. Just as the family thought they were through, one of the men looked at Raoul and said,"Where are you going?" Without hesitation he replied,"My mother is sick and we're taking her to the hospital." Ragnhild recalls that at that moment her heart was pounding and it seemed so loud, she thought everyone could hear it. The border guards accepted the story and moved to another compartment of the train, and her parents breathed a sigh of relief. The guards had tried to trip up the family, but Raoul correctly repeated what he had been told.

The train rolled into Sonneberg where their guide was supposed to meet them at the train station. When they stepped off the train, no one was there. Karin walked over to the waiting room, but it was also empty. As it turned out their guide had gotten drunk on homemade liquor. Karin and his landlady put him in the shower to sober up, but he passed out completely, and was not capable of doing anything. This also meant the money the Spiegel family had been able to scrape together to pay him was gone.

Karin returned to tell Gunnar the bad news, and he decided that they should go back before they were caught by the border patrol. As they stood there discussing their options, which at this point seemed slim, the owner of the railroad restaurant came over to Gunnar and said, "Are you trying to go into the west?" Everyone froze, not knowing if he was going to help them or if it was a trap. Considering the hopelessness of their current situation, Gunnar figured they had nothing to lose and said, "Yes." The man replied, "I thought so, you look so conspicuous with all those clothes on. Come with me, I have a room where you can sit. I think my nephew can help you."

A short time later his nephew arrived and told them there was a farmer who lived on the border, literally. When the borderlines were drawn, his farm was split in two. Half of it was in the east and the other half was in the west. The nephew then drove the Spiegel family to the farm.

They waited at the farmhouse until 11 o'clock at night, and were not offered any food, but were given coffee beans to chew. The farmer's wife told them they had to be alert to make the crossing and the beans would help. Karin decided it was time to take her codeine. Hopefully it would quell her cough until they made it across the border.

It was a bitter cold night and the moon was out as they left the farm house and walked across a field. Soon they came to a fast running brook they had to cross to get to the border. The farmer was first across and Gunnar threw Raoul and Astrid over to him, then Karin made her way over. This left Ragnhild on the other side looking over at them. She was wearing a knapsack packed with clothing, and when she attempted to jump across, she fell backwards into the brook drenching her clothes. The farmer was not pleased at all, because her pants froze instantly, and when she walked they made a swooshing sound. He became very angry and kept telling her to be quiet or they would be caught.

They continued on, walking in a deep ditch that followed a road. All of a sudden the farmer said,"Down!" Everyone dropped automatically to the ground. A swishing sound could be heard in the distance. It was the dynamo on a bicycle that rubbed against the wheel, to make the head-light glow. Then two men's voices and a dog's barking came into earshot. It was the border patrol and before long they overheard one say to the other, "We really ought to check this out." Then the other replied,"Come on, I want to get home, it's New Years Eve." Slowly, the sound of their voices disappeared in the other direction. If they had let the guard dog off its leash to investigate, the family would have been caught for sure.

As soon as the sound of bicycles could no longer be heard, the farmer informed them that it was safe to continue, they were in no man's land. He pointed and said, "If you walk down this road you will end up in West Germany." At this point he turned and walked in the other direction. The Spiegel family walked through the woods, fearing they might meet traffic on the road, and ended up at a railroad station in Bavaria, West Germany. No trains were running, but Gunnar found an official and asked for political asylum in the west and asked him to make a fire in the waiting room, because his family was nearly frozen. As they sat there, cold and tired, it suddenly dawned on the family that Karin hadn't coughed once as they made their escape. The codeine had worked!

The official made a fire in a sawdust stove and called the local police for them. An hour soon passed and two border patrol guards entered the room wearing long sheepskin coats and hats. Ragnhild remembers admiring them, thinking to herself how warm they must be in their thick jackets.

The family was then arrested and taken to the police station, where they waited for nearly 24 hours while their story was checked out. It was a fascinating place to be for an 11-year-old. All kinds of people walked in and out of the station, with every imaginable story as to why they wanted to go into the east or why they had left for the west. Some were admitted into the west and some were sent back, to who knows what fate.

Ragnhild watched as an older woman walked in with a large jar full of papers and dumped it out on the counter. She started talking to the police and said, "I have every possible paper since 1914 here. I just want to go visit my daughter in the East." The police informed her that she didn't have the proper papers, and they couldn't let her cross the border. Ragnhild will never forget the disappointed look on her face as she left the station.

Gunnar and Karin were interviewed separately, each giving their reason for escaping, and had to go before a judge stating everything they had told the police was true, as did Ragnhild. It was now January 1, 1952, and the Spiegel family was sent to a displaced persons' camp in Hessen, which was near the town where Ragnhild's grandparents lived. It was a long ride to the camp and, upon their arrival, the men and women were placed in separate barracks. Karin was put in the camp hospital and remained there for two weeks, until her health improved.

The camp was run by the West German government and it was over-run by refugees from Latvia, Estonia, and East Germany. It in turn took some time to process the family's papers and to verify their story, so they had to live there for a while. Life in the camp was boring, because there was nothing to do, but it was the first time in years that Ragnhild could remember not being hungry.

One day Gunnar announced that his parents had decided that the family could live with them in their two and a half room apartment. There were not enough beds and Ragnhild had to sleep on a chair. The kids were enrolled in school and Gunnar began the endless search for a job. In those days, once you moved in with relatives the government no longer helped you. He also applied for a visa to the United States, Canada, and Australia, because the family had friends living in all three countries that could sponsor them.

After four months of very cramped quarters Karin moved 200 miles away with relatives, and got a job selling magazines. Astrid and Raoul were put in an orphanage on what was supposed to be a temporary basis, but ended up staying there for one and a half years. Ragnhild joined her mother, as Gunnar was still unemployed.

Karin's brother's mother-in-law obtained a visa to go to the United States for one year, because her daughter was expecting a child. She offered her apartment to the Spiegels, which was a godsend at this point. The family was reunited, but her father still had only intermittent work, and her mother worked in a cafe. Money was very tight, and Gunnar pursued immigration every chance he got.

The process was a long and drawn out five year ordeal. There was paperwork upon paperwork, and interview after interview, which became increasingly intrusive. Family, friends, and community members were all interviewed. It went so far that when Ragnhild was invited to spend a few days at a friend's house, a Mr. Smith showed up one morning at 8 A.M. and was sitting at the kitchen table waiting for her. He informed her that he was from the C.I.A. and wanted to ask her a few questions. For exam-ple: Who were her friends? What did she want to do? Had her parents fled East Germany for the reasons they had stated? The questions became increasingly personal, and Ragnhild later learned they had questioned her teachers and even her minister. Apparently she answered correctly, because she never heard from Mr. Smith or the C.I.A. again.

Finally, in November of 1956, Gunnar was notified that all his paperwork had been accepted and the family was cleared to go to the United States on a green card. They quickly had two trunks made and shipped their belongings by boat. Each person packed a cardboard suitcase with a few things, and then boarded a train that took them to Hamburg. They flew on a TWA flight that was full of Hungarians fleeing their country shortly after the Hungarian Uprising (this occurred when the Hungarian people tried to stand up to the Communist government, and their efforts were squelched by Russian tanks).

One reason the paperwork had taken so long to clear for the Spiegel family was because this all happened during the McCarthy Era. Senator Joseph McCarthy held a witch hunt for Communists in America while he was in office and many innocent bystanders were affected by his relentless quest. Considering the Spiegels had come from East Germany, and Gunnar and Karin both spoke Russian, they were considered suspect. Another factor was that Gunnar had been born in Latvia and raised in Estonia, and the United States only had a small quota for Latvians entrance into this country during the 1950s. Added to this was the complicating fact that, except for Raoul, everyone had been born in a different country.

The Spiegels soon settled into life in their new country, living in New Jersey, but Ragnhild was homesick for a very long time. At first they encountered a lot of unpleasantness due to their ethnic background. Although she spoke no English, Ragnhild was enrolled in the local high school as a sophomore. One of her teachers gave her "Little House on the Prairie" to read and do a book report on. Every night she would go home and study, translating the story, page by page, using a dictionary. She was a good student and was eager to learn, which showed by her senior year, when she had caught up with the rest of the students in her class.

She finished high school and went on to a local liberal arts college, studying chemistry. On the first day of school she met a handsome young man, Peter Baade, from Portland, Maine, and they were married two years later. After a year's time, she decided that languages were more to her liking and with the help of an adviser switched majors. She soon began student teaching English and German and found she enjoyed it. After graduation, she got a job teaching German in New York state in 1963, and became an American citizen in 1964, one year after graduating from college.

Over the years she has taught at various schools, only taking time off in 1968 to earn her master's degree at Syracuse University in New York, because she had received a teaching assistantship. In 1977, Ragnhild started teaching English at the Boothbay Region High School. Since there was interest among the student body to learn German, she taught it during a study hall period. That interest has developed into a full-time German language program, and in 1996, her students and students from Germany (members of G.A.P.P., German American Partnership Program) participated in a third year of exchange programs. Ragnhild currently lives in Edgecomb with her husband of 35 years, Peter.

Author's note: *Ragnhild returned to Glisnica, Poland, in July of 1995 with her husband, Peter. Together they found the house she grew up in, and were reunited with a woman who had been her babysitter. The woman called her by her nickname "Nonja." Ragnhild had forgotten the name until she heard the woman repeat it 50 years later. When Ragnhild was introduced to one of the oldest residents of the town, Julia, she began to smile and exclaim, "Pani Reutt (Mrs. Reutt), was a great lady!" After that they were welcomed with open arms where ever they went in Glisnica. A return trip is planned for the summer of 1996.*

EMIL LANDAU
Germany

Germany started to change for the Landau family about 1933, when the Nazi party began to rise to power within the country. There had been a terrible economic

Emil Landau in Switzerland after his liberation.

depression in Germany, which started in 1927. Inflation and unemployment were very high, and newspapers started printing propaganda about Jews. They blamed them for the hard times in Germany, ridiculed them, and spread a message of hate to their readers, who were looking for a scapegoat.

Shortly thereafter, between 1933 to 1940, up to 100 laws per year were passed, sometimes several each day. They forced Jewish business owners to sell their businesses, and to turn over anything of value they owned to the Nazis. By 1938, Jews had to wear a yellow Star of David on their clothing as a form of identification. Even the privilege to use the public swimming pools and park benches was taken away. Jews were not allowed to ride the train unless they had a special permit. By doing this, the Nazis were able to suppress any group they wanted to get to, especially the Jews, by slowly tightening the noose on their activities.

As the restrictions grew tighter and tighter, the Landau family considered leaving Germany. Emil's father, Alex, wanted to go to the United States, but a sponsor was required who could put up money to support the family. Alex managed to have some money smuggled out of Germany to a relative in America, but there was also a strict immigration quota at the time. The family wouldn't have been eligible to leave until 1941 or 1942, and by then it would have been too late. Alex decided to buy a visa and take his family to Chile, a republic in South America, but all the boats were booked far in advance. In 1941, the Nazis closed all the ports, so then that option was out.

Then, in 1939, a young Polish Jew assassinated the Secretary of the German Embassy in France. This became the opportunity and excuse Hitler had been looking for to put his devious plans against the Jews into full swing. A reign of terror against the Jews soon spread throughout Europe, the beginning of which would become known as Crystal Night, the night of broken glass. Homes and stores were looted and burnt by the Nazis, but this was just a foreshadowing of what was to come.

Emil's preparatory school was closed, and he went home to Witten, Germany, where his family had lived for over 200 years. His father owned a wholesale textile business, which was taken away and sold for nickels on the dollar.

Shortly thereafter, any residents of the town who were Jewish were forced to move ten miles away to Dormund, an industrial town, where they were housed in small apartments. The Nazis kept forcing the families to move, and by doing this cut them off from their friends, and kept everyone off guard.

Their automobiles, furniture, and anything of value was either left behind or they were forced to turn it over to the Nazis. Alex did manage to smuggle a small amount of money with him when they were moved. It was here that Emil and his father were worked as forced labor, digging ditches and cleaning up bomb damage from Allied attacks. Alex had become ill at this point, but unfortunately, there was little available to help him recover.

Emil's father and his friends must have tried to reassure themselves and their families as conditions worsened by saying, "We're an important part of this community, our families have lived here for hundreds of years, they don't mean us, it must be someone else." People always want to believe prejudice and persecution can happen to others but never to them, sometimes until it is too late to help themselves.

Emil was just 16 when he and his family were taken from their home by a passenger train to the Nazi labor camp Theresienstadt in Czechoslovakia. This camp was an old fortress that had been built by the Empress of Austria. It was designated by Hitler for Jews who were veterans of front line combat during the First World War. Alex qualified for the camp because he had fought in the Kaiser's Army, and had been a P.O.W. in France for five years. Theresienstadt was considered to be more desirable than other camps. Prisoners were allowed to wear their own clothing with an identification number sewn on the outside, and their heads were not shaved.

At first, Emil was assigned the task of burying prisoners. Later, he worked in the camp bakery, baking bread. This position soon proved to be invaluable, because it gave him the opportunity to smuggle extra rations out in his clothing, which helped give his family the strength to keep working. The men and women lived separately in the camp, but visitation was allowed.

After two years, Emil was separated from his family and was sent by cattle car to Auschwitz in German-occupied Poland. The trip took two or three days, and it was extremely hot. There were no windows or toilets on the cattle car, only a few buckets to use. Many people died on the trip, because they gave up or they couldn't take the conditions.

When the door finally opened, a prisoner at the camp said in Yiddish, "The left is funeral." The new arrivals didn't understand what that meant at first, but they soon learned if you were in the left line when you got off the train, you went straight to the gas chambers. Emil and his friends were young and could work, so they were put in the right line, and were assigned to the Gypsy camp. At least that's what they called it, but at this point there were no Gypsies left.

The camp was 20 kilometers square, and was subdivided by electrified fences. Often the SS guards would pick out one of the weaker prisoners and throw his hat on the fence, then tell him to go get it while the other prisoners watched. The penalty for not taking care of your uniform ranged from standing at attention for hours on end to hanging. The smell of the crematorium was a constant reminder that you couldn't afford to make mistakes in the camp, and the fear that you might be sent to it next was with you all the time.

Workers were being picked for a transport out of Auschwitz to another camp, and Emil and seven of his friends from Theresienstadt got into line for inspection. They were told to take off their uniforms and stand at attention as Dr. Joseph Mengella made his selection. Emil was the smallest and skinniest of the group, and he was chosen to go to the gas chamber. His forehead was stamped with a rubber stamp and he was put in a holding block that was full of a couple of thousand Hungarian and Dutch prisoners. The guards had picked too many people to die that day, and the gas chamber was running behind schedule, so the prisoners were forced to wait.

There were two entrances to the building. One was a large gate, where the guards were sorting out the nationalities, and the other was a door located at the other end of the holding block. The Hungarians started to put up a fight, and at this point, knowing what lay ahead for them, they really had nothing to loose. Emil and two other prisoners broke through the door past the guard. Once outside, they rubbed the stamp off their foreheads with sand, and split up for safety. Emil got into another barracks, and came to the conclusion that the longer he stayed in this camp, the less his chances of survival would be.

The next call for a transport out of the camp was for 300 workers. Emil, having learned a valuable lesson during the last inspection, made sure he was standing between two men that were skinnier than he was.

Once again, Dr. Mengella stopped in front of Emil, this time asking him some questions and what his profession was. Emil quickly said metalworker, and made the cut. He and the other men then reported to another block, where they were shaved, deloused, and given new uniforms. Their identification number was also tattooed on their arm. Emil's is B12500. Everytime you were moved to a new camp, you received a new number. What most people didn't realize upon arrival at Auschwitz was that if they didn't get a tattooed number, meaning they passed work selection and could work, they were gassed.

A Hungarian man, who hadn't made the cut, came up to Emil and said, "I didn't make it, but my son did. You have experience in here, will you watch over him for me?" Emil promised he would look after the young boy, but later, when the prisoners were waiting on the parade ground to be transported to the other camp, a general alarm was sounded. Normally it was a signal for the prisoners to go back to their barracks immediately. The officer in charge of the 300 workers told them to stay where they were. Unfortunately that order was not relaid to the guard towers, and they started to shoot the prisoners.

Everyone tried to run for cover, but they had to cross the parade ground to get to the barracks. Emil quickly looked around and spotted a barrel, which could provide cover from bullets. He told the Hungarian boy to run towards it with him, but the boy ran the other way and was shot down by one of the guards. Emil made it to the barrel, and as he looked out from behind it at the guard tower, he said to himself, "God, if you really exist, give me a gun to kill that S.O.B."

A food ration within the camp, at its worst, was one piece of bread and a cup of watery coffee for the whole day. Sometimes a bowl of soup would be served as a second meal, and, if you were lucky, and knew the man ladling out the soup, he might serve you from the bottom of the pot, so that you would get a few potatoes in your bowl. There were two schools of thought about eating among prisoners. One was, I will eat my bread now, and it will help to suppress my hunger. The other was, I will save my bread and eat it slowly throughout the day, then I will be getting a little bit all day long. Emil lived by the first school, and ate his ration immediately.

There were several escape attempts at Auschwitz and later at Tsechowitz. Each time the prisoners were brought back and used as an example to the others in the camp, then their lifeless, beaten bodies were left out in sight as a deterrent to the other prisoners. The thought passed through Emil's mind to escape many times, but you have to realize that if he had got out, his shaved head and uniform would have been an easy giveaway. Even if he had tried at the first camp, a young man in civilian clothes who wasn't in the army would have been considered suspicious. Also, if you were successful, you were risking the lives of the people you left behind. The Nazis wouldn't blink an eye at killing 100 prisoners to set an example for the rest.

There was a Dutch opera singer in Emil's barracks, and some nights he would sing for the men. The barracks were what once had been brick stables. Seven men slept together, six lying side by side, and one at their feet. Some men attempted to keep journals, but paper and writing equipment was almost nonexistent. Fleas, lice, and disease also ran rampant throughout the barracks.

It was not a good idea to make too many close friends in the camps. People were dying all around you on a daily basis, and this factor potentially could put your own survival at risk, so Emil found it was best not to become too close to too many people. He had one friend at Auschwitz, who had been transferred with him from Theresienstadt, but they were split up in March of 1944, and he doesn't know what happened to him.

After spending three months at Auschwitz, Emil and about 300 other prisoners were transferred in 1944 to Tsechowitz, which is located in Germany. A few months after his departure, his mother, Sidonie, and sister Helga were sent to Auschwitz. His father, Alex, died in Theresienstadt on January 17, 1943. Six other close relatives also lost their lives in the camps during the war.

Prisoners were categorized in groups, by the Nazis. For instance: Jewish, Danish police, political, criminal, Jehovah's Witness, homosexual, and Russian Officers (the Russians never signed the Geneva Convention, so the Germans didn't have to follow its strict guidelines, and often Russian P.O.W.s ended up in concentration camps). Each group had a colored triangle on their blue and white prison striped uniforms, along with their identification number: green for a criminal, red for a political prisoner, purple for Jehovah's Witness, pink for a homosexual, and so on. Jews were the exception, and wore a yellow star.

The majority of camp guards were German, and were part of Hitler's dreaded SS outfits. They were diehard members of the Nazi party and militia and were renowned for their violence and brutality. Oftentimes they were volunteers, and were chosen for their cruel nature. Prisoners soon learned to look out for Rumanian, Bulgarian, and Ukrainian SS volunteers. They seemed to be out to prove themselves to the Nazis and were very dangerous. They could be identified by the insignia on their uniforms. An example of this would be "SS Rumania" on their sleeve.

Emil worked building walls around oil tanks to prevent shrapnel from damaging them during bombing raids. The prisoners were instructed to add salt into the cement while they were mixing it, so it wouldn't freeze. Sometimes when supervision was lax, they wouldn't add the salt so the cement wouldn't set well, and would crumble easily at the end of winter. It was their own method of sabotage against the Germans.

The weather was brutally cold, and you had to keep moving and working all the time in order to survive. In fact the winter of 1945 was one of the coldest years on record in Europe. When you asked to use the latrine, a guard accompanied you, and he took your winter cap when you went into the roofless structure. No prisoner wanted to be anywhere without his hat for long in that kind of weather, and the guard's actions ensured you would do your business quickly, not wasting any time, so you could be put back to work as soon as possible.

In January of 1945, the Allies were closing in fast. Since Tsechowitz was closer to the rapidly approaching Russian Army, the Nazis decided to march the inmates west to another camp, which was located closer the center of Germany. They marched for three nights, during some of the coldest winter weather in years, until they reached the town of Gleiwitz (a large railway head). Those who couldn't keep up were shot. They rode on open railway cars for several days, until they reached their new destination, Buchenwald. There were German guards posted in every corner of the railway cars, armed with either a machine gun or an automatic rifle with a bayonet. They didn't like to be near the prisoners, and when they came too close or fell towards the guards, it was often on the point of the bayonet.

Many people froze to death and died enroute to the camp. The guards wouldn't allow the bodies to be thrown off the train so they were stacked up on top of each other in the car. At one stop, a girl jumped off the train, and started to shout in Polish, "Kill me you bastards!" She was shot by one of the guards, but Emil has never forgotten her courage. He himself suffered from terrible frostbite during the trip, and his toes soon turned black and became infected with gangrene. Over 600 prisoners started out on the trip, and only 120 survived the brutal traveling conditions enroute to the new camp.

After about three weeks, Emil's feet were in such bad condition he could hardly fall out for attendance, which was held twice a day. He was then admitted to the camp sick bay by a Belgian Jehovahs Witness, who was in the first aid corps and told him, "If something isn't done soon, you will die." In Auschwitz he never would have willingly gone to sick bay under any conditions, because he knew it meant a certain death. The Belgian reassured him it would be alright, so he went.

There he met a Russian medic, a black marketeer, five Belgian policemen, and an old German Capo. Capos were the prisoners who controlled the camps internally. Some were good and some were very bad, and were often killed when they lost the protection of the SS guards. Buchenwald was controlled by the red triangles, political prisoners, but within every camp there was usually an ongoing power struggle between the Jews, political prisoners, and professional criminals as to who would control the internal running of the camp.

The Belgian peeled the skin off his frozen toes to the bone using a knife, without the aid of anesthetic, and had him soak his feet in sodium permanganate. The pain was excruciating. There were many other patients admitted to the sick bay for the same reason, and Emil stayed there for over a month to recuperate. The small medic building only held about 20 or 25 patients, so he had to leave once he started to get better.

Discussion among the prisoners often led to, "What will we do afterwards? How will we adapt back into society?" Emil credits his will to survive four concentration camps to his father, who told him, "What ever happens to you, you can take it. Don't ever become the character the SS portrays us to be." There was a gentlemen's agreement most prisoners followed in the camps, which stated that it was all right to steal from the government, but not from each other. Of course there were some exceptions, but for the most part the prisoners tried to live by this, no matter how hard or tempting it might be.

The other factor that kept Emil going was the promise he made to his mother and sister to meet them back in Witten after the war was over. His will to survive was strong, and he was determined the Nazis wouldn't break him.

While at Buchenwald, several Canadian paratroopers were captured when they landed behind enemy lines. Usually military P.O.W.s were sent to their own camp, but for whatever reason these poor fellows were not, and they were hanged in the parade ground.

Rumors ran rampant throughout the camps, as bits and pieces of information and news trickled in with the arrival of new inmates. Towards the end of the war, it became apparent that the Germans were loosing. As the American Third Army under General George Patton approached the camp, the regimental command decided to march all the prisoners that were able out of the camp, 60,000 in total, even closer to the center of Germany. The older guards were left behind with the sick inmates. Emil knew he couldn't survive another march for more than a day, so he decided to take his chances, and stayed behind to wait for the Americans. Some of the guards were killed and some were held by the inmates. Two or three were even protected, because they had been lenient or cooperated with prisoners on prior occasions.

On record the official day of liberation for Buchenwald was April 11, 1945, but actually the prisoners had liberated themselves two days before the Third Army arrived. Emil weighed only 80 pounds by that time, and was suffering from typhus. He later developed pleurisy, as an aftereffect of the typhus, but says he fully recovered from his illness after about a year's time. The SS barracks were converted into an army field hospital, and even then, there still weren't enough beds for the men so they had to sleep on the floor. One day the Colonel in charge came to Emil and said, "Emil, you are 14 years old aren't you?" Emil took his cue and said yes. He then found out about an invitation from the Swiss Army, that anyone 14 and under was invited to recover in Switzerland.

While living in the town of Davos, Switzerland, late in 1945, Emil was roommates with a man who had a girlfriend living in Sweden. She, too, had survived similar circumstances to his, and had been offered asylum in another country. A letter was sent from her to Emil's roommate, stating that prisoners' names were being broadcast over the radio in Sweden from areas the Russians had liberated. Sidonie and Helga

Landau were said to have just crossed into the west, and she wanted to know if they were relatives of Emil's.

The news was too good to be true, but there was no mail and no trains going to or from Germany, so he had no way to communicate with his hometown. Emil started sending letters out to friends and relatives in nearby countries. One day a letter arrived for him with a return address of an Army Post Office in Germany. Inside the envelope was a letter from his mother, saying she and his sister had survived, but had thought he was dead. They met a prisoner that had seen him when his forehead was stamped at Auschwitz, and thought he had been sent to the gas chamber.

Emil had been given a scholarship to study at the University of Geneva, but when he received the letter from his mother, he decided to join them in Bremen, Germany. There was one snag though. He was an enemy alien living in Switzerland, and he had to be in Germany to be able to get to the United States. The Swiss government told him the only thing they could do was deport him, but they couldn't guarantee the reception he would get on the other side. They were very nice though, and gave him a document which stated he could reenter Switzerland within four weeks, even though they were technically deporting him.

The year was now early 1946, and his mother wanted to go to either Argentina, where her sisters had fled before the war, or the United States. Since they were German citizens, not displaced persons, the Landaus soon found it was difficult to get out of Germany. They contacted their second cousins who lived in Seattle, Washington, who had saved the $500 Alex had smuggled out of Germany, and they agreed to sponsor them. In December of 1946, with a special directive by President Truman, which let "German citizens" who had been in concentration camps leave Germany, the Landaus came to America.

First stop was New York, then they traveled to Seattle to be with their cousins. After about a year, the family moved to California, and Emil became an American citizen in 1952. He worked as a photographer and in a print shop. Then, in 1957, he was hired by Time Inc. to help develop color scanners, which were used in the printing process. They wanted Emil to work in Europe, but he refused, stating he had just got to this country. So they compromised and he moved to New York, which is where he met and married his wife Carolyn in 1961. They have a son, Alex, who was named after Emil's father.

He quickly moved through the ranks at Time Inc. and went from technician to Western Hemisphere Manager. About 1970, he started his own company, Printing Development, Inc., which he later sold in the mid 1980s. Emil and his wife Carolyn currently live in Damariscotta. He has started speaking to students and civic organizations about his experiences during the Holocaust, and has lectured in his hometown in Witten and in colleges throughout Germany.

Author's note: Emil has returned to Buchenwald twice, once ten years ago, and again in April of 1995. During the first visit back, while the Communists were still in power in East Germany, Emil discovered after taking the tour of the camp that statistics were available to look at. He couldn't remember the prisoner number he had been given at Buchenwald, so he decided to see if there was any record of his arrival.

With the help of the camp historian and his wife, a statistician, Emil looked at microfiche. Much to his surprise, 40 years after his internment, he found a total record on himself. There was his name, age, and profession, metal worker, which he had made up in order to stay alive in Auschwitz. On the manifest there was no number, but on a separate index he found the cell block number where he had lived, and that the author and fellow prisoner, Eli Wiessel, had also lived in his block. He found out that the prisoners had been ordered by the SS to keep the records, right up until the last days of the war. It was a strange revelation for Emil, because he had always thought if you died in one of the camps, there would be no record of you. As it turned out, it was just the opposite, there was an abundance of information.

On his second visit, Emil decided to drive around the perimeter of Buchenwald. He had learned from the camp historian that, between 1936 to 1945, even when there were 90,000 prisoners in the camp, there were never any successful escapes. The reason for this was that the camp sits on a mountain, which falls off steeply all around it.

The radio didn't work in Emil's car, so he didn't have it on, and subsequently didn't hear any news briefs as he started out on his journey. Pretty soon he saw flashing green lights behind him. It was the German police. They waved him over, and several officers got out of the car and asked him if he had a permit to be driving here. He said, "Yes, I got one 50 years ago."

It was then that Emil found out there had been a neo-Nazi demonstration at Buchenwald just a week before his arrival. The group was con-

fronted by angry protesters and it had become a very tense situation. The police thought it was suspicious that Emil was driving where he was and thought he might be a Neo Nazi.

When he explained that he had been imprisoned at the camp 50 years earlier, the police were very apologetic, and it was then that Emil noticed the officer in charge was wearing an earring, which struck him as very funny. Keep in mind that under the Nazis and later under the Communists, it would have been unthinkable to wear an earring with your uniform, and it might have even led to your arrest. Funny how things change.

After the liberation of the concentration camps, some of the people that had been held by the Nazis ended up in the Communist East German government. Later, there was a political fight for control, and when it was discovered that some of these people had been "bad" Capos in the camps, they were shipped to the gulags in Siberia and died.

In ending, Emil would like us all to remember that no one ever thinks this can happen to them, it's always the other guy. When you let your guard down for even a minute, and hate and prejudice are given the chance to get a foothold, it is time to stamp it out right then, before it gets the opportunity to grow and poison more minds.

Johannes Tomasson and Gudfinna (Minna) Stefansdottir
Iceland

In May of 1939, the British Army came to Reykjavik. About a week later they arrived on Vestmannaeyjar Island, which is located off the south coast of Iceland. The British were soon relieved by American soldiers, so they could go home to England, and defend their own country. Johannes was 18 years old at the time, and worked for the Shell company, driving an oil truck.

Minna was staying with a friend, Karolina, the night the British arrived. They awoke to the sound of many feet tramping up the street, which drew them to the window. When the girls looked out, they saw British soldiers walking past Karolina's house towards the school, which is where they stayed at first while they were stationed on Vestmannaeyjar Island.

Minna was 16 years old at the time, and it didn't take long for the British soldiers to notice how pretty she was. The grocery store she worked in soon became very busy, and the soldiers bought a lot of Pilsner, which is beer that has a very low alcohol content. They thought they were buying the real stuff, but beer didn't become legal in Iceland until about 1985.

Iceland became an important base during the war, because of its strategic location in the North Atlantic. There was the possibility and many rumors that the German Army might try to invade Iceland. The country did not have an army of its own, so its inhabitants were really relieved when the British Army, and later the Americans, occupied their country.

Many people had been without work in Iceland, but all that changed when the soldiers arrived. Roads and houses had to be built for them, and wages went up, which improved the economy of the country. There was rationing during the war, but everyone seemed to have enough to eat. Most towns had a group of people who were trained to help and lead their neighbors if there was an air raid. These men were given some guns and helmets to use if it was necessary.

Icelanders kept sailing to Europe during the war, so in a way they took part in it. Many Icelandic boats were lost at sea, and many fishermen and sailors lost their lives during this time period. The ships tried to sail in groups both to the United States and England as much as possible, but the fishing boats did not have any protection. German U-boats sunk many Icelandic ships and fishing boats during the war.

Although Iceland didn't have a direct part in the war, she certainly played an indirect part, by allowing the Allies to set up a base on the island. Also, by saving soldiers and sailors lives whose ships had been lost at sea, and by sailing to England to sell fish, and to purchase goods which were brought back to Iceland, thus helping the British economy. Johannes and Minna currently live on Vestmannaeyjar Island.

Author's note: Icelandic women usually don't change their last names when they get married. They have their father's name, with dottir added on the end of it, which translates to "Daughter of..." In Minna's case her name means, "Daughter of Stefan." Icelandic men also take their father's name, but son is added on instead of dottir.

Johannes and Minna's daughter, Erna, was an exchange student at Boothbay Region High School from August of 1967 through June of 1968.

Her host family was David and Caroline Parkhurst and their children. In 1994, my husband Maynard and I traveled to Iceland. We stayed with Erna's family on Vestmannejyar Island for a few days, and had the good fortune to visit with Johannes and Minna while we were there.

BASILIO COSSU
Italy

Basilio was born and raised on the island of Sardinia off the coast of Italy. He was employed at the Institute of National Social Pensions as an executive in the city of Nuoro when Germany occupied Italy. He was drafted at the age of 30 into the Italian Coast Guard and served in it for one year.

During the beginning of the war, the general feeling in Italy about the Germans was influenced by fascist propaganda. There was also great admiration for their strong military, which had just taken over Poland and France. Basilio was critical of the Germans, because he felt they wanted to be regarded as superior over all men, but he was in the minority at the beginning of the war among his countrymen.

Many of his friends were sent to Russia to fight with the Germans. Many died there. Some of the survivors returned to Italy with terrible frostbite, and never regained feeling in their limbs.

As the war progressed and the German occupation became heavier and heavier in Italy, critical feelings were growing stronger and stronger against the Germans throughout the country. This was especially prevalent after their defeats to the Allied powers in Africa, Russia, and Normandy, which showed they weren't the invincible fighting force they had claimed to be. It wasn't long before the Italians felt the Americans and British could win, and would free their country.

Mussolini was very popular at the beginning of the war with the people of Italy. They believed in his politics and in his alliance with the Germans. Basilio remembers there were some intellectuals who were against Mussolini's politics, because he suppressed political liberty, but they were a minority within the country. After the Americans and British landed on Italian soil, the people became very critical of Mussolini. For a while they spoke out very cautiously, for fear of retribution from the Germans, but as the war progressed their voices grew strong. During the last years of the war many Italians became partisans and had an agreement with the Americans and British forces to fight with them as an army of liberation against fascism.

During the war many services in Italy were irregular, including transportation and communication. Also, food and coal was rationed, and in many places throughout the country there was a thriving black market. Basilio recalls the small, coal mining village of Carbonia on Sardinia. Its people suffered terribly during the war, because they didn't have many provisions. Other villages had agriculture and livestock to help them get by, but Carbonia was very rocky and there was not much that would easily grow there.

When the Italians started considering the Germans as the enemy, many were deported to German concentration camps. In fact Basilio's uncle by marriage, Luigi, left Italy to fight against the Germans. He joined the French Foreign Legion, but was captured, and was sent to a concentration camp. Luigi said the conditions were terrible and he soon found himself covered with lice. When the Germans decided to move him to another camp, he saw an opportunity to gain his freedom, and escaped off the train that was transporting him. He returned to Italy once the war was over.

By 1943, fascism had begun to dissolve in Italy. Rome wasn't free yet, and the Germans continued to control the city. Anti-fascists, who were protesting the occupation of their country, set off a bomb that killed 33 Germans. In retaliation, the Germans decided to kill 10 Italians for every German that died in the explosion.

Basilio's brother-in-law's brother, Agostino Napoleone, was a sub lieutenant in Trieste. He was 26 years old at the time, and knew it was dangerous to stay in the north of Italy, because it was still occupied, so he decided to try and get to the south. He traveled with two friends, but when they arrived in Rome, the Germans captured them. Agostino was one of the 330 people the Germans took from the suburbs of Rome and killed. They were taken to some nearby caves (Fosse Ardeatine) and were shot. Then the Germans laid land mines in front of the caves, so no one could rescue the victims. These caves are now a memorial landmark in Italy, and are honored with an annual ceremony to remember the dead.

Recovery after the war was quick in Italy, thanks to the Americans and the Marshall Plan. They provided food and materials that were critical to helping Italy get back on its feet. Within three or four years the rebirth of the country was complete.

Basilio, now 85 years old, retired from the Institute of National Social Pensions in 1975, and currently lives in Rome.

PRANAS LAPE
Lithuania

The fate of Lithuania was sealed before the war. On August 23, 1939, in Moscow, a treaty of friendship and nonaggression was created between the Soviet Union and Nazi Germany. It was not known at the time that the two totalitarian powers had also reached an agreement on the grand style of 19th century colonialism. Eastern Europe was to be divided into spheres of influence. According to the secret agreement, Lithuania, Latvia, and Estonia, the three independent Baltic states, would be placed in the Soviet sphere of influence as of the signing of the pact. Once an agreement was reached with Moscow on September 1, 1939, Hitler started the war against Poland.

Moscow demanded that the Baltic States sign with her "treaties of mutual assistance," whereby Red Army garrisons would be admitted into Baltic states. Lithuania at first did not accept the "mutual assistance," but it soon became clear that it wouldn't matter what they thought. On June 15, 1940, under the disguise that Lithuania's refusal "insulted" the Soviet Union and violated the mutual assistance pact, Moscow issued an ultimatum that "Regardless of the answer, the Soviet Union will march into Lithuania."

On June 15 at 3 P.M. the Red Army crossed the Lithuanian frontier and began the occupation of the country. Soviet tanks that were already stationed in Lithuania moved on Kaunas. It was the last day of the school year, and 18-year-old Pranas, a student at the time, had just returned home when his older sister, Elena, met him at the door with tears in her eyes, and told him they had just announced the Soviet occupation on the radio. They asked people to stay calm, and not to provoke any needless bloodshed.

Shortly thereafter things began to change very quickly in Lithuania. The President, Antanas Smetona, escaped to Germany, and later to the United States. Ministers and priests were arrested and sent to Siberia, and the Communist party forced the local newspapers to print their stories on the front page. After one month it was declared that there would only be one newspaper, the Communist newspaper.

The Soviets ordered a new Parliament to be elected, but when Pranas and his family looked at the list of candidates, they hardly knew anyone on the ballot. Years later one of Pranas' friends, Henrikas, described to him what he had witnessed during the election when he worked at their local voting center.

Henrikas said, "At the end of the day, Russian soldiers arrived and chased me out of the building." I asked, "What was going on?" They replied that the voting was already finished. Your attendance was recorded, but your vote didn't count. Any one that didn't vote was regarded as an enemy of the people. Henrikas was shocked, to say the least, and the next day when the election results were reported, the turnout was very high in some towns, 110 and even 115 percent voter turnout. It was then discovered that the Russian soldiers stationed in the country were allowed to vote.

The opera house was used as the Parliament building and was surrounded by Russian soldiers the next day. Lithuania asked to be admitted to the Soviet Union by one of the newly elected officials, and no one voted against it. That day, Pranas and his country legally became citizens of the Soviet Union.

Pranas' last year of high school was very strange. All the private schools were closed, and many Jewish, Russian, and German students were dispersed between the state schools throughout the country. This was purposely done to disorient people, so you wouldn't know who was sympathetic with Communists. It didn't take long, though, to figure out which new teachers and students you could and couldn't trust. Also, Lithuanian/German families were permitted to return to Germany, if they could prove their heritage and bloodline came from there.

The juniors and seniors were kept busy "nationalizing" things in the town, instead of receiving their normal lessons. For instance, Pranas and his friends were told to go to the bicycle shop to count and record everything in the store, because it was now state property. Pranas felt very uncomfortable doing this, but Mr. Katz, the owner, didn't seem to mind. As it turned out, Mr. Katz had been assigned to be the new boss of the local Phillips Electrical shop by the Communists, so he actually got a better job and was pleased by it.

There was a lot of brainwashing and infiltration by the Communists during this time period. They seemed to know exactly what everyone was thinking and doing. Also, anything Lithuanian was taken down, including their flag, and Pranas and all the other young men had to register for the draft.

Starting on June 14, 1941, everything crumbled around the Lithuanians. Pranas started taking his final exams that day at school, and during that night the first waves of mass arrests started. People were put on trucks, taken to the railroad station, and were shipped off to Siberia, most never to be heard from again. The Communists had lists of names, but they didn't make any sense because these people hadn't done anything; they even arrested some of their fellow Communists and took them away.

That night while walking home from a friend's house, Pranas noticed the old calvary field was full of Russian trucks. He could see the glow of cigarettes burning and could hear a few words, but it didn't seem that unusual, because the Russians always seemed to be moving around the country during the night. What he really was witnessing was the preparation for the mass deportation of Lithuanians.

About three o'clock in the morning, Elena, Pranas' oldest sister, said, "They are arresting people!" Pranas quickly got dressed and cautiously walked out of their house. There were three Russian trucks in the street, and he could see men, women, and children being loaded on them, bundled up in coats and bedding, which really struck him as strange, because it was June and was warm out.

The truck nearest to him was full, and the other two were being loaded. He wasn't sure what to do at this point, and thought to himself, "Should I go for a walk, making myself scarce, because they may stop at my house next? Or should I go back in my house?" It was obvious that this was a very big thing, and Pranas decided to return to his home, to tell his family what was going on.

The very next day he was at school, preparing to take an oral history exam. There were several teachers and people from the ministry of education there. All of a sudden the classroom door blew open and a man wearing a black leather jacket entered, followed by two Russian soldiers armed with rifles and bayonets. One of the teachers stood up, and the man approached. Pranas kept looking straight ahead, and could see the teacher had his jacket and hat laid over the back of his chair. When he

stood up, the hat had fallen on the floor. About this time, the new principal walked into the room, but didn't say anything.

The teacher asked, "What is going on? This is an examination. You
can't just blow in here without an arrest order." The man dressed in
leather took a gun out and said, "This is my arrest order!" He then
grabbed the teacher, who did manage to bring his jacket, and pushed
him out of the room. Pranas sat there all alone looking at the teacher's
hat lying on the classroom floor, and kept saying to himself, "What's happening? What's going on?"

From that point on, Pranas decided it would be a good idea to sleep
down by the river nights, in case they came to his parents' house looking for him. He took his last examination on June 21, and by that time
30,000 Lithuanians had been deported to Siberia.

He slept in the bushes with his fishing gear, so it would look better if
the Communists found him there. On June 22, there was a big explosion, which sounded like it came from the area of the airport. It woke
everyone up, and as Pranas looked around him and saw others crawl-
ing out from under the bushes, he discovered that many people in town
had the same idea he did. You could see something flying very high up
in the sky. Then three dots, which turned out to be airplanes, started
coming towards them, and as they approached, you could see German
insignia on their wings. Everyone started screaming and shouting, "The
war is on! The Germans will free us from the Communists!" People were
very happy, even ecstatic, because they thought the Germans would
beat the Russians, and the terror would end in Lithuania.

Pretty soon wave after wave of German airplanes came, and they
bombed the airport. The Russians tried to get their fighters off the
ground, but they were knocked down, back to the earth. Pranas ran
home and saw ambulances coming from the Russian camp headed to the
hospital. He woke everyone up and put the radio on. They anxiously
awaited to hear news about the war, but there was nothing. The radio
station didn't even know what had happened. Pranas' family thought he
was kidding, and didn't believe him.

Around 10 A.M. he went over to his school, but he couldn't find anyone there, so he took a bus home. On the bus, he overheard a local
woman ask a Russian officer what was going on. As an air raid siren
sounded, the officer told her it was just maneuvers and to take it easy,

nothing was happening. Pranas couldn't believe it! He knew what he had seen with his own eyes, and no one would believe him.

Midday Sunday a huge formation of German planes flew over the city. Pretty soon the air raid siren went off, and the antiaircraft guns were fired. People all came out of their houses to see what was going on, and some were hurt by falling flack, as the fragments fell back down. Finally the radio confirmed that the enemy, without warning, had attacked the border line, and the Red Army was marching into Germany pushing them back. The town of Kaunas was 200 KL from the border, so soon Pranas knew this wasn't true, because Russian soldiers were slowly dragging themselves back into town, and were trading their guns for food. They had really taken a beating from the Germans and it showed.

When the Russians blew up the bridges in town, to prevent to Germans from advancing, Lithuanian partisans seized the opportunity and formed an uprising. They took over the town and the radio station, and proclaimed Lithuania's independence. The country remained free for about three days, until the Germans arrived and took over the city. Lithuania was then occupied for the next three years of the war until late in 1944.

The first thing the Germans did in Kaunas was round up all the Jews, and confine them in a ghetto they created on the other side of the Neris River, which they surrounded with barbed wire fencing. They were forced to wear a yellow star of David on their clothing at all times, and were used as slave labor for the Nazis. They often stopped at homes in the town and asked for food. Pranas' mother, Barbara, always bought extra provisions, so she would have something to give them when they came by. It was not impossible to get food into the camp. Many townspeople snuck over to the barbed wire and brought the Jews food. Some even traded with them for articles such as jewelry or money.

Pranas started art school during the fall of 1941, after his graduation from high school. One day he returned home to find the local police turning his parents' house upside down. The man conducting the search was someone Pranas had gone to school with, so he asked him, "What is going on here?" The man replied, "One of your neighbors told the Germans your father was producing counterfeit passports and was selling them to the Jews, so we had to arrest him. Now we have to search the house for diamonds or anything else Jews would use to purchase fake documents with." Pranas then quit school and went to work at a ceramics factory to help his mother out, while his father was being held in jail.

Meanwhile Pranas, Sr., managed to get a letter smuggled out of jail with a man who was being released. He instructed his family to go and see a woman lawyer in town and to get her to help them. She was supposed to have an "in" with the Germans, and for a large sum of money, could get him out of jail. Barbara sold her diamond ring and other possessions from their household, raised the money to pay the woman, and her husband was freed.

The Lape family decided that it was no longer safe for Pranas, Sr., to live in town, and it would be better if he moved to a northern part of Lithuania. It was agreed that his oldest daughter, Elena, would accompany him, and he found a job as a caretaker for Jewish houses that had been taken by the Germans. This left his wife, son, and youngest daughter, Zita, behind in Kaunas. Petras, his other son, had joined the partisans and was living in the woods.

During the spring of 1942, Pranas returned home from work and was surprised to find a beautiful teenage girl there. When he asked his sister, Elena, who she was, he discovered that she was Jewish and had hidden when the Germans rounded up the Jews. Elena was in the process of altering her school identification card, swapping her photograph for the girl's so she wouldn't be held in the ghetto. The young woman spoke German fluently and got a job working for the German army. She was able to get to England after the war. It was a huge risk for the Lape family to take, but they thought it was the right thing to do under the circumstances.

About this time, the Germans decided to draft the Lithuanians into their army, and as coincidence would have it, Pranas hurt his knee terribly in a sliding accident. He was confined to his bed for six months with water on the knee. When German soldiers came to the house looking for Pranas and his brother, Petras, for the draft, neither was available. Petras was hiding in the forest with his partisan friends, and Pranas was bedridden.

One of the Lapes' neighbors was the wife of a colonel in the Lithuanian Army. She came by their house and took Pranas' papers and a doctor's note to the Germans to explain why he wasn't registering. They accepted her story, and Pranas was granted six months to recuperate by the Germans. Once that time passed and his knee had healed, he had to go and see German doctors at their official hospital in town.

His knee did get better, so when the time came he went to see his family doctor first, and asked him what he should do. The doctor told Pranas the knee could have several things wrong with it, and might even have T.B., if that was a help. Pranas took his suggestion, and the night before his examination wrapped his knee tightly, so when he got up in the morning and took the bandage off, the knee appeared swollen. Then he found a walking stick, and put some of his high school theater experience to use as he limped to the German hospital.

Two young doctors examined the knee and he showed them a report from his own doctor, pointing out the possibility of T.B. (tuberculosis). The doctors wrote a note which said, "Knee inflammation (T.B.?)," and sent Pranas to see the staff secretary, who just happened to be Lithuanian. She had blank examination forms that were pre-signed by the doctors, and it was her job to type in their diagnosis. Pranas asked her to save him from being forced into the German army by dropping the parenthesis and question mark around the word T.B., which she did.

He then limped into a room where several German officials sat behind a long table. When it was his turn, he handed one of their assistants his doctors' report. All of a sudden one of the officers started yelling in German – which Pranas understood fluently – "How dare you even show up in this room! You could be spreading your disease. Get out of here!" Pranas played dumb and waited for the translator to repeat what the officer had said. It was hard not to laugh because the translator was very bad and repeated everything incorrectly. Pranas received a card that released him from military duty, and as soon as it was signed and stamped, he limped back out of the room, out of the building, and when he was a few blocks away, threw his stick aside, and ran the rest of the way home. He was free!

That night he decided go to the movies. When he got there they were surrounded by Germans who were checking everyone's papers. Pranas passed his papers to an officer, who briefly looked them over, saluted, and waved him by.

In 1943, politically active Lithuanians were arrested and were sent to Buchenwald or Stutthof, which were Nazi concentration camps. Aside from that, they seemed uninterested in the Lithuanians. The Germans took over the art school Pranas attended, and used it as a training center for their women's air force corps.

In 1943, the Nazis became very irritated with the Lithuanians when they realized they couldn't get them to do anything for the Germans or their cause. They weren't able to organize a Waffen SS in Lithuania like they had been able to in other countries, and when the Lithuanians told them they wouldn't fight in German uniforms, it infuriated them. In retaliation, all the universities and institutes were closed and their former students were hunted for the German draft. The only way you were exempt from it now was if you worked as part of the war effort.

By 1944, everyone knew the Russians were coming, and were left with the excruciating decision, should we move or not? Many of their neighbors fled, and some went to the forest to fight with the partisans against the Russians. Barbara came to Pranas one night and told him, "You'd better go. When the Russians come, they will take you into their army, put you on the front, and you will disappear for no reason."

Pranas knew his mother was right and decided to escape to Sweden by boat. The Lithuanian officer's wife who had helped him before told him to wait for a truck one night, which he did, but it never showed up. As he stood in the darkness, listening to the artillery and bombs exploding in the distance, Pranas knew the front was moving steadily in his direction and he was going to have to do something fast.

The next day he was asked if he wanted to join a Lithuanian antiaircraft battery. Everyone involved thought it was a good idea, and trusted it was a Lithuanian deal, so Pranas jumped on a truck with some of his friends and headed to Taurage. After driving for a very long time, they were brought into a German camp and were given German uniforms. They had been tricked into becoming part of the German Army.

The men were loaded on trains and were taken to Witenberg am Elbe, Germany, where they were supposed to be trained at an antiaircraft artillery school. They stayed there for two weeks, received no training, and were taken by train to Danzig, now Sdansk, where they waited another two weeks for a ship. They boarded the ship and steamed to Hango, Finland. Once there, they were taken by train to Rovaniemi, where they were put to work digging drainage ditches on an airfield. As you can plainly see none of this was organized very well right from the beginning.

Then something unexpected happened late in the fall of 1944: the Finnish capitulated and told the Germans to leave their country or they would be forced to fight them. The Russians had a hand in this, because they told the Finns they wouldn't invade them if they kicked the Germans out, which they did. The Lithuanians were then marched out of the northern part of Finland into Norway. They crossed a huge tundra upon which a highway had been constructed by the Germans. It was now the fall of 1944, and it had been raining heavily. There were holes in the road everywhere, and the men were ordered to fill them with gravel as they went along.

One day a German general came speeding down the road on a motorcycle with a sidecar. He hit one of the holes and went off the road into the mud. The men scrambled to pull him out, and boy was he mad! His uniform was covered in mud and he started screaming at the top of his lungs. The first thing he wanted to know was, why aren't these men saluting me? Pranas of course understood everything he was saying because he knew German, but most of the men didn't. Many of them were farmers, ages 17 to 75, who had tried to escape and had been shipped to the north of Norway. The icing on the cake was the fact that none of them had been trained, not even to salute. Finally some German soldiers heard the commotion, and came rushing over to explain to the irate general why the men weren't saluting. Once he understood they were doing the best they could patching the roads with what little equipment they had, he agreed to send them a truck to assist with the task. The next day the truck arrived, but it took half a day's drive to get a big load of gravel, so they weren't getting any more accomplished than they had been before.

The main road between Finland and Norway had long stretches of wooden covered roads between Karasjok and Lakselv, like a covered bridge, but they kept the snow off the roads. Some stretches were five KL long, and as the Germans retreated, they ordered the Lithuanians to destroy the covers. First they were told to set them on fire, but there was so much snow on the roofs, they wouldn't burn. Then they were ordered to climb up on them and shovel the roofs off. Pranas said it wasn't very enjoyable, but at least they were able to keep warm.

On New Year's Day, 1945, the men reached Alta Fjord, Norway, where they loaded boats in shifts with Russian P.O.W.s. Most of the cargo was food and wines the Germans had looted as they retreated. The men were boarders in Norwegian homes. The Norwegians had been forcefully removed from them before they arrived. Pranas found a pair of skis in the house where he stayed and decided to give them a try. The Lithuanians were allowed to walk around the town as long as they didn't go too far.

Pranas carried the skis and walked up a nearby hill. He made one run down and decided to go back to the house. Later that day a torpedo boat came into the port, and three German sailors decided to go skiing. They walked up the same hill Pranas had used earlier that day, following his footprints, but when they came down, there were three loud explosions. The men had skied into a mine field and were blown up. Why Pranas didn't suffer the same fate that day will never be known.

In March of 1945, the Lithuanians were shipped to Namsos, where they worked in the forest cutting trees for the railroad. Their dogtags identified them as the Lithuanian Rifle Battalion, which was a real joke, because they hadn't even been taught how to shoot their rifles. The soldiers they were stationed with came from Cologne, Germany. They were all Catholic, and were all anti-Hitler. The leader of the camp was a *schtabfelfebei*, which is about the equivalent of a sergeant, and he was always drunk. For the most part the men were 40 or older and were considered too old to be sent to the front. All they really wanted to do was get home to their families, and in turn the Lithuanians had a pretty good relation with them. They even told Hitler jokes.

Once in a while German pilots would come into the town, and would start talking about how close the Germans were to having new weapons and aircraft that would be superior over the Allies. They were usually pretty fanatical about Hitler as well and the men had to watch themselves around them, even though they didn't believe a word they were saying, because it was obvious the Germans were beaten and were retreating.

One day rifle practice was announced. The men were supposed to practice sighting their weapons. Most of the older men were missing on purpose. When the younger men drew attention to them, they quickly pointed out that if you showed the Germans you were a good shot, you might get sent to the front. This point was taken to heart, and almost everyone started missing the targets on purpose. Needless to say, practice was never ordered again.

The men then moved to Overhalla, which was a small village surrounded by mountains between Namsos and Grong. Their evenings were free, and Pranas and his friend, Felix, were allowed to care for the wireless radio. They could tune in the BBC from Germany and listen to the latest news. One of them had picked up a map at a school in Finland and had carried it with him ever since. Thy put it up on the wall and used sewing pins with colored heads to represent the countries that were involved: blue for the United States, red for Russia, green for Germany, and so on. They advanced the pins as the fronts changed, and pretty soon the Germans were coming to them to learn what was going on, because they were still being fed propaganda by their own military.

Pranas could sense the war would end soon, and started investigating the possibility of escaping to Sweden. He had met the store owner's daughter, Birgit, in Overhalla one day when he was looking for some watercolors to paint with and felt he could trust her. While they were in Finland he had found some really nice watercolor paper. When the Germans saw how well he could paint, they offered to carry the paper in one of their machine gun cases to protect it if Pranas would make paintings of their wives and girlfriends, from their descriptions.

Birgit spoke some German, so they were able to communicate fairly well. She asked Pranas where he was from, and when he told her, she told him she always listened to Radio Lithuania at 7 o'clock in the evening because they played the latest jazz from America. The two formed a fast friendship and Pranas soon knew he could trust her with his plans.

Many of the men saved cigarettes or candy during the war, but Pranas saved coffee beans. In fact he had filled his gas mask container with them, and decided to give them to Birgit's family. When he brought them into the store one evening they couldn't believe their eyes, because they hadn't had coffee for over three years.

That night Pranas divulged his secret plan to Birgit. He asked her if anyone had tried to escape. She told him, "No one can make it across the mountains. People have tried, but there was nothing to eat, and they were forced to return. When they did, the Germans shot them." Pranas looked at Birgit and said, "If I go, I won't come back. I have a plan to go to Sweden, because I don't know what will happen after the war, or how the Russians will react."

In April of 1945, Pranas and Birgit discussed his escape plans again, and she told him, "You can't make it with the rainy season coming." Pranas told her, "We are going to try, because we have nothing to lose." Birgit conceded and said, "Alright, but I am going to get you a map."

As it turned out, she had connections with the Norwegian Underground because her fiance was a member, and was able to get them a military map that showed all the farmhouses in the area. Even more important, all the Quisling houses on the map were marked with a cross. (Vadkun Quisling was the leader of the Nasjonal Samling, Norwegian Nazi Party. He became Hitler's puppet in Norway, when King Haakon and his son, Prince Olaf, fled the occupying Nazi forces. Quisling's name soon became a term for someone who betrays his or her country by collaborating with an occupying enemy force.)

During the next few days, Pranas and Felix exchanged items they had for food in preparation for their escape. There were still two obstacles in front of them though. The Lithuanians had strict orders from the Germans not to leave the camp without their rifles. It was known the Norwegian Underground operated in this area, and the Germans felt it wasn't safe to walk around unarmed, and they were right. The other problem was how would the men get out of the camp with their rucksacks, without the Germans noticing?

Pranas went to Birgit, told her about their problem, and asked if she would talk to a local truck driver to see if he would help them. The man came to the camp every day and picked up the scraps from the kitchen to feed his pigs. The camp official was always drunk, and the men would be in the forest cutting trees, so Pranas figured he and Felix could pack their rucksacks and leave them near their bunks. Then the truck driver could back in like he usually did, but this trip he would toss their bags into the back of his truck with the food scraps for his pigs. The driver agreed to the plan, and when Pranas and Felix returned from working the following day, their rucksacks were gone.

Everyone in their barracks knew about the men's plans, and that evening, about 50 Lithuanians approached Pranas and Felix and told them they wanted to go too. Pranas told them they couldn't go, because it would be to obvious if most of the barracks disappeared. Also, they had to be prepared to make the trip alone, even if one of their friends fell behind. He and Felix offered to copy the map for the men, but told them they would have to make their own plans for escape. At this point a German soldier who bunked in the other end of the barracks rolled over on his cot and said, "If I were younger, I would go with you." Believe it or not, even with this many people aware of the men's plans, no one betrayed them.

Later that night, Pranas and Felix grabbed their rifles, walked out of the barracks and through the village to a pre-arranged meeting place. They waited and waited, and even began to wonder if they should go back, but at the last minute the truck driver appeared, and traded their rucksacks for their rifles. The two men walked as far and as fast as they could that night. There was a path that took them up to the mountains, and once they had climbed quite high, they came to a small summer house where they uneasily slept the first night.

The next morning the men woke up early and found a few things in the cupboards: sugar, dry bread, etc. There was a sign up on the wall that said, "Leave it the way you found it." This apparently was the custom in Norway, because they came across several of these summer houses along their trek, and they were all maintained very well.

The men started walking again. Up and up they went, climbing constantly. Soon they came to a beautiful waterfall, and as they climbed onward they reached its source. The walking was very good, because the snow was still frozen, and it would support your weight. Pranas had never been in the mountains in his life, so when they reached the top of the first ridge, he thought they were on the top of the mountain. Then he looked up, and up, and up, and realized they had a very long way to go.

As the journey continued, both men wished they had brought skis. Once they were over a ridge, the mountain flattened out like a plateau, and skis would have expedited their progress tremendously. When they looked down, they could see the house they had stayed in the night before, and it looked very small.

On the top of the next ridge, Pranas could see where the river went out to the ocean, and he paused for a minute to watch the movement of the clouds. The sun shown through them, and cast shadows over the land below, giving the illusion that the earth was moving beneath them. It gave Pranas an overwhelming feeling of freedom, something he had not felt in a very long time, and never experienced again, to that degree.

On the second day, they came to the edge of a huge lake. To go around it would have added days to their progress, and their compass indicated the direction they wanted to go in was directly across the lake. It looked like the ice was good, but when they stepped on it, it broke. Much to their surprise, they hit more ice below it, and were in the water up to their knees. Pranas got a stick to test the ice in front of them, and the two men proceeded on in this way. They stuck their matches and the map up under their hats, just in case the second level of ice gave way beneath them. By the time they got across the lake, they were waist deep in the water. They waded out and were very cold, but it didn't matter because they had safely crossed the lake. Once they got walking again and were up on the next ridge, they could look back and see where they had made a path through the ice.

By this time, the men felt they had a good jump on the Germans, but the April snow was starting to get a little mushy so the walking wasn't as good as it had been before.

They soon saw another lake below them, and when they looked at their map, discovered a notation stating a rowboat would be available so they could cross the lake. Darkness was approaching, so Pranas and

Pranas, pictured on the left, and Felix, on the right. Taken in Norway with Felix's camera using the self-timer, at the beginning of their escape.

Felix started to look for a safe place to sleep. They found a hay barn where they crashed for the night.

The next morning they descended the mountain, and came to a farm house, which was shown on the map as a safehouse. Pranas walked inside and found three men sitting in the kitchen talking; one of them spoke German, so they were able to communicate. Pranas explained that they weren't Germans, they were Lithuanians, and that they were looking for a rowboat to cross the lake. The men showed them where it was and instructed them to leave it at the house on the other side of the lake. One of the men wrote a letter and asked them to deliver it to the owner of the other farm, which the men agreed to do. Pranas and Felix took their uniforms off, so they would look more like civilians, and got into the rowboat.

The lake was about one mile wide, and as they neared the other house, Pranas started to get a bad feeling. The shore line was high and weedy, so they were able to approach undetected. Pranas crawled up on the banking and peered through the dead grass. Sure enough, his gut feeling had been right. There were two German soldiers sitting on the porch of the house, and he suddenly became very suspicious about the content of the letter he and Felix had been asked to deliver, so he crept back into the boat and told Felix to start rowing fast! Further along the shore, they found some trees and thick overgrowth where they hid the rowboat, and continued on.

The two men came to the first road they had seen in several days. It was curvy, and you couldn't see very far up ahead. They followed it, and were beginning to think there were no more obstacles between themselves and Sweden. Unfortunately, they soon discovered they were on the wrong side of a fast running river, which they had to cross to continue on. They kept hoping there would be a bridge, but instead they came to a wire with a hanging seat. You had to sit in it and pull yourself across the raging river. Once they made it safely across, they started following the road on the other side. Pretty soon they heard a truck coming, so they got off the road and hid in the woods. It proved to be a wise decision, because the truck was full of German soldiers.

The men decided they weren't in the clear yet, and they'd better continue on in the woods so they weren't unexpectedly detected by the Germans. The snow was very deep in the woods, and was deceiving to look at. What appeared to be even ground in front of you might let go under your weight, and you would soon find yourself up to your armpits in snow. This made the traveling very slow and tiresome for Pranas and Felix, but they knew by looking at the map, there was one more safe-house they could stay at ahead of them. So they set that as their goal and decided they could reach it by dusk.

The home was occupied by a very young Norwegian couple. They provided the men with food and a warm bed to sleep in. Pranas was still unnerved by the truckload of Germans they had seen earlier in the day, and checked the house for a telephone before he tried to fall asleep. Both he and Felix slept in their clothes, in case they had to make a fast escape. The next morning, they awoke early to the sounds of the woman cooking breakfast. The young couple tried to explain to the men that they couldn't possibly make the journey without skis, but they assured the couple they felt more secure walking. The Norwegians just shook their heads and wished the men good luck. Pranas and Felix gave the young couple all the German Marks they had before they left, and the couple gave them some bread in exchange.

Crossing one of many rivers during the escape. Instead of a bridge, this one had a hanging seat, suspended by a wire, which you sat on and pulled yourself across the river using the ropes.

About the middle of the day they came across another house that wasn't on the map, and found an older man splitting wood. They tried to explain to him who they were and told him about the boat they had used to cross the lake. Pranas handed him the letter to read, but his expression didn't give any indication as to what it said as he read it. Pranas, thinking of every movie he had ever seen, took the letter back and burned it, destroying the evidence. He said that action has haunted him for 50 years, because if he had just hung onto the letter, it could have been easily translated in Sweden, and he and Felix would have known if they had been set up by the men at the first farmhouse where they got the rowboat, or if it was just a harmless note.

The two continued on, leaving the old man, and once above the tree line, they found a small cottage where they were able to relax and sleep. The next morning they were awakened to the sound of a whole herd of deer grazing outside. When Pranas went to the window, the deer dispersed immediately. There was a thick fog that day, and he and Felix decided they couldn't possibly walk in it, so they stayed fogged in at the house two or three more days, and ate almost everything they had, knowing they had several more days journey ahead of them.

Finally the fog cleared, and they were able to set out again. Along the way they found some frozen cranberries poking their swollen heads up through the snow, and ate as many of the sweet berries as their stomachs could hold. Later in Sweden, they were told they shouldn't have touched the berries, because they could have been fermented from the sun, and they could have easily knocked them off their feet.

There were white birds everywhere, and they would lie still in the snow until you almost stepped on them. Then they would fly up in your face, scaring you to death. They finally reached a really nice summer cottage. It was a big old place overlooking a brook, and there was a boat stored under an overhang, which the men quickly confiscated for their cause.

The boat required some work, and they had to stuff some moss in the larger cracks so it would float. They also needed oars, so they found some shingles and attached them to some sticks they found. The river seemed very calm as it slowly flowed by the cottage, so they thought to themselves, this is going to be a piece of cake. According to the map the Swedish border wasn't far away, and the snow had become very deep, which made the traveling slow. Now they wouldn't have to walk, and they could relax all the way to the border.

It was a delight to sit down, and Felix said he would be the lookout, but he soon fell sound asleep, and Pranas decided to let him rest. The oars were makeshift and weren't very good, so Pranas used them as a rudder rather than as a means of propulsion. All of a sudden the water started running much faster, and as Pranas looked ahead, he noticed that the river was just cut off in mid air, and he could see a body of water and mountains off in the distance. Then it dawned on him, they were headed for a waterfall!

Pranas started yelling at Felix to wake up as he tried to get them to shore, but the shingle fell off the stick, and the boat was beginning to turn round and round. Felix came to and quickly threw the rucksacks on the shore, then the men spotted a birch branch overhanging the river and they both grabbed hold of it. The boat went out from under them, and they edged their way to shore, hand over hand. Pranas ran up ahead and couldn't believe his eyes — the waterfall was about 60 feet high and their boat was nowhere in sight. Finally, off in the distance, Felix noticed pieces of debris starting to surface. The boat had been smashed into a 100 tiny pieces.

Resting at one of the small cottages found in the Norwegian mountains.

Pranas and Felix gathered themselves together and discovered that they were once again on the wrong side of the river. They started walking, and the sun soon set. The wind was icy and strong, so they sought shelter behind a pile of rocks. It was so cold their clothing froze on them. After a while they came to the conclusion that this pile of rocks must be the border. They had made it, but were still in the wilderness with a long trek ahead of them.

The men built a fire between the rocks and took their clothes off so they could dry. They decided to take shifts watching the fire, but the warmth of it quickly put them both to sleep, and they awoke hours later to the freezing cold of the mountains. This happened several times throughout the night. They would rebuild the fire and would promptly fall asleep again. You can't imagine how cold it is when your fire has gone out, and you are sitting naked on a stump in the woods.

The next morning they came across ski tracks, but they were overcome by the knowledge that no one was actually looking for them. Their goal of escape had carried them all the way to Sweden, but now that they were there, they felt they weren't getting anywhere, and it was a very helpless feeling.

A heavy fog set in that morning as Pranas and Felix headed towards yet another lake. Their knees didn't want to hold them up at this point, and they just wanted to lie down and rest. Fortunately, an unexpected stroke of luck came their way when one of them accidentally fell into a giant spruce tree. The weight of the snow had laid the trees branches over, creating a sheltered area underneath kind of like a small house. They quickly took advantage of this and climbed in. At this point, they were to tired to even talk to each other, they were low on food, and they had no idea how much further it would be until they found someone that could help them.

The two weary travelers collapsed from exhaustion and slept throughout the night in the "treehouse." The next day neither of them wanted to leave the shelter of it, but they decided that since the fog had lifted, they should see what was going on. They walked on and came to a ridge, which allowed them to look out over a river that flowed into a large lake. It became obvious that they were once again on the wrong side of the river and they had to cross it. Both men were very discouraged at this point.

Pranas was using the field glasses and started to hallucinate from sheer exhaustion. He was seeing what he wanted to see, and that was houses, factories, and churches all made out of brick. He kept asking Felix, "Don't you see them?" Felix thought he had lost his mind and was starting to get worried about his friend. Finally Pranas spotted a small boat, and gave the field glasses to Felix so he could look at it. Felix took them in disbelief, but then he saw it too, on the shore of the lake. Both men were rejuvenated by this discovery, and Pranas snapped out of his hallucinogenic state.

They climbed down the ridge and came to a stream. Pranas threw his rucksack across and jumped the water with no problem. Felix followed, but when he went to jump, he slipped and fell in. The current pulled him down the stream, where he surfaced in a pool of water. Pranas quickly pulled him out and said, "Are you hurt?" Felix replied, "Yes, I hit my hip on the ice, but I can walk."

Nearby was the boat they had spotted from the ridge above. They edged it into the water, and at this point, it was a real blessing to be able to sit down for a while. Pranas told Felix to take it easy and he would row. A few minutes later, they heard gun shots in the moun-

This photograph will give you a good idea of the terrain Pranas and Felix traveled over to get to Sweden.

tains. They had been detected by the Swedish border guards. Felix said, "Turn around, we have to go back." Pranas said, "Are you crazy? Let's keep going." The men continued on down the lake, and hunger began to gnaw at them. They checked their rucksacks, and between them all they had was a can of lard and some salt, which they mixed together and ate.

Gradually they began to see summer homes along the edge of the lake. Then all of a sudden Felix said, "I see smoke, and a house!" Spirits were high in the tiny rowboat as they made their way towards the house. Pranas brought the boat ashore, and Felix went up to the house. While he was gone, Pranas fell sound asleep in the boat. Pretty soon he could hear dogs barking, but he couldn't wake up. Then he felt a dog licking his face. When he opened his eyes, he found himself face to face with a big German Shepard, and Felix and a woman were waving him towards the house.

The Swedish woman fed them, and had a sauna and a bath ready for them in no time. Pranas said it was like a seventh heaven. Once both men had cleaned up and shaved, they were refreshed and even found the energy to play with the dog. The woman brought out an album that showed the names of all the people who had escaped from Norway and stayed at her house. There were a lot of Russians and Norwegians in the book. Pranas and Felix added their names and homeland too, with the others.

Pranas and Felix started to feel uneasy, because the woman wasn't paying much attention to the fact that they had escaped from Norway. She seemed to be more interested in showing them her photo album. They asked her several times, "Why don't you call the police?" Finally, half heartedly, she did. Later, the men would learn the Swedish government was paying its citizens for every refugee they took in. This woman had several cottages built for that very reason, and really didn't want the men to leave, because she was making money off their presence.

That night Pranas was awakened by someone shaking him and a flashlight being shined in his eyes. The Swedish border patrol had caught up with them and wanted to know where their weapons were. Pranas explained that they didn't have any, and they let him go back to sleep.

The next morning, Pranas awoke and found the two soldiers sleeping on the floor of the house. The weather outside was lousy. It was raining and blowing, and he realized just how lucky he and Felix had been to find this house, and not still be up in the mountains unprotected.

After they were all fed, the border patrol told them to get in the row-boat. The wind was really blowing and they couldn't make any progress across the lake, so they returned to the woman's house and called for a truck to be sent to the other side of the lake to pick them up. Pranas and Felix and the two border patrol guards then walked to the village on the other side, and all along the way, people came out of their homes and invited them in for coffee and cakes. Pranas and Felix both remarked that this was a really friendly country. Later they decided the woman had called ahead to all the houses on the lake, and said here come some more guests, make sure they stop at your house.

Finally they got to the army truck, and the Swedish soldiers who were waiting for them starting laughing and saying, "Heil Hitler!" because they thought they were Germans. A civilian man appeared who spoke German and drove with them to Sunsvald. It took a really long time, and when he stopped to make a telephone call, Pranas and Felix got out of the truck to stretch their legs. Pretty soon they were surrounded by teenage girls bearing cakes who were very interested in them. One even asked them, "How many planes did you shoot down?"

Felix rowing one of the boats they found during the escape.

The civilian returned and informed Pranas and Felix they were going to be taken to a hotel. Pranas didn't believe it. He thought they were going to jail until their stories could be verified. Both men were amazed when the truck pulled up in front of a very nice hotel and they were taken inside. They were asked to bathe and leave their old cloths in a pile, because they would be given new ones.

The hotel ballroom was set up with cots, and the men were astounded to meet two Russians and three Norwegians, who had escaped they same way they did. Felix could speak Russian, and the Norwegians could speak German, so they all got along very well. The Russians said this country was like a fairy tale, because you could work wherever you wanted, at whatever you wanted to do, and the people even owned their own automobiles.

They spent a week at the hotel under quarantine, and then were moved just outside of Stockholm to Kummelnas. Their new home had been a resort, but it was taken over by the government and had been turned into barracks for refugees. In fact the entire fleet of Estonia's ships had fled there. Pranas and Felix were informed that they would receive help searching for a job in their own specialty. Pranas soon found a job making pottery and ceramics in Stockholm, but Felix hadn't completed his schooling in electronics yet, so he got a job cutting timber. Both men were also issued foreigners passports, because they had no form of identification with them when they entered the country.

Felix wasn't feeling well and went to see a doctor. It was then that he found out he had TB in his hip from when he had fallen on the ice during their escape. He went to a hospital on an island of Gotteborg, and was able to continue his studies while he recuperated. He eventually earned a degree in electronics, married his nurse, and became a multimillionaire in Sweden in the radio and electronics business.

Pranas, on the other hand, worked in Stockholm and tried to get into the art academy, but was told they didn't have any room for foreigners in their program. One day he saw a beautiful poster in the city that caught his eye, and he decided to investigate who had designed it. The man's name was Anders Beckman, and he ran a private art school in Stockholm. He had received critical acclaim as an artist throughout the world, and especially in Sweden, after he built the Swedish Pavilion at the 1939 Worlds' Fair in New York.

Pranas wanted to attend his school, but he didn't have enough money for the tuition. Luckily, he was able to get some support from the American/Baltic Relief Fund, and was able to enroll right away. Beckman soon discovered Pranas' artistic abilities were above the other students, and he was asked to teach drawing. It was a wonderful opportunity and it enabled Pranas to learn Swedish fluently. Through Beckman, Pranas met everyone in Sweden, including King Gustavus V.

In 1949, a friend of Pranas left for the United States, and said he would send for him. Pranas didn't give it a second thought, but one day he received a letter that said, "I've found a sponsor for you. Do you want to come over?"

At that time, the United States had quotas on the number of refugees that could enter the country. The Lithuanian quota was full for the next 15 years, but someone dropped off the list just as Pranas was applying, and he was accepted. The next thing he knew he was leaving his girl-friend and job behind, and was boarding a ship in Oslo, Norway, which was headed for America.

Photo taken at the Swedish hotel where Pranas and Felix were quarantined for a week before they were moved to Stockholm. Back row, from left to right: three Norwegians, a Swedish border patrol guard, and Pranas. Front row: two Russian P.O.W.s, a Swedish border patrol guard and Felix.

Pranas worked in New York City for the next two years at several major publishing companies designing book covers and creating illustrations. He became an American citizen in 1955, and taught art for the next 20 years at the High Mowing School in New Hampshire, the Cherry Lawn School and Thomas School in Connecticut, and at the Belmont Hill School in Boston. By this time he was ready for a change, and gave up teaching to paint, which he has done ever since. Pranas currently lives in Chamberlain, Maine, and is preparing for an upcoming exhibition of his paintings in his native Lithuania.

Author's note: Felix carried a camera in his rucksack, and recorded their escape from Norway to Sweden, which is why we have so many wonderful photographs accompanying this story.

In 1957 a letter came from Lithuania, via Chicago, to Pranas. His brother, Petras, married a girl after the war who had relatives in Chicago, so they asked them to try and find an address for Pranas and forward a letter to him. When the letter came, it was not directly written to Pranas, but in it, he detected that the letter writer was his brother by childhood phrases he used, and that he was talking about a mother's search for son.

The return address on the letter was not his parents', it was the Lithuanian Colonel's wife who had helped him during the war. Keep in mind that after the war Lithuania went back under Communist rule, and it was very difficult to get information about people without arousing the suspicions of the KGB. In 1964, Pranas was able to return to Lithuania for the first time in 19 years. His visit was restricted to his home town, and he was accompanied by two KGB agents where ever he went.

Through the years, Pranas was able to locate an uncle through the International Red Cross, but didn't have any luck finding anyone else in his family. Uncle Alexander had fled into Germany when the Russians were coming, and lived in refugee camps there for three years after the war. Then he had been able to come to the United States.

When he and Pranas were united, Pranas found out that his mother and sister, Zita, had also fled their hometown and returned to Barbara's birth place in the western part of Lithuania. Zita was very sick on the way, which made the trip extremely difficult. Pranas, Sr., Elena, and Petras all found their way to Veivirzenai, and they were reunited at the end of the war. They talked about all going to Germany, but decided against it, and stayed in their native land.

When Pranas lived in Stockholm, he met another Lithuanian who was 17 and was very homesick, so he had decided to return to their country. He asked Pranas' help in doing this, which Pranas agreed to do, but in return this man was supposed to let his family know he was all right. Apparently the man kept his promise, because according to Uncle Alexander, the Lapes knew Pranas had survived the war, but they thought he was still living in Sweden.

Barbara Lape fleeing to Veivirzenai, in the western part of Lithuania, with a wagon full of the family's possessions, as the Russians advanced towards Kaunas near the end of the war.

ANNEMARIE VAN DEVENTER APOLLONIO
Indonesia and the Netherlands

Annemarie was born in Semarang, Java, on August 9, 1938, and is the daughter of Frans and Sophia "Fie" van Deventer. Her father was a purchasing agent for the Internatio Company, which was a Dutch import business, dealing with coffee, tea, and spices. During this time period, Indonesia was called the Dutch East Indies, a colony of the Netherlands.

Frans went to work in Java in 1934, and was required by his company to live and work there for one year, before he could marry Fie. Meanwhile, back in Holland, Fie was anxiously preparing her dowry. Her father was a minister and wanted to marry them, so after the required year had passed, Frans' best friend, Bertus Havinga, stood up in his place, and they were married by proxy, which was a common occurrence years ago. Fie then got on a train that took her to Italy; there she boarded a ship, which took her to the Dutch East Indies. Four weeks later she arrived, with her dowry, and she and Frans went on their honeymoon.

By 1942, the Japanese had successfully come down from China and were sweeping through the Pacific, occupying what they considered to be strategic islands. If they had continued on with their plan, Australia would have been next. When the news came to Java that Singapore had fallen to the Japanese, the Dutch Army was alerted. Frans was a officer in the reserves of the calvary. He was moved to Salatiga, where he waited for further orders.

The women of the island quickly organized themselves, realizing the threat of invasion was becoming a real possibility. Lookout duties and a warning system was created using gongs, because the sound easily carried from one home to another across the tropical island. When Fie learned that Frans had been assigned a house to live in on the other side of the island, she decided that it would be better at this point if the family moved in with him. Because she was part of the warning system, she had to ask permission to leave from one of the community leaders. Permission was granted, and Fie became involved with a similar organization in the new community.

In March of 1942, after the Battle of the Java Sea had been lost, the Japanese invaded Java, and Frans, along with all the other males 16 and older, were imprisoned. By January of 1943, all Dutch women and children were also rounded up, and imprisoned. Frans was sent to Bandoeng, Tjilatjap, Tjimahi, Flores, Batavia, Bandoeng, and Halmaheira during his imprisonment. He later wrote in a letter back to Holland about the transportation to the island of Flores, "It's not fun to sit on your haunches for six days in the hold of a ship, but because I was an officer in charge of 250 men, I was granted some mobility."

When the Japanese came, Fie, Annemarie, and her brother Gijs (who was two years older) were told to bring only what possessions they could carry with them. Luckily, Fie had made two knapsacks for the children out of cloth napkins, which made it easier for them to carry their belongings. At the time they thought they would be gone for a few weeks. As it turned out they were held for two years in Ambarawa on the island of Java.

Their prison was actually a large stable and over 8,000 women and children were kept there. Makeshift curtains were hung for privacy, and the stable had to be checked every morning for baby rats. If any were found the women destroyed them, in the hopes that they were preventing the spreading of diseases. At the beginning of the war, boys up to the age of 16 were allowed to stay with the women, then the age

Gijs, Fie, and Annemarie van Deventer in March of 1942,
in their backyard on the island of Java.

dropped to 12, and finally 10. They had became a valuable source of labor for the Japanese, and were taken away from their mothers and siblings to work as slave labor. Fie was terrified that Gijs would be taken away from her. He would be ten in 1946, but due to the poor food the prisoners were fed, he hardly grew, and his captors thought he was younger than he really was because of his small size.

Fie had the foresight, before the occupation, to have a medallion engraved with the names and dates of birth of her two children. Gijs and Annemarie wore them around their necks throughout the war in case they were ever separated from their mother. When they arrived at the camp, Fie was given an egg shaped, aluminum tag with a number imprinted on it, which the women had to memorize in Japanese. Each adult was expected to have this tag with them at roll call, sometimes several times a day. The penalty for being caught without it was kicking and beating by the guards. The women also had to stand watch over their fellow inmates for two hours each night, while the Japanese silently crept around the camp in sneakers, trying to catch the prisoners breaking the rules. The adults had to learn two sentences in Japanese by heart. One of them started with, "Your most honorable..."

Every morning at 6 A.M. the entire camp got up and was run through a series of exercises. Annemarie can still count to ten in Japanese, because the prisoners were required to count out loud while they did their calisthenics. Afterwards, the women were taken outside the camp to work in the fields and the children were left behind to sweep and babysit. One time Fie was sick and was unable to work, so Annemarie had to do the washing for the family. She can remember how hard it was for her to wash her mother's dress, because at the time it seemed awfully cumbersome to a six-year-old.

The women were under heavy supervision by armed guards while they planted seedlings in the fields, and there was no food, water, or rest periods all day long. The seedlings they were planting would eventually produce an oil the Japanese could use in their airplanes. The women returned to the compound at dusk, and if the opportunity presented itself, they would reach down and jerk the seedlings up as they walked by, so the roots wouldn't take hold. It was the only form of sabotage they could muster, and if they had been caught the punishment would have been severe.

Women were not highly valued in Japanese society and for that reason the male prisoners were treated somewhat better than the female.
Fie is a tall woman in stature, and in fact was taller than her captors,
which displeased them to no end. Young women in the camps were
often misused and raped by the Japanese soldiers. Luckily in Fie's case,
they didn't bother her in that way, perhaps because she was older.

The women's menstrual cycles stopped shortly after they entered the
camps, which was due in part to malnutrition and to the stress of the situation. For either reason, it was a godsend for the women, and helped
to eliminate the fear of pregnancy under the worse conditions imaginable. Women and children were considered a problem by the Japanese.
If the war had continued, they planned to take the women to Borneo in
September of 1945 to work in the mines, and the children were going to
be left behind on Java to fend for themselves. This sinister plot was
uncovered at the end of the war by the Allies, and was documented in
papers the Japanese had left behind when they surrendered.

Later on, the prisoners slept on boards, and a chalk line allotted 65
cm for each person to sleep on. Their daily meals consisted of hard corn,
tapioca boiled in water, a very small scoop of rice, and sometimes vegetables boiled in water. There were several Catholic nuns in the camp
and they had brought a meat grinder with them, but they wouldn't lend
it out for fear it might get broken. You can imagine how hard it would
be to digest hard corn without the use of the grinder.

Disease was prevalent within the camp, especially cholera and dysentery. The latrines in the camp consisted of a ditch with water running
through it, covered with planks. The women tried to keep them as clean
as possible, but inevitably, disease affected everyone at one time or
another, and the oldest and the weakest of the prisoners were the first
to die. In the last camp, someone with a cart would come by every day
at 4 P.M. to pick up the dead. Often times the bodies were still warm.

A society within the camp soon formed, and people seemed to cling
to their own little groups. Luckily, Fie became good friends with another
woman and her son, and the two women tried to work together to keep
their families safe as much as possible.

Fie had brought one dress with her, and within it she had sewn
money, which was highly illegal in the camp. In fact the Japanese were
always searching personal belongings for it. Once in a while prisoners

were able to get to the fences, and if they had money they might be able to trade with a native for a banana or some other item of food. It was obviously a dangerous practice for both the prisoner and the native, but it still occurred from time to time.

The van Deventer family had a Belgian friend on the island, who was allowed to visit them once in a while during the first year. On these occasions she would try to smuggle food into the camp for them. By 1943 all Europeans in Indonesia and the surrounding islands were interned by the Japanese. Fie also had in her possession a Dutch flag. Before the Japanese invaded, she carefully took it apart and hid sections of it throughout their belongings. After they were liberated in 1946, she carefully stitched it back together, and to this day it is displayed at her home in Holland.

Another task the women were ordered to do was dig up a Chinese cemetery to make room for more fields. It was a terrible, gruesome job in all that heat, and quite obviously the Japanese had no respect for the Chinese. She and the other women also had to move stones from one end of the camp to the other on a daily basis. The Japanese are very particular about the way their yards look. They landscape with rocks and stones, and they ordered the prisoners to arrange them in a different shape and location everyday. Even little Gijs had to rake the rocks into position. It was a ridiculous task that somehow made the Japanese guards feel superior.

Later in the war, Fie volunteered to scoop food at meal time for other prisoners. She had to work for three hours, and was then entitled to one extra ladle of food. She jumped at the opportunity to do this, because Gijs was very hungry at this point, and even though the food was poor, it would help to satisfy his hunger. Also, Annemarie became very sick and wouldn't eat. There were plenty of women who were nurses, but there were no medical facilities or medicine at the camp, so all she could do was stay in bed. Her mother was in the fields during the day, so other women in the camp would check on her. They told her that if she didn't eat her mother couldn't come to visit her. After a few days without food, Annemarie finally gave in and ate something, so she could see her mother again.

There was no communication with the outside world in the camp. The women would try to evaluate the Japanese at night after their children had gone to bed, but it was nothing more than speculation. On the other hand, at Frans' camp, the men were secretly able to build a small wireless, which kept them in tune with the war. He also learned Spanish fluently from one of the other prisoners while he was there.

One day someone in the camp noticed a train loaded with women going by off in the distance. Word spread throughout the camp and the prisoners started going to the fences, standing on anything that would raise them up, so they could wave to the other women on the train. Fie took advantage of the situation and went to the faucets to get some water to do some laundry. When the Japanese realized what was going on, they were furious! Everyone was ordered away from the fence and inside, but Fie didn't hear the order until it was to late.

With Annemarie by her side, the Japanese ruthlessly beat Fie. While the other women and children in the camp fearfully hid under their beds, one of Fie's friends left the safety of the barracks because she thought Annemarie would be the next victim. She cautiously pulled her away from her mother's side, and lead her to safety. Fie's face was so swollen from the beating, she couldn't even eat for a whole week. X-rays taken after the war would show that the jaw bone had been broken.

Orders came in January of 1945 that the camp was to be moved. The prisoners boarded a train that took them to Semarang, but then the train couldn't go any farther so they were forced to walk for two and a half hours. The road was dirt and full of holes that were hard to see because it was night time. If anyone fell they were kicked by the Japanese guards until they got up.

When they arrived at their new camp, Solo, all the baggage was searched, and one quarter was found. Quickly those who also had some coins in their possession dumped them in the lavatory ditch. Everyone in the camp was punished by having to stand in the hot, tropical sun in nothing but their underwear for the rest of the day, until it was dark. It was a humiliating and inhumane punishment. The tropical sun was fierce, and no food or water was distributed. At dusk the prisoners were told they could go get some water to drink and find a place to sleep. The camp had already eaten, so there was no food left. The new arrivals had to sleep in the stone streets, because the barracks were full. Fie slept with a child on each side of her lap. A lot of people died after that terrible day.

The Japanese were always inspecting the prisoners and their belongings. Annemarie can remember standing in line with her mother behind her, and she could feel her fiddling with the straps on her pants, which seemed fine to Annemarie, who was almost seven by this time. Fie's real motive was that she was trying to hide a bobbin of thread in her clothing, so the Japanese wouldn't take it away from her.

During their imprisonment in Ambarawa, Gijs got a hold of some tomato seeds and stuck them in the ground to see if they'd grow. Before long he had some beautiful plants, and whenever his mother couldn't find him around the camp, she knew he was hiding in "his garden" to escape, even if it was just for a moment. Before long everyone started experimenting with seeds from the kitchen, until one day the Japanese came and bulldozed everything flat. Luckily, Gijs tomatoes had been harvested and eaten by all, but not the ripening cucumbers.

In August of 1945 the Americans dropped the first of two atomic bombs on Japan. They surrendered shortly thereafter. The emperor of Japan gave the order to stop the labor and guard the women. As we mentioned earlier there was no outside communication within the women's camp, so the van Deventers were not liberated until October of 1945.

On August 9th, Annemarie's birthday, several planes flew overhead. Annemarie had been collecting twigs for the fire and stopped to look up at the planes, but much to her surprise they didn't have the big, red circle on them, indicating that they were Japanese. Fie had managed to get some flour together and made Annemarie little pancakes for her birthday and coffee klop, which is strong coffee and sugar whipped together with a fork. Annemarie thought it was delightful!

One morning in October, in their third and final camp, Tjati Barang, there was a lot of excitement at the camp. Fie got up to see what it was all about, and discovered a group of recently liberated Dutch men. They had come in Army vehicles, hoisted the Dutch flag, and started to sing the national anthem. Fie went up to one of them and asked, "Do you know Frans van Deventer?" The man replied, " Yes, he's over there." Fie could hardly believe it, her husband was one of her liberators! They were reunited for about five minutes, and Frans told Fie to stay in the camp, because it was the safest place for her and the children. The Indonesians had proclaimed their independence from the Dutch on

August 19, 1945, and a civil war was at hand. Many people left the camps and tried to return to their homes, which was a big mistake because many of them were murdered. Frans then had to leave his family, and move on to other camps, and then back to his own, Halmaheira.

Annemarie and Gijs found a girl who knew how to get to Halmaheira. They decided to leave their camp, and go to see their father. The three kids trekked through the jungle, and passed over a rope bridge that was suspended across a ravine, before they reached the camp. When they arrived, Frans was very shocked to see them, because it was far too dangerous to move outside the camps. He had a vehicle, and returned them to their mothers. In November it was arranged for them to move into a house outside of the camp, but by that time the Allies, British Indians, and Gurkhas (soldiers from Nepal, serving in the British or Indian armies) had came to liberate them.

The Japanese turned their weapons over to the Indonesians, which in turn armed them for the civil war against the Dutch. Ironically some Japanese ended up protecting and fighting for the Dutch against the Indonesians because the Indonesians didn't want them occupying the island any more than they wanted the Dutch. The rebels wanted their independence at any cost, and many lives were lost during this time.

In November of 1945 the first news from Holland arrived via the Red Cross. It was then that the van Deventers learned that both the children's maternal and paternal grandfathers and an aunt had died during the war, because they couldn't get the medical attention they needed.

Frans stayed in the Dutch Army from September through May, and was in charge of protecting women's camps on the island. Fie on the other hand was anxious to return to Holland, and by this time weighed about 84 pounds. The Red Cross sent packages of food to Indonesia. There was one for each adult and one for every two children. Inside of them was cheese, butter, canned food, and chocolate. Drinking water had to be distributed, because the rebels broke the water lines. If you wanted to bathe you had to do it in the rain.

A cook and gardener, who had worked for the van Deventer family before the war, found them and wanted to work for them again, but the van Deventers didn't have any money. They had lost everything while they were in the camps. The men said it didn't matter. Since the van Deventers were not used to eating a lot of food, there was a surplus of rice at their house. At the end of the day, they paid the men in rice, who in turn fed their families.

This was a dangerous time to be in Indonesia, especially if you were Dutch. Annemarie can remember lying on the floor of their house as stray bullets whizzed through the windows. You could also hear ships firing their cannons daily in the harbor down below. Some of the Gurkhas from India lived in the house behind the van Deventers. They took a liking to Annemarie and when they needed to drive the servants home, they invited her to go with them in their Army jeep. They also let her play the piano at their house, which was a real treat.

In May of 1946 the first freighter was ready to take passengers back to Holland. The trip took about a month, and the family had to stop in Ataka, Egypt, at a Red Cross Station to be checked medically. No one was in very good shape and it was discovered about a year later that Annemarie had scurvy. They were all given warm clothes, and Annemarie was given a dress with long sleeves, which made her feel like royalty.

Fie had a sister in Rotterdam who had room for Annemarie and Gijs to live with her, and her in-laws took Frans and Fie in at their house across the street. It was very hard for the children to adjust during their first few months back in Holland. They were accustomed to living in the tropics, and not wearing shoes. On the other hand, Fie's sister lived very formally, and expected them to do so. Also her two daughters considered Annemarie to be their personal doll to dress up, because she was so tiny.

The city of Rotterdam set up Overbruggings Schools, which translates to bridge-over-schools, to help kids like Annemarie and Gijs prepare to return to school. Annemarie can remember sitting at a desk, and having no clue as to what she was supposed to do. It was devastating! It was later decided that she should be put in a lower grade, and when this was done, she quickly caught up with the rest of the children her age.

Holland had been ravaged by the war and there were no jobs and few places left to live that hadn't been damaged. The van Deventers later moved in with an uncle, and shortly thereafter, friends invited them to live at their house in the center of Holland. In 1947 a third child Frans, Jr., was born and Frans, Sr., got a job with a bank in Amsterdam. At that time you had to have proof of a job to get a place to live. The family then rented an apartment on the coast of Holland, in a town called Zandvoort, and Frans commuted to Amsterdam. The family lived there until 1949 and with the help of their grandmother bought a house in Baarn, which is located in the center of the Netherlands.

In 1957, after graduating from high school, Annemarie traveled to England to live with a family as a mother's helper, and to learn the language for one year. Dutch high schools required studies in English, French, and German, and Annemarie thought this would be a good way to improve her English. She returned home for six months of studies, and in January of 1958 went to Toulon, France, to live with a French family and improve her knowledge of that language. In September of that year, she returned to Amsterdam to attend a two year library school, and worked in a library for two years after that.

In 1962 she emigrated to Montreal, Canada, and worked with the author Anne Tyler at the McGill Law Library. During the summer of 1964 Annemarie traveled to Camden, Maine, to sail on the Windjammer Mary Day, where she met the ship's first mate, Spencer Apollonio, who was a Rockport, Maine, native. They were married in August of 1969, and moved to Boothbay Harbor, later having two sons, Tom and Taylor. She

The van Deventers in Holland after the war. Photo was taken in July of 1946. Back row: Martha (Fie's sister), Fie (Fie's mother), Fie, and Frans. Front row: Gijs, Dirk Jan (a cousin to the children), and Annemarie.

is currently the assistant librarian at the Boothbay Region High School and is an avid gardener.

Author's note: Annemarie is a member of the Dutch organization, "Informatie van de Stichting Japanse Ereschulden," which is a volunteer group that is trying to get the Japanese government to acknowledge human rights violations that occurred during the Second World War, to admit that it owes compensation to the survivors of these camps, and to help the world recognize the harm caused by Japan during that time.

Fie van Deventer attends annual reunions of the survivors of the camp at Amabarawa when they meet in the Hague once a year.

Frans van Deventer, who passed away in 1983, was in charge of the Japanese branch of the Dutch bank where he worked. Ironically, when he retired, he was given a trip to Japan as a retirement gift from the bank. It was a difficult decision, but he accepted the trip, and chose to travel alone. It gave him the chance to meet the people he had worked with by telephone and mail over the years.

All went smoothly during the trip, except for one small incident that occurred when he was walking down a busy Japanese street. Frans saw workers making repairs, which would seem harmless enough to you or me, but as soon as he heard their foreman calling out orders, it brought the war back to him in an instant, and it took him a moment to regain his composure.

JAN HAVINGA
The Netherlands

In May of 1940 Jan was attending the Naval Academy in Den Helder, Holland. He was then 19 years old, and was enrolled as a freshman midshipman. Hitler's Nazis rolled into Holland on May 10th. The Dutch fought hard but were no match for the overwhelming German forces, and, by May 15th, after Rotterdam had been flattened by the relentless bombing of the Luftwaffe, the country surrendered. Jan was put on the last warship leaving Holland with three other midshipmen and the midshipman flag, with orders not to let it fall into the hands of the enemy. The ship was a small destroyer dating from the First World War. As she made her way towards England, following the coast of Holland, the Germans tried to bomb her, but were unsuccessful in their efforts. In the evening, the men on board could see the glow of Rotterdam burning in the distance, as they fled their country.

The next morning they were in English waters and a British cruiser guided them through the minefield so they could enter Dover. The midshipmen were put ashore, where they boarded a train and were taken to Falmouth in Cornwall. Gradually, they were joined by more midshipmen, who had come over in various ships, so that there were about 40 or 50 in total. At first they were housed on a Dutch ferryboat that had operated between Rotterdam and Harwich, and was now anchored in Falmouth harbor. There were tankers and other ships in the harbor, and German bombers appeared frequently and did great damage among the ships, as well as the town itself. About a month later, the Dutch government rented a large house in the country, which was where the Dutch Naval Academy in exile would continue educating its students, albeit with a greatly reduced curriculum. In the meanwhile all the midshipmen, as well as staff personnel, also participated in exercises under the leadership of Dutch marines to become part of England's defense against the Nazis in case of an invasion.

In February of 1941 Jan was assigned to a new Dutch anti-aircraft cruiser that had been brought over unfinished in May 1940 from Rotterdam by a hastily assembled skeleton crew, to keep it out of the hands of the Germans. It had just been completed in Portsmouth, England, and after a short period of seatrials, started convoy duty in the Irish Sea and on the Atlantic. In June or July he returned to the Naval Academy in Cornwall for more training and in November he joined the crew of a Dutch minesweeper, which had been a fishing trawler that was converted for wartime duty. They left Liverpool on December 3, 1941, as part of a convoy and arrived in Halifax, Nova Scotia, 19 days later. They had terrible weather: 14 days of wind force 11, heavy rains, sleet, and snow. The continuous stormy conditions caused the convoy to be scattered over a wide area so that they soon lost all contact with the other ships.

On board the trawler was the Dutch midshipmen's flag, which was headed for the newly established Dutch Naval Academy in Indonesia (Dutch East Indies), a Dutch colony at the time. Jan was again instructed to watch over the flag, which was encased in a long wooden box and was kept above his bunk in the forward hold. Twice during the trip water came through the presumably leak proof air vents, and once the diesel engine stopped because seawater had come into the chimney. Luckily they managed after a while to get the engine started again. Water came over the forward deck and smashed against the bridge continuously, so that gradually a thick layer of ice started to form. They had to stop several times to chip the ice off the deck, because the water was not draining out of the scuppers since everything was frozen. This was a dangerous maneuver, because the ship was being tossed wildly and the slippery ice did not provide any foothold for the crew, so the men had to tie themselves with lifelines to prevent being washed overboard.

As they neared Canada they ran into a blizzard, and the ship was soon covered with more ice and hard packed snow. In order to see out on the bridge they had to heat one of the windows so that they could lower it, and then hack a hole in the ice. They arrived in Halifax on December 22nd, and soon realized they were the first one to arrive out of the entire convoy. They later heard that several ships had sunk enroute because of the storm (being empty except for ballast, heavy material placed in the hold of a ship to enhance stability), some had been torpedoed by German U-boats, and they also read in the local paper that two Canadian fishing trawlers (larger than their own trawler) had succumbed to the blizzard.

On January 3, 1942, they left Halifax headed for the West Indies. It was a three-week trip due south through the Bahamas to Curaco, Dutch West Indies. The gradual change of climate was greatly welcomed by the crew after the winter storms in the North Atlantic. Shortly after they arrived at their destination, the U-boats became active in the area, and Jan was transferred to a Dutch destroyer doing convoy duty between Guantanamo Bay and Trinidad.

In September of 1943, Jan was assigned to the Dutch Marines for training in the United States After seeing the success of the United States Marines, the Dutch government decided to build up the Dutch Marine Corps, which is the oldest Marine Corps in the world, dating from December 10, 1665. In the United States, Jan participated in a course and practical training in field artillery at the USMC base in Quantico, Virginia, from October of 1943 through January of 1944. Right after that, Jan was teaching gun fire control to Dutch Marines at Quantico and helped organize a cadre for the eventual formation of a Dutch Marine Brigade. He also spent several weeks at the USMC base in Parris Island, South Carolina, to study the U.S. method of personnel classification. During the summer of 1944, he spent some time at the Dutch Marine office in Washington, D.C., to organize and get ready for recruiting Dutch Marines in Holland, because they knew that many Dutch young men would be eager to fight the Japanese in and around Indonesia once Holland was liberated.

In the fall of 1944, they went to England, and shortly thereafter to Brussels to start recruiting in Holland, at first only in the southern part since the rest of Holland was not free until the spring of 1945. The Allies had been stopped at Arnhem because of the disastrous battle there between the German occupying forces and the British, Canadian, and Polish paratroopers that had been dropped in September 1944 to save the bridge over the Rhine. This battle was later documented in the book and movie, "A Bridge Too Far." When the town was taken later by the Allies in April 1945, very few houses were left in habitable condition; everything had been looted by the Germans, who had ordered the entire population to evacuate the city when the battle started.

Arnhem was Jan's hometown. That is where the family lived, and that is where he went to school before going to the Naval Academy in the fall of 1939. In May of 1945, shortly after the town was liberated by the Americans, Jan went to Arnhem with his jeep. It was a ghost town. Entering the city from the south and going right through the city to the northwest where his family had lived, he did not see a single soul. Practically all the windows were broken, and debris and furniture were scattered everywhere. The center of the city as well as the northwest, the direction from which the paratroopers had landed, was heavily damaged. He had difficulty recognizing his own home, which had been destroyed during the battle, but was helped when he noticed a painting that his father had done of his sister that was lying outside against the door step, slashed to pieces. He did not dare go inside, for fear of booby traps the Nazis might have left. He later learned that a neighbor's daughter had been badly injured by a Nazi booby trap trying to enter her house, so he was glad he had the foresight to wait.

Jan continued to search for his family, and one month later found out that they had gone north to Groningen, which had been his parents' hometown when they were young. His sister had married several years earlier and lived in Amsterdam. When the orders came from the Germans that everyone had to evacuate Arnhem, his parents had gone on bicycle and arrived in Groningen four days later to stay with a family. As soon as he had an opportunity, Jan went north to see his parents, and learned that his father had managed to obtain food from farmers by painting portraits of them and their homes. This part of Holland consisted primarily of large farms and wealthy farmers, so that food was not as much of a problem as elsewhere in the country, where many people survived the last and very cold winter of the war by eating tulip bulbs, not to mention many other things that we normally would consider inedible. Jan brought them food and clothing that he had bought earlier in London, and even gave his father the coat he was wearing.

Later, he brought them back to Arnhem, where in the meantime the local government had re-established itself, had started cleaning up, and had made it somewhat possible to live again in the town. His parents were appalled when they saw what was left of their house. As they entered their rubble-filled home, which had been partly restored and declared safe by the authorities, they noticed that the Nazi troops had lived in it for some time, looting everything of value, tearing up books, and destroying furniture. Jan's father had been an art teacher at their local academy and his collection of books and art treasures had been destroyed. The Germans found and stole Jan's violin and other articles that his father had hidden in secret places. What they had once known as their home was now completely destroyed. The only favorable condition of the whole situation was that the season was changing from spring to summer, and at least his parents wouldn't be exposed to the elements of winter in the shell of their bombed-out house.

Later, in 1945, Jan went back to the United States on a troopship with many Dutch Marine recruits, who were assembled at Camp David, a USMC camp near Camp Lejeune, North Carolina, where they were formed into units and engaged in intensive training. The Dutch Marine Brigade consisted of about 13,000 men, and they were soon ready to go after the Japanese. Shortly after the start of their training, however, the Japanese surrendered, and the war in the Pacific was over for all intents and purposes. Shortly thereafter, they learned that the Indonesians didn't want the Dutch to come back and, on August 19, 1945, they proclaimed their independence from Holland. Jan then was sent with the

Dutch Marines to Indonesia in October of 1945 to fight to get the colony back for Holland. Holding on to the Dutch East Indies was considered extremely important at the time by the Dutch government, because of its raw materials such as oil, tobacco, rubber, coffee, and tea. Many Dutch companies had been formed because of these resources, and became important and prosperous exporting their products worldwide.

Jan served as a battery commander in Eastern Java, with the field artillery battalion of the Dutch Marine Brigade. The purpose was to secure the bigger cities and gradually enlarge the perimeter around them. Since there was no way to distinguish friend from the enemy, who did not wear uniforms, hostilities were mostly in the nature of guerrilla warfare. After about two years, Jan was put in charge of all communications for the Marine Brigade, since he had been in that field earlier in the Navy. In June of 1949, he was sent back to Holland. The country had come to realize that it would be unwise to attempt to keep Indonesia as a colony, because of the increasing criticism from the United Nations (primarily the United States), and was in the process of ending all hostilities.

Jan had now spent ten years in the Dutch military, four in the Navy and six in the Marines, where he earned the rank of Captain at the end of the Second World War, and was promoted to Major, when he was put in charge of communications during the Dutch/Indonesian War. He discussed with Naval headquarters in The Hague what his position was and what the future had to offer, particularly since he was now six years behind his Naval Academy classmates. He could stay with the Marine Corps, but they would shrink back to what they were before, which was primarily that of commando units, in which Jan didn't have any training or interest. So he decided that it was time to get out of the military.

While in Indonesia he had visited the U.S. Embassy, and applied for immigration papers to the Untied States. He wasn't sure at the time if he would ever exercise them, but the future being as unsure as it was, it certainly wouldn't do any harm. Now, back in Holland, they came through in early March of 1950, much sooner then he had expected. So he emigrated to the United States later that month. He started working for the Dutch airline KLM as an assistant supervisor in New York City, but when he realized after some time that there was no future there, he applied to Columbia University to be accepted as an electrical engineering student. He was given two years of credit for his past education and experience, and received his B.S. in 1954. He started working in his new field in the New York City area, obtained his U.S. citizenship in 1955, and received his master's degree in 1957.

Jan went to work for RCA in Burlington, Massachusetts, in 1957, and stayed there for six years. In 1963, he started working for The Mitre Corporation, which is a research think tank for the U.S. Air Force. He retired from there in 1984 after 21 years. He and his wife of 42 years, Mimi, now live in Mount Vernon, New Hampshire, and come to their home in Southport as often as they can.

MARIA "MIMI" GOSLINGA HAVINGA
The Netherlands

Mimi Goslinga Havinga, Dutch Army, WACS

In 1937, Mimi was a teenager growing up with five brothers and a sister, living in The Hague in Holland. Her father, Wybo, was Assistant Superintendent of Schools in the city and was offered a job as Director of Education in the Netherlands Antilles in the West Indies. He informed his family of this offer and decided that he was going to turn down the position. It was at this point that Mimi's mother, Philippa, spoke up and said, "Hitler is going to march into this country and I'm not going to watch my sons being used as cannon fodder. We are going to the West Indies!"

In the meantime, while this was being discussed back and forth, the Goslinga family had a German maid working for them, who just happened to be a member of a fairly new organization in Holland called the Dutch National Socialist Party, which was sympathetic to the Nazi regime in Germany. She would attend meetings in her free time, and Mimi's mother became increasingly concerned about this. It was customary in their household, like in many homes throughout Holland, to read passages from the Bible after dinner, and the maid was asked to come in for that. Philippa started warning her husband and the children to watch what they said and read in the presence of the maid, because she figured it was being reported back to the Party.

Finally, a vote was taken within the family, and the majority decided to go to the West Indies. So they all boarded a ship in 1937, and left their homeland behind. War broke out in Holland on May 10, 1940, and Hitler's troops occupied the country for the next five years. Philippa's uncanny foresight saved her family from the ravages of war in Holland and the Nazi occupation.

The Goslinga family soon found Curacao, in the West Indies, to be a dry place without much rain and lots of warm winds. Mimi and her brothers and sister were now back in school, and everything seemed quite normal in their new home. Then, in 1940, they received the news about the German occupation of Holland. Hitler seemed to gain more strength all the time, and as German submarines had been sighted in the Caribbean, it was decided that their outdoor swimming pool would be converted into a bomb shelter. Mimi (then 16) ended up filling and sewing bags full of sand to help with the construction effort. She remembers it as a very exciting time. All the neighboring children had heard planes would be flying over to bomb their island because of the oil refinery there, so the family decided to stand watch at the bomb shelter, but when nothing happened night after night, the idea was abandoned.

When Mimi finished high school in 1942, her parents decided that she should go to the United States for further education. All foreign exchange was earmarked for the war effort, so it could only be done with a job in New York. With an allotment of only 25 dollars in her pocket, she flew to Miami, Florida, and then took the train to New York City, which cost her ten dollars. She arrived in February without a winter coat or boots, and only 15 dollars to her name. Luckily she had a job with the Netherlands Government in New York as a secretary.

During the summer of 1942, President Roosevelt invited Queen Wilhelmina of the Netherlands to the United States. The Queen and her family had fled Holland on May 15, 1940, and had been living in exile in England. The Queen's staff needed a secretary, and Mimi was picked for the job.

Working for Queen Wilhelmina was a great experience. Her daughter, Princess Juliana, and her children had gone to Ontario, Canada, for the duration of the war, while her husband, Prince Bernhard, had stayed in England. In 1942, she rented a house in Lee, Massachusetts, where her mother came to visit. The Queen's staff, official secretary, and Mimi stayed and had offices at the Red Lion Inn in nearby Stockbridge. Every morning large mailbags would be dropped by her desk containing mostly fan mail. People from all over the U.S. would write to the Queen, expressing admiration for her and her valiant resistance in leading her people in exile.

People would say that they would drink a toast of orange juice in tribute to the House of Orange (the Dutch Royalty), and one person even sent a large envelope containing yellowed newspaper clippings that she had collected over many years of Wilhelmina's upbringing, coronation, wedding, etc. This was returned, of course, with a note of thanks adding that the Queen could not bereave someone of a collection that obviously was so meaningful to that person. Mimi's job was to answer all this mail, and the official secretary would sign it. Often the Queen would have a mailbag sent on to her, and she would scribble suggestions for an answer on the letters.

The Queen received many dignitaries, military, etc. Mimi remembers two young parachutists who had just returned from a secret mission in Holland. The Queen took them for a walk in the garden, and asked them about the situation in the homeland, the underground, etc. All this involved much correspondence, and in addition she had to give many speeches. She gave a major address before the U.S. Congress. Although these speeches were mostly prepared for her, she always added suggestions and worked on them herself, making notations as to delivery.

In 1944, Mimi enlisted in the Netherlands Indies Women's Army Corps, and received basic training with the U.S. WAC in Fort Oglethorpe, Georgia. Subsequently, she boarded a troopship in California that took her to Australia, where she became a secretary for the Netherlands Indies government in exile. One evening, friends of her family in Brisbane invited her to dinner. Later that evening a military transport came to the house and told Mimi she had to leave, because she had been reassigned to Ceylon, now known as Sri Lanka. They had packed and brought her duffel bag with them.

That night she flew to Perth, and several days later on to Colombo. From Colombo by jeep to Kandy, the headquarters of Lord Louis Mountbatten, Supreme Allied Commander of the Southeast Asia Command, located in the Botanical Gardens. Mimi was assigned as secretary to the Dutch Colonel, the head of the Dutch staff. Once, when Lord Mountbatten visited the women's quarters for lunch, Mimi had the honor of getting an elephant ride with Lord Louis! She thought Ceylon, especially Kandy, was heaven.

Six weeks later she reluctantly returned to Australia – this time her boss was transferred and made Secretary of Transportation and Resources in the Netherlands Indies Government Cabinet, and they remained there until the end of the war.

The war with Japan over in August 1945, the Netherlands Indies Government prepared its return. However, on August 19, Sukarno proclaimed Indonesia (its new name) independent, and it took several weeks before the first Dutch plane would be able to land in Batavia (now Jakarta). The Governor General, the Secretary of Transportation and Resources, Intelligence Officer, a Liaison Officer with the British Forces, and two secretaries (one being Mimi) took off in a C-47 to return as the government to Batavia.

It was a long ride from Brisbane to Darwin and from Darwin to Celebes (now Sulewesi), each time stopping to get a reading on the safety of arrival in Batavia. The return of the Dutch government to the Indies turned into a very lowkey affair, and the official party was rushed to the Palace through road obstacles in a pre-war car and a truck, which did not have doors. The Japanese were still at the palace, bowing to receive the returning official government. The following morning the Japanese were sent to a prisoner of war camp. Mimi remembers a street-car rolled to the palace gates that morning with the slogan, "No more Dutch Treat!"

There were many concentration camps in Batavia where Dutch citizens had been interned by the Japanese during the war. These people were anxious to be freed – some were wives of the returning officials, including the wife of the Governor General. But it was not safe to allow them to come out and find their homes – the revolutionaries had taken weapons from the defeated Japanese, and there was a guerrilla war. Many disconcerting months followed with negotiations between the

Dutch government and the Indonesians. People were kidnapped and killed in the skirmishes with the revolutionaries. Friends disappeared and Mimi saw dismembered bodies floating in the river. Slowly the people who had been in the concentration camps were freed and transported to Holland.

In 1947, Mimi ended her term in the military and returned to the United States, to a job with the Netherlands Indies Government in New York, and later on in Washington, where she worked on the Marshall Plan. School books had to be reprinted, roads had to be fixed, and people had to be fed. Mimi typed and put all the plans for these undertakings together. In December 1949, Indonesia gained its independence from the Netherlands. The new Indonesian delegation in New York asked her to stay on, and she worked for them for three months until she was offered a position with a large Dutch company in New York.

In January of 1953, Mimi became an American citizen. In October of 1954, she married Jan Havinga from Arnhem, Holland, in New York. They had met ten years earlier, but their paths didn't cross again until 1953. Mimi continued to work for several years after they were married, then left her job to raise a family. She later returned to work as an advertising manager at their local weekly paper in New Hampshire after their two girls, Ann and Catherine, were in high school. Mimi currently lives in Mount Vernon, New Hampshire, with her husband of 42 years, Jan. The couple consider Southport their second home, and return to it often.

Author's note: Dutch people who were sympathizers with the Nazis, but were not actively involved with them, were ostracized by their neighbors after the war. The Dutch who collaborated actively, for instance by informing the Nazis as to the whereabouts of people who were in hiding, were hauled into court and received stiff sentences.

MARIT LYDERSEN PETTERSEN
Norway

When war started in Norway, the island of Tverdalsoya, located on the southeastern coast, was occupied by German soldiers. Marit lived in the town of Staubo, and was a 15-year-old high school student at the time. Feelings about the occupation were at first angry and fearful, which later grew into hatred.

Many restrictions were put on the islanders by the Germans. If you followed them all, you were for the most part treated well. On the other hand, there were posters put up on walls and the front page of all the newspapers told you,"We will shoot anyone who does not follow our orders."

So, you really didn't have much of a choice. Also, many people were arrested and sent to prison camps in Germany, where some died. They executed people in Norwegian prisons too. There were blackout conditions all the time, and almost everything was rationed including flour, butter, milk, meat, soap, and gasoline. Coffee disappeared totally, and they were given a nasty substitute. It was brown, but that is the only resemblance it had to coffee. Private cars were not given any gasoline, so they had to use bicycles. A few buses used gas that was made out of wood, and the trains were running, but everyone had to have permission from the Germans to leave their district.

Marit's father was a sailor on various ships. He spent most of the war delivering supplies between England and the United States. He was gone for five years, and in all that time, his family did not know if he were alive or not because many of the men lost their lives at sea due to U-boat attacks. For Marit, the absence of her father is the most evident memory she has from the wartime.

During the occupation, Norwegians were not allowed to display the Norwegian flag. They got around that restriction by bringing out small flags, which they placed on the table during private parties. Often parties were held behind the blackout curtains, and it was then that they got the latest news from a radio hidden in the house. Friends and neighbors would come over, and everyone would talk about the latest news and rumors, and tell jokes about the "green people," German soldiers. Everyone brought some food, and they drank that awful coffee substitute.

Marit was aware of a resistance movement on the island, and there were underground papers circulated, but you had to be very cautious about what you said and to whom. A few people on the island joined the Nazi party, and some girls made friends with the German soldiers, but as a result, they lost all their friends. Some of the Nazis were punished after the war, depending on what they had done during the occupation, but for years and years, it has been difficult for the Norwegian people to forget.

On May 8, 1945, Marit was working at a telegraph office in a small town near Staubo. Everyone started celebrating the day before, May 7, because they had heard rumors of the German capitulation. After days and weeks of joy and liberation, they had to go back to reality. Norway had to be built up again, especially the north, which for the most part had been burnt down by the Germans. They were short on everything, and it took some time to get the wheels to go round again. Imported goods and food had to be rationed for years. In 1947, thanks to the Marshall Plan, the economy in all of Europe was improved. Everyone worked together in those days and, after eight to ten years, Norway was back in shape.

VASILIJ ARCHANGELSKY
Russia

Vasilij enlisted in the Russian Army in October of 1939 at the age of 21. He served in the signal corps. He had been a student prior to that time, and was studying to be a teacher.

Hitler's plan to stab Stalin in the back and invade Russia was given the code name, "Operation Barbarossa," and began on June 22, 1941. Vasilij fought in the war from the first day until the last, May 8, 1945, when Germany unconditionally surrendered. Near Moscow, he was wounded in the legs in July of 1942, and spent two months in a very good hospital recuperating. He then was sent back to fight.

Vasilij fought from Russia, up through the Ukraine, Moldavia, Rumania, Hungary, Yugoslavia, and ended up in Austria when the war was over. In Hungary he met and fell in love with Madegda, a native Ukrainian. She had been involved with the war from its first days, and was also a signaler for the Russian Army. They married in Austria in April of 1945. When the war ended, Vasilij had earned the rank of lieutenant, and was awarded 16 medals and three orders. Madegda earned seven medals and one order for her service.

Vasilij stayed in the Army until 1960 and attained the rank of Major. They had two children, Sergej and Ludmila, and his work in the military enabled them to travel all over Russia. After his retirement from the military, he went to work as an engineer at one of the Institutes in Moscow.

Madegda passed away in December of 1991, at the age of 65. Vasilij currently lives in Moscow with his daughter, Ludmila, and granddaughter, Natalia, who has been my friend and penpal since 1992.

Author's note: *On May 8, 1995, Victory in Europe Day (VE Day), my parents, Maurice and Evelyn, received a Victory Day card from Moscow from the Archangelskys. The inscription inside it read:*

"All our family congratulates you and all your relatives with the 50th anniversary of the Great Victory! Let no one ever know the horrors of a war. Let peace and happiness always be on our beautiful earth. Dear Maurice, thank you for today's peaceful life!"

Shortly thereafter I received a letter from Natalia describing the 50th Anniversary of VE Day in Moscow. Veterans from many Russian towns and former republics of the U.S.S.R. got together to celebrate. A parade was held and a medal commemorating the 50th anniversary of VE Day was awarded to the veterans.

VE Day card from the Archangelskys in Moscow.

Natalia went on to tell me that many of her relatives were participants in the Second World War. One of Vasilij's uncles was killed in Germany, and they never found out where his gravesite was. A female cousin of Vasilij's was killed in Berlin on May 5, 1945, and Madegda's father, Natalia's great grandfather, was in the war from the very beginning.

ABOUT THE AUTHOR

Sarah Sherman McGrail is a seventh generation Southport Island native. She attended the island's three-room school house, graduated from Boothbay Region High School with the Class of 1988, and furthered her education earning degrees in Graphic Arts from Central Maine Community College, a B.A. in English and a minor in Behavioral Science, with Honors, from the University of Maine at Augusta, and a Master's Degree in Criminal Justice from Boston University.

Sarah Sherman McGrail

In 1996, Sarah founded her own publishing house, Cozy Harbor Press, Inc., and has since self-published six books—*Southport: The War Years, An Island Remembers; Heroes Among Us, A History of Boothbay Region's Veterans During the Second World War; The Littlest Tugboat; Harbor Journal, Vol. 1* (Winner Best Self-Published Book—Maine Literary Awards 2007); *Harbor Journal, Vol. II* (Honorable Mention—Maine Literary Awards 2009), and published dear friend and original Tuskegee Airman LeRoy Battle's memoirs, *And The Beat Goes On* in 2008.

In her spare time, Sarah is happiest at her island home or at the family camp in Eustis, Maine; or traveling wherever the road may lead with her husband, Jerry, sons Sherman and Jake; and often with her life-long best friend, Cory Chase, nephew Hunter, and niece Kali. Sarah also thoroughly enjoys cooking, music, photography, and being the only female Boy Scout Scoutmaster in midcoast Maine. She is very proud of the Scouts in Troop 238 and of all their accomplishments.

Made in the USA
Middletown, DE
20 July 2022